THEY CAN'T TALK
BUT THEY NEVER LIE

The Making of a Zoo Vet

THEODORE ZIMMERMAN DVM

Action Arts Press

*M*y book, with its personal anecdotes, shows the progression and accomplishment of a mission; the task of changing the environment of the wild animals in my little world, the Central Park Zoo. The victory was achieved years after I left the scene. The story tells, with subtlety, how my personal input had a small but important part in its completion.

Acknowledgements

This book is based on actual experiences. Deviations necessary for easy reading and smooth writing have been made as needed. Certain conversations and minor happenings are fiction but were written as close to what occurred as was possible from my recollection.

The following people encouraged and edited some of the work. Their advice was crucial to my decision to go forward with this effort.

Liz and Abbey Lane, Renee Steinberg, Dorothy Dritz and Arlene Isaacs did much to temper my writing. My sister, Toni, her husband Sol Linowitz and their daughter June, reviewed, recalled and corrected incidents involving themselves and contemporary anecdotes. Norman and Elana Zimmerman, Ron and Deborah Zimmerman, Ruby and Joe Zimmerman, Leslie MacMitchell and Marty Rosengarten whose recollections of ancient facts and recent events were superior to mine and much needed for a factual account. My son Rick who, with his wife Jacqui, wrote some of the pages. Finally, my wife Elaine; collaborator, ghost writer and general all-around inspirer.

I must thank all the above for making the final manuscript a reality.

ANATOMY OF A ZOO VET, revised edition, copyright © 1991 by Theodore Zimmerman. Printed in the United States of America. All rights reserved. No part of this book may be used of reproduced in any manner whatsoever without written permission except in the case of brief quotations embodied in critical articles and reviews. For information address Action Arts Press, P.O. Box 3192, Lake Worth, Lantana Br. FL 33465-3192

Library of Congress Registration Number: TXu 471 423

ISBN 0-9643084-0-1

First edition–1995

I

The Interview

THEY SAID:

"You need marks in the nineties!" "You need pull, like being the nephew of the dean!" "The state won't spend tax money for someone to treat monkeys in a zoo!"

"You can go in now, Mr. Zimmerman," the receptionist said. "The dean is at the head of the table. He will introduce you to the other faculty members."

I entered the conference room—large, rectangular and austere. Dark wood cabinets went half-way up the steep walls, topped by bookshelves stretching to the ceiling. Two shadowed windows on the east wall struggled futilely to add some light. Dean Hagan presided at the far end of a long table in the room's center. Directly opposite was the chair for me. Six faculty members, stone faces expressionless, sat three facing three. I felt their indifference down to my bones.

The dean started, "Mr. Zimmerman, have a seat and relax. I'm Dean Hagan. On my left, meet Doctors Sunderville, Milks and Udall."

"On this side, say hello to Doctors Duke, Birch, and Fincher."

Following the murmured greetings, the dean picked up my scholastic record of undergraduate studies and said. "I see you did well in the physical sciences. English, math and economics a little weak." My heart sank—weak to them are grades in the eighties!

He sat back, resting his chin on his hand, and looked at me in a friendly fashion, "Tell us about yourself. Why do you want to become a veterinarian?"

I was prepared to answer that. I began telling them my experiences in my father's pet shop in New York City, but I was nervous and knew I was talking too fast about my feelings for the suffering of sick pets of all kinds, often with no available treatment.

"Dr. Blamey (a veterinarian I was sure they knew), the pet shop's doctor, treated our dogs and cats, but admitted having little knowledge of wild animal diseases.

"I saw baby chimpanzees die of pneumonia following what seemed like a common cold. We lost puppies and kittens from distemper, without any vaccine or serum to immunize or treat them. Even pet birds and fish had insurmountable problems. It was the pleading, hopeless look in the eyes of "Uncle" my pet chimpanzee, fighting pneumonia and trying to breathe, that made up my mind."

The professors reacted—a sick chimp had sparked their interest.

"Tell us about some of your pets," the dean asked. "What was the pet shop like?"

I forced myself to speak slower. My mind's eye took me back to my youth and since I mentioned Uncle, I decided to tell them her story.

"My father was the proprietor of the London Pet Shop, a large store on Thirty-First Street and Fifth Avenue. I was allowed to work there a few afternoons a week when I was ten, fulfilling my life's desire.

"There was a traffic cop named Joe who worked the corner of Thirty-Fourth Street and Fifth Avenue. He was a big, ruddy-faced Irishman, tough when necessary but, when off-duty, a kind, sensitive man with a perpetual half-smile on his face and a twinkle in his eye. Joe was always beet-faced and smelled of beer. He was an animal lover, but aquarium fish were his favorites. On his lunch hour, he strolled through our shop sipping his beer. He paused here, whistled and cooed there, enjoying the variety of life in the store. He lingered longest over the fish tanks. Something about their perpetual motion, their varied colors and complete silence fascinated him."

My audience was attentive, but I found myself talking to Dr. Milks.

"The shop had more than puppies, kittens and goldfish. During the mid and late twenties, it was the largest pet shop in New York City. We had four, tremendous, 100-gallon aquariums, filled with graceful, busy fish, including Japanese fantails and the tropicals in many colors and sizes. Each aquarium stood in front of one of the large picture windows, one on Fifth Avenue and three on Thirty-

First Street. Their metal frames were about three feet above the floor, and under them litters of puppies or kittens played and slept."

I paused and then asked, "Should I describe some of the other pets?"

They nodded, now more alert, and Milks said, "By all means."

"The aviary contained at least two hundred birds. Canaries were the most popular. They sang constantly and almost drowned-out the noisy puppies and parrots. We also had love birds, parakeets and mynahs.

Parrots included cockatoos with their expressive crown feathers, and the huge, colorful, noisy macaws.

"Monkeys, from the tiny marmosets to ringtails, wooleys, macaques, gibbons and chimps. There were rodents like gerbils, white mice and rats, rabbits and hamsters. Reptiles ranged from baby alligators and tiny painted turtles to chameleons and snakes. At Easter time, there were always baby chicks and ducks."

I stopped again for a moment, recalling those early years. "To get back to Policeman Joe and Uncle," I continued, "that little chimp was the favorite of everyone in the shop, as well as the entire neighborhood. My sister was in the store the day she arrived, and, not knowing her sex, christened her "Uncle," because she looked so much like my mother's brother.

"She was as cute and cuddly as a baby. When I picked her up, both little arms circled my neck in a warm, affectionate hug. When I sat her in my lap, she became self-concious, and looked away, busying herself picking at my freckles. I guess she thought they were little bugs, and tried to scratch them off.

"I have a small birthmark just below my lower lip, on the left side. Here." I touched the spot. "She noticed it one day and tried to dig it out.

"Ouch, Uncle, that hurts," I told her as I pushed her finger away. She stopped and looked me in the eye. Very gently, she touched the spot with her finger, as if apologizing. 'I love you too, Uncle,' I said, and gave her a warm hug.

"My mom, watching the exchange said, 'That's her love spot for you.'

"It became a ritual that every time I left her, I hugged her and told her I loved her. Then she touched my birthmark, ever so gently, with her finger.

"I guess I spoiled her. She wanted to stay in my arms all day. She laid still during the frequent diaper changes, because she knew when we finished, a hug was her reward. When I had to put her back in her cage, she threw a mini-tantrum, screaming and pounding the floor in frustration. But after a few minutes, she picked up her doll and sat hugging it, rocking back and forth, calm and loving as ever.

"If the weather was warm, I took her by the hand for a walk outside. Either Mom or Dad would come along, as she was a rather expensive toy. My mom dressed her up in baby clothes and a little bonnet.

"Uncle's favorite adventure was raiding the outdoor fruit and vegetable stands. Pulling me close to one, she'd snatch an apple or banana, and stuff it into her mouth. Strollers were delighted with her performance, and Dad had an agreement with the merchants: he was the only customer for their spoiling or aging fruits and vegetables.

"In the shop's window, Uncle's playmates were a litter of lively puppies. The window was prepared with a four-inch layer of shredded newspaper, providing a clean, soft, absorbent playpen. Uncle was put in with the puppies, clutching the burlap sack she adored. She would lie on her back, covering herself in a 'Hide and Seek' fashion. The pups would grab the sack and, backing away, pull it off, growling in mock anger. She would take a playful swipe at them as she retrieved it, then cover herself and repeat the game."

Smiles broke the lines on those stern faces around the conference table.

"Before long, spectators outside the window were ten deep and growing. When that happened, people couldn't get past them on the sidewalk and, in the interest of traffic flow, Joe came and dispersed the crowd.

"I played with Uncle every chance I could. Her greetings, happy 'ooohs' and affectionate hugs made me her slave. It was like having a toy, a pet and a baby all in one. Mom saw to it that she was clean and diapered. Though I dreaded the realization, Uncle was there to be sold.

"It was a traumatic day when she got sick. She wouldn't respond and lost all interest in play. She stopped eating and just lay gasping for breath. A severe cough racked her body. A heavy, yellow nasal discharge soiled her face. Uncle had pneumonia.

"Dad tried every possible remedy. He telephoned Dr. Blamey, who had performed miracles with the dogs and cats, but he had no experience with apes and couldn't help. Our family doctor couldn't treat her. He knew nothing about animals. So Mom took over. She insisted we take Uncle home at night so she could have around-the-clock-nursing. Mom treated her like another child, force-feeding her soup and juices, crushed bananas and aspirin powder. She wiped her nose, changed her diapers and tried to keep the feverish little body cool with alcohol rubs. Every morning, Uncle was bundled up in blankets, and returned to the shop. We prayed, worried and waited, frustrated and helpless!"

"It was then," I said, looking Dean Hagan in the eye, "that I decided to become a chimpanzee doctor." I could tell by the way the committee exchanged glances and grinned that it was a "first."

I continued, "In the evenings, after Uncle was diapered and fed, Mother would let me take her in my arms, hugging and rocking her. With each labored breath, I felt and heard the rumble of mucous in her chest.

"Occasionally Mom let me apply menthol for her cough. Holding her with one arm, I rubbed the ointment into her back. I dreamed that some magic from my concerned hands would cure her. Nothing seemed to help. She gradually weakened and lost weight. My parents tried to prepare me for the inevitable, but I would hear none of it.

"A few days later, Officer Joe was taking his lunchtime stroll, sipping beer and greeting his friends. As always he stopped at Uncle's cage, gently fingering her face between the bars. Wearily, she lifted herself to a sitting position and uttered the first frail, 'oooh' anyone had heard in weeks.

"Zimmerman," Joe called.

"Uncle was sitting, rocking usteadily, and staring at Joe. Something about him had stimulated her. Dad took Joe's beer and poured a little into a saucer, opened her cage and offered it. He had made the same futile gesture so many times with so many tasty tidbits that all he could do was hope. Uncle stooped over and drank the saucer dry. She finished the balance of the can and from that moment, began to improve.

"When I came into the shop that afternoon and heard the news, I burst into tears. I made my dad walk me to the busy intersection of Thirty-Fourth Street and Fifth Avenue, where Joe worked. As the light changed, I rushed and grabbed him in a bear hug. In a single motion, one of his arms stopped the traffic as the other draped over my shoulders. His smile was as big as his heart, as he walked me back to Dad."

The tale almost over, I looked around and saw the light on every face. I concluded, "As Uncle's appetite returned, she slowly gained weight and strength. Soon she was playing like a normal, year-old child.

Within a few weeks she was taking her walks, dressed up like the little lady she was. She resumed her ploy of stealing bananas while playing to her public. Once again, her antics in the window helped add to the chaos of West Thirty-First Street.

"I never cared for the taste of beer, and seldom drink it. However," I told the committee, "if Uncle liked it, that was good enough for me! As the years passed, I became convinced she had covertly shared Joe's lunch, developing a taste that saved her life. To this day, a whiff of beer brings back the vivid picture of that lovable little ape."

Exchanging smiles with the learned professors, I quipped, "I thought it my duty, gentlemen, to share the discovery of that miracle drug with the veterinary profession."

Dr. Milks, beaming, said, "Hey, Zim, you ought to write a book." I finally took his advice.

Dennie Hammond Udall, BSA, DVM, Professor of Veterinary Medicine and Director of the Ambulatory Clinic

Henry Hugh Dukes, BS, DVM, MS, Professor of Veterinary Physiology

*William Arthur Hagan, DVM, MS, Professor of Bacteriology
and Dean of the College*

(left): Earl Sunderville, DVM, Professor of Veterinary Anatomy and Secretary of the College.

(right): Raymond Russell Birch, BSA, DVM, MS, Professor and Superintendent of the Veterinary Experiment Station.

II

Cornell University

The excitement and anticipation of going to a university would be overwhelming. Mom and Dad knew it and worried about my proficiency and dedication. A mediocre student at best, I was getting closer to everything I ever dreamed about, planned for and lost sleep over; the Veterinary College. Evelyn gave me a sisterly lecture, impressing on me the importance of the first step--to pass the pre-vet requirements--a group of medically oriented courses in animal husbandry and agriculture. She knew from experience how difficult the freshman year would be. She told me, her face grave with concern, how many students, elated over acceptance, let their studies slip and before they realized it, failed and busted out.

Pre-vet at Cornell, never a snap, was given in the Schools of Agriculture and Arts & Science. I assured Mom and Dad that I was so proud to be at the same university as my sister that I would never let them down.

"I'll need a job," I told Evelyn, "even with help from Uncle Stein, there are costs I must take care of myself."

"Don't worry about it," she said. "It will all work out fine."

"That doesn't mean you can't join a fraternity," she told me, "it's a little different for men."

Evelyn paved the way for me in more ways than she knew. Because of her dating Tau Delts, they were encouraged to rush and pledge me. Knowing she approved made it easy for me to join and enjoy fraternity life with its social implications (mostly coeds and dances), and the security of built-in tutors. Most importantly, it allowed me to work, as she did, for room and board.

My sister was socially popular and a very busy undergraduate, majoring in bacteriology, one of the courses sure to be in the Vet college curriculum. She told me about her job, working at Risley

Dorm for her room and board. I pictured her face, as she told me about the sororities she despised. Being active in both modern dance, under the tutelage of Martha Graham, and an intercollegiate archery champion, she had enough to keep her busy and happy.

When Evelyn was a junior, and I a freshman, Dad called to tell me about a surprise he had for his daughter. I could hear the pleasure in his voice as he talked. At no little sacrifice, he had purchased a used, 1936, black Chevrolet. He would drive it to Ithaca on a free weekend. When he handed her the keys, both hands covered her mouth in surprise and disbelief. "It's beautiful!" was all she could say as she threw her arms around him, tears of happiness streaming down her face. I got almost as much pleasure from her joy as he did.

She named the car "Jezebel." To us it was the "jewel" of the campus! I owned a part of the car, too; allowed to fix the flats, keep it gassed and in good repair, and given the honor to rescue it when stuck in the snow or marooned on Ithaca's steep hills. Permission was given, for those privileges, to use it for an occasional date or a short trip outside of Ithaca, usually to beautiful Taugannick Falls, a nearby recreation area.

During my first year, Evelyn lost her given name. She told me about it with a sad, almost mournful look. I felt terrible because I thought she was miserable. The look on my face was too much and she burst out laughing. She threw her arms around me in a quick hug. "I'm only kidding, I couldn't care less. There is another coed in my dorm named Evelyn. I bowed to seniority and accepted "Toni," a name that will be mine for eternity."

Sol Linowitz was Toni's boyfriend. He was a brilliant law student, editor of the Law Quarterly, and first in his class. Toni told me about him and how he also worked his way through school. We met one day, on the football field, where I was showing off as a varsity fullback on the 150's. He came with Toni to watch the game. I liked his mischievous grin and quick wit. "Any brother of Toni," he said after our victory, "that can play football, go to vet school, fix flats, and work his way through school, all at the same time, "is okay with me."

Our family liked and accepted him. He got the moniker "Chick," from his college friends. While still undergraduates, they were married in New York City on September 3, 1939—the day Hitler invaded Poland. Sol had three brothers. Dave, the eldest, and Bob and Harry, the two younger. Dave spent an entire week in the big city, planning the wedding with my parents, and when the lovers stood under the 'chuppa,' exchanging rings, Mom cried from happiness and Dad glowed with pride.

Back in school for their final year, Chick and Toni were revered by us Tau Delts as ideal house-party chaperones, retiring early enough to avoid seeing mischief, but always there when needed.

To this day I recall with pleasure, our fraternity house, resting about fifty feet from Fall Creek Gorge, whose roaring waterfall was a musical treat for the students living in rooms facing south. Being one of the lucky ones, I watched, captivated, the miniature Niagara, with its sheer drop of almost five hundred feet, exploding in a magnificent spray, at the street level of downtown Ithaca.

I remember with a chuckle, the constant, playful wrangle between the fraternity's steward and cook on one hand, and the rest of us fraters, on the other. The steward, Stan Kates, was a junior, appointed by the officers to manage the funds, supervise the kitchen and make sure the budget was adhered to. In truth, it was Stan, with his serious frown, not the Consul (president) who had undisputed power.

Stan was my boss and as we talked, he told me he was a lineman on his high school football team, so we had something in common. This stocky, crew-cut frater could manipulate an accordion like a virtuoso. Besides his unquestioned sagacity, his quick smile and ready laugh, he hid a politically conservative ideology. And his conservatism spread further; to conserve food and save money for the fraternity, bordering on fanaticism.

Like most undergraduates, we were in a constant state of starvation. At night, after the kitchen was closed and the refrigerator locked, our hunger was most acute. Some of the greatest minds on campus conspired to either break the lock or figure a way to get inside. I am proud to report that I, and a chosen few, nameless until now, succeeded in removing the hinges from the refrigerator door. Any onlooker, viewing the heinous activity, would swear that a bunch of safecrackers were at work. The only things absent were face masks and revolvers. I used a screwdriver on the upper hinge while Bob Witt worked on the lower. Don Sussman stood guard and Marv Steinberg supported the door as the hinges came loose. Dick Weiss was in charge of supplying dishes and silverware for the secret repast and Norm Hyman was assigned clean-up after the feast. Mouths watered as we pillaged the contents, then, replacing the door, with fingerprints wiped away and guilt forever hidden, we stole back to our rooms. The pilferage was discreetly limited to once a month, each time becoming more professional. The losses were never understood, and the mastery never revealed, due to modest gorging and pledges of lifelong secrecy.

My fraternity brothers pursued their various tasks or pleasures after meals while three of us, Chuck Lowenfeld, Don Sussman and myself, sweated for our room and board. The chef watched with a critical eye as we washed, dried and stacked the dishes, toweled the glasses and silverware and helped him clean up. Our eyes darted to the clock every few seconds but we were never done quickly enough. Waiters were finished after clearing the tables, a job we envied, but fraters were not permitted to wait tables in their own house. Occasionally, one of us had to work without help.

I was alone one evening, when Stan Kates wandered in to check his domain. It was part of his routine to look into the kitchen before he tackled his studies. He caught me staring dejectedly at a huge pile of dishes, two hundred or so glasses and a bucket of silverware. As usual, he carried an armful of textbooks. He looked at my face, then at the stack, put down the books, took off his coat, rolled up his sleeves and quipped, "If you're ever going to get into Vet School, you'll need a hand tonight."

Stan and I became chums, an unlikely association for a pre-vet freshman and a junior majoring in economics. We talked as we toiled, and got to know each other. Stan was from Long Island, the son of a butcher. He told me about high school football, but not until then did he mention his injury. He had suffered a mild concussion that ended his career. We discussed the war and R.O.T.C. (Reserve Officer's Training Corps), a two-year, optional course for undergraduates. Students who volunteered were guaranteed a commission. Stan paused, wondering how I would decide.

"It's a nuisance course," he admitted, "but if we ever go to war, which seems more likely every day, who wants to be a private?"

"You have two choices," Stan said, "Infantry or Field Artillery,"

He had already taken one year of infantry and advised me, as a veterinary hopeful, to take Horse-Drawn Field Artillery. "The Army has long since become motorized," he explained, "but they insist that students ride once weekly, until horses are officially eliminated."

I discovered that most pre-Vet and straight Ag students chose the artillery to be close to the horses. Stan and I discussed the possibilities and decided that field artillery was a natural for me, especially since I didn't know how to ride. By the time we had wiped the last dish, it was settled. "I'll take the artillery course and try to become an equestrian."

The class was given on Fridays, in the Old Armory, whose surface of natural sod had been the winter practice area for the polo team. On Mondays, we met in the Drill Hall, and learned about French 105's, the basic teaching weapon for the army.

The first day, I entered the Old Armory and saw about twenty horses standing together at the far end, untethered, adjacent to the sliding doors that led to the stalls. They stood with swishing tails and bobbing heads, disinterested in us, probably hoping an attendant would let them through those portals. I supposed they wanted to rest and eat. The smell of the stable, always pleasant to me, permeated the air. The horses eyed us as we approached, and I felt the twitter of uncertainty in the pit of my stomach. They seemed calm enough and I tried to pick out the gentlest one, as if the army would permit us to make the choice!

An officer approached holding a clipboard, and barked, "Attention!" He introduced himself as Captain Silver, and called the roll. After twenty-or-so, "presents," he reviewed the course's objectives: "We'll learn the several gaits, jumps, different leads, and simple care and maintenance of the mounts. The army assumes that most of you can ride. For those who don't, the best way to learn is to get right to it. We won't use saddles today, and we'll be jumping easy, three-foot barriers. Those who can't ride, step forward."

Was he kidding? I thought. Jump the first day? And bareback? I assumed that at least half the class would join me, and we'd all object to the exercise. I looked right and left before I stepped forward alone. I was tempted to step back and take my chances with the rest, but then I would be giving up my only excuse if they saw me struggling to stay mounted.

There were four, three-foot hurdles scattered around the track. The captain looked me over and chose my horse. He was named Midnight, jet black, stocky, with a huge, shiny mane and student-smart. To mount, we were taken to a two foot, raised area near one wall, where we could straddle the horses easily.

"Let him know who's boss," Captain Silver said, as I prepared myself. "They always know a new student and try to take advantage."

The problem was—Midnight didn't understand English. He thought he was in charge and proceeded to prove it. The captain held the reins as I mounted. I bravely threw my leg over his back and almost fell off on the other side, grabbing his mane in desperation. Captain Silver handed me the reins and stepped away. Midnight followed the other horses in line, loping toward the first hurdle. I hung on for dear life as we approached and began our jump. Somehow, in mid-air, he changed direction and I sailed right over his shoulder. The surface of the armory had been freshly plowed, and I landed feet-first, before pitching over on my face. Several horses behind us dodged skillfully, as I dusted myself off, not a little embarrassed, and looked around for Midnight. He had returned to the doors, his job done, expecting his reward - - - oats. I considered myself a fair athlete, and riding wasn't that complicated. I had to try again.

"He's just testing you, Zimmerman," the captain called out. "As soon as he's convinced you're serious, he'll stop that nonsense."

As I approached, Midnight ignored me completely, but most of the other riders were grinning and not a little interested in the only stimulating happening in what to them was an hour of boredom. "I'm going to take all the jumps today, Midnight, if it takes an hour." I muttered. Heads turned as I picked up the reins, stroked his neck, led him back to the raised area, remounted, and gripped him around the belly with firm legs. Off we went and off I flew in the same manner as before. My landings were improving, though--this time I stayed on my feet! Midnight tried for the door again. I was getting fed up with that stubborn horse and decided to be firm and more demanding. Encouraging remarks from other riders spurred me on. The captain was busy with another student and didn't seem to be watching. If so, he was the only one. I walked quickly to the doors, scooped up the reins and jerked them roughly, snapping his head around. I whispered, "No food for you till you behave, you stubborn nag."

Mounted once more, with my left hand gripping the reins short, and my right hand taking a fistful of mane, I waited for a break in the line. Pulling his head around, I kicked my heels into his side and yelled, "Giddap!"

He started for the third time and raised for the jump as I held tight, concentrating on my legs and hands. Midnight was as stubborn as I tried to be, and this time, landing on my head and rolling over on the soft turf saved me from injury.

Angry and humiliated and prodded by the students, I started for the doors again, when Captain Silver called out, "That's enough for today, Zimmerman. We only allow three falls per day. You'll have to wait till next week."

"Can you believe what they ordered us to do at the very first session?" I complained to Stan, "We had to jump three-foot barriers, bareback!" Stan grinned as he listened, "The others rode without a saddle, easy as pie, but my last mounted adventure was a slow, plodding saddle pony at Coney Island. And that was more than ten years ago!"

I got little sympathy from him, "If you're going to be a vet, knowing horses goes with the job." He was right. I fumed and fussed and dreamed, for seven days, about how Midnight could be tamed and requested him again. It was probably my foolish pride, but hoping to be a veterinarian, I couldn't allow intimidation by a potential patient.

The following week everyone in the class had sore backsides but me, not being in the saddle long enough. With Captain Silver's encouragement, I rode that black critter around the track for ten or fifteen minutes without attempting a jump, forcing him to ride around each barrier, changing direction and pace until he was compliant. By that time everyone knew my name and had a remark of encouragement or advice. We turned toward the first barrier and sailed over it easily; he stayed straight and I stayed on. There was applause and "Nice going," from all sides, and I wasn't sure whether to be grateful or flustered. They were watching my every move. I stayed on his back for one hour, and happily ate off the fraternity's fireplace mantle for an entire week.

"Any other horse would have been a snap," Stan said, as he heard the rest of the story. "You happened to get the dilly of the pack. But you'll be the better rider for it in the end. The captain knew what he was doing."

Once I gained Midnight's respect, we began to enjoy each other. I rewarded him with sugar cubes and raw carrot sticks. Soon, when I entered the Old Armory, he would give a little snort of pleasure, leave his pals at the door and greet me with an affectionate nuzzle from his warm, soft nose. He was the only one of the twenty equines to show interest in their riders. When we were finished for the day, heads turned in amusement and surprise as nineteen horses would race for the stall doors, but Midnight hung around as long as I was there, to the expressed pleasure of Captain Silver.

"I guess antagonism breeds affection," he said, shaking his head.

We had changed our opinions of each other. I stood facing him, one arm around his neck, fingering his rich black mane, my head against his powerful neck. He was such a noble, understanding creature. The captain watched approvingly as I curried him. Midnight loved the feel of the curry-comb that had the same effect as having someone scratch an unreachable itch on your back. Every few moments he received a tidbit as an extra. We had become friends and even after the course, I'd go out of my way to see him and fuss over him. I finished the riding, realizing that it was the easy part of my military training. Trying to learn how to aim a 105MM artillery piece, and figuring range and trajectory for Howitzers was very complicated. I finally got through with the minimum passing grade.

One day, on the Drill Hall bulletin board, there was an announcement about tryouts for the pistol team. I looked over and around a bunch of interested heads to read the details. It was sponsored by the R.O.T.C., but was considered an intercollegiate competition.

I dragged Stan over to read the notice and asked him about going out.

"My dad was a sharpshooter in the army, and my sister is an intercollegiate archery champion. I should be great at it. Besides, every veterinarian should know how to shoot, in case a horse breaks a leg."

"My dad was a county fair hog-caller," he teased. "My sister has three blonde daughters, and you're not in Vet School yet. I'll bet I'm a better shot than you. Let's go!"

There was a turnout of about a hundred students. We all crowded around the officer in charge as he explained the safety rules, how to load the gun, and how to hold it for firing. "We have too large a turnout for individual instruction." he said, "Each man will have ten shots and the ten best scores will qualify." We started a mad rush to be first but stopped as he concluded. "Fill out the application cards and you will be called alphabetically."

We waited our turns, and Stan went to the range first. I heard the report of the weapons and pictured Stan hitting the bulls-eye with every shot. In a few minutes, he pushed through the range curtain with a disgusted look on his face. "The pistols are too heavy," he complained. "I only hit the target once and that was on the edge. Good luck!"

It took almost three-quarters of an hour for my turn. I walked through the curtain that separated the range from the waiting area. It was smoke-filled and reeked from gun powder. A sergeant waved me to one of the ten target areas where a table held a pistol and a clip of ammunition. He must have been bored to death by the time I reached him. He introduced himself as Sergeant McGillicuddy and repeated the instructions, "The gun must never be pointed down or away from your target. When loaded, point straight up. When ready, shoot ten rounds at your target."

I considered him a model of the military. Erect stance, graying hair on a head held high, immaculate uniform and inscrutable expression. Only once was there a hint of a smile on that stern face the whole time I knew him. He talked down to the students but was obsequious to the captain. I thought about officers being better off than foot soldiers and that it's worth the extra effort to become one.

The sergeant concluded, "Don't jerk the trigger. Aim the sight above your target, lower gradually and squeeze gently. You shouldn't know when the gun fires. The smoother you are the better you'll shoot. Sign your target before you leave, and you will be called if you qualify."

The targets hung on a pulley type gadget about fifty feet away. I loaded my gun and aimed at the bulls-eye, my arm fully extended. I hoped the sergeant wasn't behind me watching my every move. The gun was much heavier when held out that way. How could I hold it steady for ten shots? The mode for shooting pistols, had not as yet allowed supporting the trigger-arm with the other hand. My dad had shown me how to squeeze the trigger at Coney Island, but they were rifles that rested on a counter. After firing ten times my arm ached, but when the pulley brought in the target, it looked pretty good. Four holes were near the bulls-eye, and all ten hit the target.

"You ever shoot before?" asked McGillicuddy, standing behind me. Damn! I thought, he was there.

"No sir." I answered.

"Good," he said, "I'd rather have natural talent. I coach the team and I want you here at least three times weekly to practice."

I couldn't believe it. I made the team! Why didn't I bet Stan? My dad would be proud that I had one of the ten lowest scores.

McGillicuddy had a compulsion about winning. He had us doing all sorts of exercises to strengthen our performance.

"Practice makes perfect!" he would repeat over and over again. I guess I made the most improvement because he always seemed friendlier to me than to the others. We qualified for the League Championship Shoot-Off and, for the first time, McGillicuddy seemed nervous. He's a good coach I thought, he really wants us to win. I didn't find out until after the season that he bet big money with the opposing mentors. We lost the match and his face looked like he would explode. He must have lost a bundle, but couldn't say a word because the captain was watching.

When the season ended we were all rewarded with a sweater with a minor "C", the large letter being reserved for major sports, like football and baseball. I was very proud and all my other team-mates were all smiles at the presentation. Our team got a framed group picture, showing McGillicuddy with that *almost* smile.

My new roommate was Norm Hyman. I was helping him unload his car in the lot just below the fraternity house porch. The boys milling around the veranda, looked down on the unlikely pair, Nor-man, six foot four in height and two hundred and forty pounds of muscle, had been an all-scholastic tackle at Albany High, New York, and a scholastic record holder in the discus. I topped one sixty in weight and stood about five foot seven. We may have painted a picture of "Mutt and Jeff," but we had an instant rapport that lasted until the army took him out of my life.

The notice for my interview to Vet School arrived in mid-April. It had me worried, knowing the appointments were alphabetical and hoping they would reach my name before all the openings were filled. Norm saw my concern.

"Don't worry, Zim." he said, comfortingly, "They'll hold a place for you."

I started for James Law Hall, the school's administration building, for my 3 P.M. appointment. As I walked uphill, along a wooded path leading toward the campus, I paused on the suspension bridge spanning Fall Creek. There were a few other students looking over the rail admiring the view. It was a poignant moment, listening to the brisk, bubbling water gathering momentum as it flowed along the gorge, finally plunging over in a sheer, noisy drop, so close to the Tau Delt House. How many more years would be left to admire Ithaca's breathtaking panorama?

Pulling myself away, I trudged up the steep footpath. The Arts Quadrangle appeared with its carefully mowed grass and crisscrossing walks. As I looked right and left I saw the Administration Building, Goldwyn Smith Hall, Boardman Hall, Baker Laboratory, and Willard Straight, the student social center, surrounding the open green lawn. Willard Straight's tower housed the busy chimes that peal out each hour, for ten or more minutes and entertain all within earshot with a variety of melodies. It played an encouraging melody for me; "Cornell's Victory March."

On the edges of the quad, two, life-size, bronze statues peered at each other across the green, founder Ezra Cornell and first president Andrew D. White.

Proceeding north, there were more ivy-covered buildings that someday, hopefully, would mark my daily route. I entered James Law Hall for the interview where I introduced my chimp "Uncle," to the weary, complacent committee.

Two hours later, dancing and triumphant, I returned to the fraternity house and Norm knew by the look on my face how the meeting went.

He shook my hand warmly, and with a huge smile on his face, said, "Nice going, Doc, I knew you could do it."

"Not so fast," I said, "it's going to take another year of Ag. Being named Zimmerman is a real drag. By the time they reached me, all the places were filled. The dean was encouraging though, and the discussion went well. Dr. Hagan said to be sure to reapply next year."

"That will give you a chance to catch up with us farmers," Norm said. "And you can take all the Ag courses we talked about and learn something about horses, swine, cattle, sheep, goats and poultry."

"I guess so. By the way, some of the guys were discussing a new Vet College in Waltham, Massachusetts, called Middlesex. It's going to open next fall, and anyone with Vet School prerequisites can get in."

Norm's eyes widened. "You'd leave Cornell?"

"It could save a year. I spoke to some of the guys who were rejected and are interested." I explained. "I may run up there to see it, after final exams in June."

About a month later, I received a call from my cousins, Jack and Janet Abelow. They were opening two summer camps near Honesdale, Pennsylvania--Todd Lake for boys and Janel for girls.

Janet asked, "How would you like a free summer at camp? I understand you can bugle. We need someone we can trust to run the canteen as well. It would require about four hours of work a day. What do you say?"

I thought fast. No pay, but a free summer. Camp is so great, how could I refuse? Two summers of working on a local farm for the farm-practice credit were required for the School of Agriculture, but only one if I made Vet School. I could postpone the credits for two years, and did.

"I'd love it, Janet," I said. "When do I start? Can I bring Silver?" They knew my Schnauzer and how much I loved him.

I discussed Middlesex with my parents: "Mom, what do you think? I can save a year if they'll take me, but my first choice has always been Cornell."

She looked at me thoughtfully and asked, "What's your hurry?" Mom was always "Mrs. Common Sense."

Then I turned to Dad, "What do you think?"

"I prefer Cornell," he said thoughtfully. "I hoped you'd follow your cousins." Mike and Sam, Uncle Stein's sons, were Cornell graduates.

But my folks agreed I should go ahead and visit the school and make up my own mind. So I hitch-hiked with Silver to Waltham, Massachusetts, and searched for the vet campus. My mind's eye had the picture of a school similar to Cornell's. I saw a building labeled, "Administration," but it was nothing like Ithaca! I walked inside and saw a lady behind a reception desk.

"Could you direct me to the veterinary campus?" I asked the young woman.

"Is your dog sick?" She asked merrily. Then, her face serious, "We don't have a campus yet. It will be built this year. We do have a barn with some animals. The dean has his office there." She was pleasant and likeable and I followed her directions to the contemplated campus.

The Dean of the Veterinary College greeted me at the barn door and gave Silver a pat on the head. He was much younger than Dean Hagan. About forty, I thought, black hair just graying slightly over the temples. "Come along," he said. "We have great plans." We toured the facilities together. I thought it strange that the dean was so young and also that he gave me so much time.

His office was just inside the door. We walked around it to the main barn where a lonely cow stood in a stall with its newborn calf. Silver was immediately interested and sniffed the calf from head to toe. "Come away, Silver." I ordered, "Mom may kick your head off."

The dean smiled proudly, looking at the animals. "We don't have horses, dogs, cats or clinics as yet, but they're coming." I asked him about the curriculum and what his plans were for teaching exotic animal medicine. I got a funny look, and I'm sure he didn't know what I was talking about.

"By September," he assured me, "the college will be fully staffed with enough animals to start the fall term."

I told him the courses I had taken at Cornell but I didn't have any papers certifying my grades. I asked him what my chances were for getting accepted. He looked at me and smiled, "I like you, your attitude and your dog. You're in!"

It was too easy, I thought. It didn't sit right. I asked him for the applications and told him I'd let him know. From Waltham, Massachusetts, Silver and I hitch-hiked to camp.

My decision to wait the extra year, on Dr. Hagan's word, proved sound. Middlesex Veterinary College lasted but four years, graduated one class, was never accredited, and the graduates were limited to practice only in the Commonwealth of Massachusetts.

The summer went quickly and, before I realized it, I was back in Ithaca, living at Tau Delta Phi and studying agriculture. Silver stayed at home, but I certainly enjoyed his company during the summer. It was too bad dogs weren't allowed in the frat, I missed that whiskered face and wagging tail.

Norm Hyman and I went over what was being offered in the College of Agriculture that would be a good background for Vet School. We agreed on several that would allow me to handle and judge draft horses, cattle, swine, sheep and poultry, plus one in ornithology for my eventual practice on exotic birds.

The fraternity pledged a new freshman class and I got one as a roommate. Ed Nightingale, from Brooklyn, moved in with Hyman and me. I'd been told, and Ed never denied, that he was scared to death of anything alive below the Phylum, Primate. I caught a box-turtle one morning and brought it into our room. As I stood at the door, the turtle between my feet, Ed jumped on his bed and scrambled to the end, back to the wall, bent almost double (due to the low ceiling under the gabled roof). His face was pained and he pleaded, "Come on, Squinch (my nick name), get it out of here!"

"Ed," I said, "he couldn't hurt you if he wanted to. Besides, you're a pre-med. You'll be working with animals of all kinds for at least six years. Get down and make up your mind to get acquainted. He's going to share our room."

"No!" he screamed. "I'm not getting near that thing. I'll get rabies! I'm allergic! Get him out! I have to study! Norm," he pleaded, turning to Hyman, "make him get rid of it."

"I think he'll make a great roommate," Norm answered seriously. "He'll be the only one in the house that doesn't require a bed and a closet."

Ed's face showed genuine anguish and, I couldn't conceive of anyone being that afraid of a *turtle*.

Suddenly, I was brought up short. I'd forgotten completely about myself. It certainly was possible for someone to have an acquired, deep-seated fear. It was ten years earlier and I had developed a phobia of my own.

Mom and Dad knew about infant mortality from the cruel statistics of European medicine. This was America, the new land where everything was perfect. Not so with the polio epidemic of 1916 nearly wiping out a generation of babies.

Rivervale, New Jersey, a tiny town nestled between Montvale and Park Ridge, was our family's "heaven on Earth." In the mid-1920's, my dad built a little cottage that was our summer escape from New York, and all its problems.

It was there and I was ten years old. A developer had planned a residential complex at the bottom of the hill on the Orangeburg Road near our new home. He had a huge, two-acre lake constructed on the left side of the road. It was fed by a little stream that ran under the road and insured a constant supply of fresh water. The plan included residential housing directly across the street. The depression stopped him cold, but it left us a wonderful swimming hole and a breeding place for aquatic nature.

I spent more time down at the lake than I did at home. I waded in the feeder spring that tunneled under the road, leading to the lake, and threw stones at tremendous spiders that had etched huge, carefully constructed webs near the concrete ceiling. I never cared much for spiders in general, although I had several "daddy-long-legs" as pets. They intrigued me the way their legs kept moving for several seconds after they broke off from their tiny, pea-shaped bodies.

On a beautiful spring day in June, following a heavy rain, the water was up to my chest as I bravely strode into the water under the bridge. My hands were loaded with stones for ammunition, when I spied a saucer-size black monster on the far end of the tunnel, near the top where he ambushed flies, moths and butterflies. I was going to knock that devil off the wall. The first couple of stones missed, then I made a good hit that knocked him down into the water. Usually they run on the water away from trouble. He must have been disoriented, because he started right at me, at tremendous speed, his ugly, bent legs a blur of motion. I was petrified because the water was too deep for me to run. The last sighting I had was when he was about two feet away and closing fast. I shrieked hysterically and thrashed at him with both hands as hard as I could, sure the huge, ugly, mean-looking beast would grab me or bite me or do whatever a spider as fierce as he looked, does to tormentors.

I was sobbing with fright and when the water quieted down, he wasn't on me or anywhere to be seen. As I scrambled out, the other kids rushed over to find out what was the matter. From that moment to this day, I suffer from arachniphobia. I stopped hunting, stoning, collecting and researching spiders forever.

I had good reason to feel sorry for Ed and the turtle. Silently I removed it and returned it to the forest. He finally conquered his fears and did go to Med School, graduating with honors.

I enjoyed the animal husbandry courses in Ag School. My marks were good and I was getting experience handling and judging the various farm animals for both the show ring and the market place. With each new course, I tried to glean information that someday I could use on exotic animal patients. I pictured the African range animals and decided I'd treat them just like I would a cow. After all, they foraged for grass and chewed their cud just like their bovine cousins. Zebras were like horses and the lions, tigers, leopards and cheetahs were overgrown tabby cats.

As summer approached, the Camp Todd Lake directors offered me a promotion to counselor, with a salary of $75 for the season. I bragged to my family. "I'm going to be rich. I'm through with the canteen and bugling."

My brother, Norman, five years my junior, would take over my previous summer's chores. He was fourteen now and I knew he'd love those jobs. I told them about my promotion to a full-fledged counselor of challenging nine year-olds with JoJo Roth, my co-counselor, a short, muscular, intense, handsome, Lawrence Olivier look-alike. JoJo and I got along well with our bright, spoiled, but gifted kids that included my baby brother, Joe.

Silver had behaved so well during the first summer, he was permitted to return. The only sound he ever made was his single "arf" to get attention. If a camper was munching on his canteen goodies, one quick yap meant, "Can I have a taste?" If he needed some attention or affection, one yelp did the talking. He was a patient pup. If his bark was ignored, he turned away, trotted to his favorite spot beside the bunk's door, spun around just once and flopped on his side. In one minute, he was napping.

I didn't find out until I arrived at Todd Lake that my greatest challenge would be caring for Max Ray, a nine year-old deaf-mute. The camp owners and his parents picked me to be his special mentor. When I met him I knew our relationship would be far from simple. He was alert, sensitive and highly intelligent. JoJo watched me try to talk to him that first day. He was very difficult and angry and turned away from my overtures. His mother insisted he be treated like any other camper. He was a lip-reader and she wouldn't permit him to use pen and paper to communicate. Max had an unsatisfactory summer at another camp the previous year but Janet assured her that Camp Todd Lake, with its excellent counselors, would be his best experience ever.

The day before Max arrived, I lectured my campers: "You boys were chosen to be with Max because you're each special. You have the privilege all the other boys will envy." I explained how the deaf are handicapped and how they must be treated. Tapping his shoulder to attract his attention, then facing him and speaking normally so he can read their lips. The boys were attentive, and excited to take him on.

His arrival with a frown on his face and a chip on his shoulder made our efforts difficult if not impossible. He was rather stocky, with dark, intelligent eyes. At first, we had trouble making him listen. He looked away and we were ignored. He liked to spend his time stroking Silver. Patiently and insistently, we touched his shoulder and talked. When he looked away in disgust, I started all over again and told the boys to do the same.

JoJo threw up his arms in disgust. "I don't have your patience," he said. "Maybe he should be in an older bunk." We didn't give up, however, tapping and repeating, tapping and repeating. Finally our efforts paid off. He became interested in camp activities and in what we wanted to say to him. His suspicions gradually disappeared.

What surprised me most was the inexplicable bond that evolved between Max and Silver. Instead of his usual resting place near the door, Silver adopted the foot of Max's bed. It was uncanny how the dog realized that Max couldn't hear. It took no more than two or three ignored yips for him to change tactics. His right paw, in a scratching mode on Max's arm, and his black, expressive eyes concentrating on his face, alerted Max that he was talking to him. Silver sensed that this boy was different, and an intuitive cognition alerted him to react. That cute gray face, with its whiskers and eyebrows lending emotion and understanding, became fixed on Max. His two-inch tail, wagging with love, accentuated his devotion.

There were rewards and punishments for the boys, meted out equally. Max had read the word "dope" somewhere, and to him it was a swear word. He used it where the other kids uttered profanity. They were punished when they cussed, and he felt part of the family when he got equal treatment. His pronunciation was "dopey," because of his training in phonetics. At first the other kids laughed. "How can you punish him for saying, "dope." They were made to understand that to Max the innocuous "dopey," was the worst expletive he knew, and therefore he was punished. Soon he was taking part in activities he had formerly disregarded. Now when announcements were made after dinner, he impatiently pulled at my arm and asked in his falsetto, "Wha he say? Wha he say?" We were thrilled the first time we heard him laugh. It was a high-pitched, infectious giggle that became a frequent and satisfying chord.

On good days, after taps and lights-out, the boys were rewarded with a story. JoJo and I alternated each night, and we conjured up tales that would intrigue and excite them. The light in the bunk was always dim at that time. Some of the boys would be sitting up as they listened, some curled on their sides awaiting the climax. One night after a story, I heard Max sobbing. My flashlight highlighted him sitting up in bed, with Silver licking his face. I put the flashlight on my mouth and asked him what the trouble was. The tears were streaming down his face and I thought his heart was breaking. I realized why. His sharp senses told him that the other boys were listening to something they loved. We had been insensitive to his needs and I felt terrible. I held him in my arms and quieted his tears. With the flashlight on my face, I told him the story of the night.

In addition to all his other problems, Max was an asthmatic, and we were warned to keep an eye and an ear alerted at all times.

He had his first attack on a damp, rainy night in mid-July. We were all asleep when Silver jumped on my bed and alerted me with one sharp bark. As I sat up, he jumped off the bed, ran across the bunk to Max. I followed. He wheezed, "I can't breathe." The look on his face frightened me. I put my ear to his chest and the musical rales sounded like a symphony. His little heart was pounding as it struggled to overcome oxygen hunger. My first thought was, "Please don't let him die!" I knew I had to get him help--and fast.

I nudged JoJo and told him what was happening. He sat straight up, groggy. "What should we do?"

"I'm getting him to the doctor."

The infirmary was up a steep hill, behind the mess hall. I bundled Max in a blanket, covered it with his raincoat, picked him up and rushed out, Silver at my heels. The other boys slept. Max was heavy, and I tried running as fast as I could. It was so dark that I bumped into bushes and once into a tree as I strayed off the path. His weight seemed to double and I was having trouble with my own breathing. I almost dropped him several times and my pace was down to a crawl. By the time I reached the infirmary at the top of the hill, I was exhausted. His lips were blue, I was limp and Silver was soaked through and through.

The doctor had been briefed and, within seconds, Max had his adrenaline. Relief was immediate and miraculous, and I sat for ten minutes catching my breath and toweling off Silver.

One wonderful day that summer, mother called me on the phone. "Congratulations," she said, "I'm not a bit surprised, you've been accepted into the vet college." I jumped a foot with delight, realizing it had finally happened. I had to go to Cornell to see for myself. On my next day-off, Silver and I hitch-hiked the three hundred miles to Ithaca. I walked into James Law Hall, this time with a smile and checked the bulletin board. The class list read: Adolph, Arnabaldi, Becker, etc. to the 40th and final name, ZIMMERMAN. The euphoria was delicious and I reveled in it all the way back to camp.

"Color War" took place on the last three days of camp. The campers and counselors were divided right down the middle, half blue and half gray. The good-natured rivalry was strong and the visiting parents sat on the sidelines and cheered their favorite teams. Our bunk was divided in half with JoJo on the other team. Max was on my side and I wanted to show him off to his mother and the camp as a whole. The competition of swimming, track, tennis and baseball was close. The teams were tied going into the last evening. The winner would be decided by the competition in dramatics.

Our team had written a play around Max. He was to be a bartender. "Do you think you can serve drinks?" I asked. "You have to pour the liquor into the glasses, after putting in ice cubes." Max was excited, and nodded that he could do everything in the script.

"Keep your eyes on the other actors," I advised. "Larry and Cliff will be talking to each other for five minutes. While they are talking, you have to serve them drinks, wipe off the tables, and get paid."

Max nodded eagerly, laughed when he saw me pouring tea into the liquor bottle, and he understood. During rehearsals, he proved to be a real ham.

"The talking will become heated," I explained. "Both boys will act like they are getting drunk. They will start a fight and you have to break it up. When Larry says to Cliff, 'I'll break this bottle over your head,' you must point to the door and shout, 'Get out!' As you push them through the door, the curtain comes down."

Timing was essential and reading Larry's lips for his cue would require concentration and timing. Max was superb. He brought the house down and a victory for our team.

Mrs. Ray was in tears from pride and happiness. Max, in one day, had erased her self-perceived guilt. What a difference, I thought, from that awful beginning. Max had real tears when good-byes were said on the last day of camp. He couldn't take his eyes off Silver, and Silver wouldn't leave his side. Max had written his mother about the dog, and she was moved and unhappy about the parting. I looked at her face, then at Max. It didn't take me long to make up my mind. I loved Max also and wasn't about to ignore his misery. I handed him the leash, and silently mouthed the suggestion that if he could convince his mother, Silver was his.

III

The College of Veterinary Medicine

Ed and Gert Driscoll lived next door to the Tau Delta Phi fraternity house on Stewart Avenue. They had a beautiful home and rented the upstairs to a Cornell professor and his wife. Ed had just completed another small apartment in the basement, and gave Tau Delt first option for its rental.

Each year the fraternity officers, with Kates in charge, assigned rooms. Seniors and grad students had the first choice, and the rest in order of seniority. Stan, now a senior, made me an offer. "How would you like to room next door at the Driscolls? Its beautiful and it won't affect your dish-washing job."

I thought for a moment. Getting out of the madhouse would be great, especially for my first year in vet school. I wondered if I'd miss the camaraderie, the bull-sessions and the horsing around with my buddies. But . . . a quiet place to concentrate!

"I'd love it, Stan, I really have to study."

"You're in," he said smiling, "but there's a hitch. We want you to room with Marv Steinberg. His marks are lousy, but if he's away from the fraternity, free from temptation, I think we can keep him from busting out."

He questioned me with his eyes. Marv was the kind of influence I didn't need. I liked him; what was not to like? He was full of hell, his first interest was having fun but he was bright with a dry sense of humor. He came from Perkiomen Prep with straight A's but in his freshman year at Cornell, he barely made C's.

"What does he say?" I asked.

"You kiddin'? He'd love it. He respects you and knows that with your influence he'd raise his marks ten points."

"Okay," I sighed and smiled, "I think it will work out fine."

"Good." Stan said, satisfied. "By the way, I'm nominating you for Consul (fraternity president) this year. Interested?"

"I never thought about it." I said honestly. "If the guys want me I'd be honored."

Marv and I moved and were immediately enchanted with the Driscolls and their pets. They had a dog, Pretzels, a purebred Dachshund, and a cat, Tizzie, a huge spayed, black and white tabby. Gert was a big woman with down to earth common sense and a heart of gold. An outsider would think we were family. Ed was a romantic and full of hell, just one of the boys. He had a bushy head of white hair, chubby, florid face and turned up nose. He was a mason by trade and used laborers language when Gert wasn't there to chastise him.

Stan was right. We loved the room. It was new and had the smell of fresh paint and newly cut wood. It was comfortable in size, with a bed on either end, each with a small desk next to it. A huge walk-in closet was off the center of the room, across from the beds, next to a large bathroom. There was wood paneling with an off-white soft tiled ceiling. Built in the basement, three tiny windows were above our heads and too high for us to have an outside view except for the sky.

Once Marv and I were settled in, it was easy to concentrate and study. All the tough courses were in the first year. Anatomy, physiology, therapeutics, materia medical, small animal medicine and bacteriology. Each course had lecture and laboratory classes. In addition, the freshmen helped clean-up in large and small animal surgical clinics.

Since my interview, my favorite professor was Howard J. Milks. I felt his genuine affection and interest. His unique sense of humor had a way of getting his point across and his practical jokes became legend. We were often the butt of his comedy.

His duties were lecture professor of therapeutics, director of the small animal clinic and of course, a member of the board of admissions. A slender man of medium height. His thinning hair topped an aquiline face with twinkling eyes, pointed nose and chin. His mouth hardly moved as he talked. He was a ventriloquist without a doll, and not a good one. It took us weeks to understand him, but soon we relished his idiosyncrasy. He had a nervous habit of licking his lips before either the quip or the reprimand and with either, the hint of a smile lit his face. He lectured on materia medica. the art of preparing, prescribing and dispensing drugs, a tough, dull subject at best. The other course was small animal medicine, where his lively eyes and unpredictability kept the interest of the class from waning.

One day he was discussing urinalyses. "You boys will learn all about the laboratory analyses of urine in physiology 1," he began, "Dr. Dukes will cover how to find abnormal amounts of sugar, albumin, acetone, specific gravity and other ingredients caused by liver, kidney or bladder disease. But you can't carry a lab on your back when making a house call or even during an office visit."

He held up a vial of urine and eyed it carefully as his tongue flecked his lips. "If you use the senses God gave you," he murmured with a grin, "You might be able to tell what's wrong long before the lab report arrives. Check the color, odor, turbidity and yes, even taste."

He dipped a finger into the sample and tasted it. His face was serious and we were convinced that, repugnant as it seemed, it was the way a serious problem was investigated.

I murmured to Gerry Bandes that I'd just as soon discover the problem another way.

Milks' searching gaze caught my lip movement and he said.

"Come on up Zimmerman and see if you can tell us something from the taste of this sample." He grinned at the class and held out the vial.

I dragged myself to the desk and stared. I waited a long moment before gingerly dipping a finger into the smelly sample, the look on my face provoked giggles from the class. Slowly I raised it towards my mouth, hesitated, then moved again. At the last moment Milks grabbed my wrist, roaring with laughter.

"You students have to be more observant!" He quipped "I dipped my little finger into the urine but tasted the index."

The class was hysterical as he pushed me to the wash basin, his face beaming. Milks was known to pull the same gag every year and every one respected his humor and kept his secret. At the end of class Milks beckoned to me. He was squatting on the corner of his desk. A beaker stuffed with pencils, pens, a small scissors and several dental scalers sat on a stack of papers. A pad with abstract doodles created by busy fingers bored by endless repititious lectures, completed the melange. His eyes twinkled and he moistened his lips.

"I hope you didn't mind." he apologized. "I didn't single you out for any particular reason. With your desire to treat chimps and tigers, I thought you merited some recognition." He grinned gleefully.

"Thanks for stopping me. I don't think I'd have relished that taste."

"Never missed in ten years. It's really a great teaching tool. I've never met a student that didn't vividly remember every detail of this class."

"I know one who won't." I said as I followed the mob.

Gerry Bandes and I decided to be anatomy partners. We had met casually the year before in pre-vet, and we became friends after the intramural boxing tournament. Bandes was a fine boxer in the lightweight division. He lost to our frater, Jerry Fried, in the finals. Our common goal brought us together.

Gerry and I had to conjure ways of remembering the hundreds of Latin names for bones, muscles, arteries and veins. One way was to give each other, and our acquaintances, pseudonyms, Latin names for muscles, to get used to their pronunciation.

"I dub thee Peroneus Tertius Zimmerman." He intoned solemnly. His face had a challenging look as he dared me to find a superior Latin designation for him.

"And you shall be, from this day forward, Gastrocnemius Bandes." I smiled, satisfied that my one, three syllable term, was a far superior muscle than his choice, a very small and insignificant fiber, located somewhere near the foot.

The anatomy lab was a huge room tiled in an uneven light brown that once had been white. The walls and floors were stained in a million spots from splashing preservative. Large hooks hung on the walls, supporting instruments like tongs and baling hooks to help manipulate the heavy carcasses. A huge wood crate in one corner was filled with the bones of previously dissected horses, cows, sheep, pigs, dogs and cats. We had been scared to death by upper-classmen's yarns about final exams. "You have to learn how to juggle bones." they teased.

"G'wan." Gerry said disbelieving.

"We're serious. For the exam, two instructors stand at either end of the lecture room tossing long bones in a high arc across the room. You have to identify the bone and the animal, before it lands!"

"It's hopeless. I couldn't tell them apart if they were lying on a table!" I said.

Gerry shrugged his shoulders. Nothing fazed him. "We can always go to med school," he quipped, "only one set of bones."

Behind the lab was the storage room. As we entered our nostrils were assailed by the noxious formaldehyde. Huge vats were filled with the preservative soaking ten horse cadavers. It was a square room that could have been a swimming pool in earlier days. It had neither windows nor ventilation. Two huge cranes lifted each horse and placed them on a long wheeled cart. They lay there dripping formaldehyde for five or ten minutes as our nostrils ached from the insult. Each team of four students pushed the creaking carts into the lab to a preassigned location. The floor was always wet and slippery and the first day Gerry slipped and found himself sitting in a stinking, nettlesome puddle. I had to laugh as I dragged him to his feet. As we rushed to the men's room to stuff toweling between his underwear and tender fanny, the look on his face was unforgettable. I could tell that he wasn't happy with his chosen profession. Especially if it required such unspeakable torture.

Anatomy professor Sunderville was a thin man with foxlike features; an unloved teacher in the equally unpopular course. I remembered him from the interview. He didn't have Dr. Milks' class, warmth or interest in students.

"Anatomy is probably the most important course you will be taking this year." He started at our first lecture. "That means work, work and more work. We'll have a quiz before every lab, so be prepared!" His voice was threatening and his face expressionless.

His assistant, Malcomb Miller, was just the opposite. He was heavy-set, light blond hair crowned a face exuding warmth and compassion. He was always there to answer questions and offer advice. Thank the lord he was there to ease our burden.

Burning eyes and sweating hands inside rubber gloves, added to our misery. We wore long lab coats and boots to protect our shoes. Our noses and eyes would have to get accustomed to the poisoned air.

One day we were standing around, goofing off during professor Sunderville's coffee break. We had been dissecting the stallion's penis. Because half the cadavers were male, the students doubled up when studing the external genitalia. Harry Burghart was holding a dissected organ that measured at least two and a half feet. He was casually leaning back, half sitting against his table, cross-legged with the weight on one foot. A group of us were standing with him, swapping stories. Included was Andrea Maul, the lone female in our class. She had wavy auburn hair, brown eyes and a slight build. Not pretty, but a very pleasant, quiet, sensitive girl. She was a good sport and was well liked.

Burghart swung the huge organ back and forth in a contrived absent-minded fashion. As the conversations continued, the swinging increased in height, arc and tempo. Andrea was directly in front of him and found it necessary to rock her head back and forth to the meter of his swing. Her face never showed what she was feeling. We empathized with Andrea but the talking went on uninterrupted.

Nobody noticed that she was holding one of the metal, three-foot, hooked rods. As one particularly close pass made her take a half step backward, she slipped the hook behind Burghart's ankle, and in one motion jerked. As he plopped to the slippery tile, he lost control of the huge phallus and it landed around his neck like a mink stole. There was a second of silence before hysterical guffaws rocked the lab. We loved Andrea all the more as she looked down at him without the slightest change of expression. We returned to our own tables happy and buzzing about the turnabout.

"Don't you think Biceps Femoris Maul should be commended for altering Latissimus Dorsi Berghart's moniker?"

"How do you mean?" I asked, never able to keep up with Gerry's fertile brain.

"His chauvinistic attitude necessitates a rechristening. From this day forward," he intoned solemnly, as we turned back to instruments and dead horses, "he shall be titled 'Equine Gluteous Maximus Berghart' (horse's ass)."

Fall fell into winter so gradually, I hardly noticed. I became deeply involved with veterinary medicine. I kept telling myself that one had to start somewhere to reach the goal of treating wild animals. Dissecting preserved horses, cows, dogs and cats in anatomy was a start. But those carcasses didn't bleed, hurt, or heal. They weren't my first choice, but before I could concentrate on the zoos, I had to start somewhere.

Gerry Bandes said repeatedly. "You'll never make a living treating wild animals, there just aren't enough of them. I'm taking over my uncle's small animal practice in New York. That's where the money is!"

I was too busy evaluating comparative anatomy to worry about money. My family didn't have much and they never worried about it. As the new Latin names became more comfortable, the realization dawned. Every animal in the world had a femur, a gastrocnemius muscle and an aorta. Learning about the horse, dog and cow inside out, would give me a very good idea of how every living creature was put together. With the realization came excitement and the incentive to study harder. For the first time in my memory, A's began to appear in my scholastic record.

Surgery was the glamour course that began modestly for us. Lectures were three times weekly, starting the second year. Each one was followed by a two hour demonstration. The class was divided into teams. The seniors held the scalpels, juniors and sophomores assisted, and a freshman observed and cleaned up. We, on the lowest rung, competed for the privilege of doing the dirty work so we could be as close to the action as possible.

When major surgery was demonstrated, Dr. Hadley Carruthers Stephenson had our attention. He picked a different group to assist each time, and on this particular day, I was the lucky freshman. The subject was spaying the pregnant cat.

The patient was brought in for her preoperative prep, a thin black and white tabby, with her distorted abdomen, grotesque in its enormity. While juniors shaved and disinfected, Stephenson lectured. His deadpan, chubby face turned this way and that, taking in all the students.

As the lecture began we were quiet, not daring to miss one word. "The spay in a normal animal has become so routine," he droned, "it is considered a minor procedure. It can be done without an assistant, in less than a half hour. The hysterectomy, however, in an advanced pregnancy, is major surgery. Almost a third of the queen's (an adult breeding female) total weight is now uterus and kittens." He pointed to her bulging belly.

"This pregnancy is practically at term. I would judge about eight weeks. The shock on the Queen's system can be profound. The surgery must be quick, the bleeding minimal and the anesthesia efficient."

He instructed the junior to begin preliminary sedation, and, finally, ether induced anesthesia. He proceeded to scrub up, inviting questions.

"Why?" someone asked, "would anybody wait six or eight weeks into a pregnancy to spay their cat?"

"Sometimes people don't even know," Stephenson explained with a shrug, "some of them don't notice obvious signs. A cat could stray from home and return when time to give birth approaches. At any rate, a client will walk in with his pet, not wanting the bother of kittens, and request the surgery."

"Did you ever consider the risk too great?"

"Yes." And he paused, looking at the ceiling, searching for the correct words. "Occasionally I've seen a frail patient with a normal pelvis about to deliver and decided against the surgery. It's a decision you will learn to make." We looked at each other wondering if we indeed will ever be able to make such a decision.

The demonstration proceeded. Professor Stephenson with his prodigious skill, removed the tremendous uterus and both ovaries, gently dropping them into the discard basin.

"Remember, this technique can be used for uterine or ovarian tumors, chronic metritis or pyometra." Then he added. "By removing the ovaries as well as the uterus, the cat will be sterile and she won't have those noisy, objectional heat periods. In addition, she can't get uterine or ovarian cancer and the chance of breast malignancy is greatly diminished."

Stephenson sutured the muscles, leaving the skin closure to his senior. He thanked each assistant, even lowly me, and gave instructions for the queen's after care before he left.

Our senior, with great showmanship dragged out the skin suturing as long as possible. "How did you like the Big Red win Saturday?" he asked. He chatted informally, hoping in that way to exhibit his supreme confidence.

"Scholl to McCullough is the best passing combination in the country." His fawning junior volunteered.

"Right, and Matuszak, the best quarterback. It takes a vet student to supply the brains for our attack."

"There! Isn't that beautiful?" He stepped back admiring the neat row of sutures. "I'll never know why God gave me such talent!"

Enviously I gazed at his work. I'll do better than that, I thought. My family were expert milliners.

"Slaves!" He ordered condescendingly. "Bandage the patient and clean up the mess." Mimicking the professor, he thanked each of us. Then smiling broadly he marched out of the surgery, tossing cap, gown and face mask in the laundry hamper as Stephenson had done.

The team finished and carried the patient off to the recovery ward. It was hard to believe that the scrawny, almost emaciated creature being returned to the ward, was the same bulging feline we saw just a few minutes before. Everyone was gone by the time the instruments were washed and dried. I waited until the last minute to discard the uterus. I approached the basin and looked down. Something moved! I stared. It happened again! Something inside was struggling.

I looked around to be sure nobody was watching, then grabbed the scalpel and slit open the womb. Six fetuses spilled out, attached by tiny cords. Five were definitely dead. All were blue, but one moved! I grabbed it, frantically tore the sac from its head and pinched off the umbilical cord. It gave a reflex gasp.

Now what to do? That kitten needed oxygen, and quickly. I tried to recall how Dr. Blamey, our old vet from the pet shop would react in a similar situation. Oh yes, I remembered now. I held it with its head down, massaged it vigorously and dried it with a surgical towel. My heart was pounding. I felt like a pioneer charting a new course in medical history.

Swing the tiny creature in a wide arc keeping its head down to free fluid from its nose and throat.

Keep rubbing it with a washcloth or towel.

Blow into its mouth and nose.

The little creature's wind pipe was suddenly clear of mucous. He was breathing. The blue was now a healthy pink. Then came a cry, its first feeble mew.

"It's working!" I cried out, "I did it! I saved it! It's alive!"

A love and responsibility for the kitten took hold. Surgical waste, a minute before, was now a precious life and I was responsible. I stared in wonderment. It was a little male.

Now what do I do? Where can I keep him? I can't even tell anyone. I'm not supposed to be making decisions about discarded, unwanted creatures. No matter! It's done! I had to keep him.

Round the clock care would be needed for the first couple of weeks.

How would I manage that? I'd think of something. First, get him home alive!

Gently I set him on a handful of discarded cotton, finished cleaning up and dressed to go out. It was a freezing day so I tucked him under my armpit, still wrapped in the cotton, slipped on my overcoat and hurried home.

Careful! Don't crush him.

I worried that he had been without oxygen too long. We had just studied the critical time of oxygen deprivation in physiology, four to six minutes. He was in the basin for fifteen minutes. There had to be brain damage. Another minute or two and he would have died. It was fate that I was on clean-up!

Thank goodness my room-mate, Marv, was out. I pulled off my coat and unwrapped the kitten. He was complaining. He must be hungry. I sneaked him up to our landlady's kitchen. Normally that room was off limits as we took our meals in the fraternity house. But, I thought, Gert is such a sweet, gently lady and a real animal lover—I knew she would understand.

I recalled the baby formula my folks used for puppies and kittens. A raw egg, a little white bread, some Karo syrup and a vitamin supplement. Luckily, I found everything easily. The cod liver oil was in a cabinet. I added a drop. With no bottle and nipple, I would have to use an eyedropper. Marv's nose drops would have one. I washed it and dedicated it to the first meal. I warmed the formula and tested it on my forearm. Marvin had better understand and help! I had no idea how he would react. Gert Driscoll was definitely a better bet. Her cat, Tizzie, was gentle as a lamb. Maybe she'd help and even adopt the little thing.

Now! Where to hide him. When Ed Driscoll built our basement room, he put shelves everywhere. Just outside the door leading upstairs, was the furnace with more shelves. It was always warm in that area. There was a cubby hole big enough for the shoe box which would be his bed. I lined it with absorbent cotton, and punched holes in the cover for fresh air.

A door slammed and Marv pounded down the stairs.

Think fast, Zim.

Tizzie was sleeping on a radiator cover in our room. I took the kitten from his box and placed him on the floor under her, then leaned over my desk and faked diligent study. Tizzie played her part expertly. She jumped down to investigate the little stranger. Out of the corner of my eye I could see her cleaning the kitten.

Marv banged his way in, as usual, talking a mile a minute. Then . . . silence!

"What's going on?" he challenged. "what's Tizzie doing?"

"Oh that," I said nonchalantly. "Tizzie just had a kitten."

"Bullshit, she's been spayed."

"The surgeon can make a mistake. There's the proof."

"Well, get her out of here. This isn't a nursery." He squirmed uncomfortably.

"Don't be so heartless. She's going to need our help."

"I'll help throw her over the gorge."

"I'm not kidding, I can't do it alone."

"What kind of help?" Marv asked suspiciously.

"He has to be fed special formula every two hours around the clock."

"Good God! That's worse than homework! What else?"

"Well, after feeding he has to be roughed up and rolled a little to stimulate his bodily functions."

"Ugh! Disgusting! If Tizzie is the mother why can't she do it?"

I wasn't sure how to answer. I should level with him, but worried that it might get back to Stephenson. How would the school accept my stealing a discarded kitten? I decided to wait.

"Tizzie doesn't have any milk." I answered.

"Well I'm not going to touch that ugly thing. It looks like a rat."

"I thought you worked with rats and mice all day. You're supposed to like them.

"I have to, to pass the course. But I don't like them. . . What would I have to do?"

"Not much." I assured him, "Just don't hurt him and don't mention him to anyone.

"Why not?"

"Well, uh,—if they find out in vet school that I didn't bring him right over for treatment, I may get into trouble. Besides, I want to raise him myself!"

"Okay, but suppose Gert Driscoll decides to bring him to the vet school clinic. It's her kitten. What'll you do then?"

"I'll tell her that she and I can give it more attention than a bunch of busy vet students."

That seemed to satisfy him but he wasn't happy about it.

I had just given the kitten a feeding and tucked him back in his box when Mrs. Driscoll arrived. Marv was upstairs and he was spilling the beans.

"Congratulations," he started, "Tizzie had a cute little kitten today. I didn't even know she was pregnant."

I pictured the grin on her face.

"Marvin don't be silly. You know she wouldn't let another cat within ten feet of her and besides, she's spayed."

"Well she's licking a kitten down stairs and Ted said it was hers."

"He's pulling your leg, Marvin. He probably brought him from vet school."

I should have known better. She's too smart to swallow that story. I'd better tell them the truth and take my chances.

"Hi Aunt Gert," I said climbing the stairs. "I brought a little day-old kitten home for us to take care of. I hope you don't mind."

The deception exposed, Marv put on his hurt look as I told Mrs. Driscoll the events of the day.

She was intrigued by the story and asked to see the kitten. I took her to its hiding place and explained how Tizzie had accepted him and licked him clean.

"Ted, you did right. You delivered the little thing by caesarean section."

"Let's call him 'Caesar'," Marv chimed in, acquiescing to the now positive mood.

"Great idea," I agreed. "You christened him and that makes you the Godfather!"

Marv smiled weakly and asked,"What am I going to have to do? Take him to church?"

"I hoped everyone would help feed him for the next three weeks or so. I'll take care of all the night feedings if someone can cover when I'm at school."

"He's so adorable," Gert said as she picked him up and petted him. "Marv, you're home most afternoons. If you could feed him at, say, noon and two o'clock. I could take over after three. Ed could feed him at 10 A.M."

"I want to get paid." Marv graced us with his mock serious face.

"You get my allowance every week, anyhow." I answered. Marv was a playboy, spending his weekly budget in two days.

"I always pay you back first, don't I?" He answered righteously. His father sent him a weekly allowance that I could have lived on for a month.

"I'll make out a schedule," I said, "and whoever does the feeding just check the time. I'm counting on you Marv!"

"He's too little and icky. I might drop him."

"I'll show you how to do it. It's simple. All you have to do is feed him a couple of eyedroppers full of warm formula. Then lay him in a wash cloth, like this." I demonstrated how to stroke the kitten's abdomen and gently roll him back and forth. "His mother would roll and lick him the same way. Then put him on the floor for Tizzie to finish the job."

In spite of his objections I could see he was excited about helping and Gert was delighted. That evening when Ed was home I showed off, telling them how a kitten develops, when its eyes and ears open etc. We would all watch for it to happen in ten days.

"I never knew his ears were closed, too." Marv said as he examined the tiny head.

"Neither did I." Ed admitted. A tough talking Irishman with a heart of mush, he readily accepted his feeding duties.

On the twelfth day Caesar's eyes opened. His little squeaks had become stronger daily and he was finally learning to walk. His little legs were bowed and spindly.

With the help of the entire household, Caesar slowly matured. Marv played with him constantly. I'd catch him talking to him while he was shaving or studying. He'd perch him up on the sink and flick a strip of toilet tissue for Caesar to paw at. On his desk he'd roll pencils back and forth with the awkward kitten trying to catch them.

"Be careful," I cautioned, "don't let him break a leg."

As I talked Caesar would cock his head to one side seeming to understand. I found myself competing for play-time.

One of the favorite pastimes in our room had been towel-snapping. We used to spend hours perfecting our technique. We could snap a pencil off a desk top without moving a paper, or flip a painful shot at each others backside. With the arrival of Caesar that play was forgotten. An errant snap could take his head off.

Everyone loved the kitten and was blind to the fact that he was failing. I researched his condition in the library, afraid to ask

Stephenson or Milks directly. Brain damaged animals suffered mentally as well as physically and life expectancy was greatly diminished.

Marv began to take the kitten to the fraternity house. Before long Caesar was an accepted addition to the membership. Fraternity meetings, always run under strict parliamentary rules, were interrupted by Marv's humor and his new obsession.

"I make a motion that Caesar be accepted in the fraternity. He has the brains to be a great rushing chairman." Or, "The food is lousy! Caesar is looking to join Beta Sig to get a decent meal. Look at him! Almost four months old and he's hardly grown."

I confided in Gert. "Caesar is stunted and has stopped growing. I'm afraid he'll never reach his first birthday.

"Oh, Ted, he's such a dear. Are you sure?"

"Look at him! He's four months old and looks like two. His legs are so weak he can hardly walk. By this time he should weigh four or five pounds and jump and climb over everything."

"Don't tell Marv yet, Ted. He really loves him and looks forward to feeding and playing with him. I've never seen him so punctual and attentive. Can't you get some medicine to help?"

"The parts of the brain that were oxygen starved, just died. There is no way nerve tissue can recover."

Caesar, regressing in health, was completely dependent on his many nurses. His appetite was poor and he had frequent diarrhea. He had stopped cleaning himself and was generally depressed. Marv spent hours petting and talking to him.

I came home after classes one evening. It was about 6 PM. As I opened the door I could see Marv sitting at his desk. Caesar's box was in front of him.

Marv looked up, his eyes moist.

"I guess we did something wrong. Little Caesar is gone."

"Oh Marv, I'm sorry," I commiserated, "but he really never had a chance. You did more for him than any of us. I guess I should never have tried to be God. I thought once he started breathing the rest would be easy. He had such a powerful urge to live, I thought he could overcome almost everything. He just couldn't develop without a normal brain. Don't ever blame yourself."

"I know," he said. He was quiet a moment, then he turned his sad, red eyes to me. "I've never lost a pet before."

"You told me you never had one, Marv. Your folks never permitted one in the house."

"That's why it's so tough. Caesar was such a great kitten." He paused, gazing at the still form. "You knew this was going to happen, didn't you? I guess you've been through this before."

"You'll have your heart broken many times if you love pets enough to possess one all the time."

My thought returned to my childhood pets.

Bill was my first, my own German Shepherd dog—a soft, face-licking, affectionate playmate. His tawny coat was warm and snuggly when I touched it. I remember our playtimes together. I would throw a ball (it didn't matter where), and he would jump with apparent glee, then make a mad dash for the sphere, stop short, open his wet, saliva-ridden mouth, grab the ball and run back to gently drop it in my lap, dripping wet. I could pull an ear, step on his tail, even try to ride bareback, and his nose would nudge me with patience and understanding.

Born in the same month and year as I, Bill took on the responsibility of our family's survival when he was only six months old. He must have been related to the fabulous Rin Tin Tin; at least he looked and acted like the movie star German Shepherd. He watched with an intuitive eye that was mystical, and saved our lives time and again, especially mine when an innate curiosity for anything four-legged got me into some dangerous situations.

One beautiful weekend, my family had a picnic near a small hotel in the Catskill Mountains. We always loved that spot--with a lake and grounds to eat and rest beside it. Never disappointed in my search for wildlife, I saw many chipmunks, squirrels, rabbits and, occasionally, a woodchuck, beaver or skunk. We sat on a blanket spread on the grass. I remember complaining about ants that arrived in hordes looking for a tidbit to carry home. Dad explained about ants and their place in nature, and how they had a queen to feed and a hilly sand-house to build. Even Bill put up with them. He didn't seem to notice as he lay next to the blanket, munching on a soupbone.

While happily eating our sandwiches, three year-old me saw something jump out of the water near shore. I scrambled up, my mouth full, and lunged for the "thing." Curious Evelyn followed. It didn't matter where or what, I just had to see what it was and maybe catch it. I tripped on the bank and pitched headfirst into the water. Thank the Lord, directly behind me was Bill. He dragged me out by the seat of my pants, coughing and sputtering, before my parents could even react to Evelyn's screams.

On my sister's fifth birthday, she got a Persian kitten. A tiny cuddly ball of fur, exactly like I would like to hold and fondle. At two years older, she wouldn't let me touch it, and pushed me away because she thought I might hurt it. That made me cry in frustration. I needed my own kitten.

Mother placated me with, "Bill is yours, and your sister needs something that is hers. It's like "Tweets," the canary, just listen to his singing and enjoy him without touching. You may pet the kitten and play with it, only when Evelyn is there and says it's okay."

My father knew that Bill hated cats, and Dad was concerned for that new kitten's welfare. But Bill knew the difference between cats and kittens and he respected babies of any kind. To be certain, Dad took the kitten over to Bill, held her right under his nose and told him sharply that it was Evelyn's, and he better not harm it. It made me miserable that my dad spoke so sternly. I put my arms around Bill and kissed him. Bill, however, understood my father's admonishment, though sorely tested, and he never forgot.

Bill's rug nestled in the hall that led from the front door to the living room. Anyone walking into that room had to pass his territory. The kitten, disliking Bill as much as he did her, followed Evelyn everywhere and, when she had to pass Bill, she'd crouch, then creep very slowly, one eye on Bill, inching past, before charging into Evelyn's arms and safety. Bill, with ears erect and eyes that followed her every move, never budged. Evelyn loved to watch the performance and would parade past Bill several times daily just to observe and giggle. Bill never once touched that kitten. He respected the silent promise he made to my father.

Occasionally Bill accompanied my mother and father to the new pet store on Broadway. He napped behind the counter and showed little concern when customers came and went. About 11:30 each day, Mother would leave to make lunch for Evelyn and me.

One day Dad noticed a man looking in the window, apparently captivated by the puppies and kittens. There were many customers milling around inside, some buying dog food or birdseed, others just playing with the pets or listening to the canaries. This particular man didn't look any different from the rest, but he waited until the store was empty, then entered. Bill stirred as if someone had poked him awake. His head come up and a deep, rumbling growl reverberated in his chest. Dad was embarrassed by Bill's behavior and told him to be quiet.

My father started forward to be of service to the customer. "Can I help you sir,?"

Bill was on his feet and stalked the stranger. His ears were laid straight back on his head, which was turned partially sideways, his eyes glaring out of the corners. I've seen that expression on dogs just before they launch a vicious attack. The growl was unrelenting and threatening, as he approached the man.

"Open the register and step away, and fast!" he said gruffly to my dad. There was a revolver in his hand and he was raising it when Bill snarled and jumped between them, protecting Dad's body with his own. The man hesitated, looked at the menacing jaws, then turned and ran, as Dad grabbed Bill's collar to restrain him from following.

"I wasn't about to take a chance that Bill would get hurt," he explained to us later, "but I'll never know how he sensed what that guy was up to."

I recall the time I got my second pet—a tiny, wild, stray kitten that somehow got under the gate guarding our West Eighty-Seventh Street basement. Hungry, mewing pitifully, he aroused my sympathy. Anxiously, I ran to Mother for some milk, sure that would save him and make him my friend. Mother warned me about the untrustworthy nature of cats, especially strays, a caution I quickly rejected. Fate had dropped the little stranger from heaven for me to care for. He was gray with black stripes, painted like a tiger. His four little feet were white as snow, making him look as though he was wearing four snowy mittens. The tip of his nose was white as well, matching his tiny paws. Long black whiskers grew from the sides of his upper lip framing two bright, hazel eyes.

As I balanced the saucer of milk, and approached slowly and carefully, the kitten, in a frenzy of hunger, jumped and landed on my chest, all eighteen claws holding fast. With a shriek of pain, I dropped the dish, milk splashing everywhere. In one great leap, Bill was at my side. He spied the little feline, voraciously lapping up every drop on the floor. Bill didn't understand my howls and alternately kissed me with that reassuring tongue, then washed the kitten clean.

Mother comforted me with hugs and kisses, and explained about hunger and thirst. The poor kitty lost its mommy and hadn't been fed for so long he was frantic.

My pain was quickly forgotten and I couldn't wait to pet that poor little baby. I knew I would have to care for him now, because he had no one else. Even Bill understood and helped. I picked him up, as Mom watched, and triumphantly carried him into the kitchen, naming him "My Kitty." At the age of three, I had found real happiness—a dog and a cat I could hold, pet and love.

My Kitty was the cutest little kitten that ever lived. He realized immediately he was mine, and sat staring at me constantly, ears erect, eyes wide and whiskers twitching. He loved to play in my galoshes, jumping inside, turning around, and appearing with just his head above the metal catches, then sit there watching me, waiting for me to approach. He ducked his head for a second, then his little striped head would pop out with two white forepaws, and the boot would topple, spilling him out. In one great leap, he would dive into the other boot, hiding for a moment before appearing with that cute, impish face.

When he couldn't find me he'd mew and search until I appeared, then he'd jump into my arms, nails carefully sheathed. He had to stay home when we went out, and he'd sit for hours right at the door, awaiting my return. Only I was allowed to feed him. Mother said he would never forget whose pet he was and would always be my responsibility.

Sunday afternoons were leisure hours for the family to take a stroll. Mom and Dad, my sister Evelyn and I, with Bill trailing behind. My Kitty wasn't allowed to come because he was too young, and cats don't like to follow a leash the way dogs do, anyway. In those days, Broadway was a beautiful boulevard. The sidewalks were wide, and crowded with Sunday strollers. Trees, flowers and manicured lawns separated the two lanes of traffic, with trolley tracks running along the cultivated center divider. Wood benches were provided at each cross street for the tired and elderly. My parents window-shopped with Evelyn, while I daydreamed, and Bill, with one leg balanced high, signed the fire hydrants.

One Sunday I stopped to survey the wonders of a toy store window and decided on some toys I really needed. I spied a little mouse that would have been perfect for My Kitty. When I looked around for Mom and Dad, so I could tell them, I was alone. I began to wail. In seconds Bill was there, but I wanted my Mommy and Daddy. Bill sensed that and dashed ahead to alert my father, while sympathetic strangers on that crowded street approached to comfort me. But Bill must have heard them, and spun around, returning to me with teeth showing and growls rumbling to keep everyone away. He stayed for a second or two, to be sure I was unharmed, and away he went once more. Dad arrived to see me surrounded by a crowd of cautious onlookers, all at a respectful distance. I was rubbing my eyes with one hand and clutching Bill's back with the other. I sobbed like my heart was breaking as I pointed to the toy store window, no longer caring about the toys, just letting Daddy know why they lost me.

Bill did become buddies with My Kitty and protected him from other dogs, even though he chased every cat in sight. One day My Kitty ran out into the street before I could stop him. He was curious about what went on outside, having forgotten the days he was lost and hungry. A passing dog backed him up to the curb, curious to smell the little stranger. My Kitty's back went up in the air, the hair on his neck stood straight out from his body and he hissed in a way I had never heard before. He fired a lightning fast paw, sharp nails exposed, at the dog's nose. He was very feisty and the dog thought twice about getting scratched, and backed away. I was proud of him and he was very glad to have me pick him up and carry him back to safety.

There were two exceptions to Bill's penchant to chase cats. One was Evelyn's pet Persian, and the other, a mean, twenty-pound tabby that lived on Riverside Drive, whose territory Bill respected. The cat terrorized the neighborhood. His owner, a janitor in one of the brownstones facing the Hudson River, was just as grumpy, and relished the reputation his killer cat had attained. He named his pet "Leopard," because his assault was initiated from low-branched trees, to pounce on unprotected backs.

Grown Toms are a peculiar breed, having cruel, antisocial instincts. Their need for territorial rights is overwhelming. Male cats instinctively attack other Toms, potential rivals, if they dare come too close, by tearing at their genitals. They even return to their own litters purposely to destroy them, the reason is a matter of conjecture. Students of animal psychology contend that the cause might be jealousy of their queen or, perhaps, to eliminate future rivals early.

Our janitor, Charlie, walked Bill every evening, when the streets were quiet and he was allowed to run free. Three months after I got My Kitty, he was now old enough to go outside himself, but he always stayed close to home. It was early spring, the temperature was moderate and tiny leaves were sprouting on the trees that lined Eighty-Seventh Street.

That fateful day, Bill found something in the gutter that worried him. Charlie called to him, but he wouldn't budge. He nudged at it and whined, and stayed till Charlie came to investigate.

Our janitor was aghast. He recognized My Kitty immediately, four white feet with matching nose couldn't be missed. For a minute, Charlie didn't know what to do. An automobile, he thought, but as he looked close, he realized My Kitty had not been crushed. There was bleeding around his genitals and teeth puncture wounds covered his body, so Charlie suspected what probably happened. He knew My Kitty was fed every evening and now I'd be looking for him. Charlie wanted to get him home without me seeing him, so he wrapped him in newspaper and dropped him near the coal bin where I wasn't allowed to go. I knew something was wrong; My Kitty's dish was still full, Bill was whining and Charlie wouldn't look me in the eye or talk to me.

Mother went outside with me and helped me look. We called, "Kitty, Kitty, Kitty," from West End Avenue to Riverside Drive. We looked under parked cars and down the stairs of all the brownstones. My father finally came home and Charlie motioned him aside. They whispered and walked to the coal bin, carefully closing the door behind them.

I crept up to the door and listened. Charlie was saying something about My Kitty, and my father, in an angry tone, said that Leopard was going to pay for it.

I ran to my mother crying. "Mommy, something terrible happened to My Kitty. Daddy and Charlie won't tell me."

Without a word, Dad took Bill out toward Riverside Drive, and gave him one command, "Go get him!" Bill understood and trotted toward the trees on the corner. Leopard silently dropped from a branch over Bill. He never landed. Bill's split-second spin avoided the talons. His flashing jaws grabbed Leopard's throat and broke his neck with one powerful shake.

When father told me My Kitty was killed, he quieted my tears with the tale of retribution. I was learning grown-up lessons about life and death, grief, guilt and punishment.

In our twelfth year, faithful old Bill was showing signs of aging. He was the equivalent of a human of eighty-four. Dr. Blamey checked him out at the pet shop during one of his routine visits. He told me Bill had arthritis and interstitial nephritis (a common kidney complaint of carnivores). Old age was eating away at his joints, and his kidneys were just wearing out. I determined to some day find a cure for both those illnesses.

At that time I was sent to study with Uncle Adam for two weeks. He was the only Orthodox Jew left in Mom's family, and he prepared me for bar mitzvah, on my thirteenth birthday. I studied about God and impending manhood, while Dad had Dr. Blamey put Bill to sleep. I was furious with my father for protecting me from that ordeal, robbing me of my need to say goodbye. I yearned to hold Bill in a last bearhug, and bury my head in his furry neck.

My sister lost her Persian cat about a month before Bill died, and Mom and Dad replaced them both with one of the first Siamese kittens imported to the United States. We named him Prajadhipok, the name of the then ruling Siamese King (deposed in 1935). "Prejie" was more like a dog than a cat. He retrieved, came when called, had a wonderful disposition, and the loudest, most consistant purr imaginable. He sounded like a speeding motor-boat. Evelyn would wear him around her neck like a stole, for hours on end, and Prejie loved it.

Time, school, the Mohawk Club (an after school boy's athletic club), and Prejie dulled the hurt of Bill's loss. Before I knew it, I remembered only the good times, and smiled when I looked at the picture Mom had enlarged of Bill astride a photographer's pony. He sat upright, just behind the saddle, with both forelegs planted in the middle of the leatherseat. After a command to mount, he proved his loyalty and obedience, and, incidently, won a bet for my dad. With a frown on his intelligent face, Bill backed away, took a running start and practically climbed the side of the equine so as not to fall off the other side. He stood for a moment, until Dad commanded, "Sit," and the photographer snapped the shutter.

Marv had been deprived, as a child, never having experienced the fascinating milieu of loving master and devoted pet. After weeks of pain, he got over Caesar's death. He forgave me and accepted my animal eccentricities with patience and humor. Marv and I grew closer than either of us could have imagined. We married sisters. As he put it, "we just switched room-mates."

The large animal clinic at Cornell was located behind the administration building, named after our founder, James Law. I had waited a lifetime to work here. Dr. Frost, the chief, and his assistant, Gordon Danks were like Gods to us. The clinic and wards were filled with cases we were going to cure.

It was my third year, the class was divided into four teams of ten students each, who worked, observed and assisted one week a month, Monday through Saturday, 8 AM to 3 o'clock.

The medical expertise that set Cornell apart from every other vet school in the world was about to be revealed. I was sure that if I took enough notes, applied myself sufficiently and used available medical principles, I would someday be able to treat any specie of bird or animal from every corner of the globe.

Unlike the majority of my classmates, most of whom came from the farm, I had a lot of basics to learn about horses: how to exercise and curry; the importance of walking to cool them off; determining how much oats and hay to feed.

We mastered the treatment of common cuts, bruises, eye infections and festering ears of all the species. We were taught to set compound fractures in the small and farm animals, except for the equines.

Serious attacks of colic and enteritis in horses and mules were covered in detail. In this course, many unanswered riddles about the farm were cleared up. The ring in a bull's nose had to be surgically installed; a twitch is used around the noses of pigs for restraint, just like in horses and mules. We learned that farmers try to do many operations themselves, allowing us to repair their blunders.

Cleaning stalls, hosing floors, polishing leather and repairing farm equipment was part of my veterinary science education. I enjoyed most of it, though the connection between farm chores and veterinary medicine escaped me.

One morning in October, as I worked the clinic, an old black Pontiac rolled up, pulling a one-horse trailer. I looked up, wondering what fate had in store. Momentarily the driver sat motionless, then slowly opened the door. He was tall and slender, stood very straight, shoulders back and head high. His close-cropped grey hair added to his military bearing. He wore dungarees and a long sleeved shirt rolled to the elbows. He looked about anxiously, not sure how to proceed.

Dr. Danks, in charge of admitting new patients, hastened to finish a hoof trimming demonstration. He would soon go over to greet the newcomer.

Leaving the car door ajar, the gentleman walked to the back of the trailer. Gnarled hands with a perceptible tremor reached to insert a key. The palsy made the simple task a painful chore. Finally he swung the door open. The backside of a small brown horse appeared, its long black tail swishing. Manure soiled the floor and spilled to the pavement. The old man swung himself up and squeezed past. He came out in a moment, carrying a ramp which he attached to the trailer. Disappearing again we heard, "Back girl, back up."

The mare backed slowly down the ramp, visibly favoring her right foreleg. She was small, fine-boned and well proportioned. A heavy dark mane, matching her tail, spilled over her neck. In the middle of her forehead was a white symmetrical spot resembling a four-pointed star. The man spoke quietly, affectionately stroking her shoulder.

Dr. Danks, clipboard in hand approached, "Mornin' sir."

"Hi, Doc," he answered, relieved that someone noticed him. "Got a lame horse here."

Danks took his name, Roger Caldwell, his address and a short medical history of the horse. Handing the clipboard to a student, the doctor pushed his glasses higher up on his nose, and slowly circled the horse. His keen eye had picked up the limp, and his hands went right to the spot. A slight swelling marred the smooth cannon. "How long has she been lame?" he asked.

"Fell yesterday while my granddaughter was riding," he said. "Just went down on one knee and got right up. Didn't even throw the child."

"Did you see it?"

"No. Carol told me. She said that she had gotten off the horse and struggled to lead her to the stable. Star must have had terrible pain with each step because it took almost an hour to get back.

"Might have stepped in a hole," Danks mused. "Maybe caught it the wrong way. We'll X-ray the leg, probably a sprain or bruise." Then turning to the students, he barked, "Arnabaldi, Becker, Fischer! Bring out the portable X-ray." To Star's owner he said. "It will just be an hour or so."

A couple hours later, Danks read the plates, with a half-dozen of us hanging over his shoulder. Our class had progressed to the point of reading X-rays. The dreaded diagnosis was obvious: transverse metacarpal fracture. Prognosis: negative! Danks showed the plates to Dr. Frost. He motioned to the students to come closer for his lecture.

Professor Frost faced every class with that dilemma. He appreciated the idealism of youth. Frost explained, "It takes six to eight weeks for bone to knit. To do so properly, complete immobilization is critical. A splint in the dog, or a cast in the human works well in most cases. Think," he said, "about the difference in weight on the legs of the lighter animals compared with even a small horse, say 1500 pounds! Our problem isn't how to set the leg. It is how to immobilize it for six to eight weeks. In horses those bones can't be kept free from movement and tension. With so much weight, it's next to impossible to keep one of four legs off the ground for very long. It's been tried. Plaster casts reinforced with metal, intramedullary pins, wiring--you name it. In the end, the animal usually has to be destroyed."

Questions began to fly: "But why just the horse, sir? We've heard of full grown tigers, wild monkeys, even deer recovering from fractures."

"Evolution," he explained patiently. "The horse has evolved to stand and run on one finger." He held one up to illustrate. "The hoof is like your fingernail. The fetlock is your knuckle. His knee is our wrist. Your second and forth fingers have evolved to be the useless splint bones on the horse's leg. The thumb is completely lost." He continued, "The lower legs are blood vessels, nerves, bone, tendon, ligament and skin. Because the lack of muscle, with its nourishing, blood-rich vascular network, healing is excruciatingly slow. The slowest to heal are the fibrous ligaments and tendons. When torn, inevitable in a displacement fracture, they take forever to heal, and demand complete immobility.

Frost then walked up to Caldwell to report the results. His voice was soft and kindly as he spoke, "I hate to tell you, sir. The leg is fractured."

We watched Mr. Caldwell. He held his grey head high, as a tear trickled down his cheek. He swallowed, looked at Dr. Frost, then at us, and began to talk. His shaking hands were more pronounced. "My granddaughter is an orphan. When she was four, her parents were killed in an automobile accident. It was in mid-winter on an icy road. An eighteen-wheeler skidded across the center divider and hit my children head-on. They never had a chance." He had to stop as he recalled the tragedy. "They used special equipment to cut Carol out. She was unconscious and came to while the rescuers worked. Her head was bleeding but the extent of her injury could not be determined. As they lifted her out she called for her parents." He paused again. "Carol kept calling for her mother and father in the hospital. We were there every day to hold and comfort her. She was now our whole life, all we had left, but she didn't seem to know us. As the weeks passed, she stopped asking and talking altogether. She became withdrawn and unresponsive. No one could tell if she was physically impaired or reacting to the loss of her parents. Carol had been a loving, sensitive and very dependent child. The doctors couldn't measure the damage. In order to rehabilitate her, the neurologists and psychologists had to reach her. She was unable or unwilling to cooperate with anyone. The medical team finally agreed there was some brain damage and they hoped that in time she might improve."

Why was he telling us this? I wondered, fascinated, unable to take my eyes off his face.

He paused again. "We took our precious baby home. Mom and I kept trying every way we knew to reach her. We read stories to her, sang to her, hugged her, with never as much as a smile for encouragement. Carol let us feed her, bathe her, dress her and take her for walks, but never uttered a word. For two years we watched her deteriorating right in front of our eyes.

"One day we walked past an equestrian trail. A horse and rider trotted by. She raised her eyes and stared. A response she had never made before. A few days later, it was Friday, I'll never forget. I took Carol over to a riding stable on a hunch. We sat on a bench alongside the beginner's track. Star was walking with a youngster on her back and she stopped right in front of us. The little filly must have gotten a hand-out from someone sitting there once before. Perhaps she was just bored or curious, whatever." As he talked his arm reached for Star's graceful neck, petting her affectionately.

"She dropped her head and gently nudged my little girl with that soft nose. Carol squealed, laughed and said 'Horsy'. I couldn't believe what I heard. It was her first utterance in so many months. This horse convinced me that things weren't hopeless. Carol might have a chance.

"We returned to the stable often, and a month or so later, I bought Star. We've had her almost two years and Carol has been improving steadily."

He looked right into Dr. Frost's eyes. "You have to save her, Doctor," he pleaded, "we can't hurt this little girl again."

Dr. Frost's head hung down. He was unable to look at Mr. Caldwell. We students behind him began to buzz. Someone piped up, "For God's sake Doc, couldn't we try?"

The rest of us took up the cry. "What will it take, Doctor, to save her?"

Frost hesitated, touched by the drama. Finally he spoke. "We'll set Star's leg in a light plaster cast supported by metal rods. The leg must never touch the ground. Do you students think you can handle such a watch? It will take monitoring twenty-four hours a day, seven days a week for many weeks.

"Weekly X-rays will monitor the healing. Not until you are convinced will we destroy the mare. Incidently," he added quietly, covering every eventuality, "to dispatch an animal with one shot, a sad task you will be asked to do many times, draw an imaginary line from each ear to the opposite eye." As Caldwell winced, he illustrated with a finger, and tapped twice where the lines crossed on the mare's head.

The word got around to the rest of the class. We mobilized, setting a schedule for round-the-clock nursing. There would be three hour shifts, two students to each shift. Other classes and duties had to be taken into account and there would be many a sleepless night. We designed a way to use folded sheets for slings. They were to be used to keep that leg off the ground. When Star appeared ready to lie down or get up, we would be there with our slings.

The first day passed and Star stayed upright on three legs. The second day she started to lie down and we were ready to help her.

She held the injured leg out, our sling in place under it, ready for support. Slowly she lay down without touching the ground or the sling. She started to rise a few hours later and again the sling was there. She was on her feet without our help.

On the second day, Mr. Caldwell told us he had to bring Carol to visit. She demanded to see her horse, and Caldwell was torn between telling her the truth or giving her the false hope that everything was going to be all right. He never lied to her and decided not to do so now. During the weeks that followed the class got to know little Carol. Day by day she came just to be with Star, and she talked to her like an adult, encouraging her to try to get well soon. She was so adorable, that all the students and faculty looked forward to her visits. Her long blonde hair, cut in bangs, framed wide, intelligent eyes that crinkled and lit up her face when she laughed. We couldn't visualize that happy angel, mournful or withdrawn and we dreaded what might happen. And with Grandpa Caldwell; only his pleading, praying eyes disclosed his concern.

Xrays were taken at the beginning of every week. One week, no change, Two, three, four weeks, nothing!

Dr. Milks, prince of the small animal clinic had an idea. He knew the prognosis and hoped another animal might assuage Carol's grief. He asked us to bring her to him, to show a litter of six-week kittens ready for adoption. The mother had been abandoned and her litter was offered to anyone interested. "Take your pick," he told the excited child. "You will have to name it and it will be yours."

One male was white, with a brown blotch covering an eye and half its face. "That one," she cried pointing, "his name is Patches."

"You've got it." Milks said, handing the kitten to its new mistress.

"I'm going to show him to Star," Carol squeeled. "I know she'll love him too."

As Carol approached, the filly whinnied, and nuzzled the kitten. "Do you like him?" Carol asked, making her offering. "Would you like to play with Patches today?" There was an instant bonding that made Star's life complete--unaware, of course, that her life hung in the balance. The three of them spent the day together. Caldwell came to take Carol home and as they were leaving with Patches, Star whinnied in protest.

Carol turned, "Would you like Patches to stay with you tonight?"

"Good idea, Carol," her grandfather said. "Star may get lonesome."

On the fifth week, we checked the X-rays again and we realized that Dr. Frost had been right. "But she never touched that leg down." I said. "What went wrong?"

"Hold on!" A familiar voice popped up. It was Ken Gumaer. He picked up the plate and held it against the viewer. "I think I see something. There's something different here. Can't you see those spicules bridging the fracture line? Let's ask Dr. Frost."

Star was the exception that proved the rule. She never needed any of us. That nimble, intelligent animal never touched her injured foot down for eight weeks.

With the cast removed and final goodbyes said, the consequences of doctoring affected the entire class for the first time. Carol left with hugs and kisses for everyone, her kitten clutched in her arms, and her horse healthy. Mr. Caldwell, his hands quieter now, smiled, threw a quick kiss to the crowd, and drove off with his grateful entourage.

A few weeks later, during the lecture preceding every surgical lab, the castration of dogs and cats was announced. Dr. Milks started the talk with the admonishment to listen carefully. This was a procedure that would occupy more time and earn more dollars than any other hospital operation. We were all ears!

The male students were chauvinists, obsessed and sympathetic to all species threatened by the loss of precious manhood. Never did we have second thoughts about the necessity for hysterectomy. The loss of that brace of tender gonad, however, sent shivers up our collective spines.

Milks, still my favorite professor, prefaced the actual anatomical description of the procedure, with a historical discourse. Beef, lamb and pork products derived from the bull, ram, and boar were, for all practical purposes, inedible! Stallions were gelded to insure strength, stamina, and tractability. The young rooster was caponized to produce a more tender and tasty bird. Tom cats were neutered to eliminate their noxious odor, and certain dogs, altered, to change otherwise malevolent dispositions.

Milks then proceeded with medical considerations. The dogs were completely anesthetized, but in cats, to my distress, there was no mention of pain control or sedation. I assumed it was an oversight, fully expecting anesthesia to be practiced, even if local.

After the lecture we rushed to the surgical lab like a herd of sheep. Dr. Stephenson, our shepherd, waited for us to settle down, his staff, the clipboard and pencil. We arranged ourselves in a semicircle and he motioned the attendant to bring in the patient, a cute six month old kitten. Stephenson held it high, its little backside up in the air. He ceremoniously lifted its tail and proceeded. "Notice the position of the testes," he began in his monotonous drone. "The feline is unique, in that nature placed the male genitalia just below the rectum in exactly the area of the female vulva. It is quite understandable, considering this quirk in anatomy, why so many errors are made by the untaught, in sexing the cat. Especially," he continued, "in very young kittens before the testicles have descended.

"In practice, make it a habit to corroborate their gender by looking carefully at your feline patients. Some laymen decide sex by a cat's facial expression. Four or five months, hence, you might find it difficult to explain how their 'Trixie" turned into 'Tom'. In addition, manually palpate to see whether one or both testicles have descended. Generally cats have more than their share of monorchids and cryptorchids."

He turned to Bernie Fischer, whose mind was always somewhere else. "Explain the difference Mr. Fischer."

"Er- ah- I know sir, if only one is present it's a monorchid. If neither is there, its a cryptorchid."

"Very good! Where are they if they are not in the scrotum, Mr. Lewis?"

"I uh guess they just don't have them, sir."

"Nuts!. . .they have them allright. . .pardon the pun. Mr. Gumaer, what do you think?"

Kenny Gumaer, knew the answer again. "Either in the inguinal canal or still inside the peritoneal cavity sir."

"Right! We don't really know why some cats, occasionally some dogs and once in a while some men have undescended testes. We know it's genetic because certain strains of cats produce one or more cryptorchids in every litter. Inbreeding is a factor and is more common in cats than in dogs. If your patient is a cryptorchid you can't alter them in the usual way. You have to search the inguinal canal or the abdominal cavity in much the same way you do a spay. Today I'm going to demonstrate castration in a normal cat. The dog will come later."

He continued, "Each of you have been assigned one dog and one cat for use in practice surgery. Consider them yours! That means feeding, cleaning cages and exercising." At last, I thought, something I know all about.

"Some of you will have female dogs and male cats or vice versa. Each partner will have the opposite arrangement, so if you spay a dog you will assist your partner when he castrates his patient. Take good care of your animals," he warned, "If you lose one or both you'll be an observer instead of a surgeon."

Stephenson then proceeded with the demonstration. He laid a bath towel on the operating table as he spoke.

"Notice that the castration in the cat is a much simpler procedure than in the dog. In canines general anesthesia is used, while in cats we just use the towel."

That shook me up. Milk's hadn't overlooked anything; there wouldn't be anesthesia! The unsuspecting kitten was laid on its side, quickly and expertly rolled in the towel so his legs and his hind end were protruding. The assistant held the animal between his elbows, each hand holding a leg. The tail was whipping furiously. The attendant timed the whip, grabbed and held it with one finger. Hair over the testicles was clipped, the skin cleaned with alcohol and an antiseptic applied. The stage was thus set and the students moved this way and that, over and around their classmates heads for a better view.

The professor's thumb and index fingers tensed the skin of the scrotum over the testicles. With the scalpel in his other hand, he made two quick slashes. The kitten screamed, and I winced. In a quick pinching move, Stephenson forced both testes through the incisions. Dropping the scalpel, he grasped them and in one motion wrenched them out, arteries, veins and nerves attached.

I couldn't believe the casual inhumanity of the procedure. He unrolled the towel and held up the quivering little creature like a magician climaxing his rabbit act. "Notice the lack of bleeding. When an artery is torn deep within the body the pressure of the surrounding tissues controls hemorrhage."

"Sir," I asked shakily, "Why don't you use an anesthetic on cats too? Don't they hurt just as much as dogs?"

"Zimmerman," he answered, "giving a local block would hurt as much as the entire operation. General anesthesia is too expensive and is relatively more risky. We do what's been done for years. In five minutes the cat has forgotten the entire experience."

"But he screamed, there must be another way to do minor surgery so it wouldn't hurt so!"

The class was hushed as the many minds tried to decide which side to favor. Some agreed, others couldn't have cared less.

"Come on Zim," Dan pulled me away. "No point in getting in dutch with the prof."

I turned away muttering, "It's not right! In Vet school you would think they'd lean over backwards to be compassionate. I'm going to talk to Dr. Milks."

"You're just looking for trouble. They're not going to change their whole curriculum just cause you're a little squeamish."

Walt Matuszak, another student and quarterback of the varsity football team approached. He was six foot six, weighed two hundred and forty pounds and was gentle as he was big. A fellow athlete, he placed a comforting hand on my shoulder, "I come from a farm and they castrate pigs the same way. They stuff them into a boot, and don't even use antiseptic. It used to make me sick too, but you get used to it."

"That's just what I'm afraid of, Walt," I answered miserably. Somehow, someway, I thought, I'm going to do something about it!

A few days after the episode with the cats, Matuszak and I ran into each other, practicing, on upper alumni field. He trotted over with his helmet propped atop his head like a professor's miss-placed glasses. "Hey Zim," he kidded, "next Tuesday in large animal surgery they are going to demonstrate castration in the horse. I wanted you to know that they have to use anesthesia or get their heads kicked off."

"I knew they'd never find a towel big enough to roll those babies in, but I'll be there to observe." I appreciated Walt's concern about my feelings in the matter. Some of my other classmates labeled me a softy.

The class met outside the Horse Barn on the Ag campus. Dr. Frost, and Dr. Danks, presiding. Most classes in large animal surgery were given in the main operating arena in the rear of James Law Hall. Whenever possible, however, demonstrations were given sim-ulating field conditions. Such was the case that day.

Four beautiful young stallions, there to be gelded, were tethered nearby, happily munching on rich green grass. Dr. Danks called the roll and Frost waited for attention.

"We will cover castration today because as you can see we have four fine volunteers from the Batavia Horse Farm. Think of yourselves right at the farm. Farm hands, when available, help out. Don't get spoiled by the man-power here. Many a time you will have to do everything yourselves, from rounding up patients to necessary restraint for your doctoring! The exception will be the rare sophisticated racing stable.

"In equines, anesthesia is more critical than in other species. A horse can't lie on its side longer than one hour at a time because its great weight will cause hypostatic pneumonia. I'm sure many of you students spent many a sleepless night turning horses every hour."

No wonder some horses sleep standing up, I thought.

Frost continued, "We use epidural for this procedure because of its safety, speed and ease of administration. It's similar to the spinal used in humans, except that procedure is much more dangerous. This method, given by injection into the epidural space, doesn't jeopardize the spinal chord and blocks sensory as well as motor nerves to all structures behind the umbilicus" (belly button).

Why don't they use this on cats? I wondered, I guess it couldn't work or they would certainly have tried it. I made up my mind to ask Dr. Danks about it.

Frost continued, "With his hind end completely relaxed, you will notice that the wakeful horse still tries to stand. While in the sitting position, we force him on his side, one man controlling his head to keep him from hurting himself. He will hold the head in his lap, keeping it from thrashing by hugging it to his chest, nose up."

Dr. Frost removed a 10 cc syringe from his medical bag and held it so all could see.

"For the average horse about 10 cc of 2% procaine injected into the epidural space is sufficient for a complete posterior block. That is sufficient time to shave, scrub and operate. The surgery is simple. The only area of concern, besides infection, is hemmorrhage. Arterial bleeding is controlled with crushing forceps. For this demonstration, half the students will come with me, half go with Dr. Danks. Lets say, A through M, follow me, the remainder, Dr. Danks."

I hearkened as Dr. Danks prepared the procaine and lectured. It was difficult to compare a five pound kitten with a 1500 pound stallion, but one's imagination makes anything possible.

"The epidural space is just posterior to the spinal cavity. First I am going to demonstrate the injection site."

He walked to where the young stallions were grazing. Picking up a pair of reins, he motioned a student to hold the animal's head high (a horse can't kick without dropping its head). He strolled around to its back end and took the tail in one hand.

"Notice as I raise the tail, a wrinkle is formed just in front of it's base. Right here," he said demonstrating, "on the mid-line of the fold, is the entry point for the needle.

"Remember it's the first wrinkle. If you press a finger on that spot you can feel the space between two vertebrae. Every one come up and feel the depression."

He stepped aside as each student took his turn. As my chance arrived, I was thinking about the procedure in a cat. I was hoping the injection site would be as easy to find on a five pound kitten as it was for a one ton horse.

"The same technique as well as the surgery, is identical in bulls, rams and boars."

Danks demonstrated, and invited our questions. In less than a minute the stallion's hind legs began to buckle. He sat. As the block took further affect, his bladder emptied, its powerful odor permeating the area. I realized the epidural block would be effective in all types of surgery involving the rear end.

Dr. Danks motioned Dubois Jenkins, one of the huskier students, to force the sitting animal to lie down. He then controlled his head, as previously instructed. Danks demonstrated the use of crushing forceps and in five minutes the procedure was over.

A team of students was selected to operate on the second stallion. One gave the anesthetic, a second did the surgery, the third applied the forceps and the fourth restrained the horse. By the end of the semester every student would have to perform or assist.

Within an hour the geldings were back to grazing, their only concern how much and how fast they could eat the tender green lawn.

I cornered Dr. Danks. "Doctor, has epidural ever been used on dogs and cats?"

Danks never answered a question without careful reflection. He thought, pushed his glasses up on his nose, and finally answered. "Theoretically it should be a feasible procedure. All vertebrates have an epidural space. I would check the library if I were you, then ask Milks or Stephenson." He concluded, "I can't recall ever seeing it used on small animals."

My heart sank. "It would have been so perfect." I thought. Nevertheless I made up my mind to pursue it.

For the next two weeks I made a pest of myself at Flower Library. The patient and gracious librarians searched the old journals, any and all text books, including the translated German texts. About a week later I was met with a triumphant smile from Miss Guilford. "Is this what you wanted?"

I looked at an old copy of the AVMA. The date was from the early 1900's. The article was headed, "Alternatives to General Anesthesia," by a Dr. C. H. Wood, DVM. In it was a chapter about epidural anesthesia in small animals. It described the anatomy of the epidural area and showed how to find the site for injection. It wasn't specific about needle size, usable drugs or clinical trials. But the summary, "This procedure, in the hands of an experienced practitioner, is a valuable alternative to general anesthesia. It is safe, simple and quick to administer, and the recovery is complete in thirty to sixty minutes," was all I needed. I was jubilant as I carried my borrowed journal to Dr. Stephenson's office.

"Can I try epidural on my castration?" I asked after showing Stephenson the article on epidural.

"Sure you can Zimmerman. I told you you can do anything rational with your lab animals. Remember to be careful about preparing the area for injection. I don't know how it will work, but give it a try."

My big day arrived the next week. Only Dan Woolf and Dr. Stephenson knew what I was up to. The surgical lab was busy and noisy as usual. The twenty or so operating tables, four students per table, were covered with instruments, towels for wrapping the cats and antiseptics for disinfection.

I had practiced for a week on my kitten, palpating the point near the pelvis where the injection was to be made. The needle had to be at right angles to the top of the back and exactly in the center. The article said that if the entry was correct the tail would twitch once and there would be no resistance in the syringe as the barrel was depressed, indicating the anesthetic was in the epidural space.

I told Danny to hold the kitten over the table's end with one hand on his back and the other holding both legs straight down. I prayed that the article was correct in that minimal discomfort was felt by the patient. I could hear the muffled screams of cats at other tables as the students performed their surgery.

I filled the syringe with 2% procaine. Dan cleaned the area with alcohol, swabbed tincture of iodine on it and then wiped it clean with alcohol again.

I took a deep breath, placed my left hand on his back and felt the little depression that was supposed to be the injection site. The syringe was in my right hand and I inserted it at the correct angle as gently as possible. The needle struck bone as his tail jumped once. The barrel of the syringe started to empty by gravity. There was no resistance to my right index finger, as it sat lightly on the barrel's end. After about ½ cc of solution was injected I removed it and stepped back.

The room had become quiet as the word got around. Dan released the kitten and it sat up as we all waited expectantly. The tip of its tail was waving back and forth in a light show of emotion. In less than a minute the tail was flaccid and the back end of the kitten collapsed much as the stallion's, the week before.

"Danny! Scratch her neck while I clean and shave."

I proved my point as I slashed the skin, forced out the gonads, and pulled them free. Everyone was talking at once. One wanted the library article, some a demonstration and others asked more questions than I could answer.

Through the years, I perfected the technique and expanded the procedures for spays, posterior fractures, feline urolithiasis (blocked urethras) and anal gland surgery, to name a few. Thousands of operations were performed with no pain, no deaths and no spinal damage.

In small animal medicine, Milks and Stephenson were molding my thought, and were important in planning for the future. I was now in my second year still desiring to specialize in exotic animal medicine. They encouraged me to read and apply everything learned to every specie of the animal kingdom.

A Seminar in small animal surgery was scheduled for November 10, 1940. I was thrilled to be on the inside track of developing new medical procedures. Our professors, role models "who could do no wrong," and the object of our adulation, were to be spotlighted. The seminars were held in the James Law Hall amphitheater and were exciting and prestigious conferences. Scheduled once or twice yearly, they were reserved for any new research discovery, a new or innovative technique in surgery, a breakthrough in blood chemistry, an advance in bacteriology or virology, or almost any new and important approach in any subject of medical importance.

The subject was a speedy and sutureless spaying technique for young cats, that would work for small wildcats as well. Not exactly an earth-shaking topic for Cornellians in general, but for us, an insight on a significant medical advance. As a sophomore I was given the privilege of being part of the show. The freshmen weren't included and I was the only sophomore on the supporting team. I carried a bucket of disinfectant and cleaning towels as my badge of eminence. I would keep such an important event clean-smelling and spotless.

The amphitheater was constructed like a huge cone with the stage at its base. There, an operating table, a movie or slide screen, a chemistry table or pertinent paraphernalia, was set up. Steep rows of desks arched towards the windowed ceiling. Bright illumination and an unobstructed view were afforded everyone in the hall. I sat there many times, when trepidation rather than anticipation was my reaction. It was the arena where we took our formidable, written exams. The instructors placed us two seats apart, as we struggled to decipher the impossible. It was a rendezvous with fear that only a few enjoyed, such as Kenny Gumaer, who always knew the answers. Today was different however; I would be an observer.

Professor Stephenson was hoping to be the demonstrating surgeon. That decision, however, was up to the boss, H.J. Milks. Quite by accident, it was Stephenson who created the surgical procedure to be demonstrated. Accident or not, I felt that he earned the right to perform. Why shouldn't he be the center of such a highly publicized and prestigious event? It might even put a smile on his face.

The procedure evolved during one of our class's routine surgical labs. Nick Paddock and Don McGown, lab partners, were conniving to get Stephenson to their operating table. They wanted some hints and personal instruction for their first cat spay. Stephenson was spread thin among twenty surgical teams, and never seemed to be available.

Jerry Bandes had busted out, and Danny Wolfe, my new partner and I knew something was up when Stephenson spent more that just a few minutes at their table. We were working next to them and asked Nick about it afterwards.

He grinned as he told us what happened.

"We had to figure a way to get some attention. I told Don the only way to get him over to our table was to get in trouble."

Stephenson had approached, gowned and gloved, arms half raised in the classic surgical posture, with that omnipresent annoyed look on his face. Paddock said sheepishly. "I must have made the incision in the wrong place, sir, I can't locate the linea alba."(the thin white ligament visible on the midline separating the right and left abdominal muscles). It was the landmark for the initial cut.

His answer, laced with sarcasm as thick as pea soup, was, "You see those little pimples lined up on either side of her belly? Well those are called nipples. You may recall that people have them also, though if you think real hard you'll recall that we are disadvantaged by nature, owning just two. Now draw a parallel line between the two rows of nipples. You can't be far off now can you?" Then sternly, "I should make you suture that skin incision and let you start again."

Stephenson must have suspected their pretext as he settled over the cat and studied the problem. He played with the cut edges, forceps in one hand and scalpel in the other. He pulled the skin bordering the incision toward the midline, then let it snap back. He repeated the motion absently several times attesting some deep thought.

Suddenly his hands stopped and a rare smile transformed his face. The forceps grasped the skin again and once more he pulled it over to the linea alba. He made a stab wound of not more than a half inch through the white fibrous line between the muscles. He then let the skin snap back covering the incision. He repeated the motion again, exposing the stab incision with a small retractor and inserting a small spay hook through it. He then proceeded with the spay. In young animals, blood vessels are narrow and crushing forceps control bleeding.

When Stephenson was finished, he let the uterine and ovarian stumps slide back inside the abdomen. The skin then slipped back,

completely covering the linea alba. Neither incision required suturing, because of their size. He put a snug bandage around the
abdomen and instructed the boys to leave it for five days.

"I'll remove the bandage myself." He told them, "If it heals the
way it should, you may have bumbled into a technique that may
cut the spay time for young cats to under five minutes. The off center
skin incision negates the use of sutures in either skin or muscle."

Nick grinned recalling how well the ruse worked. On the fifth
post-surgical day Paddock and McGown excitedly brought the kitten
to the lab. Paddock said condescendingly, "It's a good thing for the
veterinary profession that I'm such a brilliant surgeon. Who else
could possibly conceive of such an amazing innovation."

"The most remarkable exhibition of dumb luck ever recorded in
medical history." Mc Gown answered.

"And you Mac, of all the nice, intelligent classmates available as
my partner, I chose you. You should be eternally grateful and for
a small stipend. . .say ten bucks, you can watch me perform magic
with the scalpel for the rest of the year. . .Uh oh, here he comes.

Their faces and demeanor changed from cocky to humble pie
as Stephenson, without a word or change of expression, removed
the bandage and surveyed the scar.

It had healed perfectly!

He met with Milks that day, and explained the technique. He
thought it would be a timely subject for him to use in a seminar.
Milks was interested but reserved his decision until he did several
trial runs himself. "After all," he cooed, licking his lips and grinning.
"If I give a demonstration I want to be sure that it works."

"I thought I might do the surgery since I discovered it." Stephenson murmured hopefully.

"As head of the department, it's my duty to perform the demonstration." Milks retorted abruptly, "But don't worry," he added licking
his lips and grinning. "I'll give you, Paddock and McKown full credit."

Stephenson's face fell. Frustration turned to anger and he thought
to himself, "Its too humiliating. I won't watch him exult over my discovery."

He said, turning away, "Well I won't be there. I have some
important research to check in the library."

Milks retorted. "You be there! Do research on your own time."

Milks practiced the new procedure several times and finally set
the date for the seminar. The day was clear and cold. The audience

was excited and expectant. The Dean, surrounded by his staff, added diginity and influence to the proceedings. Stephenson sat with them, his face expressionless. Most students were excused from routine chores and classes so they could attend. The exception was the unlucky few who had routine or emergency assignments. I was excited because I had seen the entire drama unfold and was part of its presentation. I liked Milks, but my sense of fairness was wounded by his treatment of Stephenson, who complained to the class that he really deserved to be the surgeon.

Milks, gowned and capped, but as yet unscrubbed, entered the staging area from the wings. The buzzing ended abruptly as all eyes focused on center stage. Milks gave the usual predemonstration talk. He mentioned Hadley and the circumstances leading up to the novel surgical approach.

"The average practitioner should benefit greatly from this procedure." he continued, "spays make up 75% of all the surgery in most small animal hospitals. This operation can be used only on the young feline. But so many are spayed every year that a five minute exercise will be a great time saver. Stab cuts on both skin and linea alba preclude the need for sutures. The offset skin tissue incision, slipping back into place, protects the muscle like a tissue bandage. After the demonstration there will be a question and answer period. I'll scrub up and we'll be ready to start in just a few minutes."

The silence was broken again as everyone buzzed. The potential of the procedure, the risks and the doubts, were intriguing. The senior assistant wheeled in the operation table, the anesthetized cat draped and in position. Intravenous nembutol was used so the ampitheatre wouldn't reek from ether.

Milks, gowned, masked, gloved and wearing his sterile cap followed in a few minutes. The arena grew quiet. He picked up the scalpel and glanced at the clock. It was 3:20.

I had the best view in the house. I stood on the stage, off to one side holding my bucket, the envy of my class.

Milks began the demonstration. He indicated the line of the skin incision with the gloved index finger.

"Notice the skin incision off the midline. The elasticity of the skin allows flexibility. I've been as far as one inch to the side with no problem."

As he proceeded he kept up a relaxed mumbled chatter, enjoying his role as absolute center of attention. He deftly made the stab incision, picked up the spaying hook and went in after the left uterine horn. Hooking the horn required experience and feel. He was usually successful in his first try. The clock read 3:25 as the came up empty. Licking his lips he tried again, and then again. Still no uterus. The compulsive tongue worked faster.

He stopped his chatter and concentrated on the hook. It was 3:27. The hall was quiet as a wake. Still no luck. His peers began to squirm in sympathetic embarrassment.

A voice from nowhere, "Check the sex."

Burns, the assistant reached under the shroud. Every ear in the amphitheater heard the tortured words as his fingers found the testicles.

"I'm sorry doctor. She called it her little girl. I should have checked." Milks, who always reexamines, was attempting the impossible! The cardinal rule for pre-surgical examinations in felines had been breached, and by its arch proponent.

I was embarrassed, sick and hurt. I felt it was my personal, private defeat. I looked over to where Stephenson had been sitting. I didn't see him leave.

Milks looked up at the towering arena. His eyes twinkled as he stared at Dean Hagan. "It's a lesson you'll never forget. We'll bandage this little fellow as if he were a lady. The exercise of the day was to illustrate the stab incision and its healing without suturing. That we did, and now we'll bring out a cat we operated on five days ago."

The little male was released from its ties, bandaged quickly and removed from the stage.

Milks nodded to an assistant who disappeared for a moment.

He returned with a bandaged cat and set it on the table. Milks, with one swipe of a bandage scissors, pulled the dressing away.

"You are all invited to examine the abdominal area. No sutures were used and the healing is complete."

Professors, grad-students and underclassmen filed down to see for themselves, surrounding the demonstration table.

Milks was murmuring away to his heart's content. Pointing to the incision, greeting fellow faculty members and thoroughly enjoying himself. I heard him say laughingly, "nobody's perfect."

To this day I'm not sure that the program wasn't a set up. It was just like Milks to pull off a stunt no one would forget. It was also in the realm of possibility that Stephenson arranged it. That night in the senior league at the Ithaca Bowling Center, Hadley Stephenson rolled his first perfect game.

I joined Marv at the Driscoll's to start 1941 and my junior year in vet school. My parents were assured that I wouldn't play football for four years after leaving high school. I kept my word but it was the fifth year at Cornell and the yearning to try out for the 150 pound football team was overwhelming.

Assistant Professor Alexander Zeissig, of the Bacteriology Dep't, didn't think much of me as a student but he adored football. He was assistant to Dean Hagan who gave the lecture course while Ziessig ran the lab. Alexander Zeissig was a short stocky man that wore ill-fitting eyeglasses so he was forever adjusting the lenses. He had thin graying hair, short pudgy fingers that mirrored his build. Wearing dark wrinkled suits that suited his disposition, and a rather high irritating voice, he reigned over his students like a despot. He seemed to resent students asking questions about anything.

I liked bacterilology and was good at it, probably a genetic gift. My sister was a bacteriology major and always got straight "A"s. After the first term I got an easy A from the Dean and a low B from Zeissig. I was sure I deserved better. It wasn't until he called me aside one day that I realized he knew who I was. "Zimmerman," he squeeked, "the germs we are studying are quite universal. They may not be identical to those found in other parts of the world, but they are probably similar to those that attack monkeys, predators and range animals."

Somehow he had heard about my special interest and was willing to talk to me about it. "I'm sure you'll find streptococci, coli and staphs in the jungle," he continued, "so study with an eye to adapt what you learn to all species." And that was the last and only time he ever talked directly to me.

Zeissig never missed a 150 pound football game or a practice. He would sit on the bench with Coach Grant and soon became an endless presence. I could understand him never giving me an acknowledging glance when I was only a scrub, but he didn't change even after I moved up. He was there when the jump was made from scrubs to the first team. During a particularly rough scrimmage, Williams, the varsity fullback was tackled hard. The impact caused him to suffer three cracked ribs and it knocked him out for at least three weeks. The second team fullback had the flu so coach Grant, rather reluctantly, moved me up because I was the only one who knew the assignments.

I waited, hopefully, for Zeissig to react. He said nothing to me then and never alluded to it in class.

I started the Princeton game with the entire fraternity proudly watching. My sister and her fiance were there for the second time. I played well, throwing and completing seven passes in a row, scoring a touchdown on a pass interception and playing the full game as safety. In those days, we played both offense and defense.

Phi Zeta was the Veterinary School's Honor Society. Five or six outstanding students were chosen from each class. A faculty member proposed a name and a committee of professors and members of the society voted. One blackball from either faculty or student eliminated the prospect. The applicants were chosen for scholastic ability, character, and extra-curricular achievement.

A week before the election, the twelve nominees were posted on the James Law Hall bulletin board. It was a week before Christmas. I was thrilled to see my name on the list. It was a very special honor to be considered for the society. I knew my chances were nil because Zeissig was one of the committeemen. Dr. Milks was also a member and I felt he might be sympathetic. The following week the six lucky names were on the James Law Bulletin Board with faculty sponsors listed next to each. Alphabetical order put my name on the bottom of the page. Next to it was my proposer. . .Dr. Alexander Zeisseg!

The selection to Phi Zeta completed a dream year. I made varsity on the 150's and now could look forward to my senior year, graduation, the army, (if the war was still on) and finally the practice of veterinary medicine.

Captain Wilson, our ROTC commander, called us together in January of 1943 with a proposition we couldn't refuse. The Army had taken over the vet school. They would pay our fees, and eliminate the summer hiatus enabling us to graduate in February, 43'. Our class would be immediately commissioned second lieutenants in the reserve, and when we were inducted we would be first Lieutenants in the Veterinary Corps, Medical Department, Army of the United States.

Myron Gustin Fincher, D.V.M.,M.S., Assistant Professor of Medicine and Obstetrics, was head of the Ambulatory Clinic of the

Veterinary College, large animal section. The clinic served the farmers in the Ithaca, New York area, in a radius of almost 50 miles. Dr. Fincher was a tall, wiry, soft spoken man. He had an almost preacher like appearance and demeanor. He wore glasses and was forever cleaning them. When lecturing it seemed to help him concentrate. As he reached into his mind for the right work or description, the circular motion of handkercheif on glass seemed to be the catalyst that helped capture the elusive phrase.

He used his own beat-up private car to make his rounds. It was a black four door Dodge with a huge overloaded trunk. A senior usually accompanied him, although on occasion, an exceptional junior would be asked to go along. They learned first hand, how to talk to the farmers, how to reassure them, explain medication and treatment regimes to them. Most important they learned how to charge for their services. He explained when not to mention money and when and how to press for delinquent payments.

The practice of medicine on a typical New York State dairy farm was different from what any of us could anticipate. No clean smelling barns, freshly hosed down treatment wards, or handsomely landscaped pastures. There were no spotlessly attired assistants to help restrain the cattle or immaculate instrument cabinets to hold the endless number of medical tools and medicines that might be needed. A student couldn't possibly attempt to practice large animal medicine without the kind of experience Dr. Fincher afforded. There was constant competition among the seniors to be chosen as his assistant.

One day in November of 1942 the clinic received an emergency phone call. Dr. Fincher was tied up with a serious obstetrical case and I was the only student present. The other students had gone home for the Thanksgiving holiday. I hadn't gone because I couldn't afford the round-trip fare for the long weekend.

Dwight Van Nest from Ludlowville had a sick cow. It had calved a week before and had not expelled the afterbirth. We had studied the condition, "retained placenta," which was failure to eliminate the after-birth after calving. If untreated it could become serious as decomposition and subsequent putrifaction could cause severe toxemia. The very least would result in loss of milk production, and the inability to produce a calf for the entire year. Fincher needed an experienced student to take the call.

Dr. Fincher nervously cleaned his glasses as he walked over to me. "Zimmerman, here are the keys to my car. Dwight Van Nest's farm is about 20 miles down the north shore of Cayuga. He has a downed cow, probably retained placenta. All the equipment you might need is in the car. Rubber sleeve, forceps, sulfur drugs and soap. Do you have a driver's license?"

"Yes sir, but I've never gone on a case before, not even as an observer. I'm not sure I'll even know how to start, . . .or charge or any thing!"

"Zimmerman, the best way to learn is to just go ahead and do it. I have been watching you work around the clinic and you handle yourself with knowledge and confidence. Don't let Van Nest think you don't know what you're doing. You've read all about removing a placenta.

"When you put on the surgical sleeve lubricate it with the sterile jelly and feel for the button-like areas that attach the placenta to the uterus. Be very gentle so you don't tear the tissue. You'll find that it separates quite easily. Be slow and careful. When the after-birth is completely removed, drop a bolus of the sulfa into the uterus to prevent infection. Get a urine sample for the lab. I wouldn't let you use my car and instruments if you didn't have my complete confidence."

I gulped. How did Dr. Fincher have the nerve to trust me with a real case. If I do manage to get the placenta out, I thought, how in the world would I get a urine specimen from a cow? I had seen the seniors collect it in cups from hospitalized animals, but suppose the cow isn't ready. I could see myself holding the container for hours with nothing happening.

"How do I go about getting a urine specimen, sir? Suppose she doesn't have to go!" I asked nervously. I realized I was conceivably worrying about the least important item of the whole trip; but I was nervous and grasping at straws.

"Have you forgotten the urinating reflex from Physiology I? We can't use a catheter because it may introduce infection into the bladder. Severe cystitis leading to pyelonephritis will surely result. Take a piece of gauze or cotton and gently rub the anal area. Reflexly she will fill your container within a few seconds. Anything else?"

"Yes sir. I don't know what to charge."

"Tell Van Nest I'll send him a bill at the end of the month."

"I haven't any money sir. I mean for gas or an emergency or anything."

"Here's ten dollars." He said digging into his pocket. "You can return what you don't spend. The gas tank is full. And Zimmerman, stop trying to think up excuses why not to go. This is really a great opportunity for you. Usually a junior just stands around watching the Doctor or the senior do all the diagnosing and treatment. Now you can do it all with no one but yourself to answer. Now get going, Zimmerman," he paused putting his hand on my shoulder, "Good luck, and don't worry, it's going to turn out just fine. Now remember, even though we think it's retained placenta, be sure to give her a complete physical just the way we do here at the clinic. And don't forget to examine the calf."

I took the keys, found the car and got started. The only time I had driven in the last two years was my sister's "Jezebel," borrowed for an occasional date. I had never driven off the campus and here I was going on a professional house call, half way around Cayuga Lake. I was sure I would get lost!

I drove from the Vet Clinic through the Ag School, then the Arts campus to Stewart Ave. Down the steep hill into Ithaca and south until I reached Cayuga. It was a beautiful glistening jewel when viewed from Cornell's great height. I had butterflies in my stomach as I drove along the lake's north shore towards Ludlowville. A little over a half hour later I was deep in farm country. The roads wound around with gorgeous views of the lake, then the landscape changed to farm scenes with barns and silos silouetted against the hills of upper New York.

I knew I was getting close because the odometer showed twenty miles. My heart skipped a beat as I spied an old mail box on the right of the road showing the name "Van Nest."

I pulled into the driveway, an old dirt and rock strewn road. There was a steep incline towards an unpretentious farmhouse on the left. It was a large three story structure badly in need of paint. A porch extended across its entire front. A four step staircase lead from the road to the porch directly in line with the front door. The porch was littered with children's toys, several unpainted wood chairs, one rocker and a hammock.

Standing on the porch was the welcoming committee. A tall middle aged woman with gray unkempt hair that was constantly being pushed into place with one hand, showing the world that she really cared. I could see that once she had been a beauty. A skinny little ten year old girl in a very plain dress leaned over the wooden railing trying to get a good look at the stranger. A little six or seven year old lad holding the hand of a fairly well dressed and very attractive teenager. They watched intently as I pulled to a stop.

"I'm from the Cornell Veterinary Clinic to look at a sick cow. Is this Dwight Van Nest's farm?" I asked. I hadn't the slightest idea about how to proceed.

"Aya, we've been expectin ya. I'm Olive Van Nest. These here are Irene and Lloyd and my niece, Fern Buckingham. Dwight is straight down the road to the barn. You can see it from here just on the right side."

"Thank you Mam," I responded and drove the car towards the barn scattering cackling chickens and guinea hens in all directions.

I could see Fern in the mirror starting down the stairs toward the roadway. "I'm going to watch him treat the cow." She called back to Aunt Olive.

"Me too," Irene said.

"Me too," echoed Lloyd as all three started toward the barn.

"He looks like he's all business, Fern." Olive called after them. "Don't cha go gittin' in the way."

"We won't Mam."

I parked the car near the barn door, opened the trunk and proceeded to gather what I might need. I looked around the barn yard trying to appear casual and experienced. I could see and smell the pig sty off to the left with six or eight hogs snorting and squeeling. As I glanced back at the farm house I could see the three youngsters approaching. Damn! All I need is an audience, I thought.

Dwight Van Nest appeared at the barn door. "Hello," he greeted, "spected Dr. Fincher."

"Sorry, he had an emergency at the clinic and couldn't get away. I'm Ted Zimmerman, one of his students."

"Well come on in. Doc usually has one of you boys with him. Hadn't met one that wasn't a nice fella. One of my milkers is down. Hasn't passed her afterbirth and won't let the calf suck."

"How long since she calved, Sir?" I asked professionally.

"Today is the sixth day. Only stopped eating yesterday though."

I carried the gear into the poorly lit barn. There were five stalls freshly washed down. In the third was a Holstein lying on the floor.

An electric light bulb on a long wire was hanging from a nail over the cow to afford some light. In one corner lay the calf on a pile of straw. There was no milking machine in sight. I should have known this was a hand-milked herd.

"I'll be needing a bucket of boiling water, Mr. Van Nest."

"I know. I'll be gittin it whilst you look her over." Dwight turned and left the barn. He knew the procedure from Dr. Fincher. He was on his way to the kitchen as he passed the children on the road.

"We're going to watch the doctor treat the cow, daddy." Irene said excitedly.

"I think he'll do an operation," Lloyd volunteered seriously.

"Just don't be no bother. Keep them out of trouble, Fern, till I git back."

"I will Uncle Dwight." Fern answered dutifully.

The three hurried to the barn door in time to see me examining the cow's head. There was a thick mucous secretion in the corners of both eyes. Lowered resistance from the infection, I thought. Her ears were cold to the touch. Cold ears, high temperature. I recalled my medicine notes. I forced her mouth open to examine her teeth, gums and throat. The mucosa was dry and hot to the touch. Dehydrated too. I wondered why he waited a week to call the clinic?

I went to the medical bag for the stethoscope. Her heart rate was rapid, lungs congested. I took the rectal thermometer to check for fever. Three minutes, I hummed as I timed it.

"Why don't you put the thermometer under her tongue?" Fern asked with mock seriousness, a big grin on her face.

"Cause she won't hold it there while I'm busy with other things."

"Would you like me to be your nurse so you can do other important stuff?" she asked.

"No thanks."

"My name is Fern." she said, "I live in Ithaca."

"Hi Fern. I'm Ted."

"I'm Irene." the little lass interjected, "My dad owns this farm."

"I'm going to be a farmer too," little Lloyd said seriously, "or maybe an animal doctor, like you."

"That's nice. I think you'll be a great doctor. Be sure you get good marks in school."

"I hate school." Irene chimed in.

"I'm going to kindergarten this year," Lloyd said. "I love to ride in the school bus."

Three minutes were up. 103.6 degrees, as I suspected. I'd better get started with that afterbirth, I thought to myself. I reached in the bag for the rubber sleeve, an ingenious extention of the rubber glove. It went all the way up the arm and over the shoulder. I reached for the sterile talcum and prepared my hand and arm.

While waiting for Van Nest to arrive with the water, I tried to clean the cow's soiled backside and legs with alcohol. Much of the exudate had dried, making it difficult to do. The soap and hot water would be needed to wash her down. I had sterile towels to pat the area dry. Small talk continued with the children as I walked over to examine the calf. She seemed okay, warm to the touch and eager to suck my fingers. Good, I thought, she's hungry.

"Isn't she cute?" Fern said. "Aunt Olive said I could help Uncle Dwight nurse her if necessary."

I liked Fern and wondered if I would ever see her again. She was much better looking than most Cornell coeds! I learned later that Fern was wondering the same thing about me. Her girl friend, Trixie, was always boasting about her dates with a Cornell Engineer.

What luck! she thought, that she decided to visit her cousins today.

Dwight arrived with the water a few minutes later. The audience wasn't about to miss a thing. They sat down on the hay near the calf and watched eagerly.

I scrubbed down the vulval area and hind legs. The sticky, crusty skin required elbow grease to clean. Finally I was satisfied and used the towels from the medical pack. I slipped on the rubber sleeve, lubricated it with sterile jelly and gently inserted my hand through the vagina, the dilated vulva, into the uterus. I felt for the buttons, they called them cotyledons, that I had studied in anatomy and Fincher had described.

Suddenly I felt one. It was like a little growth on the surface of the mucosa. Carefully, my gloved fingers separated the placenta from the button and searched for the next one. Sure enough, just as Fincher said, the retained placenta came away easily. These attachments, so important for the nourishment of the fetus during pregnancy, should separate and fall away in a normal delivery. Nutrients for the fetus pass through the myriad blood vessels at each raised area. In retained placenta for some inexplicable reason the uterus remains attached.

I proceeded slowly until my arm was inside the cow up to my shoulder. I strained to reach the most distant attachments, and finally the last one parted. With my free hand I lifted out the entire placenta, dropped the tissue into a waste bucket and heaved a sigh of relief. My first case was a success! With my ungloved hand I took a bolus of sulfa out of the medical bag, transfered it, and gently dropped it into the uterus. The smooth muscle, so flaccid during the entire procedure, was beginning to contract.

"I think she'll be okay now Mr. Van Nest. I felt her uterus react. I'll take a urine sample back to the lab to be sure."

"Thank ye Doc. I sure would like to git away from hand nursing her calf. I ain't been gitten much sleep this week."

I took the sterile container used to collect urine samples and approached Bossie again. Now! I thought, this better work. With cotton in one hand and the container in the other, I rubbed the rectal area as instructed. A voice piped up, "What are you doing now?"

"Just getting a urine sample for the lab."

"You going to ask her to cooperate?" It was Fern.

"I've already asked her." I answered confidently. I was hoping that it would really work. Almost the next moment my prayers were answered. My cup was running over.

"That's terrific. You're really a good vet!" Fern said.

The flush of satisfaction swept over me as Dwight joined in, "I always wondered how Dr. Fincher got his samples. He asked me to git one for him once and I wasted an hour coaxing the stupid cow."

He grinned at the recollection. "Thank ye, Ted, 'preciate the treatment. I'll tell Doc you did just fine."

I was glowing. All the trepidation and concern was for naught. As I gathered up the gear and carefully replaced it in Dr. Fincher's medical case, I felt what all students experience after their first successful case. My gratification was complete and I knew I was on my way!

"What do I owe you Doc?" Dwight asked.

"Dr. Fincher said he would send you a bill or stop by the next time he's in the neighborhood."

"Thanks again, Ted, would you mind dropping Fern off in Ithaca on your way back? Her folks wanted her home in about an hour. Olive doesn't drive and with chores coming up I'd really have to rush."

"I'd be happy to Dwight, if she doesn't mind." I said smiling at Fern. She agreed with all the plans.

The trip back to Ithaca was quiet. I was preoccupied with my triumph and too shy to respond to Fern's artful overtures. We did exchange phone numbers and I promised to call as soon as I had time.

As I entered the Clinic I saw that Dr. Fincher was finished with his emergency and was scrubbing up. He looked up as I approached. I guess I looked kinda proud.

"How'd it go Zimmerman? You look as though you accomplished a medical miracle."

"Everything went just as you said it would, Doctor. They are a nice family and asked to be remembered to you. I think the cow and the calf will be all right. And here is the urine sample." I handed him the waxed paper cup.

I gave him the car keys and went digging in my pocket for the ten dollar bill. For a minute I thought I'd lost it.

"I told Mr. Van Nest that you'd send him a bill."

The following day Fincher heard from Dwight. The cow was eating, the calf suckling and I had made a hit with the entire family. A month or so later I was invited to Fern's high school prom. It was on a free weekend so I accepted. I was the only Cornell student there. Fern was radiant and I felt like a grandpa.

For three interminable, troubled years, our class looked up to the seniors. It was hard to believe that finally we had reached that elusive plateau. Now it was our class that ran the clinics, did the surgery, studied jurisprudence, looked down on the underclassmen, prepared for our State Boards and finally had time for a social life. The only blot on our future calendar was the comtemplation of World War Two. Private plans for practicing medicine would have to wait because I wanted, above all, to wear the uniform and serve my country.

I was awarded a minor letter for 150 pound football and with it came the privilege of ushering varsity football games at Schoelkoph Stadium. "Wearers of the C," were given beautiful sweaters of cornellian and white, the background was like snow with the red letter C lighting up its face. Wearing it I saw all the varsity football games and showed off my insignia to the world.

One day in October, Renee Wolf, a member of the sorority, Sigma Delta Tau, was at our fraternity house with her date, Len Rafael, one of our fraters. Renee had always been one of my favorite coeds. Bright and attractive, we saw a lot of her thanks to Lenny and I got to know her well.

Len mentioned to her that I ushered varsity football games. One day she asked me if I would mind showing her guests to their seats at Saturday's game. "My family is coming to Cornell for the first time and I know the chaos of Schoelkoph on a Saturday afternoon."

"I'd be glad to, Renee." I said, happy to be of help. "I'll do everything but guarantee a victory on the football field. We have a pretty good team and I'm sure it will be a great game."

The evening before the game Len invited the Wolfs for dinner at the fraternity house and I got to know them. Papa Wolf was a fun loving, fine looking gentleman and Mrs. Wolf a small blonde lady, with rather stern features, seemingly a little shy. Elaine, the kid sister, was a cute, skinny, buck toothed and enthusiastic fourteen year old, wide-eyed and thrilled with the entire college experience. Little did I know then what the future held.

The next day, proudly sporting my varsity letter, I showed the four to their seats. Cornell cooperated to make the day a memorable one, and with my classmate, Walt Matuszak quarterbacking, we were victors on the field.

I was taking a graduate course for extra credit with Dr. Hayden. Compared with the rest of the faculty, he was relatively old, slow talking, excruciatingly precise and very caring and thoughtful. I can't recall ever seeing him without his immaculate, white laboratory coat. His hands were always locked behind his back as he paced slowly and thoughtfully back and forth across the lab. Retirement was his option but he loved working with the students. We all realized that learning from him was a privilege. He seemed to like me and my work. He almost convinced me to go into laboratory research as my life's endeavor.

The project I worked on was with the wonder drug, sulfadiazine. The sulfa drugs were one of the new modern miracles of medicine. Penicillin came first. Initially it was given by injection every four hours around the clock. Sulfanilimide was the first drug to be taken orally, and many new formulas in the sulfa family were synthesized. Sulfadiazine was effective for certain strains of bacteria that were resistant to Sulfanilimide. It was difficult to imagine that by swallowing a tablet it was possible to actually kill germs. This was the new concept in the practice of medicine and Hayden was in the forefront of research. He was a professor emeritus and in addition to his work in the laboratory, he lectured in our jurisprudence class. He joined most of the full professors, who gave us insights concerning their specialties.

The course in jurisprudence was innovative and important. It taught us the principles of client-patient relations, the proper way to handle difficult clients, and the science of running a practice. It included how to charge and most important, the ethics of practicing medicine.

One day the entire student body was buzzing about two kittens admitted to the emergency room of the small animal clinic, victims of strychnine poisoning. There was a bizarre story circulating about murder and suicide in relation to their family.

As usual, rumors spread like wildfire, and the entire school was captivated by the two stricken felines. They were immediately given names by the students caring for them in the clinic: Amos and Andy, both being black males. We could tell them apart because Amos had two white feet. We rushed to our books to learn as much as possible about what could be done about strychnine poisoning since both had arrived convulsing. Small doses of barbiturates controlled the seizures and the following day both kittens seemed to be resting comfortably.

Dr. Hayden brought up the subject in his weekly jurisprudence lecture.

"Amos and Andy are a good example of how mother nature works. Amos seems to be doing fine but Andy is failing. His liver was damaged and doesn't seem able to detoxify the poison. "Remember," He paused to allow his ideas to sink in. "Except for their marking one couldn't tell them apart but it seems as though Andy is the weaker of the two and Dr. Milks feels that he may not make it."

"It isn't always weaknesses that make the difference," he reminded us. "Amos was blessed with kidneys efficient enough to eliminate the poison, a heart strong enough to survive the stress of severe convulsions, and a better than normal liver to detoxify the blood of a noxious poison." He stopped again and this time looked right at his audience.

"Amos has no family to return to. All were lost and Dr. Milks is looking for someone to take him. Anyone interested?"

A half a dozen hands went up as one and Hayden smiled. "I'm not a bit surprised. If you folks will see Dr. Milks after class today, he'll decide the winner. Now to get back to business."

He paused, his hands locked behind him and his face staring at the ceiling. "Medicine can help many conditions. In others there is nothing man can do. Nature does a pretty capable job in overcoming its weaknesses." Hayden paused, every eye riveted on his face, every ear tuned in to his voice.

"Be sure, as you travel the medical road, that you don't do more harm than good. If you do nothing in your practice but pat fannies, 90% of your patients will recover, a pretty fair rate of success. The object of todays talk is for you to appreciate, in spite of all you've learned these past four years, that nature is on your side. Try not to do more harm than good. Learn when it is better medicine to do nothing than to invent a treatment that can hurt the patient though it earns you a fee."

We left Dr. Hayden's lecture wondering why we had worked so hard and so long when we could only help ten percent of our patients. I asked him about it in the privacy of the laboratory and he told me that the real art was recognizing the ten percent that can be helped, then curing them with skill and understanding.

Graduation and the State Boards approached and the entire class was frantically preparing for the trick questions we had been warned about, such as: "Name five varieties of turkeys." or, "What is a caprine? porcine? ursine etc."

The class learned by rote, the different breeds of chickens, pigeons, ducks, geese, sheep, pigs, cattle, dogs, cats, deer, ruminants, carnivores etc., in addition to the thousand of medical facts accumulated over the past four years. The only category I was better prepared for was in the knowledge of exotic animals. I was sure they wouldn't ask me the weaning formula of an orangutan or gorilla or if I knew that camels and llamas were related as were pigs and hippos, but I was prepared if they did.

Finally, we learned the procedure for throwing a horse without gadgets, using only a rope. The trick question was asked every year in the practical section of the state board exams, failing more than 90% of out of state applicants.

January, our last month of college, was cold and snowy as usual. I became increasingly nostalgic about Cornell and Ithaca, even before I left. I had six wonderful years and a peculiar sadness began to permeate my thoughts. One afternoon, bundled up with overcoat, mittens and ear muffs, I climbed to the upper tier of Schoelkopf Stadium. I brushed away the snow from the highest bench, right over the fifty yard mark, sat down and daydreamed. The view was overwhelming. Starting to the north of Ithaca and extending as far as I could see was Cayuga Lake, glistening in the afternoon sun.

I was painting a picture that I would never allow myself to forget. I was just a sentimental jerk, I thought. But six years of the wonderful aura of Cornell, the fantastic gorges and waterfalls, the magnificent campus of the School of Agriculture, and Willard Straight's chimes singing to me constantly, was overwhelming. I almost cried, but I told myself I could always return. I shivered from the cold but was refreshed by the tangy, fresh air. Gradually I returned to the real world.

Our last day of school was routine. The Army didn't believe in ceremonies, parchment certificates, or faculty oratory. On the James Law bulletin board our names appeared on an alphabetical list, preceeded by "second lieutenant." That was our graduation.

Bill, astride a photographer's pony, winning a bet for my Dad

CORNELL UNIVERSITY
ITHACA, NEW YORK

REGISTRAR AND
DIRECTOR OF ADMISSIONS
EUGENE F. BRADFORD

July 24, 1939

Mr. Theodore Zimmerman
209 W. 97th St.
New York City, N.Y.

My dear Mr. Zimmerman:

I am glad to inform you that the Committee on Admissions
to the College of Veterinary Medicine has approved your application for entrance to that College in September 1939 by transfer from the College of Agriculture.

Very truly yours,

Arthur Gordon Danks, DVM, PHD, Instructor in Surgery

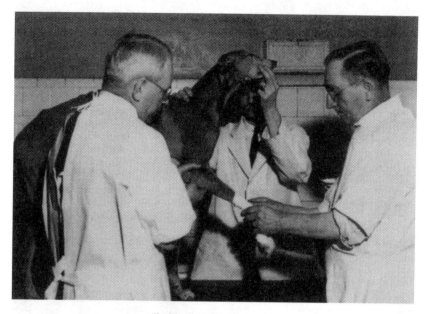

(left): Dr. Stephenson

(right): Howard Jay Milks DVM, Professor of Therapeutics and Director of the Small Animal Clinic

Malcom Eungene Miller, DVM, BS, in AGR, MS, Instructor in Anatomy

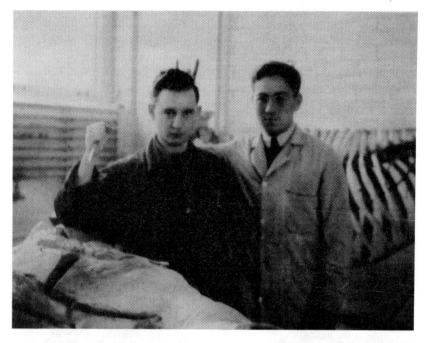

(left): Jerry (Peronius Tertius) Bandes

(right): The Author, Ted (Gastrocnemius) Zimmerman,
Anatomy Class 1940

IV

Drs. Thompson And Corwin

As the termination of studying veterinary medicine approached, the class of '43 was obsessed with the customary, dual agonies of state board exams and finding employment. The Second World War caused the first accelerated class in the school's history, creating a unique predicament. The army was already our employer but they insisted that we become more efficient employees. We were allowed six months to follow up our studies with jobs in the private sector, to determine our specialties and sharpen our medical skills. Passing the boards was first and foremost. Should we fail, our title of second lieutenant or doctor, would be reduced to "private," or "Mr."

By the time I had completed cramming for the State Boards, I knew so many facts and so many cures, that I was sure any doctor looking for an assistant would be happy and lucky to get me as his aide. The problem was that all that knowledge didn't show on my face and I didn't have a resumé describing my brilliance. So having passed the boards, when I arrived in Honeoye Falls, in upstate New York, and met Dr. Thompson, my new employer, he had no idea how lucky he was. He was a large animal practitioner and I was captivated by the opportunity to use my knowledge on his patients: cows, horses, swine and sheep. My penchant for exotic medicine would have to wait. First things first. I would take what fate meted out and learn all I could.

I arrived in the middle of a snow storm. The temperature was twenty degrees and a hard driving wind made it feel like twenty below. The train to Honeoye Falls had plowed through the heavy, blowing snow and I stared out the window daydreaming about the future. The day was gray, bleak and depressing but anticipation kept my emotions high. After all, I was expert in domestic animal diseases and elated that the Army was allowing a short respite for practical experience.

I'd always loved train rides. Being met by family or friends at the end of a long, clattering, swaying ride was romantic and spine-tingling. Many of my trips to Cornell were by railroad and the final station stop was always exhilarating. Dr. Thompson was to meet me at the station, and that would be the start of my new adventure. There was no way we would know each other except that I was the only passenger to get off and he was the only one waiting.

Dr. Thompson was a tall, bespectacled, taciturn man, who spoke exactly like Dwight Van Nest of Ludlowville. Long one syllable words and three word sentences.

He shook my previously gloved hand with a heavily mittened one and a disarmingly flaccid grip, and uttered one of the longest remarks I was to hear for the next few months. "Howdy. Nasty day. Glad you're here. Dinner's at 6."

He bundled me into his car, my bags sitting on the back seat, and bumped me to his home in the suburbs. He said nary a word as I waited for him to ask me all sorts of intriguing questions about my experience, my aptitude and my attitude. Not 'till we pulled into the driveway of a huge Colonial type, three story structure, did he venture to say anything. He answered my "Nice home," with, "Been here twenty years."

The house was tucked between snow covered trees dwarfed by hills on three sides. Must have a large family, I thought, counting the ten or more windows, all with shades drawn staring at us from the front of the austere mansion.

He showed me to my tiny little room, hiding in a corner wing of the second floor of the old house. He carried my small bag and I lugged the heavy suitcase. Tramping up the stairs behind him, I stared at the dark, old portraits and bleak landscapes that hung on the walls. I listened for sounds of the family. Not a murmur. It was eerie. My room was poorly lit, and contained a bed, a chair, a small table with a radio and an alarm clock. The house was heated to 68 degrees during the day, and, as I soon discovered, turned down at night.

Thompson sat on the bed as I opened my bags and filled the closet. The doctor asked me if I had leather boots. "The ground's frozen hard," he said, "With a thaw, there'll be lots of mud. And manure never freezes."

The veterinary college never mentioned mud, and even working the ambulatory clinic there wasn't any need for heavy boots. I really wasn't too well prepared for what lay ahead, but that was the excitement and challenge of the veterinary profession.

The first night I wore two pairs of sweat socks and a T-shirt under flannel pajamas to keep warm. As I lay uncomfortable and wondering, sleep finally took over just in time for the alarm that jangled at 6 AM. We ate breakfast at 6:30, dressed in an overcoat, warming my hands around a jug of coffee.

Dr. Thompson was a widower and a Mrs. Woosen, his housekeeper, served us. She was short, heavy, hair tied in a bun, her face wrinkled and tired. We ate in silence that first morning. No radio played and no one talked. I made up my mind to ask for a couple of more blankets. I joined in a repast of home canned beef, potatoes, vegetables, eggs and apple pie for dessert.

We then drove to Honeoye Falls to purchase boots. Everyone knew Dr. Thompson. The store was open at 7:30 AM. "Mornin, Doc. New assistant?" and to me, "Glad to see you. Better stomp the snow off your shoes." then, "What size?" They were all friendly and curious. I got my new boots and we were on our first farm by 8:00. We visited two or three more before noon, grabbed a quick lunch in a small town restaurant, and finished about 5 o'clock in the evening.

Dr. Thompson's practice was strictly large animals. There wasn't even a dog to pet and talk to. Most of our time was spent with cattle. We TB tested herd after herd, vaccinated heifers, the milk producers of the future, and steers that he had castrated the previous spring. We went to farm after farm that had filthy fenced enclosures, where there was an abundance of unfrozen fresh manure, trampled and splashed by nervous suspicious cattle constantly adding to the bad scene. As a rule, the farmers never thought it necessary to help. It dawned on me why Dr. Thompson needed an assistant. I had to rope the animals and restrain them so the veterinary surgeon could give the shots. Rarely did I get the chance to be doctor. I was pushed, stepped on and shat on by anxious, unruly animals. Most of the time I felt like a cheap cow hand. How could I put all my knowledge to work in a situation like this? It was humiliating and frustrating and my compensation was but $15.00 a week. My salary was sweetened by free room and board, a questionary stipend for six years of college and a degree in Veterinary Medicine.

Unhappy and lonely with no one to converse with and only my room radio to listen to, I prayed that the Army would call me to active duty a couple of months early. I suffered in silence. Dr. Thompson was reluctant to use his voice. If a pointed finger or a hand sufficed, that's what he used. Mrs. Woosen could talk and would occasionally ask if I wanted more coffee or vittles. Or was there laundry she could wash for me?

I decided to write to a small animal practitioner that I'd heard about from my classmates, who favored former Cornell athletes. It was a hopeful dream to get out of Honeoye Falls. His name was Dr. Louis A. Corwin, from Jamaica, N.Y. He was a Cornell graduate that hired one or two students every year. Being an athlete himself, he would hire Cornell graduates, if possible, who were "Wearers of the C." I mentioned in my letter that I had a few months before army induction and asked if he were interested in hiring me. I explained that I was working on large animals for a month or so to get some experience. So I waited, ready and anxious, for Dr. Corwin's reply.

On a particularly nasty day, with gray skies, high winds and temperature in the mid-teens, Dr. Thompson interrupted his usual routine by telling me about a call from a farmer with a sick horse. He put off the usual TB testing and we made the "house call."

The barn sat high on a bleak, windswept hill about a half hour drive away. The farmer was a small, slight man about seventy years old, dressed in a huge overcoat, high boots and Eskimo gloves. As we trudged up the hill Dr. Thompson listened to the medical problem.

"She's my best brood mare and overdue. Not ovulating, I guess." We entered the barn, cold but protected from the wind. The farmer was correct, his mare was having trouble ovulating. Dr. Thompson took off his coat in that sub-zero barn and pulled on the rubber sleeve he used to perform rectal examinations. The farmer held the horse's head steady and I held the tail high. Dr. Thompson lubricated the glove and gently inserted his hand into the mare's rectum. He worked his hand and arm slowly until his entire arm disappeared up to his shoulder. He told us that he felt a huge ovarian cyst and told me to put my sleeve on so I could identify the mass also. "It's on the left. Feel it before I rupture it."

I remembered reading about that procedure in Dr. Frost's course. It amazed me that it was possible to grasp and rupture an ovarian cyst, (the approved treatment for that condition), through the colon, with frozen fingers encased in a rubber glove.

Reluctantly my overcoat came off, my heavy sweater with its long comforting sleeves were rolled up. I was numb. My fingers were so cold, I couldn't feel the rubber I was supposed to powder and lubricate. Finally, the sleeve slipped over my shoulder. I greased my hand and inserted it, followed by my entire arm, into the mare. A welcome sensation of warmth and comfort flooded my limb. For the first time in weeks my entire arm felt good. I pushed as far as I could so as much of me as possible would benefit from her body heat.

Dr. Thompson was instructing me in how to feel for the ovary but I wasn't interested. I just wanted to stay there and keep warm. Finally, the powerful pressure of her rectal muscle cut my circulation and my arm began to fall asleep. Reluctantly I withdrew.

My memory recalls, to this day, about Dr. Thompson and the only way I could find to keep warm in Honeoye Falls: up a horse's ass.

The letter from Dr. Corwin arrived with the affirmation of a job. Hiding my glee, I told Dr. Thompson and Mrs. Woosen that I was called by Uncle Sam and was off to the war. Traveling to Jamaica, New York, where Dr. Corwin lived and practiced, was one of the happiest journeys of my life. I sang all the way, while the train rumbled and the heaters warmed me from head to toe.

At Dr. Corwin's, my salary jumped to $55.00 a week. I slept in a warm bed in a little room off the hospital area and ate meals with the family. Dr. Corwin was a short stout man with grey hair, pudgy hands and an infectious smile. As a varsity baseball player at Cornell he was known as "Shorty" Corwin. His Mrs. was a doll, the same size as the doctor and always solicitous about my comfort and happiness. The two Corwin boys, future veterinarians, had been told that I had played varsity, lightweight football. They insisted on playing touch football with their friends and me every afternoon. I taught them how to pass, block and run. Dr. Corwin encouraged his young teenagers to play and allowed me as much time off as necessary to keep them happy. Now, I thought, this was how to practice veterinary medicine!

I learned more about the practical medicine of small animals in three months than I did in my entire senior year. I assisted in at least two operations a day, and marveled at the skill and dexterity of the pudgy fingers of my employer. The doctor's second car was at my disposal and I went on house calls all over that section of Long Island; I became more confident every day. I worked hard and was on call twenty four hours daily for six out of seven days and I loved every minute of it. I was a half hour subway ride from home and I visited every week. On April 2, 1943, I was notified that I had been appointed First Lieutenant in the Army of the United States. Orders arrived for me to report to the Brooklyn Port of Embarkation, April 19. Finally, I was going to war.

Dr. Corwin said I should have one week off at home to prepare myself for overseas duty. He liked me and my work and told me there would be a job waiting for me when I returned.

The night before my induction, Mom, Dad, Little Joe and Elise prepared a surprise going away party for me. Norman was away at school and I spoke to him on the telephone. Elise cooked my favorite meal. Thick vegetable soup, leg of lamb with spaghetti and home made apple pie a-la-mode. Mom and Dad each made a little speech. We drank toasts and my baby brother wished me luck.

The next day, with bags packed, hugs and kisses for Mom and Elise and hand shakes with my Dad and Joe, I was off. The Port of Embarkation meant overseas duty and I was anxious and ready. Norman and Joe were envious. I knew Norm would be called soon enough. He was nineteen and ripe for the draft. Joe was the baby and at fourteen was safe.

The subway ride to Brooklyn took about a half hour and I checked into the Port of Embarkation. I was directed to the Adjutant's office who signed me in, told me where to get fitted, and gave me directions to the Post doctor for shots. I was carrying two heavy suitcases with everything I thought I'd need for the war. As I bent over to pick them up he laughed.

"Lieutenant, we don't have quarters for you here. After you get your uniform fitted and the doctor checks you out, you can go home. You will be part of a Veterinary Corps' pool, awaiting orders. Just report every morning at 9:00 AM. There is basic training every new officer must go through, how to use a gas mask etc. You will be notified. If your orders haven't arrived you will be free for the day."

The look on my face made him laugh again.

"I said my goodbyes already." I explained. "How can I go back home the same night?"

I found the Medical Department and got some shots. I received typhus, small pox, typhoid and tetanus vaccine. Now I was ready to go overseas. Next was my fitting for an officer's uniform. They gave me a summer outfit I could wear immediately. The dress uniform might take the tailors a week.

Almost immediately I began to feel queasy. The doctor mentioned that most of the men had a reaction to the typhus shot. I struggled back to the subway with my bags and I began to shake. The shivering caused my arm muscles to get so tired, I had to put the valises down and rest every few seconds. My problem was an anaphylactic reaction. I had to get a seat, but in New York nobody cared or knew what I was going through. The bags had to be moved frequently as the subway crowds ebbed and flowed. Finally the Ninety First Street station of the IRT appeared. God, I thought, how will I ever get home? I struggled from Broadway to West End Avenue, resting every few steps. Now, two short blocks more to Ninety Third Street. They seemed like two hundred miles.

It was an eternity before Elise answered my ring. She took one look at me and knew something was dreadfully wrong.

"Lord, you look awful. You wounded already? I'm going to call your folks. They are at Mrs. Stein's at the seder."

"No. Please don't bother them. Just let me get to bed. I had a reaction to some shots."

The bags were left at the door and I dropped like a pile of lead. I was chilled and nauseous. I stayed in bed for three days, unable to eat or walk. My arm was sore and swollen.

My folks had tried to phone the Port to explain my absence but no one knew what they were talking about. On the fourth day I donned my summer uniform for the first time and back I went to the subway for the trip to Brooklyn. As I went to report, numerous GI's passed. To my surprise they saluted me; I returned the salute awkwardly. When I arrived no one seemed to know or care that I had been AWOL for three days.

The adjutant grinned when I told him what happened. "No harm done. No orders yet. Report again tomorrow. Oh, by the way, the Veterinary Pool is meeting tomorrow at 1800 hours for instructions, and don't forget to pick up your dress uniform."

Then he told me about the tradition of the first salute. "The first enlisted man to salute a new officer must be presented with a dollar."

I had already messed up that tradition so I just gave the dollar to the next GI that passed. I realized after throwing a dozen returns, why we got inoculations on the left arm.

I decided to take a room at the nearby YMCA. It was close enough to walk to the Port and I wouldn't have to ride the subway twice daily. The next day I met twenty of my classmates. It was fun to see them and talk about the months between graduation and army induction. We were handed questionnaires. One query was where we would prefer to serve. The married men (there were three) requested stateside service and the rest of us bachelors checked off the overseas duty.

When the orders finally arrived we had our first example of the "army way." All the married men and three singles were shipped overseas, the remainder were assigned stateside. It was June, 1943. My orders read, "Report to the Fourth Service Command, Fort Benning, Georgia."

V

Veterinary Corps, Army of The United States

Upon leaving the frenetic Brooklyn Port of Embarkation, I drove Jezebel, which I finally inherited, along the busy roads of New Jersey, Delaware, Maryland, past Washington, D.C. and on through Virginia. Then I took the leisurely drive along the picturesque, winding roads of the South, enjoying the vivid colors of wild flowers and the sight of newly greened trees.

Nearing Columbus, Georgia, my reverie was broken by the sight of hundreds of billowing parachutes swaying on the horizon. Getting closer, I saw the mother transport spitting out tiny dots that seconds later exploded into white careening flowers. It was the Parachute School we'd heard so much about, part of the multifaceted training machine that was Fort Benning, the military suburb of Columbus. At last I'll be face to face with the real war effort.

A half-hour later, as I drove through the city, four tall, metal structures in the distance were silhouetted against the sky-parachute training towers.

I drove to Fort Benning's security gate, manned by efficient, business-like M.P.s. I got a snappy salute from the man at the shack's open door. Another MP, clipboard in hand, circled the car. He jotted something on his pad, the license I figured.

He approached my window. "Can I see your orders, sir?"

I handed them to him and he made more notes. "Just a minute, sir!" He went into the security shack and picked up a phone.

He leaned backward to catch something the man on the phone said, then. "Please pull over to the parking area, sir." He motioned to a space inside the gate, out of the traffic lane.

Finally, after five minutes of whispering, phone calls and nodding in my direction, the M.P. handed back my orders. "You may proceed, sir. No one answered from the veterinary detachment office. We checked with the adjutant at the commanding general's office. Your master sergeant will give you a security pass if you are permanently assigned."

"Can you point me in the direction of the detachment?" I asked. "I'm sure that's where I have to report."

"Yes sir," he said, and he walked ahead pointing, "take the main road through the post, about two miles. You'll see a sign directing you to turn right."

"Thank you, private," I said as I turned away, got into Jezebel and headed down the main road in search of the veterinary detachment. The post was alive with GIs: colorful squads of jogging paratroopers in different stages of training everywhere on Benning's tracery of roadways. They were shouting their crisp, rhythmic cadence. Strolling infantrymen, off-duty, but fully armed were everywhere. Others marched in platoons, their order-barking sergeants nursing them along. Half-tracks and jeeps rattled in both directions. Military Police, on foot or patrolling in well-marked jeeps kept order and insured discipline.

The fort had expanded from a sleepy, peacetime outpost to a huge, World War II Training Center. The excitement generated by thousands of eager young men, preparing for war, showed on their faces. The Infantry School, Officer's Candidate School, Tank Warfare Training Corps, and Elite Paratroops were all quartered and trained here.

As I proceeded, signs appeared every hundred feet, providing information to every conceivable Army service and practice area. Headquarters to the right, Tank Training Area left, Post Hospital and OCS straight ahead, Infantry Training Center Headquarters five miles left, etc.

About two miles down the road, "Veterinary Clinics" appeared, an arrow indicating a right turn. My sensitive stomach felt butterflies. Then a hundred feet around the corner, was a large, two-story, red brick building. I pulled over and stopped behind a large, new Cadillac. A Brigadier General's star glared from the rear plate. I wondered what he was doing at the clinic.

My new headquarters had open windows on either side of a large, center door. Smaller, curtained windows surrounded the second story, probably the enlisted men's dormitory. Over the front door hung the "Vet Detachment" sign. Another, with "Lieutenant Colonel S.G. Kielsmeier" printed on a copper plaque, was just to the right. My new boss, I thought. Behind the building was a paddock, with several horses grazing quietly, enclosed by a wood fence.

I got out of the car, stretched my legs, put on my cap, straightened my tie, cleaned the toes of my shoes on the back of each calf, took a deep breath and started for the building.

The reception area was deserted, but dogs were yapping, a child whimpering and a woman talking in a room beyond the doorway to my left, topped by a carved plaque reading, "Clinic." On the opposite side of the waiting area was a closed door, protected by an enormous desk. It was piled with papers, files, a huge calendar and a beer mug crammed with pencils and pens. A brass desk marker labeled "M/Sgt James Vance," sat in front of the desk. At the main entrance was another desk; neat, tidy and feminine. Probably the receptionist's. A small name plate, "Beulah Mae Carlucci," proclaimed its owner.

What do I do now?

"Can I help you, sir?" a deep voice drawled behind me. Startled, I turned to see a paunchy, bespectacled G.I. in Army khaki, a soiled towel over one forearm, and a pair of surgical scissors in the other hand. Both sleeves were rolled half way to the elbow. Master Sergeant's stripes adorned his sleeve. He stood at the clinic door, his brow wet with perspiration.

"I'm reporting for duty, Sergeant. Am I in the right place? My orders say, 'Veterinary Detachment.'"

"You must be Lieutenant Zimmerman," he said with a half-smile. "I'm Sergeant Vance. The colonel was expecting you yesterday. I'm glad you're here, we've got an accident case and no officer."

I could see why the MP's at the gate didn't get an answer, "I understood there were over twenty officers assigned here," I said.

"There are," he replied, "but they're all meat and dairy inspectors and they're off on Sunday. Defibrio and I were trying to make do. Would you take a look at this puppy?"

"What's his trouble Sergeant?" I asked, my concern and fatigue forgotten at the thought of a clinical case. "Who's Defibrio?"

"Dom is in charge of the small animal clinic and the Officer's Club Farm," he said as he stepped back. "I'm administration, trying to help."

"Where is the colonel, Sergeant?" I asked without moving, "Shouldn't I report to him first."

"That's the usual procedure, Lieutenant, I think he'd rather you handle this first. I was about to call him to take a look." He paused, "He's a little squeamish about handling dogs and cats. It's been a lot of years since school. His expertise is horses. This pup was just hit by a car and is in pretty bad shape. It belongs to one of the infantry generals, and the commanding officer here. He is a golfing partner of the colonel's. His wife and daughter are here and worried to death."

"Okay, Sergeant, I'll see what I can do," I worried that my month of interning at Doctor Corwin's might not have prepared me for what lay ahead.

Vance held the door, and I entered the clinic. The pervasive odor of small animals and disinfectants, familiar to me for most of my life from pet shop to Veterinary Hospital Clinics, hit my nostrils. The puppy was lying on a towel, on a stainless steel examining table, in the center of a large, square-tiled room. A staff sergeant was busy cutting strips of adhesive tape and sticking them to the side of the table. I figured he must be Defibrio. He was about fifty years old, tall and slender, with graying hair and a kindly, worried face. On the other side of the table stood the ladies. The mother was an attractive blonde, and very agitated. She must have been giving Defibrio a hard time. The daughter was about seven years-old, and rubbing her tear-filled eyes. Heads turned as I entered. When Defibrio saw I was a veterinary officer, his face softened.

Vance said, "Hornsby's replacement, Dom, Lieutenant Zimmerman. Lieutenant meet Sergeant Defibrio."

"Hello, Sergeant."

"My pleasure, sir."

"And this is Mrs. Wilson and her daughter Kathy. Their puppy was hurt this morning. We're sure glad you're here."

"Yes," sobbed little Kathy. "Please don't let him die!" She reached out and grasped one of the legs of her unconscious puppy.

"Don't honey." Her mother pulled the child to her. She buried her head in her mothers arms and cried desperately. "The doctor will help him."

Putting the emotion aside I turned my attention to the first small animal patient I'd seen in over a month, since Dr. Corwin's.

A black and white, fox terrier puppy, about five months old, rocked rhythmically, with extremely labored breathing. There was no sign of blood, but his little backside was soiled and stained.

"Mrs. Wilson," I asked, trying to sound as professional as possible, "was the puppy actually run over, or just struck by the car?"

"I really don't know, Doctor. Kathy just ran in screaming that Terry was hit by a car. The driver didn't even stop. Maybe he didn't know he hit him; he's so tiny. Please do something for him!"

Kathy, her face stained with tears turned to face the table.

While her mother talked, I examined the puppy. He was in shock, eyes pale, skin cold and clammy. I felt for fractures, nothing. As I turned him over, a huge, tense, uneven lump stuck out grotesquely from his abdomen. I could palpate intestines just under the skin. With more probing, I felt the edges of a muscle tear. A hernia caused by the impact. Luckily the skin was unbroken. Gas must be building up in the displaced bowel, I thought, causing poor circulation, severe pressure and shock.

I volunteered my diagnosis in language properly medical that I hoped would impress, and still be understood by, this very nervous lady.

"It's a traumatic hernia." I said aloud. Probably strangulated, I thought to myself.

"The blow split the abdominal muscle. There may be internal bleeding or a ruptured bowel. We'll have to operate immediately. I can't feel any fractures, and if there are no crushed organs he may have a chance."

Was that me talking? I was proud of myself, and a little nervous. Our course in jurisprudence taught that we instill confidence but always leave enough doubt to cover one's self.

"I think you and Kathy should leave now, Mrs. Miller. We'll call as soon as we're finished. If all goes well, Terry will have to stay for at least a week."

Kathy had stopped crying and wiped the tears with the back of each hand.

"Thank you, Lieutenant, I know you'll do your best. My husband is the commanding general. He knows Colonel Kielsmeier. As you can see, we're all very attached to the puppy." She looked me in the eye as she took Kathy's hand, "Nice meeting you."

This isn't a private's puppy, she was telling me. Better be on the ball!

"Come on, honey," she said as she walked to the door. "Terry is in good hands. We'll pick him up in a few days."

Kathy turned at the door and made a small wave of her hand to her dog.

I'm not officially on duty and I'm stuck with major surgery, I thought—for a general, no less. I didn't want that child's heart broken if I could help it. I remembered how I felt when "My Kitty" died and Bill was put to sleep.

"Sergeant, do you have instruments and a sterilizer? I'll need gloves, a mask, a gown, ether and a small cone for anesthesia. Also saline and I.V. apparatus. We can X-ray the puppy after the surgery."

"We have everything, Lieutenant, except X-ray. We have to use the medic's machine over at the hospital. Pick out what you'll need and I'll have them sterilized in a half-hour."

Defibrio showed me to a complete-looking instrument cabinet.

"I'll need retractors, sergeant. I don't see any here."

"Most of our surgery has been spays and castrations. We can get anything you might need in the future. I'm sure we can borrow retractors from the Post Hospital."

"We don't have time for that, Sergeant. If we are going to save this pup, we have to go in now! I'll improvise for retractors."

In a few minutes the sterilizer, fully packed, was steaming away. Vance had gone back to his desk, and I was busy shaving the puppy and applying antiseptic. Nervously, I planned the surgical approach. I would have to go in just lateral to the puppy's penis, which necessitated catheterization during both surgery and recovery. Why wasn't it a female, I fretted, that would have been too easy. The male's penis lay just behind the umbilicus, right over the hernia, where I planned the skin incision.

What I faced was never demonstrated in school. It would have been a comforting feeling, should something go wrong, to have Professor Stephenson look over my shoulder.

I'm a big boy now, I thought, the sooner I do it myself, the better.

"Sergeant, have you ever given ether?" I'd be able to supervise the anesthetic if I had to.

"Yes sir, many times. We have quite an active, small animal clinic here, and I've been assisting with spays for years."

I thanked God for Professor Fincher and his ambulatory clinic! These guys will never know it's my first solo operation.

The I.V. was started and the puppy was wrapped in warm towels under the surgical shroud. I thought I put on a pretty good act, scrubbing up like a pro, donning the gown and snapping on rubber gloves while waiting for Terry to go under.

Defibrio was good. He was confident and careful--important when anesthesizing an injured animal. He monitored the vital signs, and nodded when the patient was deep enough. There was something about this soldier I liked. I felt comfortable working with him and he seemed to like me.

I catheterized the puppy, and clamped the penis off to one side. A long incision was made over the herniated bowel, and accumulated blood spilled out over the shrouds. Sponging revealed a bleeding artery at the edge of the muscle.

"We'll get that spurter first," I said, half to myself, clamping and tieing the artery. I sponged again and surveyed the damage. There was a rent in the ventral abdominal muscle. The edges were frayed. That would make it difficult to suture. Another small tear to the side had a loop of strangulated bowel protruding. I eased the gut back and, as it slipped into the abdominal cavity, more popped out at the larger opening. It would be impossible to hold them in place with one hand and suture with the other. I really needed help.

"I can't manage it alone, Sergeant. You'll have to get me another pair of hands. We have to repair the small tear first, then do the larger. The muscle has to be raised, this way," I demonstrated, holding one finger of each hand like retractors, lifting the muscle so the suturing wouldn't injure the underlying bowel.

At that moment, Vance stuck his head through the door having heard the exchange. "I'll run upstairs and see if I can get one of the men," he said.

I continued probing. The internal organs were normal, and there were no more bleeders. In a few minutes, I heard the sound of scrubbing and gloving behind me. Soon a gowned and masked figure appeared across the operating table. I looked up into a pair of steel-blue eyes, glowering between face mask and cap. I guessed Vance had gotten a volunteer with a little experience, as he held his hands in a professional manner.

"Have you assisted before?" I asked, knowing the answer.

"A long time ago."

"Well, don't be nervous. Just do as I say, and you'll be back in your dorm in no time." I proceeded to demonstrate what to do.

"The pup is pretty small so just use a finger from each hand and gently lift the muscle so it is clear of the bowels." I demonstrated. "Your fingers are taking the place of muscle retractors, and I'll be able to sew more easily."

Defibrio was grinning as he watched the lesson.

I thought to myself: he knows I'm a beginner, giving instructions like a college professor.

I closed the small muscle tear first. The large rip required forty-five minutes to sew; only mattress sutures would hold the frayed edges. I stopped for a moment to admire my work—nothing like coming from milliners, and I thought of my Aunt Rose.

I was relaxed and in command. There's always small talk when a good surgeon is working. "You have a very nice surgery, Sergeant. A little chintzy on the equipment. Buy a couple of retractors so we don't have to inconvenience the enlisted men."

Defibrio cleared his throat, "Uh. . .um. . .the officer of the clinic buys all the equipment, sir. The money comes from the Kennel Fund."

"Well, we'll have to tell the powers that be not to be so stingy." I whispered as I completed the muscle work and stepped back to rest my arms.

I complimented my assistant, "Good work. The skin closure will be easy, so you can leave if you like. Thanks very much."

"Thank you, sir," he replied and slipped away, leaving me to close. Half-way through I looked at Defibrio, he looked uncomfortable and I guessed he was getting tired. "Sergeant, ease up on the ether. We're almost through. He's been under long enough."

"Right, Lieutenant," he said, taking a deep breath, while removing the cone.

After the last knot was tied, we undid the restraints and proceeded with the bandaging. I applied a layer of cotton, completely covering his abdomen. At school the surgeon always stepped aside and permitted the assistant to apply the bandage. I wondered if I should do the same here. I didn't want to hurt any feelings but this bandaging wasn't routine.

"The bandage is covering his penis," Defibrio said. "The little guy has to go occasionally."

He *was* upset I thought, I'd better explain. "We'll leave the catheter in. Bandage right over it with the end of the catheter dripping up here, near his chest." I pointed to the spot.

"Ingenious!" he said.

I had to give Doctor Corwin the credit—only two months before, I watched him do a monorchid the same way, as the removal of a retained testicle required the same surgical approach as a spay.

I decided to keep quiet and take the acclaim. After all, I reasoned, this success might help bridge the unforeseen predicaments of tomorrow, since I was a greenhorn in both the army and the practice of medicine.

Defibrio expertly manipulated the tiny puppy from hand to hand, keeping the I.V. tubing from entanglement as I wound the gauze around the cotton, leaving the catheter facing forward between his forelegs. We finished with the strips the sergeant had prepared earlier.

"We'll leave this on at least five days." I said as I pressed the tape on all sides insuring a snug adhesion.

Defibrio set the precious, sleeping, wrapped pup on the operating table and we waited. This was the time of apprehension, especially for a young surgeon. The dread that maybe something could still go wrong. Maybe the anesthetic, the respiratory system or the circulation. Perhaps a rare allergy that filled medical journals with sensational articles.

Then Terry began to stir and we breathed again. The first movement was the tip of his tail, wagging as if in appreciation. Then he raised a very wobbly head as he tried to focus. He rolled all of his five pounds to his sternum, steadied himself with his forepaws and gave us a proper look in the eye. I knew puppies and I was sure he wondered where his mistress was. He must have adored and followed Kathy everywhere. That might have been what did him in; chasing her in thoughtless, playful circles unmindful of speeding automobiles.

"I'm sure he'll make it," I said confidently. "Post-surgical shock is our next hurdle. Let's keep the I.V. dripping at one per second."

"Right, Lieutenant."

We stood back, and this time I sighed deeply, my first test completed and hopefully, passed. We had done our best.

"Thank you, Sergeant." I snapped off the gloves, untied the mask and removed my cap and gown. I rolled them up and tossed them into the laundry hamper, simple moves I'd seen Stephenson do a hundred times. He would put all three garments into a ball and toss them like a basketball into the open wicker as he left the lab. I had

seen seniors mimic the professor in college, and I relished the envy
of *my* under-classmates. Now, in the real world, the simple finale
lifted me, at least in my mind, to the status of a Stephenson.

"You're welcome, Lieutenant." Defibrio answered. "That was a
dandy bit of surgery!"

"Thanks! Let's wash up, I haven't reported in yet."

"Take your time, Lieutenant," he said, as he lifted Terry from
the table, hugged him to him with one arm as the other wheeled
the attached IV apparatus toward the recovery ward.

"You've earned a little rest." He said to me. "How about a drink?"

Defibrio told me how worried he was a couple of hours earlier
when he feared for the life of the pup. He forced himself to cut
adhesive tape strips to hide his concern as he tried to reassure the
anxious client and her daughter. Now he felt relaxed and smiled
as he leaned against the swinging door, opening it as he looked
back. I knew I was going to like this soldier. He was considerate
without fawning. The army wasn't supposed to be so pleasant.

"I don't drink much" I said gratefully, "and I wouldn't dare before
meeting the colonel."

I walked into the reception room with a glow. Vance was busy
at his desk. I liked him also. Any master sergeant that would roll
up his sleeves and pitch in as he did, was all right with me. Besides
he had a little twinkle in his eye that made him special. He looked
up and smiled. "Good job, Lieutenant. The colonel is waiting to
see you." He ushered me into the sanctum.

It was finished in natural wood with a plain rug covering most
of the floor. There were two windows, one behind his desk and
the other on the adjacent wall facing the paddock and ball field. I
noticed a golf club leaning on the wall near the window. I marched
up, trying to be especially military, snapped to attention and saluted.
"Lieutenant Zimmerman reporting for duty, sir."

His head was behind a newspaper that slowly lowered 'till his
eyes appeared. Casually the colonel touched his forefinger to his
eyebrow and dropped the paper. "At ease, Lieutenant," he said,
smiling. "Have a seat."

His face framed against the bright window light was just an outline
and his features were indistinct. I relaxed, glanced around his plush
office and sat on a comfortable easy-chair facing him. I stared. His
face came into focus and it seemed to have a perpetual grin. He
had a huge scar that ran down his left cheek to the corner of his

mouth, leaving him with an omnipresent leer. Defibrio told me later that in vet school he was kicked in the face by an intractable horse that tore his face. He required over a hundred stitches. The side of his mouth was twisted and his lower eyelid sagged. It reminded me of the occasional droopy lids of Springer Spaniels and Saint Bernards. I wondered how he shaved and why he never had cosmetic surgery.

He was speaking. "Nice bit of surgery this morning."

I'd heard that voice somewhere, and something about him was familiar. Those eyes! My God, I thought. He was the assistant! My face turned beet red and perspiration formed on my upper lip. "I'm sorry, sir," I sputtered. Had I called him chintzy?

He slapped his thigh and roared. Finally controlling himself, he said, "Relax, lieutenant, no way for you to know. Tell me about yourself. Where did you go to school?"

"Cornell, sir."

"Fine school." He proceeded to ask about my veterinary speciality. When he heard "exotic animals and birds," he looked at me with surprise and asked. "How much experience have you had?"

"Not much yet," I told him, "most came from the pet shop when I was young and my aspirations were to work in a zoo some day."

"You're the first officer I've met with that in mind." He said. "What about hobbies, are you interested in sports?"

I had to admit that I was a jack of all trades and expert in only one, football, and that game I'd never play again. I noticed a pen and pencil holder in the shape of a golf bag sitting on the desk. Two golf balls sat in an ash tray near the miniature bag. I wasn't interested in golf and wondered if he was looking for a companion.

He never mentioned anything about himself, just let me talk, prompting me from time to time with questions. After a while, he sat back, hands locked behind his head. "I am appointing you property officer, custodian of the kennel fund, company commander and clinician. Your duties will include running the small animal clinic and helping me with the large animals. I do the horses and you the cows, sheep, pigs and mules from the farm. And Lieutenant," he smirked, "let's not be too scrimpy about ordering needed instruments for our surgery."

Why couldn't I keep my mouth shut.

The colonel was still speaking. "Sergeant Defibrio can show you all you need to know about the animals. As company commander, you pay the men, run classes for them and are responsible for their welfare. Sergeant Vance will help you there. Any questions?"

I had several, but all I could sputter was, "I don't have any quarters yet, sir."

He hit the intercom. "Sergeant, the lieutenant needs help finding quarters. Call the BOQ." Then to me. "Stop by the sergeant's desk. He'll take care of your billoting." He paused, "You can go now, Lieutenant." The colonel was smiling. "I think we're going to get along just fine." Then, as he thought about it, his eyes narrowed and he barked, "But you're gonna do the gettin' along!"

I signed myself into the bachelor officer's quarters and unpacked Jezebel. My room was about the size of a college dorm's. It was clean and comfortable, with a nice view of a nearby forest. There was a bed and night-table, a bureau, a table, an easy chair, an adequate closet and a telephone. The plasterboard was unpainted but clean. The window had a plain curtain that was tied on each side with a ribbon in the middle and tacked to the wall. Someone had papered the closet shelves and the bureau drawers. I unpacked my two valises then carried in the dress uniform and civilian suit that swayed on a hanger all the way from Brooklyn. A cardboard box filled with all the loose junk that I couldn't part with was put on the closet floor. As I looked around the room I thought how great it would be if I had a dog. There was plenty of room for him to sleep and play and how I missed the adoring eyes and whipping tail to greet me. I thought about my childhood and growing up with Bill.

I reached into my box of memories and pulled out the horseshoe I had made in vet school. This would hang over my door for luck.

Suddenly I realized that I was famished. I followed Vance's directions to the Officer's Club and sat alone at the bar with other singles. The main dining room was buzzing with conversation, occasional laughs and other friendly sounds but I felt very alone. I gulped down a sandwich and a coke.

I drove back to the clinic that afternoon. Defibrio took me in hand. Each time I was with him I liked him a little more. He was fatherly, concerned about my feelings without patronizing. His eyes twinkled when he spoke of the colonel. He had more nerve than I did on that score. Nothing seemed to phase him.

Dom walked me through the building and we climbed the stairs to the enlisted men's area. He introduced me to the men as we proceeded from room to room. As he called out their names and they stood and shook hands, I realized that they were a microcosm of America. There was an Irishman, a Scot, a German, one sounded Czechoslovakian and of course, the usual Americans, like Miller, Jones and Smith. Some of them had dogs. Lounging about the room was a well behaved Setter and a black and white Spaniel.

"I see the men are permitted pets," I said to Defibrio. "I like that."

"Only the well-behaved can share the dorms. Some of the guys have snakes, a couple have pigeons and one has a tame duck. But they are not allowed in the common areas."

Most of the men were relaxing, reading, writing letters, playing cards or just talking with their buddies. I especially liked Corporal Stern from upstate New York. He was in charge of the hounds and kennels. He had a huge pot belly but no behind. A glistening bald pate but huge bushy eyebrows. A contagious grin and lively personality made him a favorite with the men who called him "Pot."

He was in the midst of a noisy poker game and took the time to get up and greet me. "I'm glad we have a small animal man in charge, sir. I've worked under a few who believed that horses were the most blessed creature on earth." I'm sure he was referring to the colonel. He then explained, "I volunteered to help with the surgery on that pup this morning but the colonel insisted on doing it himself. He said the best way to judge you would be if you didn't know who he was."

They loved the story of the morning's emergency and Kielsmeier's masquerade. Defibrio had narrated the mornings events with exaggerations permitted by his position. I was accepted with smiles as I shook friendly hands time and time again. Defibrio mentioned with a big grin that not many people talk down to the colonel, knowing or not, and get away with it. It felt good not to be resented for invading their weekend privacy. Only Calder, a wiry, mean looking corporal who worked under Defibrio at the farm, seemed a little put out by an officer parading through their quarters.

We walked to the rear of the building where I toured the large animal clinic. It had several stalls, a large animal operating table with enough floor space to treat three horses at once. I noticed how much cleaner it was, compared to the vet school surgery. Lots of free help, I thought. The paddock behind the building was for grazing, and the baseball diamond next to it, for the enlisted personnel's recreation.

Defibrio explained, "We occasionally get a softball game going in the late afternoon. One of our WACs loves to play, and drags the rest of us out. You'll meet her, Pat Murphy. She works in the large animal clinic and is quite an athlete."

I drove back to my quarters pleasantly exhausted and I suddenly got a feeling of deja vu.

I felt that I had been here before. Something somebody said, something about the room or the building, something about those names sparked a recollection. Then I realized: it was the mention of a pet duck that took me back to George Washington High School in 1936.

That year the George Washington High School football players were labeled "the scoreless wonders." My teammates were a typical, New York, ethnic mix. Al Suarez, Hispanic; Vinny Reitano and Phil Simonetti, Italians; Buddy Naidus, Rosy Rosengarten, "Oink" Kaufman and myself, Jews; "Moose" LaBosse, French; Johnny Smith and Tom Carrol, Irish; Dutch "Whitey" Froechtenicht, German; Bernie Jovans, Czech; and "Tex" Guilliland, Southern Baptist American. We were a damn good bunch of football players, better than the record showed. George Jolley, our coach, didn't think I was big enough to play, but I made the squad and thanked him for that. I could sit on the bench and thrill to the crowds, with the bass drums' vibration buzzing in my chest. The high-stepping cheerleaders exhorting the demoralized home crowd to cheer, no matter what. The stands were full for our opener, but interest diminished with each loss, and attendance plummeted.

Weighing but 147 pounds, my teammates knew I could make it. I was fast enough to evade lumbering 250 pounders, and able to block effectively by tangling up the legs of potential tacklers. During scrimmages, when I caught a punt, recovered a fumble or intercepted a pass, my broken-field dance carried me, triumphantly, for many a gain.

One September day, Coach Jolley was asked to cut everyone under 150 pounds. Pressured by the principal, the PTA and the Budget Committee, he had no choice. But Jolley respected every boy that came out for practice. If left to him, he would have a varsity squad and two hundred scrubs. And he understood the importance of being a coach. Many guys had busy fathers who couldn't give them quality time, so a coach was their father image.

Encouraging fearful youngsters to overcome the test of their peers, he knew the terror that turned young men into bullies—cowards who browbeat the small and weak.

Dave Monaghan, my first coach, gave me the knowledge that built confidence and erased fear. When I knew how to block, tackle, pass, punt and run, I was no longer afraid.

Boots Astor refined what Dave started. His Claremont Club put us to the acid test of tough competition. We proved to ourselves that we were better than average and smarter than most. Marty, Les, Al Suarez and I had played for Boots. When Marty and I tried out for high school football, we were ready! After two weeks, I was third-string halfback. Rosy made second varsity guard and, I knew, in time, we'd be playing together on the first teams.

Jolley found a different way to cut the squad. He called a special practice--the first team against the lightweights.

Rosy took me aside the day of the massacre. "Any guy that doesn't shine today will be cut," he warned.

The coach told the varsity not to hold back, "Hit 'em hard. Play like the city championship is on the line!"

Rosy parked himself alongside Jolley. He wanted him to notice me. I knew I was faster than most of the varsity, but I'd have to out-run all the little guys, too. God, how I yearned to stay on that bench.

The play was brutal. We scrubs had to use our heads to keep from being blown off the field. I made the first four out of seven tackles, desperately trying to excel.

Rosy was smart enough to make the coach think he knew me only casually, saying, "Coach, that kid is a great defensive player."

Al Suarez, chimed in, "And he's one of the best broken-field runners on the squad."

Rosy reminded Jolley that I could punt and pass if needed, and fleet enough to play safety. He was mighty convincing because that afternoon all the other lightweights were cut. What finally did it, I think, was a tackle I made on Conlin, our all-city center. Although he weighed about 200 pounds, he was a good broken-field runner. Conlin intercepted a pass and came charging up the field, right at me, faking one way and, when I didn't move, decided to barrel right through. I knew I could never get my arms around those churning, bony knees, so, as he came over me, I grabbed one leg, pulled it to my chest, and wrapped my legs around it as well. I shut my eyes and waited for the shock. Lucky for me and tough on Conlin, the impact was his head hitting the ground. He was momentarily stunned and, as time was called, I hopped up and thankfully jogged away.

In addition to being a fine leader, Jolley was a clever, football tactician. He couldn't fathom how we could outplay every opponent and not score. He worked hard teaching physical education all day, and then coached two hours after school. Nervousness and frustration made him sneak a swallow or two of booze before Saturday's games. He kept a pint in his hip pocket to "keep out the cold." Before the final whistle, he was so potted that Rosy was making substitutions from the field.

Jolley, in a quandary, had to break the cycle of losses. Someone suggested that the team get a mascot, something to stir the souls of the crowd, the band, the cheerleaders, and most of all the team. It broke his heart to look into the eyes of his defeated gladiators, week after week, when they knew in their own minds, they were good.

The Friday before the St. Francis game he called a field meeting. "Guys, I know, and you know, that we're a better team than our record shows. We need something, some kind of a mascot we can use to change our luck. Any suggestions?"

We looked at each other. Many of us had pet dogs and cats, but he wanted something more provocative.

Following a prolonged silence, Rosy piped up, "I've got a pet duck by the name of Joey. He can follow a leash and is even house-trained."

There was a loud hush. Who ever heard of a duck mascot? Rosy had gotten it from my dad's pet shop the previous Easter. He trained it as a house pet and had come to love the little bird. His folks never allowed him a dog or cat, but how could they deny him a little Easter duckling?

Rosy was the only parent Joey knew. He bonded early and followed him everywhere. It wasn't an easy decision to offer his pet to the team, and, for a minute, no one spoke.

The coach, hoping for a ram, a donkey, a tiger cub or even a pit bull, had to settle for the bird! Disgusted, he told Rosy to bring him along for the St. Francis game. "It will be different," he said. "The first duck mascot in the history of football. Put an orange and black collar on him, and bring his leash so he doesn't fly away."

On the Friday before the game, Rosy carried Joey to the practice field so all concerned could meet him. He had a long rope attached to his collar. He put him down in front of the bench before the scrimmage. Actually, Joey was really quite a beautiful duck. A white ring separated a bright green head and neck. His chest was chestnut and his back gray-brown. His white tail jumped back and forth with each pigeon-toed waddle. Joey was understandably nervous, and immediately ran between Rosy's legs and wouldn't move.

The team crowded around and someone said,"She's cute, what kind is she?"

"Joey is a Mallard drake (male duck). He is very special," Rosy said. "There aren't many ducks that will follow a leash, fly away and always return to their masters."

Rosy assigned one of the football team's assistant managers to hold him, while he left for practice. Joey started after Rosy with his typical pigeon-toed waddle, and had to be restrained. After a half-hour or so, he settled down and patiently awaited Rosy's return.

The next day, he was back for the St. Francis game. The game had a familiar pattern as we pushed the opponents all over the field, without scoring as much as a field goal. Like all the other teams, they got lucky, getting seven points early. A tipped pass fell into the hands of a defender, with no one between him and the goal. One of our weaknesses was not having a safety fast enough to catch potential scorers.

With two minutes left in the half, they scored again. As they were about to kick off, Jolley paced in front of the bench looking for a substitute. He wanted someone to fill in until halftime. For the first time, he stopped and looked me in the eye, "Zimmerman, go in and give Smitty a rest."

I was finally going to play and had two minutes to prove myself! I was so excited, I ran out on the field without my helmet. They called me back, and I remembered Joey. It was his first game, too. I ran over and patted his head, ran my hand down his smooth neck and prayed.

Joey, terrified by the noise and the attention, let out a muffled "Quack," and went winging straight up. His feathers were beautiful, with blue patches showing against the chestnut. He was limited to the length of the rope lead and made a crash landing behind the bench. I'm sure he meant to wish me luck.

As fate would have it, the kick-off came toward me. I went for the ball on the dead run and it hit me in the chest, bouncing straight down before I could grab it. Miraculously, the ball caromed right back into my arms. Without breaking stride, I ran it back with the exhilaration of a liberated prisoner. I picked up a block by Jovans and, sensing daylight, reversed the field, cutting down the sideline, hoping no one would touch me. Two more blocks and I was free. I felt a moment of invincibility as I crossed the fifty-yard line, to the growing roar of the stands. Only their safety remained a threat. He was fast and clever, and I couldn't wish him away or lose him. I saw him coming from the other side of the field. He dragged me down at the 20-yard line, two long seconds away from our first score. As I lay panting and exhausted, I thought, 'Joey is my lucky charm.'

We took a time out and, in the privacy of the huddle, discussed the play we hoped would score. The crowd thundered encouragement! Johnny Smith came back in with the play. He would take a pass from quarterback Phil Simonetti, after faking a line buck. I couldn't believe that Jolley let me stay in. Our entire line rose and erased the St. Francis defense, as Smitty caught the pass all alone in the end zone.

The crowd went wild, the cheerleaders did gymnastic maneuvers I never saw before. The drummers pounded and the band played our victory march over and over. One would think we were winning.

We missed the extra-point and lost to St. Francis that day, but we were finally on the scoreboard, and I had made the team! From that substitution on, I played every minute for the rest of the season. "Tex" Gilliland was injured, so I took over the kicking chore and played safety on defense. It was a fitting climax to my senior year.

Joey changed tradition! Our previous appeal for luck was the starters kissing the football before the kick-off. Now we stroked Joey's silky neck to insure good fortune. At first, strange hands frightened him, but he soon got used to the attention and gave each player a "Quack" as a send-off. All, that is, except "Oink" Kaufman. Oink was the team comedian. Throughout the season, win or lose, he kept us in stitches. When he petted Joey the first time, instead of the usual "quack," there was a "splat," as Joey fertilized the turf. Oink's hurt look broke-up even staid George Jolley.

The next week, we beat Roosevelt 12 to 7, our first victory in a stadium, now three-quarters full. It was a sight to see thirty-five football players fighting to carry a little Mallard around the field.

Our final, home game was against Evander Childs, the 1935 City Champs. We were two-touchdowns underdogs, and it turned out to be the most exciting game of my life. The tension was thick as we warmed up on opposite ends of the field. The stands were packed with students, faculty and press, all anxious to watch Evander execute the slaughter. We were loose, riding the momentum of one victory. They were tight, needing a win to repeat as champions.

The intimidation began early: "I hear you guys eat duck shit for breakfast; we're gonna pluck your feathers and bury them with that bird."

Our boys kept their mouths shut and practiced harder.

Evander went on, "why don't you send out your pussy cheerleaders to play?"

Suarez finally answered, "You fuckers are scared shitless we're gonna take away your championship. And you're right, we're gonna beat your asses with football, not words!"

The first half was a war. They were clearly stronger as they pushed closer and closer to our goal. With two minutes left, beaten and sore, we were backed up to our one-yard line. They had four chances to score.

Jolley called a time-out and we circled him to hear the last pep talk of the season: "You linemen, from tackle to tackle, submarine their line. Ends, be careful for reverses and naked quarterback sneaks. Linebackers, wait and look for holes developing in front of you. And Zimmerman, you're our last resort, move with the ball and hit the runner high. All they have to do is fall forward and they have a score. If the linemen can just stop them, the linebackers and safety's job is to put them on their backs. You can do it! You've done it a hundred times this year. This is our last chance. Do it for the crowd, do it for our school and do it for yourselves!"

He extended his arms, and eleven pairs of hands pyramided excitedly to show our loyalty, affection and hope.

The whistle blew, and an inspired eleven crouched for battle, too tired and intense for the expletives exchanged since the opening kick-off. The Evander team was quiet, as well, determined to capitalize and score. The first three plays were straight runs into the line-- that we stopped cold. Our line, obeying orders and playing their hearts out, submarined the offense while the linebackers knocked back three different carriers. As free safety, I ranged behind our crouching gladiators, slapping their fannies and yelling encouragement.

Evander took a lot of time in that last huddle, their final chance and time was running out. If I were quarterbacking, after three failed line-bucks, I'd try something different.

I ran from one end to the other, Carroll to Reitano, saying, "Watch for a naked reverse, let the line handle the bucks."

To the three linebackers, I said, "They may try a pass, be ready to back up and cover your zone."

My job would be to watch for anything and everything, and cover all eventualities. Thank God I guessed right. The quarterback appeared to hand-off to their huge fullback. The line submarined, but he leapt high over the tangled linemen, untouched, into the end zone—without the ball. After an interminable interval, the quarterback, with the football hidden against his thigh, turned and raced around our left side. I saw him move and followed laterally. Reitano, playing left end, wasn't fooled either. He met him head on, five yards behind scrimmage, and flattened him for the loss, as the gun sounded.

The angels sang and the orchestra played! We did it. We held the City Champs! The crowd cheered as we raced for the locker room.

The second half was an exact reverse. We pushed them all over the field and held their offense to twenty-five yards. We scored in the final quarter, made the extra point and held them off for the greatest upset of the year.

In the locker room ecstatic and proud, we poured the ritual champagne over Coach Jolley. We took showers fully dressed, and sang the Trojan victory march, as gleeful, school photographers flashed their bulbs. We were interviewed by Cherry Tree staff reporters, and congratulated by the principal and alumni reps. When the sports reporter asked Jolley why he had kept me on the bench for two years, he swore I could never master the playbook. He quipped it was Joey who caused the turn-around. Anyone could be a hero with him on the sidelines.

I made my varsity letter, and was nick-named "Tiny Ted," by the newspapers. I modestly thanked Joey for everything.

After a lonely dinner at the Officer's Club, I got myself back to my room and flopped into bed. The local radio station supplied quiet music as I shut my eyes and waited for the news. Less than a week ago I was at a port of embarkation ready to go to war. How lucky can one get? Safe in a fourth service command installation, practicing medicine on small animals and assigned to a large animal farm as well. I met people I liked and . . .a soft comfortable slumber embraced my tired body.

The alarm sounded at 7 A.M. and I wondered where I was, then, when my head cleared, I got excited about my first day of active duty. Suddenly a knock.

"Come!" I called pulling myself up on an elbow.

The door slid open slowly and a face appeared through the gap. I squinted my sleepy eyes and repeated my invitation. A short statured fellow wearing a military cap stepped into the room. I reached for my glasses, adjusted them on my nose and focused on a handsome young officer wearing captains bars and a veterinary caduceaus.

"Are you Ted Zimmerman?" he asked half apologetically, "Dom Defibrio gave me your room number. I'm just down the hall. My name is Hornsby, Bill. You're my replacement."

"Any friend of Dom's is a friend of mine." I said smiling. I liked Hornsby. He had a slight southern accent with the hint of a lisp, pleasant to my ear.

"I wanted to meet you before I left. In a few days, I'll be on my way to the Southwest Pacific with a load of mules." Bill, like many short men stood very straight, shoulders thrown back and head held as high as possible to increase his height.

I sat up and offered my hand. "Defibrio mentioned you had a run-in or something with the Colonel."

"Everyone has a run-in with Kielsmeier. I was appointed clincian when Doug Crane refused to give a sick horse a cold-water enema. Can you believe it? This mare had colic, it wasn't even severe. An occasional kick at her belly and a head-turn with each cramp. Crane was a small-animal man back home, he wasn't exactly sure how to handle it. He's a good man and careful. He was standing next to the horse with an open text book in his hand, reading up on the treatment when the colonel arrived. He gave the mare a quick look and said, 'Put your book away, Captain. Just give her an enema. She doesn't need a shot.'"

"Crane said, 'Yes, sir,' and began looking for the equipment. He came up with some small animal enema apparatus he found in his medical bag. It was the size used on an infant. You should have seen the look on the colonel's face.

"He waved him aside, took a regular garden hose, shoved it up the horse's backside, nodded to Murphy, the attendant, to turn on the water and ran in cold water. It's against everything we ever learned, but damn if it didn't work! Crane's specialty was small animals and Kielsmeier sent him back to food inspection and I took over. He got rid of me for another reason."

"I know. I'm sorry." I said apologetically.

"No sweat! The colonel is impossible to please and he got mad at me because of too much publicity when a couple of my men got hurt by Willy the mule. I was in charge and in the army you are responsible for your men. Now you're the boss and Willy's all yours."

"You mean I have to walk a tight rope too."

"Prepare yourself." he said, still seemingly irritated, "He'll give you pretty free rein with the small animals and the cows but he's the boss when it comes to horses." Hornsby pulled off his cap, dropped it on the table and sat. He continued talking about what happened. Finally he stopped and took a breath.

"I heard all about it from Dom." I said, and I swung my feet to the floor and decided to change the subject. "So you're going to get a chance to see the real war."

"I'm getting out of here if that's what you mean. I just want to get finished and go back to Memphis. Got a mixed practice there, hated to leave."

"You married?"

"To the best little ol' gal in the world." His eyes were far away. "Got two kids."

"You're lucky. You won't see much action taking care of mules. Before you know you'll be home."

"Sure hope so. Well . . .I'll let you get dressed. Just wanted to say hello. I'll be shipping out in a day or so . . .Say, how about joining me for breakfast?"

"Thanks Hornsby, I'd like that. I'll just be a minute." I would have hated eating alone again. I thought how nice of him to be so friendly, especially when I was his replacement.

We discussed the world over his hot coffee and my hot chocolate. I was lucky to chat with someone who could fill me in on Benning from an officer's point of view. I asked him about the office, Defibrio, Beulah Mae and my new job as company commander.

"Defibrio's great. Best man in the outfit. He'll help you through everything. Really knows his animals. Runs a great Officer's Club Farm. He's regular army like Vance and Kielsmeier, but you'd never know it."

"He sure helped me yesterday." I gave him a quick run down on what had happened.

He laughed. "Kielsmeier will do anything necessary to impress the brass. Most of the officers and men at Benning have pets, but the colonel doesn't treat dogs and cats. He tries to have a good small animal man do it. By the way, are you married?"

"No."

"Well, you mentioned Beulah Mae. She's the only civilian in the detachment. She's the receptionist. Built like a brick shithouse. Must be a great bang! I never could figure how she got the job. Spends most of the time filling her nails. Mean though. Wouldn't go near her with a ten foot pole. There's enough ass around the post without getting involved with her."

"Thanks." I thought. He was discouraging me before I even met the girl. I changed the subject again. "It must be tough going overseas and leaving your family." I told him about my classmates at the Port of Embarkation and how the Army screwed the married ones.

"Typical army. Well . . .I've got to get going. I'm glad I met you. If you get a tough small animal case, call Crane." He got up, grabbed the check before I could and stuck out his hand . . .we shook firmly and he started away.

"Thanks, Hornsby," I said, "and good luck."

"By the way," he stopped as if recalling something, "if you're interested, I know a great little gal that works here at the post. I think you'll like her better than Beulah Mae."

"I thought you said you had a wonderful wife?"

"I'm married," He said with a twinkle in hie eye, "not dead."

"Okay," I laughed, "what's her name?"

"Helen Modell, a cute little blonde. I'm sure she'll like you. Here's her phone. She works over at the Tank Training Center." He scribbled on a slip of paper.

We shook hands again, I thanked him, wished him luck, then headed for the office.

Beulah Mae was at her desk, legs crossed, busily filling her nails. She had a typical Italian face, broad, with high cheekbones framed by wavy brown hair. Her nose was bulbous and her partly open lips showed large white teeth.

She looked up as I approached, never missing a stroke. So far Hornsby is right, I thought. "I'm Zimmerman, I work here." I looked over and saw Vence, busy at his desk.

"Nice to meet you, Lieutenant."

"I met your desk yesterday." I told her lightly.

"Ah declare, you're quite a surgeon, and the first bachelor officer since ah've been heah."

"There's a pretty good looking bunch of enlisted men in the detachment," I teased. "They must keep you pretty busy." I agreed with Hornsby. I didn't like her looks or style and was thankful for the notion that officers shouldn't fraternize with employees. I wondered what she and Vance were arguing about.

"I don't go out with soldiers too much." She said haughtily as she scanned my record. "I see you're a Jew. You're the first one I ever met."

"I hope you're not disappointed."

"I judge people by their character not their religion." she blurted. "It ain't easy be'in a catholic either."

"I'm sure there are some nice soldiers you could go out with." I said getting back to her remark about GI's. "You must be breaking a lot of hearts around here."

"Ah guess ah've helped a few guys prove they were men." Then, changing her tone and putting away her make-up kit, she pulled the chair to the desk, "Ah have some routine forms for you to fill out, Lieutenant."

"Really, what kind?"

"Billeting, pay and allowance, the usual for new officers. Then the colonel wants me to brief you on the small animal clinic procedures and how to manage the Kennel Fund." She handed me a manila folder. "There all in thaya."

"Thanks, How long do I have to complete them?"

"A couple days will be fine. About the clinic." She gave me the pertinent details.

"Thanks. Do you like being called Beulah, Beulah Mae, or Miss Carlucci?"

"Beulah Mae, if you don't mind."

As I moved toward Vance I checked her from the side. She was both nobly breasted and curvaceous. I was sure she thought she was gorgeous, endowed by nature for something better than a veterinary clinc receptionist.

"Mornin, Sergeant, how's our patient this morning?" After yesterday I felt like I'd known Vance forever.

"He's still down and on the IV," Lieutenant, "The colonel has seen him already. He talked to him and got a little wag. He has to keep the general informed because Mrs. Miller nags him to death. She wants the pup home, like yesterday."

"She looked like she rules the roost." I said, as I started for the recovery room. "I'll check him. The catheter should stay in a while. If he starts to pull at it we'll use a Queen Elizabeth collar."

He looked at me questioningly. I loved showing off my knowledge.

"It's like it sounds," I explained. "It's round with a hole for his head, made of cardboard and sticks out so far he can't chew anything behind his head."

"Well, Defibrio said he doesn't need anything yet. So far he looks okay!"

"Good. Do we have office hours today?"

"9:30 till noon as usual. We don't have any surgery scheduled. It should be quiet."

In recovery little Terry slept. The IV bottle hung on the stand in front of his cage with its steady, relentless drip. I pinched the skin on his neck and he woke up, looked me in the eye and I got a little wag. The skin was warm and pliable. I petted his head, lifted a lip to check his gums and he licked my hand. What a cute little guy, I thought. His mucous membranes were pink. Too good to be true.

Defibrio appeared. "Mornin' Lieutenant. Have a good night?" He was smiling but seemed tired.

"Fine Sergeant. I see the patient is doing fine."

"I think so. I spent most of the night watching him. I think he'll make it okay."

Just what I'd expect from Defibrio. I felt that he did enough yesterday without staying up all night. "That wasn't necessary, Dom," I said, "he only needed an occasional check. One of the other men could have done it."

"I know, Lieutenant, but I would have worried and gotten no sleep anyhow."

"Well, he looks pretty good. Once he starts eating we can rest easy."

After clinic hours I decided to look in on the Colonel to report on the patients condition. A WAC enlisted woman was talking to Vance.

"Lieutenant, meet Private Pat Murphy. She helps out at the large animal clinic and is the post athlete. We have about twenty WAC's assigned here. Most work downtown on meat and dairy."

"Glad to meet you, private, I've heard about you." She was a cute, slightly built girl, big hazel eyes, little turned up nose, brown hair peeking out from under her military cap. She was all Irish and wore no makeup. What a contrast to Beulah Mae!

"Same here, Lieutenant." She answered shyly.

I turned to the sergeant, "I thought I'd talk to the colonel before I left."

"Go right in, Lieutenant, he's waiting for you."

The colonel was smiling, "The pup seems to be doing fine. Mrs. Miller was happy to get the good report."

"He's not out of the woods yet but he's young and I don't anticipate any problems." I said.

"I've arranged a social evening tonight with the other officers. I thought you should meet them and make some friends. We'll meet at the club after dinner. Mrs. Kielsmeier will be there also."

"Thank you, sir, I'd appreciate meeting them."

I met all twenty three Food and Dairy inspectors. Hornsby wasn't there, I supposed he had gotten his orders and had all he wanted of the colonel. Kielsmeier introduced me to his wife, a tall slender woman with curly gray hair and rather stern countenance.

I singled out Captain Crane from Westchester, New York, Hornsby's clinic predecessor. He had years of experience in his own practice before th Army grabbed him. His staring, red rimmed eyes made him look like he hadn't slept a wink. After several meetings I realized it was his normal look. He had a wife and three kids at home and resented being away. I asked him why he wasn't doing his specialty now. I wanted to hear him tell it because the cold water enema intrigued me. He was very friendly and told me he had been away from large animals so long he couldn't, in good conscience, treat them properly. And once the colonel was disenchanted, he didn't get to do the small animals either. Not a word about the garden hose and the colicky horse. The way he told it, he quit himself.

A week from the day of my arrival, Terry was discharged from the hospital. Kathy and Mrs. Wilson, all smiles, picked up their Fox Terrier, still bandaged, but wagging and whimpering with joy. The colonel just happened to be there to greet Mrs. Wilson and her daughter.

"Say hello to the general," he said. "We've enjoyed your puppy and the lieutenant says he'll be just fine."

"Bring him back in five days, Kathy," I said, addressing the joyous child, "we'll check him once more and take off the bandage for good."

Mrs. Wilson said to Kielsmeier, "You run a fine hospital here, colonel, and your staff is very professional and efficient. I'm going to tell the general that you all should be commended."

I thought the colonel would bust his scar from the smile that stretched from ear to ear.

After Terry's departure and the high that we all felt from Mrs. Wilson's accolades, I thought I owed myself what had been on my mind for a week and headed for the parachute towers. I parked Jezebel and examined the structures carefully. Each was T-shaped, about 150-feet high, accommodating a parachute on each end. The men waited in line, taking turns like customers at a carnival. They strapped themselves into the seat-harness under the chutes and waited impatiently for their chain-lift skyward. The units crawl up, swinging the manned gear under it. I followed the swift descent to a bumpy landing. Would I ever get the chance to try one? The towers would probably be busy from dawn to dusk, plenty of time for me to sneak a ride.

My attention suddenly shifted to the base of the nearest tower. Men were strapping a dog into the harness. They were petting and talking to him as if he were something special. He was an English Bull: huge head and shoulders, with tapering hips and a tiny, twisted tail. He wasn't happy about being confined and struggled to get free. One of the men barked, "Stay," and he quieted for a moment, his eyes fearful. They started him upward, his head whipped right and left as he twisted to get loose. One of his legs did pull free and he might have fallen but for the quick reaction of the soldier in charge. The lift was brought to a jarring halt. The man that strapped him in rushed to his side. He was shoulder high when the lift stopped, and opening the straps to redo his restraint wasn't easy. The belts were tightened, a few pats on the head and reassuring words from the corporal quieted him. Up he went again, this time staying secure through the entire ride and the jarring landing. The men crowded around, cheering and hugging him as if it were his first jump. He was "Geronimo" the class mascot and it was his first. He showed his relief by wagging the tiny tail and hind end as hard as he could as he licked the face of his corporal.

As I approached the scene, the men stiffened and fired salutes. Damn! It wasn't easy getting used to the obsequiousness of army custom. How the devil can you get friendly with someone who glares at you behind a facade of resentful respect?

"Mornin'," I said, as friendly as possible, "your dog is a beaut. I'm a new veterinarian on duty and had to get a closer look. How old is he?"

The young corporal stepped forward. He was a small, wiry Midwesterner, with hawk-like nose and dark, penetrating eyes. Somewhat relieved by my inquiry he replied, "Thank you, sir, he's about a year-old. I got him as our mascot."

"I'll probably be seeing him professionally. What's your name, Corporal?" I asked.

"Hector, sir, and I hope not. He's going through training with us. He is in very good health."

I laughed, "I'm sure he'll do fine, but there are shots and stuff he'll need from time to time." I petted him, admiring his fine breeding. "Nice meeting you and your circus pooch. Good Luck."

Geronimo, I discovered, was not only the dog's name but the corp's battle cry as they stepped over that scary threshold, their ultimate test of courage. When looking down those thousands of feet, that yell was the emotional release as they plunged toward uncertainty. The fearless and fabled Apache chieftain of yore thus inspired today's warriors.

My duties soon brought me into close contact with this unique outfit. Parachute school requirements were for men mostly under five feet, five inches tall. Transport planes were relatively small, and the more men that could be carried aloft, the better. So smaller, lighter men were recruited. What they lacked in height, they made up in spirit. Always in double-time, their tough training molded them into the finest physically conditioned branch of the armed forces, according to the army brass. Their camaraderie changed shy recruits into aggressive, self-reliant fighters, fiercely loyal to each other and their corps. The object of their greatest pride, like caps to the Green Berets, were their glistening, brown, jumping boots. Except when sleeping, thy wore them everywhere.

As I had predicted to Hector, a directive from the commanding general to the veterinary detachment as well as the commanders of the units at the post, ordering all pets be examined and vaccinated by the Post Veterinarian.

"How many are there? Does that mean every kind of pet?" I asked.

"Only the ones that are susceptible to rabies." Dom estimated that about 2,000 dogs, cats and other house pets belong to military personnel. "It's an educated guess," he said, "because many of the troops never brought their animals for shots, or if monkeys, birds or reptiles are involved, they aren't required to."

The unusual pets were the ones I was anxious to treat, and I would just have to wait for them to show up.

"When men are away from home," Dom explained, "scared and lonely, the first thing they do is adopt a pet. It could be a puppy, a kitten or a baby alligator. Many abandon them when they get shipped out and the local humane society keeps busy tryin' to place 'em. At the clinic we take care of them, try to keep their medical histories straight and treat them when necessary."

"And don't forget the thousands of civilians workin' on the post that take advantage of our clinic." He stopped for a moment, smiled, and I knew he relished his place in the complex mix of men preparing for battle.

"The post civilians," he continued, "are from the surrounding towns and villages and almost all of them have pets or horses. We don't compete with local vets, but so many have been drafted that people are desperate for any animal doctor. We don't charge much either. For them it's like another bargain 'Post Exchange.'"

"It sounds like it might be a madhouse." I said.

"It will be hectic." Defibrio warned. "Clinic hours will be expanded and appointments are a must."

I finally got to see the animals I loved to treat the most. Dogs and cats were routine, then came canaries, parrots, crows, hamsters, squirrels, snakes, descented skunks and baby raccoons. Southern colored troops brought in baby opossums. They raised them, fattened them up, and then feasted.

It was a hot, humid, rainy Monday in Georgia, the kind of southern discomfort we had become used to. The clinic was open and usually when it rained, the traffic was light. People called and cancelled appointments, hoping for a better day. Geronimo arrived with three of his two legged buddies who came along to stand a careful and uneasy watch. One of the men was Hector, the trooper I spoke to when I visited the tower two weeks before. I knew he had a love for his charge and soon discovered in addition that he had a deep suspicion and fear of veterinarians.

He faced Defibrio, his cap and shoulders stained from the morning's downpour. Geronimo sprinkled the clinic floor with rain water, with a determined shake, starting with his head and ending with his little pig-tail.

"Sergeant," Hector asked, wiping his brow, "are these shots really necessary? The guy who sold him to me said he already had them."

"If you want to keep your dog," he answered, "he's gotta have his shots. 'Army Regulations!'" As far as Defibrio was concerned there was nothing to discuss, Army Regulations were the law.

I heard the last exchange as I entered the waiting room.

"Hello Sergeant. Hector, isn't it? We met at the training towers a few weeks ago." His face lit up. "I see you've been promoted. Congratulations."

"Thank you sir," he answered. "You said we might be seeing you soon but I didn't believe it."

"Don't be nervous, Hector. Only one rabies shot a year is necessary. Show the sergeant your certificate. He really doesn't need them again, though it wouldn't hurt him."

"I never got a certificate, sir. The guy who sold him to me told me he got them. Distemper too."

"It's a lot cheaper for someone to say he got his shots than to give them," Defibrio said, "If you don't have a certificate and he bites someone, there will be two weeks of quarantine. And if he gets distemper you could lose him for good. Why are you so worried about a couple of shots?"

Hector started to explain, then thought better of it. His concern was obvious. He was frowning, perspiring freely and shifting from side to side uncomfortably. There wasn't much he could do about it if he wanted to keep his dog, but I waited for his approval. Finally he shrugged his shoulders and said.

"OK Lieutenant, sir. You might as well go ahead. I just don't like doctors, hospitals, shots or medical talk."

"When you getcha leg blown off in combat, you may change your tune." Defibrio mutter sagely.

It was obvious that something traumatic had colored his past. I tried to put him at ease with a reassuring smile as I motioned him to lift Geronimo to the table. "Good boy." I said as I opened the huge jaw and looked in. I pushed his tongue down in the limited space allowed in his throat to get a look at tonsils and palate. It was easier to check his teeth under those loose and floppy lips. He seemed to enjoy the probing. English Bull's ferocity were usually limited to comic strips.

"Don't you ever get bitten, sir?" Hector asked, disappointed that Geronimo didn't as much as growl.

"Don't be upset, Corporal. He'll only let me do what he thinks you approve of. One can usually sense when you'd better be careful," I answered. "They can't talk but they never lie!"

A few more minutes of looking and fingering proved him a fine healthy specimen. With a clean bill of health, Hector's concern now focused on the vaccinations. He dreaded them for himself and more so for his pet.

The rabies shot was given intramuscularly in the heavily muscled thigh. I could see Hector wince. Geronimo never stirred. Then the distemper shot, given subcutaneously near his massive shoulder. Again, only pain for the soldier.

I turned to Hector with a shoulder shrug and a silent 'See?' I dismissed Geronimo with an affectionate pat on the rump. Hector put him down, smiling with relief and said, "That wasn't too bad, was it, boy?" He looked at me with an almost friendly glance as he left. Geronimo's reaction from tension and restraint was a vigorous rhumba as they hurried out the door.

June 28, 1943, will always remain vivid in my memory. It centered around the paratroopers, both in combat and those stationed at Benning. As Jezebel carried me to the clinic, the morning news covered the RAF raids on the Reich. It was the eighth straight night of bombing. What caught my ear was the third raid on Messina, with mention of paratroopers landing behind the lines. I passed the barking, rhythmic squads of young troopers in double time and realized that training at Benning was for just that kind of softie and those men probably trained here.

Later that day, Buelah Mae took a phone call from Corporal Hector who reported a landing accident involving Geronimo.

Funny, I thought, as I took the call, it happened at the same time their comrades were parachuting into enemy territory.

"We were making low jumps for a couple of weeks," he started, "and coming away in fine style. Geronimo was becoming a real veteran. You know how the weather turned," he said, "a strong swirling wind was blowing and Geronimo landed awkwardly, rolled over several times, and got to his feet, blood pouring from his mouth."

Hector continued, breathlessly, "I was nearby and screamed for the medics. They told me that a fang tooth was broken in half and three small incisors were gone."

I reassured Hector that if the nerve in the fang wasn't exposed we could file it smooth. A fighting parachute dog didn't need a full length fang anyhow. We could fill the pulp cavity if necessary, and I assured him that he would never miss a few small incisor teeth. "Bring him in and we'll take a look."

I never did get to see Geronimo and I found out later why he didn't show. It seems as though a month or so before his induction, Hector had spent half his savings on the show-prospect English Bull puppy. When he was drafted his parents told him he would have to leave the dog behind. He had become so captivated by the pooch, that he decided, in order to stay together, he would present him to his parachute class as a mascot. His commanding officer thought it a great way to take his men's minds off themselves. Hector planned, if they survived, to put him on the dog show circuit and parlay his investment into a grand champion. A good stud could make a lot of money and fulfill his dream of owning a breeding kennel. Geronimo's mouth, if not repaired cosmetically, would eliminate him from competing in any important dog show. He assumed that I did not know how to replace dog's teeth and unaware of his aspirations, I never considered a dental reconstruction. Obviously he wasn't happy with my advice and decided to look elsewhere.

Dental repairs for the men in the paratroops were routine. Several free-for-all's caused enough damage to keep the dental clinic as busy as the mess hall. Captain Dan Miller was an orthdontal specialist in civilian practice and his oral surgery and repairs were magnificent. The need for his expertise was too infrequent for his talented fingers and he yearned for cases that would keep his hand "in." Hector called and said someone recommended him as a specialist for fixing damaged jaws. Something had to be done for Geronimo and Hector was convinced by his buddies that Captain Miller was the man. Would he please treat Geronimo? Hector described his dog's jumping ability and blamed the weather for the mishap. "The vet can't fix it," he said. Sight unseen Miller agreed. As in most dental schools, practice surgery and dental repair is done on dogs.

Geronimo was ushered into the examining room of the clinic with elaborate fanfare. Miller and his staff had heard about the canine parachutist and couldn't wait to see him. They watched wide-eyed as he pranced in with his handler, back end and tiny pig-tail swaying. Hector lifted him to the dental chair where he sat, looking like a waif on a throne. Geronimo loved the attention and as long as his master was there he was like a child at the circus. Captain Miller rolled up his sleeves and cooed at the new patient. Hector held his collar, while the professionals crowded around trying to get a look inside his mouth. The bleeding had long since stopped and there was no pain. Luckily all the damage was in the front and could be easily seen.

"I've worked on a lot of dogs in our college surgery lab." He admitted, "but they had jaws and teeth that were normal. Not at all like this guy. He's all lower jaw."

"He's a show dog, Doc. And his teeth have to be perfect. Can you help him?"

"I think so." Miller said as he eyed the damage. "We'll have to make an impression, then fashion a plate with false teeth." Miller had done a couple of dozen plates while in school. The dogs were the terrier type, however, with normal bites and had been anesthetized for the procedure.

"The technical part will be simple. The trick is having him hold still for an accurate mold. It would be a lot simpler if we could anesthetize him." His assistants nodded approval, a sleeping patient would be ideal.

"No way! Captain." Hector said emphatically. He had heard tales of bull dogs and anesthesia. He might let a qualified veterinarian do it in an emergency, but never a dentist. He looked askance at the two assistants then back to the Captain. "He's very good with me, sir. Just tell me what you'd like him to do."

"Okay. We'll get the material ready. Then we'll pack his mouth with cotton and gauze rolls to absorb the saliva. His mouth must be perfectly dry to get a good impression."

Dan Miller and his associates busied themselves with the composition. Hector watched the preparations and was quickly joined by four or five enlisted men and another dental officer from the clinic. It seems that the word got out that Captain Miller was up to something strange and they weren't about to miss it. They buzzed about it among themselves and got some clues from Miller's helpers. From Geronimo's point of view, he had about ten humans making a fuss over him and he loved them all.

Miller explained for all to hear, especially Hector, who hadn't seen army dentistry before. "This sticky stuff will be pressed around the area of the incisors and both canine teeth. We send the impression to the lab where the technicians fashion a plate that will fit over his gum, right here," and he pointed out exactly where it would go. "False teeth will be copied from the undamaged teeth and incorporated into the denture. "The finished plate will be attached to other teeth by wire clips. It can be removed and replaced easily."

Soon the material was ready, and they all crowded around again. Captain Miller was about to get a practical lesson in canine anatomy and physiology. Geronimo was the professor and even though Hector was steadying his head, he watched his master out of the corner of his eye, nervous about being handled by a bunch of strangers.

Geronimo was salivating profusely, a natural reaction to the cotton and gauze that four pairs of hands were trying to jam into his mouth. As soon as they got them into place, his huge slippery tongue pushed them out.

"Corporal Hector," he pleaded, "can't you de-activate the tongue? He's playing games with us."

He bent over, ready for another try. A perfectly timed thrust of that tongue affectionately washed Miller's face.

The captain stepped back, as everyone giggled. He dried himself with one of the sterile towels.

Suddenly Miller paused. An idea evolved that he thought might work. He rolled up one end of a small sterile towel, just like the one he had just used. He put the rolled end between the back molars for Geronimo to bite on, the loose end he left open to absorb the saliva. Hector talked softly to Geronimo who finally let the staff proceed. Success!

The lab constructed a very usable dental plate with artificial teeth, well fitted to Geronimo's jaw. A week later Geronimo was back to receive the finished plate. They stepped back, proud of their achievement. Hector couldn't have been happier.

A few weeks later on Geronimo's first jump following the accident, the paratroops prepared to strap him in. The men crowded around Geronimo admiring his dentures. "Good as new!" was the general opinion. "He doesn't seem to mind false teeth at all" they marveled. "Modern dentistry at its best." On his first landing, however, Geronimo hit hard and rolled over. His plate jarred loose and was swallowed. A day or so later Geronimo began retching.

"The men looked for the plate but there was nothing but dry heaves. It had passed through his stomach and into the small intestine. Because of its peculiar shape and size, it could not fit through the narrow portion of the bowel and became lodged. Hector and his pals had to watch as persistent vomiting, accompanied by severe depression resulted; classic symptoms of intestinal obstruction. Three days after the accident, three sheepish paratroops arrived at my office, carrying a limp Geronimo."

Hector's face showed his worry and exhaustion. He began to speak, apologetically. He couldn't understand why I didn't suggest replacing those teeth. Knowing he was a show dog, I should have suggested it. He then called Dr. Miller who told him it would be an easy job, so Hector said, "Go ahead."

I asked Hector, "How many dogs has Dr. Miller treated?"

He answered, "Except for practice in Dental School, he never did one before. But he really did make a beautiful plate."

"If Geronimo was preparing for a dog show, instead of active combat," I told him, "I might have suggested such a procedure. I thought it was pure stupidity for him to wear it all the time, but then, how were you to know? You should have been warned to remove the plate before a jump or just keep it in a safe place until after the war. Dogs can't spit things out the way we do. They just swallow them like an infant. You have no choice." I told him. "From what you've told, and the way he looks, if I don't operate immediately, he's a goner."

"Hector surprised me. 'Lets get on with it, Sir.' He said, then pleaded, 'can I stay with him and watch?'

"I don't mind," I told him, "but you'll have to be masked and gowned like the rest of us."

The preparation for the operation meant reviewing everything I had ever read, seen, or heard about intestinal anastomosis, and necessitated another session of cramming, but this time I only had an hour or so to do it. If the bowel wasn't necrotic, a small incision in the elastic gut was all that would be necessary, I knew that the past three days of pressure was too long for a simple procedure to work. I warned Defibrio about the seriousness of the surgery as I prepared for a resection.

In about an hour we were set to proceed. We routinely used ether with a cone, but that would never fit over Geronimo's nose. I gave the anesthetic, Numbutol, intravenously, freeing Defibrio to assist.

After a few minutes I glanced at Hector standing at the foot of the table. His face was wet with perspiration, green in color, and eyes glassy. As yet, hardly a drop of blood had been shed.

"Sergeant!" I called sharply to Vance, standing just inside the door. "Get him out of here!"

Vance caught him as his legs buckled. The procedure for fainting spectators was well practiced; smelling salts and a soft couch. In a few minutes an embarrassed young man would wonder what happened.

Defibrio held our shiny new retractors as the scalpel cut through skin, fascia, muscle and peritoneum. I hoped a six inch incision would be adequate for me to see and treat the pathology. I had one practice anastamosis under the watchful eye of Dr. Stephenson and observed two more while working for Dr. Corwin. My stomach was a little queasy but I was confident and ready for the test.

Defibrio expertly placed the retractors as I felt for the dental plate through the intestinal wall. "Just what I feared," I mumbled to Defibrio as I gingerly exposed the blackened, necrotic bowel. "A resection is a must. I'm glad they didn't wait 'till tomorrow and more glad I spent a little time reviewing the procedure." We were finished in about an hour.

I handed the plate to the embarrassed Hector. Geronimo proved his mettle with a normal recovery. Ten days later sutures were removed and Geronimo was discharged. Curious onlookers were treated to the sight of the jubilant corporal who trotted homeward, mascot at his side.

A few weeks later, Dr. Miller was astounded when Hector handed him a package with a "Thanks but no thanks, Doc," and left without an explanation. He was surprised by the return of his rare, museum-piece dental-plate.

Hector also thought it appropriate to express his gratitude to me. I received a complimentary pair of beautiful jumping boots that I showed off to the world, and finally, what had been hoped for from my first day at Fort Benning, a signed permit to ride the training parachute. Most important of all, Geronimo, toothless but happy was jumping once again. Within a month the entire class, including the mascot, graduated and were flown to England to await their turn in helping the invasion of Hitler's Europe.

Long after Geronimo and Hector were shipped overseas, I was having a drink at the bar of the Officer's Club. Next to me was a captain nursing a tall, ice filled cocktail. I noticed that he was wearing a dental caduceus. We looked at each other. I said, "Captain Miller?"

He glanced at my veterinary caduceus, paused, looked up at me and asked, "Lieutenant Zimmerman?"

Together came the name, "Geronimo!" We laughed and shook hands.

"We have to talk," I said, "but I'm due back at the clinic in five minutes".

"How about a drink tonight before dinner? I'll be with my wife; about 6:30 Okay?"

"It's a date."

We met that evening and he introduced me to his wife, a tiny, attractive, well dressed and perky lady. After a few drinks, he sighed deeply, and recalled to me his vain attempt to help the parachute school's mascot.

"Don't blame yourself." I told him, "God had a hand in it. He just messed up on the creation."

The expression on Ruth Miller's face made me wonder about her notions on theology. Both looked at me, quizzically.

"I don't mean to be irreverent," I said, and when she smiled, I continued. "He made two mistakes. I guess just creating man was the worst." And I laughed. "The other was the way he designed the mammalian throat."

"Why do you say that?" He asked. She looked curious, now very interested in what I was driving at.

He laughed, but had to agree that there were some problems with the throat. "Let's hear more," he said.

"The pharynx," I lectured, "where traffic is congested at best, has to manipulate food, water, and saliva, over the windpipe and down the esophagus into the stomach. Couldn't God have directed air to go directly to the lungs and food right to the stomach?" I looked at Mrs. Miller for moral support. "It's a terrible system," I continued. "A horse that regurgitates is doomed. They inhale the vomitus and get inhalation pneumonia. If a man talks too much while he is eating, he can choke to death."

"You're absolutely right," she said, clenching her fist and rapping it playfully on the table. She's a good sport, I thought.

"And that slippery, canine mouth that he created!" Miller said cheerfully. "Why so much saliva?"

"That was partly man's fault," I explained.

"English Bulldogs are classified as brachycephalic, having very long palates and short noses. Others like them are Boxers, Pugs, Boston Terriers and Pekingese. For years, we veterinarians have implored the fanciers to breed away from those exaggerated features. Besides the very distinctive look that it affords, the result is a snoring, wheezing, and excessively salivating dog."

"Well that makes me feel better. I thought the entire fiasco was my fault." Miller said relieved.

"Yes, Lieutenant." Mrs. Miller added. "Thanks to you, he can blame the Lord and his fellow men, the dog-breeders, as well as himself. Maybe my husband can sleep better now."

"We really can't blame all breeders for making improper decisions. I think they did a wonderful job on Airedales." Dr. Miller said. "We've had one for seven years that we wouldn't give up for the world."

"Oh, Doctor." Mrs Miller, agreed passionately, "We couldn't live without our "Whiskers." He is the most precious animal alive."

"I guess every breed has their good and their bad." I said.

"He's one of the family, we love him like our own child." The thought of their pet, never-the-less, brought me back to my first and traumatic experience with Airedales. I remembered them as anything but cute and adorable.

Rivervale, New Jersey, our little summer-spot of heaven was far from the crowded city, far from school with their mean, tenacious teachers. But it also had its share of hazards. Ebony, the Linderman farm's stallion was just one of them. Another was farmer Volk's dogs, our neighbor's brace of brown bewhiskered canines. The Airedales jealously guarded their road. But it was our road, too. I was eight years old and had to pass their house to go anywhere.

The dogs would run at us, barking furiously and brake to a sliding halt, dust exploding around them. Their noses touched our legs as they made their identification, then, disdainfully, they turned and trotted back to the shade, under their porch, allowing us to proceed.

My dad told us that any time they charged, we should freeze, "Stand like statues till they sniff, and they won't bite."

Dad was right. We obeyed his instructions, shutting our eyes and holding our breaths. When Bill was with us it was different. He would glare at them, the hair on his neck and back would stand up stiff and ominous, his upper lip would curl, exposing shapely, fearsome fangs. The Airedales would slink back to their nest, tails between their legs.

Our neighbor in the other direction was Marie Zeller, Sonny's older sister. She played with Evelyn at our house. I had a crush on her even though she was two years older than I. She was slender with sleek, auburn hair, black eyes, a sparkling smile, and could run like a deer. "Will you race me to that telephone pole?" I challenged time and again, just wanting to be near her. I knew she was fast and loved to run. We raced and I always lost. I didn't care because she was so pretty and I loved to watch her move.

Once Marie walked with us past the Volks. Bill stayed home and the Airedales charged as usual. We stopped dead as instructed. I was getting accustomed to the confrontation, knowing they weren't so fearsome. I even kept my eyes open and watched them, acting very brave to impress Marie. It must have been her first encounter, because she was terrified. I tried to reassure her.

"Don't be afraid, just stand quiet and they won't hurt you."

Marie couldn't bring herself to stand still with two snarling dogs seeming to be on the attack. She turned and raced away. I'm sure she felt that she could out-run any living creature. One of the dogs chased after her and nipped her behind. When she got home, she tearfully told her dad what happened. He paid a call to the Volks immediately, and warned them that if his children were molested again, he would use his shotgun. After Mr. Zeller's visit, the Volks put a fence up around their yard.

I explained to the Millers about my experience as a child and why I disliked Airedales to this day. "But if and when they ever need me for treatment, I won't turn them away."

They understood and Mrs. Miller said as they got up to leave, "I guess there are good and bad in every breed, just like with people. Let's have a drink again, soon."

I learned the hard way, that day or night, I was on call for emergencies. I had just fallen asleep when the phone jarred me awake. It was Defibrio, apologizing. He had a colicky horse that had to be seen immediately.

"What do I do, Dominick?" My mind began the run-through of possibilities. Trauma was common when horses run together. A kick to the abdomen, or head. A laceration from a fence or a barn door. I stopped the conjectures. Wait and see, I told myself as I got dressed. I felt better knowing Defibrio would be there. He would know what to do and what to bring and probably how the colonel preferred to minister a belly-aching equine. His presence gave me a sense of security and assuredness. I awaited his answer, almost guessing it.

"Meet me at the large animal clinic behind the office. This one is an overeater. We see him once a month like clockwork. We don't have to bother the colonel for this one. He probably got into apples again, and a high colonic will fix him up." We checked him and Dom was correct. I was old-fashioned. I made sure the high-colonic was body temperature.

I was back in my room about 3 A.M. Wrote a quick letter home describing the post, my duties, all the new characters I met and other trivia I knew they loved to hear about. I went on about Defibrio, this pillar that I trusted, because I knew they would like him and feel better about me being away among strangers.

About a week after reporting, the colonel called me and Defibrio to his office. Vance told us that he wanted to talk about the farm and find out my experience with large animals. I was confident with the memory of Dr. Thompson's freeze in Honeoye Falls fresh in my mind. The season's annual examinations and vaccinations were coming due and a trip to the farm was on the colonel's "must" list.

Defibrio, as usual, filled me in on the pertinent details. We met in the small animal clinic lounge where we could relax and talk. It was 1:00 P.M. and the colonel wanted to see us at 3. We settled into comfortable chairs with cokes, coffee and cigarettes for Dom. Detachment men drifted in and out, some nodding as they approached, some backed away from the lieutenant's bars.

"The farm," Dom started, "has the ridin' horses for the soldiers, the wives, girlfriends and children. Most of the horses are gentle and feel at home on our track. Some are used for the weekly boar hunts durin' the summer." Dom's eyes lit up as he told me about the weekly cross-country challenge. He was sure I'd love them too.

"I'm not so sure, Dom. Riding over hills, jumping fences, dodging plants, rocks and water holes, chasing wild pigs?"

Midnight and R.O.T.C. was the last time I rode, not exactly a training ground for a rough trip on horseback. But, then again, I'll be sitting in a saddle, it might not be too bad.

"Huntin' wild boar is a great sport." he reassured me. "We ride and the hounds do the trackin'. Our steeds are very experienced, so don't worry. There is a delicious cook-out afterwards, fresh roasted pork with all the fixins. Mrs. Kielsmeier supervises and you'll get to meet the officers and families from all the other services."

He went into a description of the draft horses and mules, the ram and his family of sheep, some cattle, a sty with a dozen or so hogs, poultry and finally Pot's kennel of twenty hunting dogs. For some reason, he put special emphasis on the donkeys and his eyes implicd something memorable. Then he told me about Willy the mule, a favorite among the men, who was the only individual man or beast, that dared put the colonel in his place. I thought I'd like to meet that animal.

Hearing about mules, I thought of Hornsby and brought up his name. "He's pretty feisty, isn't he?" I asked. "He wasn't too keen on the way the colonel runs the shop."

"Hornsby's a rebel. I liked him and we got along fine but he hates takin' orders so the colonel does the easiest thing. You can't fire anybody in the service," he said, his eyes sparkling, "you either court martial him, shoot him, or ship him out."

I mentioned about my concern about taking over company commander's duties. "It seems like a lot of responsibility for a greenhorn. Where do I come off teaching the facts of life to men older than myself? And the colonel mentioned I'd be paying the men as well. How does that work?"

"Vance takes care of everythin' in his quiet efficient way." He assured me. "We all depend on him. He makes most of the administration decisions and helps the colonel on officer assignments."

"Are you married, Dom?" I asked.

"No way! I'm a confirmed, army bachelor."

Defibrio loved to talk, and I was a good audience. I really felt that he liked me and was, in a way, taking me under his wing. I sipped on a coke and he lit a cigarette and went on about the detachment.

"Was it Vance's idea that I be assigned clinician and company commander?"

"Yep." He said, "Vance thinks the quickest way for one to learn about the detachment is to be put in charge. Of course it was the colonel that got rid of Hornsby, but you impressed him with the small animals and he's hopin' you're as good on the farm. But don't worry, I'll show you everytin' you gotta know."

"What do the other officers do?" I asked.

"They inspect foods with the help of the enlisted men and W.A.C.s.

"What is so difficult about inspecting the food?"

"Have you ever candled an egg, or graded a chicken? Do you know what 93 score butter means?"

I shrugged my shoulders.

"The other officers are in the same boat. You learn from the enlisted men until you go to the meat and dairy school."

Defibrio reasoned, "Who is better qualified than veterinarians to judge healthy meat and dairy products." He continued, "For convenience, the Quartermaster includes vegetables, fish and canned goods. We also inspect the food that goes to the Navy and Marines. The army realized that some sort of trainin' was necessary for the officers, so they ordered the Quartermaster to start the school in the Chicago stock yards. Every state-side veterinary officer must eventually attend a five week crash course there."

"Are you a food inspector too?" I queried.

"Thank God, no!" He answered emphatically. "I just care for the animals! I hate railroad cars, frozen food warehouses and inspectin' poor, filthy, local farms. You won't be so lucky. In the past, officers in charge of the clinics have been assigned to the Columbus cold storage plant twice a week. You got to observe and learn about inspectin' and gradin' frozen produce. They all hated it and you will too." He checked his watch again and motioned for us to go in before I could question him further about why I'd hate the frozen food warehouse.

The colonel answered our salutes and waved us into two easy chairs. He talked quietly about routine duties at the farm, his scar jumping with each stressed word. He saved last years problems with Willy, the mule, for last. His pace quickened and his tone was stronger. I could see traces of whisker glistening on his scar that the razor couldn't reach. The blemish seemed to come alive as he waxed emotionally. "That stubborn, idiot jackass put two of our men in the hospital last year. Why the men like him, I'll never know. They're scared to death to go near him!" I looked at Dom and he gave me that 'I told you so' expression. I recalled that Hornsby was relieved of his duty as chief clinician over that same incident.

The colonel rocked back on his desk chair, hands locked behind his head. The omnipresent leer on his face made him look angry. He was talking to me but I could tell there was an undercurrent of complaint for Defibrio. I watched the sergeant's face. I had the impression he had heard these ramblings many times. He wasn't even listening.

"He's too smart for his own good," the colonel continued, referring to Willy. "I wanted to sell him last year and I told those bastards down at Quartermasters he was too unpredictable." He paused a moment, letting his chair rock forward as he put both hands back on the desk top. He grinned and suddenly changed his expression.

"They sit around all day with their thumbs up their asses," (he gesticulated, fist raised, thumb pointing straight up), "and I let them talk me out of it."

He looked me straight in the eye and I knew he was thinking that I was just another inexperienced city boy. He finally came to the point. "How are you with large animals?" I had the feeling it was a mule or jack that scarred his face when he was a student. He was testing me, as I'm sure he did most of his subordinates. I had been fore-warned by Defibrio and wasn't about to let on. As I groped for an answer, without boasting about how good I was, he dismissed us with a casual wave.

"Sergeant, show the lieutenant around the farm and brief him on the spring round-up." I wasn't too sure what he accomplished by our talk but I supposed he had to get something off his chest.

I jumped up and gave a snappy salute. The sergeant's was more relaxed.

The Colonel responded, his eyes back to the work in front of him.

The next day as we rumbled out of the Post on our way to the farm, Defibrio and I got better acquainted. He settled back in his seat and lit a cigarette. He was as relaxed in his driving as he was with everything else. One finger on the wheel eased the jeep to the center of his lane. His free hand caressed the smoking cigarette. It was a beautiful spring day. Trees passed, with Spanish Moss decorating their branches like silver streamers on a Christmas tree.

"Where is the farm?" I asked.

"Across the Chattahoochee. We gotta go through Phenix City. It's off limits to the troops but it's the only way to get there."

"Very far?" I asked Defibrio.

"About five miles. We take the bridge just ahead there, and through town to the outskirts." After crossing the span, he slowed to the posted limit as he spied a police car hiding on a side street.

"They don't like us since the commandin' general took all their customers away." He explained. "Cost them a lot of money."

"Why?" I asked curious about the details. I had heard about "Sin City" long before I got there.

"Too many GI's got taken. Picked up VD or got beat-up. You know, rolled by prostitutes or cheated by gamblers. They got some mean dudes in this town."

Dom Defibrio was the most relaxed and matter of fact enlisted man I had met. Nothing seemed to fluster him.

He talked about fishing and told me about a little pond that was full of hungry ketaufel fish (sunnies). "They're delicious." he said, his mouth watering. "I catch at least twenty every time I go out."

"I'd love to go fishing." I said. I hadn't fished since those carefree days in Montvale during the summers of my youth.

We were eleven years old when Sonny Zeller taught me how. He had a wonderful, secret place in the Hackensack River and he was taking me because I was his special friend. We started by walking to the far end of the field, across the road that had the daisies, buttercups and bumble-bees. It was a one hour hike through woods, heavy brush and marshes until we found a narrow stream he called the Hackensack. I was expecting a *river*, I was used to the wide, majestic Hudson in New York City.

Sonny had gotten a little fat since last summer, and he seemed unusually quiet.

"How are your folks?" I asked, breaking the silence.

"They're fine," he said, as he stopped for a moment. "We have a new baby brother."

"That's great. Marie okay?" I still liked her a lot.

"She's fine. . ."

"Come on. Lets fish," I said, anxious to catch something.

Sonny knew the best place and allowed me to share his secret. He cut branches for fishing poles from a special tree. It had to be the correct thickness and length, and bend freely without snapping.

"These will make good poles. You tie the string to the end, attach the hook and we're ready to go." He carried safety pins that he adapted as fish-hooks.

"What about bait?"

"We'll get some earthworms under rocks near the bank."

When we reached the river, he rolled over several rocks, exposing big, wiggling earthworms. He dropped some into a tin can filled with dirt.

"Okay, we're all set. You see that bend just ahead?" He pointed to a shaded area in the river. The Hackensack at that point was little more than ten feet across.

"It looks deeper there. Is that the secret place?"

"A two-pounder lives there. I've been trying to hook him for a year."

We scrambled up a steeper part of the bank just over his target.

"Shhh," he whispered. "No more talking. He can hear us."

We sat and I watched Sonny bait the hook. He held the frantic insect with one hand and forced the point of the homemade hook through its fatter end, threading it through about half-way. The hooked half of the worm was quiet but the free end wiggled desperately. At last we were ready.

The only movement in the water was a rippling that came from the edges of the river where the water was shallow and ran over the pebbles and rocks. Suddenly a huge trout came into view. I was thrilled—what a beautiful sight! We could see the fish settle in the deepest part of the pond, constantly fluttering his side fins and gills. Sonny swung the pole over the water and let the worm settle on the bottom just in front of his nose. The worm wiggled and the trout contemplated the meal.

I decided to bait my hook. As I held the slippery, firm insect in one hand, I got ready to stab its thick end. I paused for a moment, wondering how much it would hurt the struggling creature. I rationalized it was a necessary torture because humans have to eat, and killing the worm wasn't much worse than catching the fish. The skin was tough and the pin pushed the worn almost inside out before it finally yielded. The worm's insides spilled out on my fingers as I tried to thread the bent needle through its body. I couldn't do it right. The point kept coming out the other side of the wiggly, slippery, icky creature. I had to keep pulling the pin back to re-aim it. Finally half the worm was impaled and I let go, swinging the pole out, allowing it to fall to the bottom behind the fish. That startled our victim and, with a swish, it kicked up a cloud and disappeared.

"Be careful!" Sonny shouted disgustedly. "You scared it away."

"I'm sorry," I said apologetically.

"That fish is pretty smart," he said. "I've been teasing him with worms for weeks. We'll just have to get him when he's hungry."

I kept trying, but the only movement I could see were schools of tiny fish no larger than the bait. I sat with the pole in the water, content with the fact that I was finally a fisherman. Sonny got bored and walked down the river to try his luck in another place.

Then the dark shape of the big trout came swimming slowly back toward its original position. I held my breath and waited for it to stop, easing my pole, so the worm was in front of his nose, just the way Sonny had done. Suddenly, he struck. I screamed and frantically jerked the pole out of the water. Sonny ran back to find me staring at the empty hook.

"He just pulled the worm off the hook and swam away," I said sheepishly.

"You jerked it up too fast, I guess. These safety pins don't work too good on big fish. We'll have to get "store bought" hooks to nail that bugger."

We didn't catch the trout, but instead pulled in a bunch of brilliantly-colored, flat, sunfish. Sonny taught me how to handle them without hurting myself. The dorsal spines were sharp as needles, and had to be folded back before picking them up. I decided they'd make great aquarium pets. As I filled a glass jar with water and put in a couple of the freshly caught fish, I thought of Policeman Joe. As we walked back, I told Sonny about Uncle and my other pet monkey, Suzy. I don't think he believed me, because he acted as though I was making the whole thing up. By the time we got home, the fish were floating belly up in the jar. I never have discovered how to keep them alive for more than a couple of minutes.

The sunnies were the same type of fish that Defibrio had described, a decade later. After a few minutes of silence I thought I'd better stop dreaming and play officer. I asked him about the round up.

"Don't worry about it, Lieutenant. "It's no big deal. The colonel likes everything to work real smooth. We get the same pep-talk every year."

"Well tell me about it, anyhow."

He gave me a rundown of early spring at the farm. "Once a year the farm machinery gets tuned up. The blacksmith sets up his forge, bellows and rods to make shoes. Then we round up the horses and mules. They get their shots, some new shoes and they're set for the season. The other animals are checked and vaccinated too. Only the chickens are exempt. They are too hard to catch," he added smiling.

"Its sounds pretty simple. What happened last year that has the colonel so edgy?" I asked.

"Everything was fine," he explained, "until it was Willy's turn. Willy was the new kid on the block. He's smart and high strung. He gets wary! I Ie don't like shots! Hitchin' him to a wagon or plow is one thing, and it took a lot of patience and training to do that. Standin' in front of the Vet with a suspicious lookin' needle and the smell of alcohol was different."

Defibrio reached for another cigarete, "So when it was his turn for the shot, he backed away. He didn't trust Hornsby." Defibrio looked into his rear view mirror. The cop had pulled out and was trailing him. The jeep slowed more. "He'd love to ticket me," he muttered, "I'm not about to give him an excuse."

"To get back to Hornsby. Once, when treating Willy for a simple shoulder bruise, he whipped him because he objected. He should have let Calder or me calm him. Calder is in charge when I'm away. Willy knew us and trusted us. Instead he went over Calder's head and ordered two big stupid privates to hold him."

"Didn't he like Calder?"

"Calder is a funny guy. You met him that first day in his quarters. He has problems. He drinks too much. The colonel had to bust him from sergeant because he sneaked into Phenix City after it was put off limits. He was turned down for O.C.S. because he was too unstable. He resents all the new young officers and shows it. Hornsby wasn't about to take any crap and just ignored him.

I didn't remember who he was. "So I'm going to have a problem with him too." I said.

"Maybe. I hope not. I've talked to him about you. I think he'll be okay."

"To get back to Willy." He resumed, and laughed as he recalled the incident. "Hornsby shouted, 'Grab his ears and hold the son-of-a-bitch.'"

"Willy reared back, lifting both them lunks right off their feet. He shakes 'em loose, spins, ducks his head and gives them a one-two combination. One gets it in the gut, the other on his backside."

He took a deep drag and continued, "With both of them on their backs and Hornsby sputterin', Willy saunters back to the meadow."

He reflected a moment. "Hornsby's a good officer, lots of fun and a real ladies man. He should stick to small animals though."

"So then what happened?"

"The men went to the hospital. Just bruises and black and blue marks for one, a ruptured liver for the other, but too much publicity as far as the colonel was concerned. The entire post, so busy with the business of war, loved the story and took special note of Willy-the-mule. Nobody was sorry for the men who got hurt and they all cheered Willy. The colonel couldn't do a thing about it."

"So the colonel thinks the same thing is going to happen again."

"Well, he hates to take a chance on anythin' that might hurt his promotion. He's been waitin' five years to get silver chickens." (Full colonel's insignia). "He's been passed over so many times he's afraid any flack, no matter how minor, will hurt him. That's why he's so tickled with the general's dog and the way you handled it. About two weeks ago," he continued, "Hornsby got orders, and the colonel requested a replacement that turned out to be you."

When we arrived at the farm, the police car turned and went back to town.

Dom gave me the quick tour. Horses, mules, some cows, and a ram with several ewes were grazing inside a huge fenced area. I smelled the sty in one corner, a dozen hogs grunting with satisfaction over the morning's slop. Searching, scratching chickens were everywhere, hens cackling and roosters crowing importantly.

Off to one side was the kennel of howling, tail wagging beagles and bloodhounds. The stable housed the horses and some mules. A quarter mile fenced circular track lay in front of the stable area. I recognized the manure spreader parked behind the stables. Collecting fertilizer for the crops, I reflected, was as common here as in Ithaca and the rest of the world.

Defibrio pointed out Calder. I recalled him from the enlisted men's dorm on my first day and eyed him carefully but he seemed respectful and normal. Corporal Stern waved to us from the kennels. I greeted the enlisted men, some of whom were in the dorm that first day.

Defibrio briefed Calder about the next day's routine. "Save Willy for last," Defibrio said, "everything else will be easy. Maybe he's forgotten last year's roundup." Calder nodded but he looked skeptical about Dom's last remark which gave me a slight sense of foreboding. We then boarded the jeep for home, and sure enough, close to the city we picked up our escort.

"He certainly is looking for an excuse to stop us, isn't he?" I asked uncomfortably.

"Forget him." Defibrio replied soothingly reaching for a cigarette. "He's got nothin' else to do."

He loved to talk about Willy. "A couple of years ago the farm needed another mule to help do the heavy chores. Plowin', haulin' logs, loadin' manure and general farm work. The colonel bought Willy for the army, and boasted about the bargain." Defibrio chuckled. "He never realized why he was so cheap. When the men tried to work him they couldn't get close without gettin' kicked or what's worse, bitten. The colonel belittled the stories and decided to show the men how an ornery mule should be handled. He got us all together and gave a lecture on donkeys, burros and mules."

"'They're usually super-intelligent" he started, trying to ease their fears. 'They never step in a puddle or put a foot where they are unsure. They're too careful to be used in combat. Their reputation for being stubborn is unfair. They are just too smart to follow what they think are dumb orders. Horses, so loyal and willin', can't reason. They will follow their master anywhere. On the steep treacherous trails of the Grand Canyon, burros, not horses, are used.

The same is true in the Southwwest Pacific where artillery pieces have to be hauled up such rough terrain that even tanks are useless."

"It sounds as if he likes them," I said, "and he's right." I recalled the terrible fire in the horse barn on the Ag campus in my senior year. "We had to blindfold the horses to get them out. Three of them shook them off and rushed back to their deaths while the donkeys and mules walked out quietly." The mule was a perfect example of man's creation of hybrid-vigor.

Difbrio gave me a run-down on their breeding. "As a beast of burden he's got more stamina and endurance, can carry heavier loads and is more sure-footed than either the ass or the horse. As the sire of the mule, the donkey has made his contribution to man. A mule is the offspring of a male donkey (jackass) with a female horse (mare). (A hinny is the offspring of female donkey (jenny) and a male horse (stallion)." I remembered reading about them when I was cramming for my state boards.

Defibrio continued the story, "After the lecture one of the men brought Willy over. 'Even the mule can be mastered.' the Colonel said. 'You may have to twist an ear or use a twitch but never let them bulldoze you.'"

Defibrio stopped to take a puff. Then he smiled. "That mule made such a fool of him, the colonel never forgave him. He was standin' with the reins in his hands, lecturin' and jerkin' this poor donkey's head repeatedly, . .needlessly. A horse would just stand there and take it. Finally, I guess Willy had enough. Before the colonel had a chance to show the men anythin', Willy put him where both pride and backside were hurt. He reared up, practically liftin' the colonel off his feet, spun around and let both legs loose in a wild kick. The colonel's past experience saved him. He threw himself aside and landed on his back. The men were stunned. They didn't know whether to help him up or laugh at him. He got to his feet, brushed off his backside, and left. "Anyhow," he continued, "the men loved that mule for his spirit and for showin' up the colonel."

We drove the rest of the way in silence, Defibrio smoking and I thinking about tomorrow.

The next morning we packed the jeep with medical supplies and started for the farm. "How do you think Willy will take to the injections now?" I asked.

"God knows." he answered, as he blew a smoke ring into the windshield. Defibrio didn't seem the least bit worried. He had more concern for the Phenix City cops than he did for the intractable mule.

Calder supervised that day's activities. He was well respected by the other enlisted men and Defibrio just stood aside and observed. Calder was very business-like and competent. The men roped the cattle and sheep and held them for the inoculations. The cattle were T.B. tested and released to the pasture.

Our jeep was set up inside the track about twenty feet from the swinging wood door. Between the track and the barn the harrier had his equipment.

Calder had the men walk the horses and mules to the jeep. I examined them, calling out information for Defibrio to enter in the log. One of the draft horses had bowed tendons, another fistulous withers, a third an infection inside the cheek caused by sharp molars. My confidence was rising with each recognized condition. Being on my own was fun and for each malady I had an effective treatment.

I'd need a speculum (a gadget to keep an equine's mouth ajar) and a file to float his teeth. I wondered if the equipment were available. I asked Dom and he assured me that the colonel had everything available for the treatment of his favorite specie. Each horse and mule got two shots, one for tetanus (lockjaw), the other for equine encephalitis (sleeping sickness). After the injections they were led to the blacksmith.

As Defibrio suggested, Calder kept Willy for last. Like the colonel, he disliked but respected him. Being a horseman all his life he didn't have the patience for unmanageable and undisciplined mules. Calder chose the strongest and most experienced men to help, hoping for the best.

I looked up and saw the cause of the colonel's displeasure.

He was beautiful; black shiny coat over a powerfully muscled body, silvery grey bordered his ears, colored his nozzle and each fetlock. His eyes were brown, bright and intelligent. What a model, I thought, for an artist or photographer.

Willy looked towards me, ears erect. His eyes met mine in what I felt was curiosity. From the stories I'd heard, I could imagine him thinking: "Ha, another one to take care of!" Calder motioned the men to lead him to the jeep and cursed when Willy pulled up sharply, prancing nervously back and forth. Calder was certainly right. He hadn't forgotten. The men were hard put to hang on, and did a little jig to avoid being trampled. Other enlisted personnel, not otherwise involved, began to congregate in small groups to watch what they thought would be a repeat of the previous year. The dust began to fly from Willy's stamping and sliding on the dirt track. The air was still as if everything, including mother nature, awaited the outcome.

Calder was ready this time. He slipped a twitch (a club similar to a policeman's nightstick, a loop of stout cord attached at one end) over one ear and proceeded to twist it like a tourniquet. He was quite skilled and I marveled that he looped the ear on the first try even though Willy's head bobbed up and down in nervous frustration. "Hold still," he threatened, "or I'll pull your god-damn ear off."

At last, Willy, quivering with pain, froze.

"Hold it men." I commanded. "Keep him right there. I'll bring the shots to him." I couldn't see them dragging him by one ear, humiliating him further.

"Bring the stuff with you," I said to Defibrio, over my shoulder.

Walking the ten or so paces, in my mind I could hear Professor Danks.

"Talk to them," he said. "Animals are less suspicious of a noisy stranger. A silent approach implies stealth and possible danger. Remember the equine's blind spot. Because of the position of their eyes they can't see directly in front for a few feet. Always approach from the side."

Willy and I looked at each other again. He eyed me suspiciously and I talked softly as I prepared the shots. "That's right Willy, you're a good boy." I continued, as I reached up and stroked his neck working my hand down to his shoulder. Calder was on the other side twisting his ear.

I reached behind me, Defibrio slapped a wet cotton swab into my palm. Still talking, I dabbed his shoulder then slipped the needle under his skin. He never moved! I reached for the second hypodermic. Another minute and it was over. I had triumphed over uncertainty! I doubted if I made a friend, but at least I talked to him and touched him. I wondered how I would do without that twitch.

"Let him go." I said to Calder. "He knows we're finished. Let the men hang on to the bridle."

Reluctantly Calder obeyed and stepped away. I reached to pat his neck and he jerked his head away. "Come on, Willy, it's all over. How about letting me pat you for your good behavior?" His head came down and I tried again. He jerked away again, not quite as fiercely. He would have no part of me. "Okay Willy," I said as I stepped away, "next time maybe we won't need that twitch."

I turned to Calder, "Have the blacksmith give this mule two new pairs of shoes!"

"Whew! I'm on a roll." I thought out loud. "The general's pup went home good as new and there was no crises with Willy. The colonel might be getting his chickens after all."

On a quiet Sunday morning, I was finally off duty. My alarm was turned off and I was sleeping late. The phone jarred me awake, interrupting a deep repose. My mind cleared and I remembered where I was. Reluctantly, I reached for the phone. Still drowsy, I snapped to attention at the sound of the colonel's booming voice.

"That crazy mule of yours got himself hung up on a fence. Get over to the farm and see what you can do!"

That "mule of yours" must be Willy, I thought.

"Yes sir," I replied as I started putting on my trousers with one hand. "I'm on my way."

"And don't take any chances. If you have to shoot the bastard I've already ordered the MP's over there with men and rifles." and he slammed down the phone.

MP's with rifles! What did he think that mule can do? How could he even consider harming that beautiful animal. The colonel must have heard about Willy and our first meeting. He probably resented my modest success. The picture of Willy hung over a fence, bleeding to death from barbed wire cuts made me shudder.

I called Defibrio, "Dom, the colonel is on the warpath. Something about Willy. He says he is hung-up on a fence and I'd better get out there to check on it. Can you pick me up?"

"Of course, Lieutenant," Dom said. "Right away."

The jeep swayed and squeeked at high speed, then suddenly slowed as Dom remembered the Phenix City police. They wouldn't be sympathetic to any of our problems. We came to a halt at the farm's security gate and were waved through. "He's up at the north field." They yelled, pointing, and we raced the jeep to the fenced-in pasture.

About a half mile away and along the fence we made out the crowd and some vehicles. There were about ten or twelve people, standing together about ten feet from the dark, still form of Willy.

Also an MP automobile and a couple of farm trucks. Willy was standing quietly, one leg grotesquely stuck high on the fence. When they heard us coming, all heads including Willy's turned toward us.

Defibrio jammed on the brakes and I leapfrogged over the door in one motion, waving the men back. Four MP's were among the group, one holding a rifle. Calder was there as well. They stepped back a few yards wondering what we could possibly do.

"You're only making him more nervous." Defibrio said. "Give him some room and maybe he'll let us help him."

Willy stood motionless. He had long since realized he couldn't free himself and had stopped struggling. "Thank God it wasn't a horse," I thought. He would have thrashed himself to death in ten minutes.

I approached, talking quietly as I sized up his predicament. "Whacha doin' big boy? Trying to high jump? You ought to know better." Both hind legs were planted, holding most of his weight. He was wringing wet, his nostrils flared with every whistling breath. His eyes were frantic and pleading. I knew he couldn't kick, even if I got close but there was nothing wrong with his jaws.

We were eyeball to eyeball again. "No shot today, Willy." I said softly as the sour smell of mule sweat hit me.

"Hold still, old boy," I continued, "we're going to get that leg free."

The fence was constructed of two layers of heavy wire. As the men watched I fingered the wire, several feet from where Willy was stuck, trying to figure out what to do. There were no cutters and no time to fetch them. Now I would have to manipulate that hoof, and quickly, before someone decided to use a gun. One strand would have to be lifted with one hand and the other pulled down to release his hoof.

I cautiously put my hand right below his knee and slid it towards the hoof. It was wedged higher than his shoulder. I felt Defibrio at my shoulder. It was just like him to stay near in case I needed him. Willy's skin was hot, and twitched nervously as if chasing off a fly. "Easy boy, easy." I cooed. He remained still. A close look told me I would have to lift his leg with my shoulder so I could use both hands to work the wires. I could have Defibrio help, but two people that close? Better try alone. It was evident that during his earlier, futile tugs he had caused his fetlock to tear and bleed. Blood ran down his hoof making it slippery. His jaw touched my head. Flecks of saliva wet my head and neck. As my hands strained to part the wires, my shoulder began to ache. After an eternity the wires loosened slightly. I begged half aloud, "Now, Willy, now!" He understood and responded as the wires slackened. He suddenly reared back and jerked free as I ducked and threw my arms up to protect my head. There was no need. He deftly twisted away and dropped to all fours. He limped, backing off a few strides, disdainfully eyeing the cheering humans. Only Calder was unmoved. Willy's eyes turned to me as if to say, "I owe you one." He whirled, limped a few more steps and raced off.

Wise old Defibrio pulled me into the jeep and started for the office. Now, I was shaking. He knew the colonel would want a full report. "We'll treat Willy's leg tomorrow." He said. "It'll take a day or so for him to calm down."

As the leisurely moving jeep hummed along, he mused. "I wish the colonel cudda seen Willy's reaction under all that stress. I'm sure he would appreciate him more. You were as cool as he was, Lieutenant and the men respect you for it, except maybe Calder.

"Now what's his gripe?"

"Calder shudda taken care of the incident and been done with it. He knows where the wire cutters are. He wouldn't stick his neck out and went over my head when he called the colonel. He wanted to show you up, Lieutenant, never anticipatin' how you'd handle it." His voice turned harsh. "I'm gonna take care of him!"

"Well, I guess I can thank Willy's brains and temperament. I hope we can convince the colonel to keep him"

"I'm sure we can, Lieutenant. He'd have to sign too many papers and give too many explanations. As long as he's bucking for full colonel, Willy is safe."

Willy stayed and Calder got a laying out from both Defibrio and Vance. The colonel never said a word to me about Willy and the fence. I had the feeling he was a little disappointed.

The day was uneventful and I ate dinner at the Officer's Club. That evening I phoned Helen again. She had been out on my first call and I spoke to another girl.

"Iris speakin". . .Her roommate again.

"Is Helen there?"

"Shucks!", aside and muffled, "It's for you, honey."

"Hello."

"Hi. I'm Ted Zimmerman. Bill Hornsby gave me your number."

"You're Bill's friend. You called before. Ah like him. He's cute and lots of fun. Haven't heard from him in weeks."

"That's why I'm calling. He was ordered out and he wanted me to explain. Can we have dinner some evening?"

"Well uh," She hesistated, "Ah'm goin with a major now." Uh-oh I thought.

"So Iris said." I thought fast. "But it's your duty to see me at least once."

"Mah duty?" She giggled. "How come?"

"Well, when a man is serving his country and is shipped out, and he makes a request, it's only patriotic to grant it.". . Come on Helen!

She laughed and said. "Why don't we have lunch some day. Ah work at the Tank Training School Administration Building. Ah'm off from 12 till 1.

Whew! "How about Thursday? Lunch at the Officer's Club. I'll pick you up at noon."

"Okay. How will ah know you?"

"I'm young, in uniform, and very handsome." I kidded. "Seriously. Look for a black '36 Chevy. I'll be right in front of the entrance. Thursday, at 12 noon. Okay?"

"Okay. But ah'm goin with a major, okay?" She left herself an out.

"Okay."

The end to a perfect day, I thought as I turned out the lights, I hoped she was as cute as Hornsby promised.

At 11:30 AM Thursday, a half hour early, I parked in front of the Tank Training School's administration building. There went my stomach again. I wondered what she looked like. I waited 'till 12 noon and no Helen. . .Well, she's not late yet.

I paced back and forth in front of Jezebel. She's going with a major, I thought! Maybe she won't even show up. 12:07. . .I noticed a cute little blonde approaching.

She was about five feet two, and I found myself very pleased.

"Ted Zimmerman?" She asked her eyebrows raised questioningly.

"Hi, Helen." I said, "Bill Hornsby was absolutely right. You're cute as a speckled pup."

"That Hornsby could convince a Tom turkey to lay eggs." She giggled. "An you sound jus lak him."

I liked her. She was direct, honest, and unafraid to speak her mind. She spoke with a cute Georgia accent. As we made small talk over lunch, I asked her for a real date."

"Ah'm free Saturday." She grinned. "Ma major is on a two week training bivouac."

"Saturday is fine. Where should I pick you up?"

"Ah'll be workin. Right where we met today."

I drove away singing happily. Maybe I found me a girl."

That afternoon I made my first trip to the provision company in Columbus, a frozen food storage plant in the heart of the city. It was a typical 90 degree, humid June day and I couldn't wait to get out of the heat.

I was assigned an Army sedan and Sergeant Harold Taylor, an expert on frozen foods. The plant was kept at twenty degrees below zero and we were given long furry winter coats and gloves. The change from ninety degrees to twenty below was an experience I was soon to get used to. The first minute or two was heavenly but after twenty minutes I was frozen stiff.

One day I told the colonel that the plant manager had offerd me a ham. "Of course I refused," I said. "How does an officer handle those overtures?"

"I meant to talk to you about that." He said. "Don't accept a used hot dog from anyone. You'll have to make decisions for the army that can't be compromised by those bastards. They take advantage of every trick on the book. They 'up' their grades on meal and poultry, try to sell shit to the troops. You and your men have to say no! Save the government a fortune and keep them honest in spite of themselves." The colonel showed me how one grade difference on a carload of chickens could save or lose up to $30,000.

That Friday, I was scheduled to give the detachment my first lecture and I was worried about Calder. Since the incident with Willy, there was an undercurrent of resentment. He still wouldn't look me in the eye. I discussed him with Defibrio.

"I think as time goes by, he'll be okay." He said. "Especially after he sees you work."

In the Army's "chain of command," Calder took his orders from Defibrio, whose immediate superior was myself. I was under the colonel, who kowtowed to the post commanding general. Calder, senior to the enlisted men working the farm, had a lot of influence on them. I was fighting my own battle with a new kind of life and unasked for responsibilites. I was a twenty four year old, lecturing and counseling men thirty five to forty years of age, on topics including sex education, current events and personal hygiene. My classes would be held at the company quarters and occasionally at a different location convenient to the occasion. The topics were usually selected by the post comander, occasionally by the colonel or myself. I thought it wise to talk to Doug Crane since he had some experience with the lectures.

"You're in for a shock, Zim." he confided, "There's a world map in the lecture room. Try asking them some simple questions like; where's Texas, or Europe or what are we fighting for?"

I discovered the truth for myself. First, bringing them up to date on the progress of the war, I asked some of the men to point out Sardinia, our first major invasion target. There was silence. I tried other simple questions that might as well have been designed by the Encyclopedia Brittanica. Calder wasn't much better than the rest but at least he knew where the Southwest Pacific war theater was.

I gave up, disappointed. Trying not to show my disenchantment, I read to them directly from the Army manual, "Ways to protect one's self from contracting venereal disease."

Crane's assessment was correct. The average education of middle America was not good. I decided that for our next class, I would pick the subject. After a short lecture on current events, I decided to talk about something that might interest them: the health and treatment of horses and mules. I decided to have it at the farm where we could have a live demonstration.

On a routine farm visit, I cornered Calder. "I'm planning a lecture and demonstration next Tuesday at 10 o'clock. Round up the men and a couple of horses for a lecture. I plan to show the men how to give medications using the speculum, and how to file molar teeth. If there's time I'll demonstrate the army way to throw a horse, alone." He nodded and said "Yes sir," in a way that showed his annoyance. He obviously thought he was better qualified than I to give such a talk.

The day of the meeting Defibrio piled the stuff I'd need into the jeep and we rode to the farm with our usual police escort. The men formed a semi-circle. The horses were gentle and would make good subjects. I half expected Calder to slip Willy in to make the entire exercise impossible. I wanted to show them procedures they could use without undue restraint or sedation.

"Liquids are given by stomach tube." I told them as I lubricated the slender rubber catheter, then passed it through one of the horse's nostrils, down his throat, inducing the swallow that passed it into his stomach, I pointed out the outline of the tube as it passed along his neck, in the esophagus, like a pelican swallowing a fish. I had each man put his hand on the horse's neck to feel it going down.

I hoped they got the same thrill I did when I was a freshman, learning to deal with equine medicine and physiology. I had given them all the positives about medicating through stomach tube, then I mentioned the possible problems, before Calder had the chance to criticize behind my back.

"A complication would be if the horse didn't swallow the tube and it went down the wrong way. If that were to happen you wouldn't see or feel the tube, and the animal would cough his head off. We wouldn't want to pour liquid into a horse's lungs, now would we?"

The way to check that it was in the right place, I told them, was by putting the end of the tube to one's ear and listening for breathing sounds. They would be loud and clear every time the horse took a breath, and more-so if he coughed.

I had each man hold the catheter to his ear and listen. When all were convinced that it was placed correctly, I attached a funnel to the exposed end and emptied half a bucket of water into it, like adding a pint of oil to an automobile engine.

The experienced horsemen had seen and used the tubes many times. The neophytes were as incredulous as I had been.

"As you can see," I concluded, "the foulest tasting medicine can be given without objection."

I pulled the feeding tube out, and continued.

As I talked, Calder was carrying on his own private conversation with some men to the rear of the group. When I stopped and glared, he paused, only to resume when I did. Defibrio walked back to shut him up.

"Boluses (large horse pills) are given directly into the mouth, either by bare hand, with the help of a speculum, with a dosing gun or both. The safest way is with the speculum and the balling gun."

I held the gadget up and proceeded to demonstrate. By placing the straps over the head and the metal grips into the mouth, it worked just like a bridle.

"God created the perfect mouth for the bridle and the speculum." I lifted the horse's lip to illustrate. "Notice the space between the front teeth and the molars. A man can slide his hand through there without the danger of being bitten. With a little experience you can reach through there, grab his tongue and pull it to one side between his back teeth, to keep his mouth open."

I illustrated again and continued. "The bit' rests in that space, and the horse learns that when the right reign is tugged, he must turn right and vice versa.

"When the speculum is in place you can force the mouth open by pressing the jaws apart with your hands. The gears have several teeth so you can keep his mouth open from one inch to four or five. When the jaws are forced open, the gears lock like an automobile jack and hold fast, like this." I showed them. "They can't close their mouths until the catch is released."

I was sure Calder had used it a hundred times, and only Defibrio's presence kept him quiet. "You take a bolus this way." I held the attached speculum with one hand, reached far into his mouth with the other, holding the huge pill, and dropped it into his throat. The horse swallowed easily.

"It's only sugar, men," I assured them, "we're not forcing them to take medicine.

"The balling gun is an ingenious gadget that does the same thing except one doesn't have to put his hands into the mouth at all. As you can see it's like a huge hypodermic syringe with a plunger that shoots the bolus into the horse's throat. Like this." I showed them again.

"There is one more use for the speculum," I concluded, "that you will all get a chance to practice. It's filing sharp molar teeth. Horsemen use the term "floating". As you can see floating is a simple procedure when the speculum is in place." I took a huge rasp and demonstrated by filing a few of the back teeth.

"Any questions men?" I asked.

One of the men held up his hand.

"Yes Hanson."

"Isn't it good for a horse to have sharp teeth? Why file them at all?

"Good question. Sharp molars can cut the insides of the cheek causing infection and soreness. When you notice a horse chewing gingerly, or if he stops eating, report it and we will use the speculum to examine him. If his cheeks are cut, a few strokes of the file will correct the condition."

"Anything else?" I asked.

Calder couldn't restrain himself. "The speculum is fine for floating teeth, but why waste all that time attaching a speculum when you can dose a horse without one?" He walked from the back of the circle and picked up a bolus, reached into the horses mouth barehanded, a bolus between his thumb and index fingers, backhanded the horse's tongue, forcing it out and back between his teeth. In that position, he deftly dropped the pill into the back of his throat.

The men were impressed and Calder reveled in his hotshot exhibition.

"If you don't mind, Calder." I said, "In the army we'll save our fingers and use the speculum." I continued, "A horse will never bite his own tongue so that procedure is safe if one has experience and the animal is gentle. However, I know of someone who tried that method on a mean old mule and had his arm bitten off."

I proceeded to my final subject, "Occasionally you will find it necessary to throw a horse, alone. The gadget I have here," I pointed to a heavy halter, surcingle and crupper lying at my feet, "is what the army recommends, called the Galveyne's method."

It was a clumsy but effective way for one man to throw a horse or mule. As I prepared to demonstrate its use, Calder interrupted again. I was becoming more and more upset and wondered how far to let him go before pulling rank; not my style in handling men.

"Using straps and rings," he said, "attached to each fetlock is better and quicker. It takes all day to attach that gadget."

I glared. "Calder, are you implying that your method is better than the Army's official choice?"

He shrugged his shoulders. "It is with a good horseman using it."

"Would you condede that every soldier may not be a 'good horseman' and would be wiser using the Army's choice?"

As he shrugged again I remembered the trick question the professors taught us while preparing for the New York State Board's practical examinations.

I picked up a coil of rope lying close by and tossed it to Calder.

"Let's see 'the good horseman' throw that horse alone with just the rope. No rings, no halter, no bridle."

As he caught the rope he glared at it. The men crowded close, intrigued by the bandying. He eyed the horse, the rope, then me. "No way Lieutenant." he said with conviction. "It can't be done."

There was something he didn't know.

I took the rope from his hands and looked at the men. "Any good horseman can do it." I said casually. I looped the rope around the horse's neck and tied a slip knot at the shoulder. With one hand I placed a half hitch around a hind fetlock, with the other, lifted the leg to a raised position keeping the rope taut. The horse rested on three legs. Then I looped each of the remaining fetlocks, again with half hitches. Pressing my shoulder against his side, a sudden push towards the raised leg sat him down. Another pull of the rope and his front end followed, throwing him on his side. Two more half hitches and he was hog tied. I exulted but kept a straight face.

The look on Calder's face was worth a month's pay.

The men had been uncomfortable with his arrogance, and they looked at me, first with surprise, then respect.

"That's it for today, men. Calder! Undo the horse. Have them walked, bathed and curried before feeding."

That evening I couldn't resist telling Helen the story. We were at the officer's club and we sat by ourselves near the dance floor. Glancing across the room. I noticed Beulah Mae sitting with several officers and girls.

"That girl across the dance floor works in our office. She's the Small Animal Clinic receptionist." I said pointing her out to Helen.

"Ah went to school with her." Helen said with a distasteful look. "Ah never liked her."

"Neither do I. But I have to work with her."

We danced and talked and laughed till midnight. I took her home in the thickest fog I ever saw. I had to drive with the parking lights on and my head out of the open window. I couldn't see where we were, so she had to direct me.

The next morning I got a very frigid shoulder from Beulah Mae. She filed her nails furiously, frowning, legs crossed as usual.

"I understand you know Helen Modell?" I ventured.

"One would think an officer could do better than date po' white trash. You might as well take out a nigra."

"She's a great date." I said.

"She's nothing but trash, always has been. Po', Georgia, fuckin' 'white trash!" She was irate, threw the file into the top drawer and slammed it shut, spun in her chair and began typing furiously.

In a few weeks the workings of the hospital routine began to gel. Mornings were devoted to small animals. Two afternoons a week, Mondays and Fridays were for large animal clinic. Tuesday and Thursday were for working the Columbus Provision Company.

Visits to the farm were rare, I never seemed to have time to check out the animals or the kennels. Occasionally Defibrio and I took the slow trip through Phenix City to visit with Calder, Stern and the other men. There never was a problem and we always hurried back.

My lectures began to bear fruit. The men were learning to read a map and follow the war's progress. Most of them were happy to learn and anxious for current event's reading assignments.

One morning Defibrio told me he had a call from Calder. The ram was sick. He had stopped eating and looked peculiar. He couldn't walk and couldn't lie down.

"Let's drive out after lunch." I suggested.

"Good idea."

As we drove into the compound we looked toward the pasture. The ram was standing apart. His problem was obvious.

"He has tetanus, Dom." Frozen in the typical 'war-horse' stance we had been taught to recognize. At that stage his condition was hopeless.

"Is it treatable?" Dom asked.

"I'm afraid not. Tetanus, is like our "lock jaw". Like hydrophobia or rabies, it's a deadly neurological disease. He's in the terminal stage. He'll have to be destroyed. He must have been injured within the last two weeks from a deep, penetrating wound that didn't bleed. There's Calder. Let's ask him about it."

"I don't recall anything unusual till this morning." he told us, shifting his weight from side to side. He obviously thought my questioning was a reprimand.

The animal couldn't move. He was frozen upright. His eyes had a staring, desperate look. I checked each leg separately and found a weeping wound between two clod hooves. He was so rigid I had trouble examining them. He was shedding excessively and a sour unhealthy odor emanated from his body.

"He must have stepped on a sharp object. Had we discovered it within a couple of days, vaccine would have protected him. It's like the tetanus shots you men get after a deep wound. Before paralysis sets in, antiserum is effective. I'll come right back later and put him down. No reason for him to suffer."

I always resented preventable death. It was an insult to my profession and to me personally. As I left I said half aloud, "He has such beautiful horns." A few days after, Defibrio had a surprise package for me. "Calder prepared this for you," he said, "I guess he's apologizing and making his peace." I opened it to find the horns, cleaned and mounted: a good luck momento I cherish to this day.

Pay Murphy was assigned to the large animal clinic. She was the post athlete and the baseball diamond she loved was just outside the clinic door. One afternoon, late in June, we had completed treating some horses. Pay Murphy assisted and had such a sad look on her face I visualized all sorts of tragedies. "What's the trouble, private? You look awful."

"Nothing serious, sir," she said with a winsome smile. "I just don't have anyone to play catch with. Lola is in sick bay, and Mary is on ten day pass." They were the other WACs assigned to the clinic. Pat had drafted them into her baseball world of late afternoon play. "It's such a beautiful day." She sighed. "We should be playing softball!"

"Have you an extra glove?" I asked. I hadn't played ball since college, and besides I wanted to see if she was as good as everyone said.

Her face lit up and we played catch for a few minutes. I hit grounders, then fungoed fly balls. She was fabulous. Her enthusiasm was catching. By the following week good players from other outfits were enticed to join. Occasionally the ever-present GIs were dragged out of the spectators ranks to coach or bat grounders to the girls. Before long there were two softball practices a week.

One afternoon I joined the girls and started a game. Their contagious screams of delight attracted enough GI's for two teams, twelve WACS and six men. Colonel Kielsmeier heard the racket and came to investigate. He loved to watch his girls cavort, and suggeseted after several sessions that they join the local WAC Benning softball league and that I, the only officer on the field, be the coach.

That week, events unfolding elsewhere and seeming completely unrelated, would become a momentous part of my life.

The New York Times explained that on Monday, July 19, 1943, (the same day we were holding an afternoon baseball practice), Miss Elaine B. Wolf, a Davis High School senior in Mount Vernon, New York, smashed a bottle of champagne against the bow of the new sub-chaser, PCS 138 at the City Island shipyards. She won the privilege and honor by selling the greatest number of bonds in a war bond selling contest. She said as she launched the ship, "Here's a Mount Vernon blow against the Axis. Lets hope it helps bring all our boys home soon."

Elaine was the skinny, buck toothed, kid sister of Reneé Wolf. I had met her and her parents at Cornell the year before. I didn't see the article or her picture in the papers until long after the event. Four years later, in fact, when I came home from the war. At this time I was treated to a "blind," date by my former roommate, Marvin and his wife Reneé. I was enchanted with the transformation of the family "baby", to an attractive and provocative young woman.

Before the start of the small animal clinic, one morning, Vance motioned me to his desk. "The Colonel wants to see you before you leave." he said, "And don't look so worried, it's probably just routine."

I headed for his office before lunch, hoping my fears were groundless. I glanced at Beulah Mae, and just to spite her, I smiled and nodded a greeting that was still ignored.

"The colonel left word for you to go right in." Vance said. "I told you not to worry, he just wants to brief you on the wild boar hunts."

"Dom mentioned them a couple of times." I said, "What are they like?"

"Don't ask me. I don't ride. Dom loves them though. I've tasted the fresh roast pork, and it sure is delicious." He smacked his lips at the thought and looked at Beulah Mae, "You were there once, with that infantry officer."

"I remember," she said and went back to her work.

I entered Kielsmeier's office, interrupting a putting session on the rug. He had moved the arm chair to one side leaving a six to eight foot clearance for the ball.

"Good morning, sir. You sent for me?"

"Yes Lieutenant," he rested his club and sat. "Have a seat. Pull that chair up. How are things going? By now you should be comfortable with your duties."

"Yes sir, everything's fine."

"Can you ride horseback?" Here comes the wild boars, I thought, and I wasn't sure how to answer it.

"Uh,. . .yes sir." He should have asked how well I could ride.

He continued, "One of your duties is to accompany the horses and dogs on our summer boar hunts. The event means a lot to the officers. Gives them something exciting to look forward to on Sundays." The colonel settled back in his chair, elbows on the arm rests, fingers entwined under his chin.

"It's a feather in our caps, Lieutenant, because there wouldn't be a hunt without our horses, dogs and men. That's where you come in." He leaned forward to impress me with its importance, "The chase can be hazardous for the animals. We hope it will be for the pigs," he grinned. "But you won't have to treat them." Then seriously. "A wild boar can be pretty nasty, especially if his family is nearby. The dogs, howling and barking and sniffing, pick up their scent and run them down." He rose from his chair to better illustrate the movements of the dogs and their quarry. "They surround them or back them into a corner." His arms gave emphasis to the action. "The dogs never attack but they must be agile and alert." He had paced around the office and was behind me. I half turned to watch his face, his disfigurement accentuated by the intensity of his chatter.

"You know the boar's reputation. The horses, dogs and even the men have to be on their toes. We've only had a couple of minor incidents in the past, but it pays to be prepared."

"Will you be riding with us, sir?" I asked. I had never seen him on a horse but Dom had intimated that he was an expert equestrian.

"I'm afraid not, Lieutenant. You're on your own. I let the younger men chase the boar now. They're full of piss and vinegar and its good for them to get out and ride. You'll be the first veterinary officer in charge of the hunt in over a year.

"I don't want the horses run too hard or too long." He continued. "Most of them belong to the army and they're our responsibility. Six of the mounts are the personal property of the officers. They pay for their feed and board. If you see any signs of abuse to the Army horses by anyone," he stopped to emphasize his remarks, "that means any rank! You are under my orders to consider the horse first and act accordingly!"

He was frowning. "That's all, Lieutenant." He reached for his putter and I knew he would resume his practice.

"Yes sir!" I answered, getting up. "Pardon, sir. Are the boars close to the post? Do the men have a long ride to find them?"

"About ten miles in the spring," he explained, "as the summer progresses, the pursuit drives them further into the hills." He set his golf club down again. "They had been domesticated at the end of World War I and turned loose after the armistice. Now there are hundreds, wild as tigers. So we have sport for the men who love horses and dogs and crave the hunt." He paused, turned to gaze out of the window and continued. "We kill the boar and barbecue the sow and piglets. It makes for quite a Sunday night feast." He turned back and looked me in the eye. "The wives and kids come to what's become a tradition and Mrs. Kielsmeier runs the show."

He grinned. "You got a girl, Lieutenant?"

"I uh, have a few friends back home." I wouldn't ask Helen until I was sure I wasn't going to make a fool of myself.

"Well, if you meet someone," and his eyes twinkled mischievously, "be sure to invite her."

"What does Sgt. Defibrio do on the hunt, sir?" I asked, quickly changing the subject.

"Defibrio is the expert. He'll fill you in." He started to wave me away, thought for a moment, and continued.

"There is no rank on these hunts, Lieutenant, except yours. You're on duty! You'll probably be the only officer in uniform and as I said before, you'll outrank everyone there."

I turned to leave, wondering!

"By the way, Lieutenant," he called, "be sure to check the dogs. I don't want any hounds infected with heartworm dropping dead on the run. That's all."

I pictured myself taking charge of a bunch of officers I didn't know and had reservations about riding on a furious cross-country chase. In addition there was boning up to do on heartworm disease and not much time for testing the dogs. My experience with that ailment was cursory. We covered the subject in parasitology but not in much depth because the disease was only endemic in the south.

That night, it was 2:00 A.M., the M.P.'s on night patrol noted a light in one of the rooms at the BOQ. My text books and college notes were all over my bed. I was cramming, just like I did in school, to refresh my memory of a thousand details. After going over the notes, I realized that it would be best for me to make mental lists the way I did in school. I began.

First: Heartworm is a tropical parasitic disease contracted like malaria, spread by mosquitoes that inject hundreds of larvae (filaria) into the blood with each bite.

Two: They grow into huge worms that live in the heart and interfere with the closing of the valves.

Three: The first signs are a cough, then progressive weakness and, if untreated, certain death.

Four: It is diagnosed by history, heart sounds and a direct blood smear.

Fifth: There is an effective preventative pill, that must be given daily. I stopped. There's one more. I concentrated, holding the first finger of my other hand.

Oh yes, once infected, the only cure is intravenous therapy.

There, I had my six facts, gave a sigh, closed the book, put my college notes away, turned out the lights and slept untroubled until 7:00 A.M.

The next morning at the office, before clinic hours, I cornered Difibrio. "Dom, the colonel ordered me to ride on Sunday's boar hunt."

"Good, Lieutenant, glad to have you along." He grinned. "I wondered when he would talk to you about it."

"He isn't sending me to enjoy myself, Sarg." I was frowning. "He said I would be in uniform and in charge. He made it sound like I'd be running a roving ambulatory clinic. I really don't mind, but I haven't ridden a horse in six years and I've never been good at it."

"Not to worry, lieutenant, I'll let you have Shamrock. He's General George Marshall's horse. He asked me to have good men ride him to keep him in shape. He's a big, strong, intelligent and very gentle animal, already gelded and just ideal for an inexperienced rider. Even if you should get lost, just drop the reins and say 'home boy.'"

"Sounds good to me." Then I turned my attention to the dogs.

"Sergeant, would you arrange a time for me to see the kennels and check the hounds?"

"How about tomorrow, Lieutenant?"

"Great," I said, "the sooner the better."

The following day we took the jeep and drove to the farm. Defibrio's eyes followed Phenix City's omnipresent police car through the mirror.

"Tell me about Corporal Stern." I said.

"He ran an A.S.P.C.A. shelter as a civilian in upstate New York. It had the reputation of being the best run shelter in the state. He really knows his dogs. He was assigned here primarily because of his experience."

"That's rare for the army, isn't it? I would expect him to be assigned to inspect a hot dog factory."

Defibrio laughed, "It was a rare assignment but we can thank the colonel for that one. He demands quality men for all his services."

We approached the kennels, unusually quiet for a change. "They must be napping." Defibrio mused as we entered Stern's office. It was neat as a pin and I was sure there were G.I.'s doing cleanup every day. Defibrio had called ahead and Stern was expecting us.

"Corporal," I asked as I spied him bent over a file on the far side of the room. "The colonel asked me to check the dogs before the hunt next week. Any problems?"

"They all seem okay, lieutenant." He said, slamming the file shut and approaching us near his desk. "There's always an occasional case of diarrhea or once in a while, one or two will catch cold."

"I'm sure you didn't have much experience with heartworm disease in New York," I said, "but, down here there must be lots of mosquitoes, and you know what that means.

"There are, sir, but I never saw a case of heartworm since I've been here."

"Are they getting their medications daily?"

"Yes sir!" he said emphatically. "Every dog, every day."

"What about their rabies and distemper boosters?"

"Everything, sir, we have records with dates on every hound here." He pointed back to his files.

"When were they tested for heartworm, last, corporal?"

"All were negative six months ago, sir."

"Let's test them again. At Cornell we read about negative tests that were proved false two weeks later. It won't take long. We'll do five or six a day and be finished by Friday. How about 3 o'clock tomorrow at the clinic?" Stern nodded.

"Now let's tour your kennels." I said. "I should have done this weeks ago but never seemed to have the time."

Stern jumped up, anxious to show off. Defibrio had mentioned how proud he was of the dogs and the kennels. He held the door open and we entered the immaculate indoor quarters of concrete and tile. Each kennel was a comfortable size and backed up to a self-operating swing-door that opened to its own outside exercise run.

As we walked outside, a huge, brown, handsome, dog was waiting with a wagging tail. He was the only canine not confined. A beautiful wrinkle-faced Bloodhound whose eyes never left Stern. I reached down and petted him and his nose touched my leg. He sniffed Defibrio and the wagging increased in tempo as he acknowledged an old friend. Dom reached down and fondled his wrinkled forehead.

"Your dog Corporal?" I asked. "He's a beauty. Looks like a show dog."

"He's good enough to be, lieutenant. He's Brany, our lead hound. He was here before I was but we just hit it off and now he's my favorite."

The other dogs heard us and when we appeared, happy bedlam ensued. As we walked around, the friendly howls were accompanied by wildly wagging tails.

"Very nice, gentlemen." I yelled, "I'm sure the colonel is more than proud of these kennels."

"Thank you, sir." The corporal shouted over the happy din. "The dogs like company and they love to hunt. I think they just live for summer Sundays, and to tell you the truth, so do I."

The twenty dogs were Beagles, Bloodhounds and Foxhounds.

"How come there are no Setters, Pointers, or Spaniels?" I asked Stern.

"To track the boar," he explained, "ground scenters are needed, and Setters, Spaniels and Pointers are air scenters."

Stern lowered his voice as the hounds, after their initial excitement, settled down to quiet tail wagging and an occasional yelp.

I learned something never taught at Cornell. I decided to test him further. "What about other great hunting breeds, like the Russian Wolf Hound?"

Stern was ready with the answer, "Salukis and Borzois (Russian Wolfhound), are also sight hunters."

I wondered about my old pet, Silver. "My dog was a Schnauzer," I said, "he was quick as lightning, I bet he would do well against wild boars."

Stern shook his head. "The terriers are useless for chasing pigs," he volunteered. "They 'go to earth' or follow prey down burrowed holes."

He certainly knew more than I did about hounds and their specializations. I turned to the huge Bloodhound at our feet and rubbed his ears. His wet nose touched my arm, reinforcing the cognition that added me to his list of two-legged friends. I liked Brany, and Stern was happy to have someone interested in his favorite hound, he filled me in on the Bloodhound's history.

"They are the oldest and the progenitor of all the hound dogs." He lectured. "They were carefully bred in Europe, long before the crusades. They were known as the "blooded hounds," the dogs of royal ancestry. They never attack, they just use their magnificent sense of smell. Most of us are acquainted with their finesse in hunting down criminals."

As we returned to the quiet of the office, Brany at our heels, Stern motioned for us to sit. Brany curled up under Stern's desk.

Defibrio explained. "Corporal Stern directs the dogs. He scouts the hills with Brany a day or so before the hunt. On Sunday he knows exactly what direction to start the pack." He turned to Stern.

"Tell the lieutenant how you and Brany work."

Stern loved to talk. He smiled, settling comfortably in his chair. "The Saturday before the hunt I look for some pig droppings or just footprints with Brany, and that is enough for his nose. Off he goes in the direction of the boar's family. There is other game out there but he knows it's the pigs we are after. I keep him leashed for the practice run so he doesn't scare them away."

Stern continued the lecture as he stroked Brany's head affectionately, "We usually track a family on Saturday evening. When it gets dark they stop, nest, and remain until daybreak. Sunday morning Brany starts the pack off in the right direction. The dogs have become so expert in finding their quarry that there has never been a wasted hunt since I've been here. They back the swine into a corner and hold them until Dom arrives with the other horsemen."

"Pot's right, lieutenant," Defibrio chimed in, "the dogs make the chase a success."

I looked at Brany. "Is he agile enough to keep out of trouble? He seems such a quiet, deliberate animal."

"He and the other two Bloodhounds just do the tracking. They back away once the pigs are cornered and leave the harrying to the other hounds. Stern and Defibrio were excited as they talked and explained the finer points of catching boar. They left the climax of the hunt to my imagination.

Defibrio explained the logistics. "The men gather at the stables at 9 A.M., warm up their horses and await the start. The dogs finally move, and in an interminable five minutes, the horses follow." It sounded exciting and I was beginning to understand their anticipation.

Monday morning Stern arrived with the first five hounds. They had been to the clinic before and showed their fear with flattened ears and tails tucked beneath their legs.

The next day, four others came. Brany was one of them. He knew and greeted me with a lick and a wag. I drew his blood sample. There wasn't even a flinch. Brany was a purebred through and through.

By Friday we were finished. Two of the twenty tested positive. They were brought back and left in hospital cages for treatment. Both were sad-eyed beagles.

Sunday was almost at hand. I could see the suspense in the eyes of the enlisted men and the excitement was contagious. Though not in the hunt, they reveled with vicarious pleasure. They were the chosen few who would serve the food to the hunters as they returned from the hills, breathless, flushed with excitement on sweating, prancing steeds.

Those in charge of the cook-out had the grills, fireweed, dishes and silverware ready to go. Mrs. Kielsmeier had been there late Saturday and her house-wife eye had planned every detail. Picnic tables were unfolded and set up in prearranged positions. The butchers and cooks had their tools assembled. They were responsible for slaughtering, bleeding and preparing the meat. The quartermaster would supply the lettuce, tomatoes, peppers, onions, carrots, parsley and grated cheese that made up the delicious salad that accompanied the roast pork. Candied yams, turnip greens, grits and sausage rounded out the southern style feast. Mrs. Kielsmeier had a long list that was followed and checked off like battlefield orders from the commanding general. Finally, there would be an apple for the pig's mouth while roasting.

Sunday morning at 7:45, I met Defibrio at the Post Hospital. I watched him pack a saddle bag with instruments and medical supplies.

It had rained hard all night and Defibrio mentioned that sometimes scents are diluted by a rain. A cold front had moved through and the temperature was a cool 65 degrees. As we drove he rambled on about horses, hunting, fishing, the dogs etc., little of which I heard. I had my own thoughts about the unknown.

The stables and track looked different. The place was buzzing with activity. The enlisted men had saddled the horses and had them lined up outside their stalls. They showed their excitement by prancing about and little deposits of manure scattered at their feet.

I watched some of the officers warming up their horses. By 9 o'clock most had arrived, dressed in civilian clothes or riding habit. The silver bar on my military cap was the only emblem of rank. Some of the men drank coffee as they chatted in small groups. Before long. they mounted and joined the early-birds.

I didn't know a soul and couldn't tell an officer from a guinea hen. Defibrio took me over to the railing and whispered for me to observe the horses as they circled the track. "Once we get moving," he said, "it will be impossible to see any medical problem or pick up a lameness. When and if all is okay, you can mount Shamrock." He pointed to a steed standing quietly in front of his stall. His only movement was a swishing tail.

"The riders will see you in uniform and they'll know you are the officer in charge." Defibrio said. "I'll introduce you to the men before we start."

The excitement mounted. I looked over to the dogs who were howling and yapping, tails wagging non-stop. They were in a small fenced-in area about a hundred feet from the stalls. Stern was already mounted, his pot belly hanging over his belt, waiting for the starting signal. He kept one hand on the gate that he would throw open, the minute the signal came.

Most of the men wore side-arms. Four or five had hunting rifles tucked into their saddle bags. As I watched them ride by, some walking, some cantering, and a few in full gallop, I noticed one horse favoring a foreleg. Here goes, I said to myself as I slipped between the railings. I walked onto the track and flagged down the rider.

"Pardon me, sir," I said to the young blond officer, about thirty years old. "I'd like to check your horse. Have you noticed him limping?"

The soldier was dressed in civilian sports clothes, wore high boots, and carried a riding crop and side arms.

"No lieutenant. Chief's fine. I rode him last week and all he needs is a ten minute gallop to warm up."

"I'd better look at that leg. It will just take a minute." I walked around to his left side, stroking the horse's shoulder then ran my hands down the left foreleg from the shoulder to the knee. Chief stood quietly, obviously used to handling. I examined the knee, lifting it and flexing it as far as it would go. There was no pain to the touch nor flinch to the flex. The cannon down to the fetlock was cool and sound. I picked up the hoof to examine the frog and the shoe. The hoof was hot. Recalling Professor Frost's advice: "Never trust one hand to test temperature. If your hand is cold the hoof will seem hot, and if hot, the reverse is true. Feel both hooves together, one hand on each."

For sure there was a problem. The left hoof was burning, the right, cool to the touch.

"I'm sorry, sir." I said, "This horse shouldn't be ridden today. He has laminitis. Running could cause permanent damage. We'll get you another animal."

"Bullshit, Lieutenant! There's nothing a little workout won't correct."

Like magic, we were the center of attention. Cantering animals slowed to a walk and walking horses close by came to a halt. I picked up the leg in question, and held it firm. The animal didn't mind and couldn't move.

"Is he your horse, sir?" I asked looking him in the eye. "If he is, go ahead. But if he is army property I'm ordering you to dismount!"

Two or three of the riders who had slowed, sauntered over.

"What's the trouble, Lieutenant?" One of the older men, obviously of higher rank, asked.

"This horse is foundered, sir. He shouldn't be ridden today."

"I know enough about horses to tell if one is lame." the young officer retorted angrily. "He's just lazy and needs a good hard run!"

"His left hoof is burning up sir," I answered, ignoring the outburst. "It should be in an ice bucket, not running cross-country."

Where was Defibrio when I needed him?

The older officer addressed the complainer. "Captain Merritt, are you questioning the judgment of a veterinary surgeon? I'd advise you to get another horse."

That seemed to settle the problem. Thank God for rank! I released the hoof, returning the animal to all fours.

Just then, Defibrio approached. He had noticed the disturbance from the paddock and figured I might need him.

"What's the trouble, sir?"

"The captain's horse pulled up lame, sergeant. Can you assign him another mount? Then have that left foreleg soak in a bucket of ice till we get back."

"Fine lieutenant, no problem. We have two or three horses we can saddle in a minute. Gentlemen," he said addressing the officers, "this is our new veterinary officer, Lieutenant Zimmerman. He's been assigned by Colonel Kielsmeier to supervise the hunt."

They all nodded and a couple smiled a greeting.

Merritt dismounted and glared at me. I stared back, not about to be intimidated. Defibrio led the horse away, with Merritt trudging behind. While walking he rhythmically and angrily slapped the riding crop against his thigh. I hoped Defibrio would give him a tired old nag. In my estimation he didn't deserve a good horse. Defibrio passed the lame horse along to an enlisted man and relayed my orders for ice and rest. He must have told him to get another mount for Merritt because they both entered the barn as Defibrio turned and walked back toward me.

"He was really giving me a hard time," I complained. "One of the senior riders backed me up."

He grinned as he heard the details. "So you met Captain Merritt. I guess you can see what the colonel meant."

"I'm going to suggest that he ban Merritt from future hunts. For the good of the service of course." I growled, still hurt that he didn't take my word.

"The trouble is," Defibrio said, "he's a damn good soldier. Absolutely fearless. Has a chest full of medals already. He's just too intense. I'd rather have him next to me in combat than some of the others."

The riders wheeled their mounts and the warm-up proceeded again. Dom turned and waved to Stern who pushed open the gate for the chafing, howling dogs. They took off in a frantic rush led by the bloodhounds, each straining to reach their prey first. I remembered that we had about five minutes before the horses would follow.

I turned to see Merrit on his new horse. He wasn't happy with him. I could tell because he kept jerking the reins from side to side. I thought I'd talk to him again if he continued to abuse the poor animal. The other riders waited for Defibrio's signal, their animals pranced impatiently, heads bobbing and tails swishing.

I finally mounted Shamrock and got myself ready. I rode straight toward Merritt who was finally sitting quietly in his saddle. I wanted him to know that I was watching him. At the same time, like the others, I kept an eye on Dom. I was the only rider that didn't get the chance to warm up and that griped me. I was the one that really needed it.

Defibrio's horse suddenly reared, turned and charged after the dogs, the others thundered behind. I trailed the field, riding carefully, keeping the men and horses in sight. I noticed that Merritt was one of the last riders in the group. He must have gotten a slow horse because I saw him using his crop, whipping his steed, trying to keep up with the pack.

The ground was wet from the rain and Shamrock's legs were soaked after running just a few feet in the deep brush. I could see clearly about 300 feet, peering over the low growing vegetation. Shamrock was obedient and smooth and I gained confidence with every stride. I felt exhilarated, riding a wonderful horse, chasing men, horses, dogs and wild boar.

It was ten minutes into the ride when I noticed a few of the horses had changed direction and speed. They appeared to be milling around. One of the riders braced a rifle under his arm and discharged it. Then they all broke into a gallop, riding back in my direction.

I was in a clearing in the underbrush when suddenly a dark, stocky animal, dripping wet, burst from the rain-soaked, underbrush. He ran in my direction. Shamrock and I spied the boar at the same moment. The horse planted both forelegs in a sudden stop, the momentum sending me flying headlong. As I landed on the soggy, wet turf, the cold mud soaked through my trousers. There wasn't time to think or move. I was thirty feet from two fearsome, razor sharp tusks. The beady eyed boar was bloody and furious. We stared at each other for an instant. I didn't dare move. The boar glared over my head at Shamrock, whose usual quiet demeanor had changed. He pranced nervously, shifting his weight from side to side, then shook his head and snorted. The boar then lowered his head and charged. He was so close I could smell him. I was frightened to death. I tried to rise again. All of a sudden Shamrock, with flashing hooves, reached over me and with both fore-legs, struck at the boar. The charging animal rolled over backwards. He struggled upright, angrier than before, blood pouring from his shoulder. It ran down his foreleg making a small crimson puddle around one leg.

I rolled to my side and stood up. At that moment two of the riders burst through the underbrush. Both men had guns drawn. The boar held his injured leg just off the ground for a moment, then lowered his head again.

One of the officers dismounted, leaving the safety of his horse. He shouted and waved his arms, distracting the animal again. The boar hesitated, changed his direction, and went for the noisy, moving form. The selfless man, in one motion, raised his revolver and calmly fired two rounds. The boar quivered for just a second, then lay still.

"Why are you off your horse, Lieutenant?" Said Merritt with a satisfied grin on his face.

I looked at him sheepishly. "I'm certainly grateful you found another horse, Captain. I sure do owe you! That took a lot of guts and a damn good shot. Thanks."

"You're welcome, Lieutenant." He said as he remounted, wheeled his horse, his riding crop flailing, and left in a wild gallop. I followed slowly, stroking Shamrock's broad neck, grateful to be alive.

It wasn't long before I neared the dog's excited howling. The hounds had been successful and the riders converged from all sides. In a small clearing I saw the action unfold. The dogs had their prey backed up to a cliff-like formation of rock. Twenty riders watched the very nervous boar protecting his family: a sow and about eight small pigs. The boar lowered his head, swinging it from side to side, razor sharp tusks parrying the charging dogs as they alternated their thrusts. He was smaller than the one Merritt shot. The sow paced back and forth behind him. The little ones squealed and tried to stay beneath her as she moved. Something inside my head recoiled from the ritual. The animals hadn't been bothering a soul and were being harried and frightened to distraction.

The dogs never got close enough to be hurt. Defibrio and one armed officer dismounted just behind them. As the dogs taunted the snorting male, Defibrio walked towards him. Timing his action like a professional wrestler, he grabbed both hind legs from behind as the boar slashed at a charging hound. In one skilled motion Dom lifted, twisted then threw him on his side and sat on his hip, hanging on to the struggling limbs. Unable to get up, the boar frantically pawed the air with his forelegs. One rifle shot and all was still.

Stern ordered the dogs back. Their work was done. The sow cowered against the rocks, her pigs fighting each other for cover. One of the men waved his hat at the sow's head to distract her while Defibrio got in position. He threw her in the same way and sat on her, grinning. Two hunters dismounted and within seconds had her hog-tied. She would be slaughtered and bled later. The sow was lifted and draped over the back of one of the horses. A couple of piglets were captured and the rest allowed to scamper away.

I watched disbelieving, amazed at the drama.

My experience with hunting had been limited to a simple wild turkey hunt with Sonny Zeller as a child in Montvale, New Jersey many, summers before.

What innocence, I thought, as time evaporated like mist in a windstorm. Watching that turkey for weeks had made my adrenaline flow. His nest was about a hundred feet from our parking spot, opposite our neighbors, the Volk's. The weeds were taller than my head. I watched that turkey come and go—a huge, graceful bird that floated back and forth several times daily. The need to catch a wild turkey was overwhelming but no one could get within ten feet of the nest without it taking off.

I told Sonny about it and showed him some of the feathers picked up near the nest, and asked him to help me catch it.

"You have to grab them at night when they're sleeping." He said. "Wild turkeys are smart and can fly like eagles."

"But how can you see them in the dark?" I asked, excited by the prospect.

"We'll memorize where the nest is. You have to draw imaginary lines between four trees that we can see against the sky, then, when it's dark, we just go in and grab where the lines cross."

"It's pretty big," I said, "about thirty pounds."

"Between us, we can handle it. Let's try tonight!"

"Okay, but who gets it, if we catch it?" I asked.

"Let's share it. My mom will cook it, and you can have any part you like."

"Okay," I said satisfied. "My mom doesn't cook anyhow, so I'd like to have the neck and the gizzard." The parts I loved most.

That night we stalked our prey. I approached from the side near my house, and Sonny came the other way. I looked up at the trees and could barely make out their tops. We planned that when we were about five feet away, Sonny would whistle and we'd lunge at the nest.

"Approach very quietly," he warned. "If he hears you, he'll get away."

I tried to walk as quietly as possible, looking up to be sure where the imaginary lines crossed. About five feet away I stopped. The only sounds were the crickets, and their buzzing got louder and louder as my heart pounded. We were both ready to leap.

Suddenly the whistle came. I took two steps and dove. The bird, with a squawk, started to take off. I grabbed at the dark form as it rose from the nest. One of its wings caught my arm with tremendous force, hurting me. I grabbed at it and held tight to a fistful of feathers.

Sonny tackled it from the other side, falling on it and pinning its wings behind its back so it couldn't thrash. I came up with just the feathers, but we had our bird. Mrs. Zeller cooked it the next day and I triumphantly carried my neck and gizzard home; the victorious hunter returning with the pickings. The spoils were delicious and I wouldn't share a single bite with the other kids.

Now the boar hunt had my less willing attention and I was happy to have survived the initial chase. Would the colonel expect me to take part in the feast? A boar is not a turkey, I thought.

The weeks of June slipped away. The war news continued on the positive side. The Sunday hunt became routine. I hated myself for not objecting directly to the colonel. I rationalized that my disapproval, especially during wartime, was pointless.

I became so fond of Brany, that I asked Stern about taking him to the BOQ, for a visit. He agreed so I bought him a new leash and collar and marched him back and forth in Stern's office. He followed the lead like a house dog. Going out the door he stopped and looked back at Stern. My little tug was all that was needed as inducement. I thought I saw a flash of disappointment on Stern's face, it wasn't hard to see he loved that bloodhound.

"I'll have him back soon." I promised.

I took Brany to my room and he stayed with me for about a week. I fell in love with that big, awkward, lovable pooch, in spite of his shed hairs covering everything. His adoring eyes followed me the way they did Stern. He just had to love someone.

Dogs were forbidden in the B.O.Q. but my fellow officers liked him and nobody complained. Helen, Brany and I went on picnic lunches. His tail wagged constantly and his big wrinkled head rested happily on Helen's lap as we settled on the blanket. She would plant a big kiss on the top of his brow and tell him very seriously how much she loved him. She paid more attention to him than to me and I told her I'd get her a puppy if she behaved herself.

On a Saturday afternoon three weeks later, Defibrio and I spent the morning at the farm treating a couple of sick mules and colicky horses. We were back at the small animal clinic by 10 AM and worked 'til noon. Surgery began at 3 o'clock and by 5 we started cleaning up. I was fantasizing about my date with Helen when suddenly, stamping feet and loud excited voices broke the silence. I looked in to see Stern and Defibrio straining to lift a bloody, bulging army jacket onto the examining table.

"Lieutenant!" Dom called, despairingly!

I rushed over to see what the trouble was.

"When we are tracking boar. . .I never let him off the leash. . ." Stern got out between gasps. "He wanted to run and we were just starting for the hills, so I let him go."

The jacket fell away and I saw Brany. My god! I wondered, is he dead? My heart sank, he's not breathing! He was lying in a pool of fresh blood. I saw the deep, clean gash across his lower abdomen. From the wound, loops of intestine spilled out, soiled by mud and debris. I could see a small artery spurting from the muscle, proof of a beating heart. He gasped. Maybe we had a chance. Most of the blood seemed to be from that artery. Brany let out a soft moan and as he strained involuntarily more loops of gut were forced out.

He tried to lift his head.

"He'll need morphine to stop that straining and an IV for shock." I barked to Defibrio who left on the run for the medicines. I pressed a clean towel to his abdomen to prevent any further prolapse until the sedative took effect.

"It was such a nuisance to hold him on that leash." Stern tried to explain, his chin quivered as he looked down at his fallen comrade. "I wrapped him in my jacket and got here as quickly as I could." He paused, catching his breath, recalling the details. "He was only ten feet ahead of me." He explained remorsefully. "He caught the boar's scent and went into some heavy bushes. I was sure they were miles ahead. I just heard a yelp and when I dismounted and looked for him, the boar was gone and he was down, the bastard eviscerated him."

Defibrio rushed in with his hands full. Plunking it all down on a stainless steel tray he said, "Here's the morphine, lieutenant, and the saline IV."

I looked down hopelessly wondering where to start. The insult of filth, septic shock and blood loss was too much for that loyal, gentle, majestic canine. Brany's weakening body was trying its best to rid itself of the poison. He vomited and diarrhea poured from his bowel, soiling himself and creating an overpowering stench. Standing over the table, with Dom across from me and Stern at one end, I watched helplessly as Brany expired.

We cried shamelessly for a few long moments before I left and walked, heartbroken, to report the incident to the colonel.

Our softball team improved, as did my coaching. We continued to demolish all in the Benning league to the joy of our fans. Somehow, Commanding General Wilson heard about us and there was a phone call to Kielsmeier.

"Colonel," he said, "the Fourth Service Command is sponsoring a W.A.C. softball league in Atlanta. Each military installation is invited to send a team and I think that our team should enter."

Early July was hot and humid. I was told by the colonel to spend as much time as I needed to coach the WAC baseball team. The colonel was playing up to his superiors again. His veterinary detachment team had turned into an important vehicle for advancement. The Fourth Service Command tournament was a week away and he had to do what he thought would insure, at the very least, a good showing.

At the office, he gave me my pep talk in front of Vance, Defibrio and Beulah Mae. "Keep up the good work, Lieutenant, I like the way you are handling the team. The general asked me and the Mrs. to drive to Atlanta with him and Mrs. Wilson next week for the first game. "You'll be taking over, Vance." he said over his shoulder, "Lieutenant Zimmerman and I will be gone for two days, starting Friday afternoon."

The semi-final baseball game in Atlanta was hectic. We won, but had a couple of injuries to some key players.

A week later we returned to Atlanta for the final game. I had prepared my lineup. I walked to the umpire and handed him the roster. Nine starters and two wounded subs.

The game was close and in the bottom of the ninth we were one run behind. We managed to get two runners on base with two out. Our injured slugger limped out to the batter's box knowing she could never run out a hit. On the first pitch the ball soared towards the left field fence. It hit just in front and skipped away at a crazy angle. Both runners tore around the bases and scored. We were the champions. The Veterinary detachment and Benning would never be the same.

A week later the colonel called me into his office. There was a funny look on his face as he engaged me in silly small talk. I knew something was up, but what? Suddenly, two shiny silver eagles that for years had been burning a hole in his dresser drawer, adorned both shoulders. The colonel had his chickens!

"Congratulations, sir." I sputtered. He had the broadest grin his scarred face would allow. "Thanks Lieutenant." he beamed as he jumped up and wrung my hand as if I were the recipient.

I received a worrisome letter from my folks. Elise had been ill for a week and was in the hospital. They thought if I could get away to see her, it would do her good. I put in my request for leave.

Within the week I was on my way to New York, worrying all the way. I couldn't remember any time of my life without Elise. I took her as much for granted as I did the rest of the family. We never asked her age and she never told us but I realized she was no youngster.

My destination was the Salvation Army's hospital on Welfare Island. I had to take a bus, then a ferry. A taxi took me to the buses where there was a long line of people in front of me, all anxiously waiting to board. I was the only soldier, and the crowd wouldn't permit me to wait. They pushed me to the front of the line. The ferry ride was short and after debarking I was at the hospital door in less than five minutes.

The information desk gave me her floor number, ward and bed. An elevator took me to the third floor. "Coronary care" caught my eye and the strong smell of disinfectants and ether assailed my nostrils. I preferred the odor of veterinary clinics.

I stopped at the nurse's station and inquired about Elise's diagnosis and condition.

"Heart failure." A businesslike floor nurse announced after looking up her chart. "Her prognosis is guarded. She must have complete rest and quiet."

"Is there anything she needs? What can I do to help her?"

"Nothing. We have everything she requires."

When I got to Elise's bedside she was sleeping. As usual, when she napped, she clutched her Bible. For the first time that I could remember, she didn't have her fingers inside, marking her page. Her Bible had always put her to sleep and was the first thing she read when awakening. I kissed her cheek and she opened her eyes. They filled with tears and she cried silently for a few moments. I was sure it was because she was so happy to see me. I learned in a few moments why her heart was breaking. They had taken away her eyeglasses and she couldn't read the Bible.

"Why did they take them?"

"They said I would hurt myself with the glass. I begged them to let me have them for just a few hours."

Infuriated, I marched back to the floor nurse and demanded to see the head nurse or the doctor in charge. My uniform allowed me entrance to the head nurse's office.

"I'd like to know why Elise McLean can't have her eyeglasses?"

"It's against the rules. Patients are liable to hurt themselves. None are permitted."

"How would you like to be deprived of your eyes?" I asked, enraged at the stupidity, "Especially if you had to lie in bed all day with nothing to do but contemplate God and impending death." The more I thought about it, the madder I got. "Since I was a child Miss McLean got her greatest pleasure from reading her Bible and serving the Salvation Army. I'm not fighting for my country to have loved ones miserable because of some stupid rule. I'm not leaving this place till I'm assured she can read at least two hours a day. If necessary I'll pay to have someone sit with her."

She looked up with disbelief. I guess she couldn't comprehend this army officer making such a fuss over an old colored lady.

Embarrassed, she left to consult higher authority. When she returned, she went to a cabinet holding personal effects and handed me the eye glasses.

"I'm sure we can make an exception for our fighting men." she said smiling. "I'm sorry for the trouble and incovenience."

"I think you should review your rules and procedures, especially for a loyal and dedicated worker that spent twenty five years in your service." I said quietly. "I've always respected and supported the Salvation Army because of its profound regard for human feelings. I'm sure there are some patients that should not have glasses, but to make a general rule without considering the individual and their needs is cruel and unacceptable!"

I walked back to Elise and handed her the glasses.

"If they ever take them away again you ask for the head nurse. She promised me you can have them as long as you like."

"Jesus love you." She said wiping her eyes. "I need to read my Bible. I can't walk anymore and I think the Lord will be taking me soon."

"Don't be silly. When I get home I want some of your soup waiting for me. What do you think I'm fighting for?"

We talked for an hour. I reminded her of all the fun we had through the years. She finally smiled as we reminisced about her beloved Montvale.

She liked my uniform and told me she was worried about Norman and especially Joe, if the army were to call them. Joe was the baby and she was closest to him.

"Don't worry about them." I told her. "We are winning the war and soon I'll be home, also. When they come to see you be sure to report about your glasses. And remember," I said seriously. "I expect you to be all better and waiting for me."

She smiled, "As usual, you hear but you don't listen. If God wants me I'm ready!"

I squeezed her hand, kissed her cheek and backed away as she embraced her book with a contented look on that lined, weary old face.

I never saw her again but I knew she would be happy with her God. She was an exceptional lady and I will never forget her.

On returning to Benning, orders had been cut for my five week course in Meat and Dairy Inspection to start Dec. 2, 1944 at the Chicago Stock Yards.

Chicago lived up to its reputation. It was windy, cold and smelly. I got a room in a small hotel on the Southside, not far from the yards. The classes started at 8:00 AM. sharp and on the first morning we met our forty classmates. They were veterinary officers from every corner of the U.S. We were handed a fistful of mimeographed notes covering every kind of produce imaginable. White smocks were a must, and gloves a necessity to protect us from the freezers. Besides meat and dairy we would be taught to inspect and grade fish, vegetables and canned foods. The teaching staff were young G.I.'s, enlisted men skilled in their own specialties, also dressed in long white coats.

The first day we learned how to score (grade) butter. I couldn't believe there were so many different tastes. 93 score was the top grade and had the finest, purest taste. We had apples to bite, chew and expectorate after each sample tasted, "to clear the palate." We were warned never to swallow a sample. Tastes were identified, like bitter, metallic, sour, acid, rancid and other descriptive terms. They were impossible to remember and associate with the ever worsening gooey, sickening glop.

We went to the slaughterhouse for cattle and hogs. A huge, noisy, smelly room filled with the animals programmed for that day's butchery. They were fenced into areas that had an opening at one end that narrowed into a chute. There was a giant, muscular, perspiring Negro, wielding a huge mallet as he straddled the cattle chute. One captive beast at a time was goaded down the runway till they were blocked by a gate just under those sinewy legs. He swung the sledge with almost uncanny accuracy, striking the unsuspecting creature between the eyes with a sickening "plop".

Hooks attached to one leg lifted the limp animals and swung them away to the "bleeding platform". A deft swish with a razor-sharp knife sent a crimson spray spurting to the vats below.

We watched in horror wondering what would happen if there was a miss-hit. We discovered all too soon that it occured frequently. The powerful sledge, glancing off the head of the poor creature

causing excruciating pain as an eye might be torn out or the top
of the nose smashed. The hammer would be thrown repeatedly
trying to correct the errant stroke as the wounded animal, now
down on its knees, bawled in agony and terror. It wasn't easy for
a class of graduate veterinarians to watch.

The vivid recollection of my first encounter with needless cruelty
to living creatures welled in my memory. I wasn't ten years old but
I remember it graphically.

Harry Zeller, my friend Sonny's father, owned and operated the
farm next door to our Montvale, New Jersey haven. He was built
like an Adonis and I looked up to him like a God. I was at his
farm almost every day, transporting chickens and eggs for Elise,
or playing with Sonny. Mr. Zeller's tanned, muscular arms carried
heavy buckets of chicken-feed or water like they were feathers. He
had a new joke or riddle or story for me on every visit.

One day I told him a joke I heard from my Uncle Leo. The story
was told in Yiddish, easily understandable to a German. It was about
a young man who emigrated to New York and was walking in
Central Park, when suddenly he had the urge to go to the bathroom.
He didn't know what to do, so he stepped behind a bush, dropped
his pants and defecated, not an uncommon practice in the old
country. A policeman caught him and brought him to the police
station where he was fined $5. He wrote a letter to his brother
back home, telling him of life in the new world. The punch line
was, "My antira Bruder. Et hat mir gecost funf tollar fur esgacockin
in America." "My dear brother, it costs five dollars to defecate
in America."

The joke broke up Mr. Zeller. He roared, slapped his thigh and
patted me on the back for a joke well told. Every time he saw me
for weeks afterward, he repeated the punch line and laughed. That
joke made us buddies.

Before Sonny was allowed to play, he had chores to complete.
He collected eggs from the hen houses, washed and packed them
in special egg boxes. I was allowed to accompany him on his rounds.
I learned that eggs didn't originate in a grocery store, and that the
eggs he collected could never become chickens. Only the hens that
ran free and were exposed to roosters would lay eggs that hatched.

Marie, Sonny's sister, had to care for the baby chicks that came
from commercial hatcheries. They were only a few days old and

needed special mash for fast growth. She fed and watered them, and transferred them to regular coops when they were old enough. I watched her one day, and marveled at the melifluous sound of hundreds of young birds, all peeping at once, begging for food and sounding like a symphony. They adopted Marie as their mother and crowded around her as she fussed over them. She let me hold one and I was amazed by the soft, cotton-like feathers. I yearned for Marie to ask me to help her every day, but she preferred my sister's company.

Once a week I picked up a package of fresh chickens to take home. They were neatly wrapped (never plucked, as that was the customer's chore). One day the package wasn't ready and Mr. Zeller invited me into the chicken coop, to show me how he caught and prepared them. He carried one outside to a blood-stained tree stump that was the chopping block. He held the bird with one hand and chopped his head off with one quick stroke of a razor-sharp axe.

What appalled me was the way he threw the bird in the air, headless, and bleeding, before going after a second one. The headless bird actually flew a few feet before landing and running several steps, sometimes defecating, before collapsing. Mr. Zeller could see by my expression that I was sickened.

"There is a kosher way to slaughter," he told me, sure it would be better received. He took the second bird, holding its wings together behind it, and bending its head all the way back, so one hand held the head as well. With his free hand he plucked the feathers over the throat, and tensed the skin.

"At this point," he said, "the rabbi takes a razor, says a prayer and painlessly slashes the throat." After Mr. Zeller made the cut, he tossed the bleeding bird in the same fashion. It gurgled and flapped its wings as it ran in circles several times before collapsing. Zeller then took both birds, tied one leg from each to a nearby tree till they were completely bled out.

I watched silently. My stomach was sick and my heart disillusioned. My face must have shown my feelings because Mr. Zeller draped his arm over my shoulders and led me to Marie's baby chicks.

"How about taking one of these babies home?" he asked quietly. "They make real cute pets."

"No thanks," I answered. I realized then that things aren't always as they seem.

At the Chicago stockyards, the bleeding of the hogs was quieter. No anesthesia and no sledge hammer here. At least the swift accurate slit of the throat was painless.

The other unforgetable class was on grading fresh oysters. Huge number ten cans, fresh from the coolers were opened for our perusal, smelling, tasting and grading. The instructor explained the procedure and had three grades for us to distinguish.

"Try the best grade first," he advised. "Chew them and register the flavor in your mind so you can compare the tastes. Spit into the waste buckets when you are finished." I had a problem with oysters. I had never tasted them because the sight and thought of them made me ill. Never the less, as a good student, I chewed and tasted one trying to be as objective as possible, knowing I could expectorate when finished. The bitter taste wasn't as bad as my shock when the slippery thing slid down my throat. That swallow ended tasting for the day. It took years for me to gather the courage to try even a fried oyster.

I sent Helen and Defibrio a picture postcard of the stockyards and my folks received a detailed condemnation of modern slaughterhouse procedures. The five weeks in frozen windy Chicago passed quickly. We posed for a class picture and were given certificates of accreditation. We were now official Army meat and dairy inspectors.

The following Monday I reported to the colonel about the school in Chicago. I complained about the slaughterhouse and asked what could be done to change things.

"There's a war going on, Lieutenant, things are happening and changing fast. I'd forget it and try to do something about it afterwards. By the way, 4th service command headquarters has asked for you. New orders are being cut for a post where you can use what you learned in Chicago."

I was stunned. Fort Benning was like a first love. What about the farm and the small animal clinic. What about Defibrio, the baseball team, Helen and all the enlisted men and officers I had gotten to know and like. What about Willy. Who would look after him and the dogs. I'd have to say goodbybe to them all? Pot and Calder and Vance and even the colonel? I was there only one year but I felt that I was losing my family!

The colonel saw it all in my face and softened for a moment. "I've enjoyed your stay, Lieutenant. I'm proud of what you have accomplished. You're a good officer and you will do well wherever you go. We'll miss you."

Then, back to business. "You will be relieved as company commander, finance officer, kennel fund custodian and clinician. 1st Lieutenanat Lester Jackson has arrived and will be taking over those duties."

He saluted, but I could barely move. For the first time the salute was never returned.

"Have my orders arrived yet, Sergeant?" I asked, my voice barely audible.

"They'll be here in the morning, Lieutenant. You've been assigned to Foster General Hospital in Jackson, Mississippi. I'll have Dom drop them off for you in the morning."

He held out his hand and we shook warmly. I doubted that he had anything to do with that decision.

"I'm going to miss you guys, Sergeant."

"Likewise." he said simply and threw his last salute.

I almost cried as I shook Defibrio's hand. I put my arm around his shoulder but for a moment couldn't talk. I had gotten to like and depend on him so much. "Say goodbye to Pot and the farm," I said hoarsely. "Wish the girls goodluck with their baseball team."

"Keep in touch." He said quietly.

I could never take regular army life, I thought. Too many goodbyes and too many moves.

I called Helen and asked if I could see her that night. She hesitated but sensed the urgency. I hadn't seen her for five weeks and wondered how she would take my transfer.

"I cain't go out," She said. "Why don't ya drop over about 6. We can have a drink and chat."

We talked about my move and I told her how upset I was. She kept checking her watch.

"I'll be in Jackson, Mississippi. It's not too far away. I bet I could drive here in a couple, three hours," I said.

She walked me to the door, reached up and kissed me on the cheek.

"Don't come back, Ted. I'm marry'n the major."

*July 19, 1943, Miss Elaine B. Wolf, of Mt. Vernon, NY launches
the new Sub-Chaser, PCS 138, at City Island, NY*

ERNEST I. PUGMIRE
COMMISSIONER EASTERN TERRITORY

BRIGADIER WILLIAM MALTBY
DIVISIONAL COMMANDER

FOUNDED 1865

THE SALVATION ARMY
(INCORPORATED)

MAJOR AND MRS. DACOSTA
(OFFICERS IN CHARGE)
50 WEST 135TH STREET
NEW YORK 30, N. Y.
PHONE AUDUBON 3-2570

July 1st, 1947

Mrs Zimeman,
New York City.

Dear Mrs Zimman,

        This is to inform you of the death of Miss E. Mc Lean. We are arranging a Funeral Service for her on Friday night at 8 .30 O/Clock at 48 West 135 St.

        Yours sincerely

        Major.

VI

Jackson, Mississippi

The cliché is trite, but it "poured cats and dogs" from Columbus to Jackson. Half way through Mississippi, old Jezebel's window-wipers died. She crawled on endless highways, with me straining to see through the blurry windshield, wondering what lay ahead. The weather matched my mood. I was depressed about Helen. There never was serious love, but we liked each other and I had someone to talk to, dance with and I was rarely lonely.

Finally the signs, hazy through the rain, proclaimed Jackson, the capitol of the most backward, bigoted state in the union. I drove through the business section looking for a service station. Suddenly on the right loomed a sign, "Jones' Gas Station," and under it another smaller one, "mechanic on duty".

I pulled up to the gas pump and hit the horn a short blast. The lights were on but the station seemed deserted. After a long moment a youngster, huddled under a raincoat and rubber hood, came out to service the car. I lowered the window and he looked at me. "How can ah hep ya, soldier?" He looked to be fourteen or fifteen years old.

"Lousy night." I apologized for dragging him outside.

"Right! and ah'd be home, warm and dry if that damn nigger hadn't taken off."

He must have seen me wince. He walked around the back of Jezebel and glanced at my license plate. "Long way from Noo Yoke!" he said as he returned. He had a toothpick sticking out of the corner of his mouth. He kept sucking at it as if a morsel of food was stuck between his teeth.

"I've been in Columbus, Georgia for a year." I explained. "Fort Benning. Just got transferred. Am I headed right for the Foster General Hospital?"

"You're on the right road, half mile straight ahead."

"Are you the mechanic?" I asked dubiously.

"Na. Mah dad. What'sa trouble?"

"My window wiper just broke. I can hardly see. Can he fix it? And I have coupons for ten gallons of gas."

"Shore can. Ah'll get him. You a doctor?"

"I'm a veterinarian."

His eyes lit up and his expression changed. "All our vets are away in the army. Can you look at our dog?"

"What's the trouble?" I was tickled that he seemed to be impressed and needed some professional help. Maybe I'd get a break with my windshield wiper.

"Ba the way, mah name's Babe. Babe Jones. That's mah nickname. We got a black Labrador. Hunts lak a tiger. He's lame bout a week. Paw's swollen and he wasn't even huntin'."

"Is he here? Maybe I can look at him while your dad does my wipers."

"Come on," he said, turning his back and waving over his shoulder as he marched to the garage door.

I opened my tattered umbrella and followed him in. It was more chaotic than any service garage I had ever seen. Tires, lying everywhere. Tools and oily rags on the floor, some on beat-up chairs and a few more on several work tables in the back of the room. Soiled newspapers were crumpled up and scattered everywhere. A pair of legs protruded from under a tattered pickup truck. A voice called up. "Babe, hand me them large pliars. Ah left them on the floor near the fan."

"Dad! Come on out. There's a fella here from the army. Got a broken windshield wiper on a Chevy. He's stationed up at the noo army hospital. He's a vet and he'll look at Smoke's paw."

The legs wheeled backward and Babe's father rolled off and stood up. He held out his hand. It was filthy but I thought I'd better take it.

"Jim Jones. Glad to meet ya. Think you can fix up our pooch?" He was short with black hair and eyes. I noticed a joint of his right thumb was gone as we shook hands.

"I'll be glad to take a look at him. Tell me what happened."

Babe popped up. "It started last week after a Sunday cookout." He kept talking over his shoulder as he walked to another door where I suspected the dog was. "Ah thought he stepped on something sharp. Come on Smoke!" he spoke sharply as if to wake up a sleeping animal. "It didn't bother him none 'til late Monday and his paw began to swell. He's been lickin it since."

A black Labrador limped slowly into the garage, his tail between his legs and ears laid back.

"Come on, nigger-boy." Jim said and gave him a couple of affectionate pats on the head. "Come ova heah to the light."

The dog obediently shuffled slowly after Jim, his tail still between his legs, the tip wagging tentatively.

I knelt beside Smoke and picked up the tender leg. Jim unhooked the portable light, hanging at the end of a long wire and held it close as he spoke.

"Ah checked it mahself for splinters but there was nothing sharp under his paw."

I ran my fingers between his foot pads and the skin was smooth and unbroken. His pads were uncut and spongy with no sign of tenderness or a foreign body. The paw was grossly swollen up to a point just below the wrist. A slight furrow at that point completely circled the leg. I pulled gently at either side of the furrow and found that the skin was broken in almost a complete line.

"Were there any kids at the cook-out last Sunday?" I asked, I had a feeling about what may have happened.

"Sure!" Jim said. "Mah nephew and a couple of nieces. Why?"

"Did they play with Smoke a lot?"

"Sure did. They love 'im. Won't leave 'im alone."

"I'll get my bag." I said. "I think I know what happened." Both Jones' looked at each other. I picked up my umbrella and walked outside. It still poured.

Back inside, I searched my medical bag for a tiny splinter forceps. Then I pulled out a scalpel handle and a #11 disposable blade, narrow with a tapering sharp point.

"One of you can help." I said as I slipped the blade on the handle. I motioned Babe over as Jim was holding the lamp, "put one thumb from each hand on either side of this furrow, like this." And I showed him the break in the skin. "Pull the edges apart, gently but firmly just like I'm doing."

Smoke was a trooper. He never moved as I reached inside the skin edges with the forceps and grasped something. I withdrew the forceps slightly and stabbed gently with the knife. Something snapped and I put the instruments down. From the bottom of his wrist, at the other side of the furrow, I pulled out what was left of

a severed rubberband. It had circled the wrist twice, gradually breaking the skin and shutting off the flow of blood.

"The swelling is called passive congestion." I told the open
mouthed Jones boys. "Lucky I had a couple of kids pull that trick
on me once. They don't do it purposely, but they forget to take
the rubberband off. Sometimes its just too tight and as you can
see, it squeezes slowly."

I applied a soothing ointment to the wound and taped a light
bandage in a circle around the paw. "Take this off in a couple of
days and let him lick it clean. Tomorrow the swelling will be gone
and in a week he can hunt."

Jones couldn't thank me enough. He blamed the "damn niggers,"
two colored maids that had been working there. "Ah don't think
the kids did it," he said, "they're too smart."

"How come you blame everything on the colored folk?" I asked,
a little annoyed.

"You're a Yankee. You don't know or understand niggers. They
got to be kept in their place!"

He fixed my wipers though I'll never understand how. The thumb
on his right hand making it awkward to hold the tools. Yet he deftly
worked through a small opening in the Chevy's dashboard and in
a half hour the repair was finished. Babe watched carefully, sucking
the toothpick through the corner of his mouth as if it helped him concentrate.

In less than an hour they sent me on my way to Foster General.
I was stationed there for two years and I got to know the Jones
family well. Mrs. Jones was a delightful lady and I never heard her
say "nigger," once.

The next morning I was in the office of Colonel Sam Parker,
my new commanding officer. He had a kind, tired, weatherbeaten
face. He was the fatherly type and seemed genuinely interested
in me.

"How are you, Lieutenant? Glad to see you." After returning my
salute with one finger, much the same as S.G. Kielsmeier. Then
he stood up and offered me his hand.

"I hope you'll like it here. Are you married?"

"No, sir. Just got out of college and spent a year at Fort Benning."

"Well you won't be lonesome, Lieutenant. We have almost one
hundred nurses, another twenty-five Red Cross volunteer ladies and
Jackson has some of the prettiest women in the south."

"I have your service record." He said fingering a page he had taken from a manilla folder. "You have an excellent report as clinician of the Post Veterinary Hospital, from the looks of this directive." He pulled out another thick type-written sheaf. "Your duties here will be Post Veterinarian. It will involve meat and dairy inspections of foods of animal origin." He read slowly from the directive. I could see that he was trying to digest something new in his experience. "That is checking and approving farms and processing plants that supply food products to the armed forces. Their list included milk, butter, eggs and meat products, including beef, pork and lamb. Also, the many sausages and frankfurters that are processed in those establishments."

He read on silently, his expression changing to a more or less quizzical look. Then he looked up at me and continued.

"I must caution you, however. Your reports must be treated top secret. It may sound silly, but the War Department mentions that most carloads of frozen produce that are inspected and passed, are shipped directly to the New Orleans' Port of Embarkation. They say that convoys leaving for Europe are having problems with German subs. Convoy departure dates unknowingly repeated to Nazi agents by loose tongues can wreck our supply lines.

"You will have an office, a secretary and three enlisted men. Be sure to inform them not to discuss their duties with anyone. Especially their girl friends and wives. If any of your men drink, let me know. Too much is at stake."

Suddenly a pained expression crossed his face. He clenched his jaws and his face paled.

"Are you allright, Sir?" I asked rising.

He waved me back.

"I have twenty-five crack orthopedic surgeons, five of the best radiologists in the Army, at least ten anesthesiologists and as many psychiatrists, one veterinarian, not to mention a fine group of well trained nurses, but not a single cardiologist." He smiled grimly and admitted sadly. "I have heart trouble, Lieutenant, I live on these two pills." He pulled out a tiny pill box, opened it and popped a couple of white pellets into his mouth. He leaned forward and peered intently into the box. He was counting. "I shouldn't be taking so many. They lose their effect after a while."

"I haven't practiced medicine for years, Lieutenent. In the last few years, the army needed administrators with my background more than practicing physicians. It took a couple of hard years to put this hospital together. I think we have the finest orthopedic center in the service. We'll need it God knows." he said sadly. "The poor lads come in here so torn up, so mutilated. . ." He opened a desk drawer and took out a flask. "Like a snort, Lieutenant?" "No thank you, Sir. I don't drink much. Got sick in college once and swore off." "Good for you. I don't think I'd get through a day without a few swallows. Well, good luck, Lieutenant. Come to me with any problems. I'm sure you'll do fine." He waved me out not even bothering to return my salute. Little did I know at the time that a year from that day, I'd have a new commanding officer. Colonel Sam Parker died of a heart attack in less than six months.

The next day I searched for my office. Foster General was a very large military complex that could pass for a small city. It had its own theatre, gymnasium, swimming pool, and baseball field in addition to the orthopedic treatment areas. Operating rooms, with observation balconies that I knew I'd be sitting in when I had the time. Recovery rooms, rehabilitation wards, Xray rooms, diagnostic labs, a tremendous rabbit hutch for research and diagnosis that I would be in charge of. The morgue, a necessity at a war-time General Hospital, made me shiver and I didn't bother to inspect that facility. A tremendous mess hall and kitchen with huge freezers and cold storage facilities. A motor pool with ambulances, staff cars, and stretch limo's. Barracks for the enlisted men, nurses quarters and the Bachelor officers quarters where I lived.

I walked around acquainting myself with the layout and introducing myself to the officers in charge. Lt. Peterson was the mess officer. I should have guessed it by his build. A very fat Georgian with cheeks that my Uncle Stein would have loved to pinch. He wasn't too happy with me. He already knew, though I didn't, that the colonel was about to assign me to monitor him as food service supervisor, and, in addition, we would be competing for the one available captain's bars allotted to the hospital that year.

Lieutenant Adrian McKenna was the hospital adjutant. I met him the day before. He was very bright, bespectacled and efficient. He was too young to be Regular Army but he was as good as Vance. I'd need him for leaves, motor pool privileges and gas coupons.

In radiology I met Captain Peter J. Washko. His eyes lit up when he saw that I was a veterinarian. Washko was an equestrian and a tennis player. He was married and owned a black female Cocker Spaniel. "I was looking for a local vet, but they are all in the Army." he said animatedly. "We want to breed Blacky, and she'll need a professional obstetrician." He was a short man, stocky, with dark hair and horn rims that needed pushing up every few seconds.

I met Captain Rake Rodholm, an orthopedic surgeon. He was a tall, blonde, former varsity tennis star at UCLA. He asked me if I played tennis and when I said I "played at it," he promised to teach me so he'd have someone decent to volley with.

In the administration building I found my office and my staff. This wasn't the usual office with a door and four walls. My secretary had a desk in a tremendous room, shared with at least ten other girls. She was as big and round as Lieutenant Peterson. Her name was Chris Childers and she wore glasses, a light, flowery, print dress, was very shy and had the thickest and slowest southern drawl I had ever heard.

Standing around her desk were three GI's; my staff. They had been waiting almost a week with nothing to do.

Chester J. Jozefiak was from Chicago. Chester and I rode our staff car from one end of Mississippi to the other as well as many parts of Alabama. Frozen beef, lamb, chickens and pork were purchased by the army in carload lots, costing millions of taxpayers dollars. We saw to it that Uncle Sam got his money's worth.

Herbert Kirk was a red-neck southerner. He was a staff sergeant specializing in the inspection of butter, eggs, sausages, frankfurters, fish and canned foods. He would accompany me on inspections of farms, dairy plants and butter processing plants. I liked most GI's but could never bring myself to find one redeeming feature in Kirk's character.

Sergeant Harold Taylor was an enlisted man with class. He was soft spoken, neatly dressed, well educated and good looking. He was the administrative genius of my office and we needed one. The number of reports for Chris to type every day was mind-boggling. Taylor checked each and every one like a Scotland Yard sleuth before it landed on my desk for a signature. Poor Chris was always misplacing reports and apologizing. Sergeant Taylor never failed to find them and was as patient and forgiving as a Labrador Retriever.

Peter Washko set up a date at his home for me and a "cute" southern belle. He invited us both to dinner. I met Mary Jane, his lovely wife, five months pregnant with their first child. Blacky, the black Cocker Spaniel who's love-life I was supposed to supervise and finally my date, Melna Nichols.

They knew Melna and her family from church and were charmed by her looks, dress and temperment. She was delightful. She laughed easily with a bell-like, joyful tone that was euphonic.

Blacky, the Cocker Spaniel was as cute in her own way, as Melna. With long ears and wagging tail she couldn't get enough petting. She went from person to person to collect a caress, then, as if she had forgotten, she started her rounds all over again. Peter finally had to put her outside to give us a rest. I went with him to get some air and tell him that I liked Melna.

Life at FGH was busy and fascinating. My duties allowed free time to visit the orthopedic surgical arenas. Our staff of psychiatrists were brilliant and, as I imagined, grossly overworked, convincing dismembered young men that living was, nevertheless, worthwhile.

My trips to the countryside and the myriad of farms we inspected was a shocking experience as only one in ten could begin to qualify as acceptable. The cows as well as the horses and sheep looked neglected and ill-fed. Hand milking, under filthy conditions, were the norm. My experience was limited but even Sergeant Kirk was appalled by the lack of basic sanitation. Milk, butter and cheese needed a better starting point than most of the farms could supply.

I compared our visits with the farms of New York State and the memories of my youth, when unpasteurized milk was delivered to our front door in clean sterilized glass bottles. Even mean horses, like Ebony, had been well cared for.

Our new Bajan housekeeper that summer in Montvale, was Elise. She insisted Dad find a dairy farm to deliver milk and butter to our door. She didn't drive and thought we youngsters had to carry too many heavy bottles over a mile from Scarengeli's, the closest grocery store. He found the Linderman's Dairy at the top of the hill on the Orangeburg Road, in the direction of the Montvale Village center. Dad asked Elise to make the necessary arrangements, so she took us all for a walk to meet the owner. On the way, we passed a fearsome black stallion that we had seen for weeks, never realizing there was a dairy associated with the rambunctious black horse.

Mrs. Linderman was a tall, slender woman with a goiter the size of a grapefruit showing in her neck. It caused her voice to be creaky and high-pitched. Her half-gray hair, was fashioned into a bun, framing a tanned, wrinkled, kindly face, and her long, full, dark skirts reached her ankles.

Elise told her we needed fifteen quarts of milk daily, and asked if she could deliver them to our door. Mrs. Linderman was thrilled to have such a good customer so close to the farm and readily agreed to Elise's terms.

When we left, we joked and ridiculed her deformity, until Elise explained that it was caused by an iodine deficiency and, but for the grace of God, we might have goiters, too. We were ashamed and showed our contrition by being especially polite to our milk lady.

Mrs. Linderman's helper delivered the fresh milk every morning. It was before the days of pasteurization and homogenization, so three or four inches of fresh cream would rise to the top of each bottle.

After a few weeks, our manners paid off and Mrs. Linderman allowed us into the barn to watch her milk the cows and see where milk really comes from. The barn had a separate stall for each cow, and a huge loft with delicious-smelling hay stacked to the sky-high ceiling. There were cats everywhere and Mr. Linderman said they are important to control vermin. It was an unbelievable revelation to see and hear those gnarled, old hands coax streams of fresh milk into gleaming metal buckets. There were always some of the cats sitting close by, watching the milking very carefully. We soon found out why. Every now and then, Mrs. Linderman directed a stream right into their mouths, saying, "Here you babies, open up and drink." Sometimes the milk would miss and their heads and bodies got soaked. They never minded and licked each other clean before sitting again and waiting for more.

We fashioned a path to the Linderman Farm, through the woods behind our house to avoid passing Ebony, the black stallion. It was an uphill and difficult task to cut our way through the wild, virgin forest, on a line parallel to the road, but we finally found ourselves in the berry patches behind her farm house. We feasted on strawberries, blackberries, huckleberries and raspberries for weeks, before Elise figured out what caused the berry-stained faces and fingers, accompanied by poor appetites for lunch and dinner. She told us they were Linderman's property and not there to be pillaged. Elise apologized for us, and ordered berries to be delivered with the morning milk. The paid-for berries never tasted quite as good.

Ebony, the huge, mean horse that seemed to be guarding Mrs. Linderman's home, had a large mane and ever-swishing tail. The first time he saw us was on our walk to Montvale Village--my sister, four first cousins, Bill and I were there. Just below the crest of the hill, we saw the log-fence corral, about five feet high. As we passed, we heard a squeal that turned into a screeching neigh as the nervous horse reared up on his hind legs, pawed the air and charged the fence. We were terrified he would jump over it, so we ran past as fast as we could. Even Bill was wary. He barked bravely as he backed away, following us to safety.

Ebony had a fearsome expression, ears laid back, nostrils flaring and eyes glistening with hate. I loved horses, but I was afraid of Ebony. I wished I could pat his nose. I fantasized myself riding him, to the envy of all the kids. I complained to Elise, not knowing what to do. She told me he was a sinful animal and not to fool with him.

I paid attention to her advice until the following summer, when one day I walked up the hill alone. Bill was napping and the other kids were playing their silly games. I had to try Ebony by myself. Maybe the others made him nervous. As I approached and he heard me, he lifted that magnificent head and I held my breath awaiting his charge. His ears pointed straight up and his eyes appeared softer and more gentle. He surveyed me in a curious detached manner. The kids and Bill were who he didn't like! He didn't hate me at all!

Going home, I skipped past the corral, smiling and whistling, and looked back. I saw the branches part and another horse strolled into view.

I told Mom and Dad. "I finally tamed Ebony. He has another nice horse with him now." I added.

Dad explained that Ebony had a wife and was so happy he didn't have to frighten children anymore. My father was right because the next time Bill and the other kids walked by, he hardly looked up.

In Mississippi and Alabama it wasn't easy changing local, primitive farming methods to the standards I was used to and the army would accept. Sanitation was the principle fault and eventually a few of the farmers complied and were accepted as sources of meat and dairy products for the Army.

The colonel liked my work and added the Officer's Club to my duties. Now in charge of that body, I found myself thrust into the social life of Jackson.

Lieutenant Conners, the post recreation officer, was in charge of the Hospital radio show. It was a half hour program that Colonel Parker initiated to acquaint Jackson's citizens with our patient's needs and thank them for their interest and support. He asked me to help formulate a meaningful program. The first broadcast had to be different and exceptional and I agonized with him over the format.

"I think it would be a good idea to have an interview between a town person and one of the hospital's officers about the problems that have to be addressed." I said.

"Good idea," he replied, "then we can inject some sort of entertainment. We have a class-act band and I bet many of the hospital personnel and even some patients may be talented also."

"The local newspaper is sending a reporter to cover the event," Conners said to me. "I met her last week and I'm sure she'll cooperate." He stopped as a slender, attractive young lady came through the door, followed by a tacky, bushy-haired, and disinterested looking person.

"That's her with that fellow carrying the camera."

She came toward us smiling, pad and pencil ready.

"Say hello to Ann Buchanan, of the Clarion Ledger and Jim DeSilva, official photographer."

Then to Ann, "Lieutenant Ted Zimmerman is our Officer's Club chief. He'll help us set up a program to get some pictures of our wounded and have them meet some of the officers and towns people."

Everyone nodded a greeting and DeSilva set his apparently heavy equipment at his feet.

"Colonel Parker wants to thank people for their generosity in raising money to entertain and help our men." Conners began. "Many were seriously wounded and some will be in wheel chairs for life. The Army, Navy and Marines are grateful; we treat them all," he said. "We are an orthopedic center so we have a lot of men who need transportation to town for movies, parties, USO dates etc. Your townspeople arrange for cars and station wagons with volunteer drivers that accommodate wheelchairs, supply lunches and snacks and generally go out of their way for the men."

"It's a great story!" she said enthusiastically, "I'd like to get some of their war experiences on paper. I'm sure some must be decorated heroes. Maybe I could speak to the doctors and nurses treating them. I could run a series about the activities in the hospital, besides medical treatment, for rehabilitation and entertainment."

"What do you do?" She asked politely. "How come a doctor is running the Officer's Club?" I saw her stare at my insignia, a medical cadeucous with a large V imposed over the serpent.

"I'm a Veterinary Officer with no animals to treat so the colonel asked me to run the Officer's Club."

DeSilva perked up when he heard I was a vet.

"Boy! Do we need you. I've got two dogs and all the vets are away in the army."

"And I've got a cat that could use some professional help." Ann added. "The only vet left in town is Dr. Chadwick and he only does large animals. I'm afraid to take my cat to him. Would you look at him?" she asked shyly.

"I really don't have any equipment, except what I carry in my bag. Maybe I could meet Dr. Chadwick and use his office."

"It seems that Jackson people are animal lovers." Conners interjected, "Maybe we could use that theme for one of our radio shows."

"The people will love it," Ann said, "we could work through the humane society. We've used pets as companions for our patients at Jackson's hospitals for years. The animals took their minds off of themselves and healing and rehabilitation was much quicker and less stressful."

"For your radio show, I could read a wonderful tribute to dogs." DeSilva said, "I know it will be a hit." His whole attitude had changed as soon as animals were mentioned.

"That's not a bad idea." Conners said, "We could have part of the time interviewing you, Ann, as the local reporter telling some of the GI's war stories as they were told to you. Jim here, could take pictures that would appear in the Ledger, showing the interview."

"What would you read?" I asked the photographer.

"Senator Vest's Tribute to a Dog. It's a wonderful statement he used in court to defend the animal in a dog-bite case. They wanted to have the dog put to sleep. I'd like to read the senator's argument."

"I remember that from school," I said. "He won the case without using a single witness. And you're right. It would be a hit."

The first show was planned for Monday night and we were as nervous as players at a Broadway opening. Conners introduced Ann who promptly stole the show with a provocative interview with two wounded veterans.

While she talked DeSilva took pictures that appeared in the early edition of The Clarion Ledger the following day.

When the interviews were completed, the FGH band began playing soft background music and Jim DeSilva read with skill and emotion,

Senators Vest's Tribute to a Dog

The best friend a man has in the world may turn against him and become his enemy. His son or daughter that he has reared with loving care may prove ungrateful. Those who are nearest and dearest to us, those whom we trust with our happiness and our good name may become traitors to their faith. The money that a man has, he may lose. It flies away from him, perhaps when he needs it most. A man's reputation may be sacrifced in a moment of ill-considered action. The people who are prone to fall on their knees to do us honor when success is with us, may be the first to throw the stone of malice when failure settles its cloud upon our heads. The one absolutely unselfish friend that a man can have in this selfish world, the one that never deserts him, the one that never proves ungrateful or treacherous is his dog. A man's dog stands by him in prosperity and in poverty, in health and in sickness. He will sleep on the cold ground, where the wintry winds blow and the snow drives fiercely, if only he may be near his master's side. He will kiss the hand that has no food to offer; he will lick the wounds and the sores that come in encounter with the roughness of the world. He guards the sleep of his pauper master as if he were a prince. When all other friends desert, he remains. When riches take wings, and reputation falls to pieces, he is as constant in his love as the sun in its journey through the heavens. If fortune drives the master forth an outcast in the world, friendless and homeless, the faithful dog asks no higher privilege than that of accompanying him, to guard him against danger, to fight against his enemies. And when the last scene of all comes, and death takes his master in its embrace and his body is laid away in the cold ground, no matter if all other friends pursue their way, there by the grave side will the noble dog be found, his head between his paws, his eyes sad, but open in alert watchfulness, faithful and true even in death. "

The word had gotten around that I was a small animal veterinarian. Before long, I was getting calls from friends and strangers alike, to please look at a dog or cat or bird, as there was no one to treat their pets.

I couldn't charge anything and I told them I'd be glad to contribute my services working with Dr. Chadwick.

Ann had mentioned him. It was purely coincidence that I met Martha Chadwick, his daughter, at a post dance at Foster General. She was a tall, skinny blond that was one of the best dancers I had ever met. A few weeks later the post ran a dance and both Melna and Ann were busy. I asked Martha to come. When I stopped by her home to pick her up, I met her dad.

We talked shop for a while, then he asked, "Why don't you drop by when you can. I'd like to discuss some of the cases that are flooding my office. It has been so many years since I did small animals, I'm really not comfortable with them." I thanked him for the opportunity, and told him I would.

A few days later he phoned and asked me if I had time that day, to drop over. "I have a case of urolithiasis in a tom cat that worries me."

It's a condition quite commonly seen in a small animal practice. The urethra, very narrow in the feline, becomes blocked with gravel from the bladder and the cat strains but can't urinate.

I dropped over, anxious to help him and at the same time, keep my hand in. "Why don't you tell me this guys history while I look him over."

He was a huge black, seven year old tom, depressed, cold to the touch and dehydrated. I palpated the huge hard bladder. The smell of urine as on his breath, indicated a developing uremia.

"He's a pet at the farm I was at yesterday." Chadwick explained. "They had the usual complaint, constipation. He just sat in his pan, straining. One feel and I knew it wasn't that simple. They always used Dr. Norris, a small animal man away in the service. I've treated cases like this before." he said sadly, "Never had no luck with them. They never wake up from either anesthesia or even sedation."

"Did you ever use epidural on the small animals?" I asked, "I'm sure you use it on horses and cattle."

"Never heard of it for cats." he said.

"Do you have 2% procaine solution?" I asked rolling up my sleeves. My obsession with epidural at Cornell and the year or more at Fort Benning had given me the experience and confidence I needed.

Chadwick nodded.

"I'll need a one-inch 21 gauge needle for the epidural and a blunt 19 guage needle for flushing the urethra, sterile saline, sterile lubricating jelly, tincture of iodine and alcohol."

Chadwick motioned to his assistant to get started.

"Then an IV drip, assuming we can unplug him. He's dehydrated and shocky. If you have a feline urinary catheter we'll leave it in place for a day or so."

I showed him how to hold the patient for the injection. In less than a minute, the cat was relaxed and I demonstrated how to flush away the plug. After the blockage was cleared, gentle pressure on the bladder emptied it. A sterile catheter, well lubricated, was slid into place, its open end sutured to the anesthetized skin near the end of the penis. An IV drip was inserted into the jugular and taped snugly in place. The cat was wide awake during the entire procedure. To Chadwick's delight, he recovered completely. I told him about the new commercial, low mineral diets for cats that were prone to forming bladder stones.

"I'd advise Hill's CD diet and slightly salted food to encourage drinking as a good follow up for your clients." I concluded.

For the rest of my stay in Jackson I spent four to five hours a week working with Dr. Chadwick. The experience was invaluable.

One day he said, "The people in Jackson think a lot of you. How would you like to open a practice here? There's money in the budget for a zoo. You mentioned how much you'd like to work in one. What do you say?"

I was flattered, but I had to return home. My plans for the future didn't include working in the deep south.

It was August of 1944 and I hadn't been home for over a year. I missed my folks and my letters couldn't adequately describe all the activities and duties at Foster General Hospital. Helping my mother at the pet shop was fun and I looked forward to witnessing her in action again. Mom was a joy to watch, never wasting a move, nor a morsel of food. If the puppies left scraps in their dishes, the birds or the fishes had their chance to wipe the metal clean. Despite the fact that it was a small, one person operation, there was always something new and innovative to enjoy. Dad worked at the new Gimbels Department Store pet shop most of the day and I knew Mom would appreciate my company.

With this in mind, I dropped in on our adjutant, Adrian McKenna. "There aren't any orders for food inspection for the next week or so," I started, "what are the chances for leave?"

"Good, I think." McKenna smiled. He loved his role as power-broker for the officers but we were friends. "Let me check with the colonel. I'll put you down for ten days starting August seventh. If you don't hear from me, it's okay." I didn't hear from McKenna and my orders came through.

My first stop was to see my Mom at the London Kennels on Sixth Avenue. It was with eager curiosity that I whiffed the inimitable fragrance of our newest pet, "Inky". My parent's pet shop had never harbored a skunk. That may not sound unusual, but as a small boy in a large pet store, something had been missing.

Actually the "Kennels" were quite a come-down from the London Pet Shop on Fifth Avenue that I knew as a boy. It was about a quarter the size. It had mostly dogs and cats for livestock, except for an occasional parrot, some goldfish, a marmoset monkey or a baby skunk. As I entered, I saw Mom sitting at the counter playing solitaire and eating sunflower seeds. The puppies were quiet after enjoying their lunch and all the kittens slept.

Mom jumped up all smiles and happy. "You look great, soldier-boy," she said as I got my hug and sniff. Mother never kissed. She would bury her nose in our neck and give us a big sniff. She was a great hugger though and I lifted her and swung her around in a warm, affectionate embrace.

"Tell me about the baby polecat," I demanded. "I smelled him at Idlewild as I got off the plane."

Mom gave me that little half-smile, denoting an admission of naughtiness, or guilt, or adventure, or all three. Actually mother could never refuse any offer from anyone for any kind of four legged creature or bird for a refuge. She was an easy-mark for the homeless, the strays, the orphans and the discarded animals of the city. That was exactly how she adopted "Inky".

Most people would think that owning a skunk would be an exercise in self-abuse. But then most people are not like my parents. They were equal opportunity pet owners and didn't in the least look down on Inky just because he smelled a little different. And, after all, couldn't their son with one well placed slice of his trusty scalpel, forever relegate Inky's unusual odor to history? Besides, Inky had an exceptionally good personality, even for a skunk.

I opened the cage door to coax him out. Losing all shyness, he jumped onto my hand, ran up my sleeve, and parked himself under my right ear. Instinctively I froze in place, reaching for him very gently, praying that he wouldn't be offended as I placed him back in his little house.

"Well, I guess we'll have to sweeten him up before you lose your business, Mom." I said, "Dad can help. We'll do it some evening after work."

My father's pride in his son couldn't be expressed in words. His little boy, his number one son, was an officer, and a surgeon. And he was going to assist him! He was understandably nervous and worried about his ability, especially without a chance to practice his new roll.

We set up the make-shift surgery at the back of the store, behind a partition that separated the storage area from the livestock. The sink in the small bathroom was where we scrubbed, and the stacks of crates filled with the paraphernalia of the pet shop had full view of the operative theater. The patient sat on a chair in a small holding cage, excited and curious about all the special attention.

In full view of Inky, in neat rows, were all the tools and equipment I would be using. Dad took him out of his cage and set him on the operating table. Fearless Inky was not in the least intimidated. He remained calm and playful as Dad helped me administer the ether. We used a make-shift applicator improvised to fit over his tiny mouth. Our special skunk was soon sound asleep.

"Hold his tail up, like this." I showed him. "And watch his chest. His respirations should remain constant."

Everything went smoothly until I noticed the slight blue cast on his tissues. I glanced at my dad who was frozen speechless. Without warning, Inky had stopped breathing. Pop was sure he was gone.

"It never slowed up," Dad said sadly. "I hardly noticed it. He just stopped breathing."

I had never given artificial respiration to anything of that size before, but it worked better than I thought. After two or three squeezes with a couple of fingers he resumed breathing on his own.

"Don't worry Pop," I assured him lightly. "It's a very common occurrence. Just keep the anesthesia light, he's more sensitive than I thought."

My father heaved a deep sigh. As far as he was concerned, Inky had come back from the grave. "Are we almost finished, son?" The emotional strain was telling.

"Almost. Just hold the cone over his nose lightly for a minute or so. If he starts to fight add a drop or two."

"How can I hold the ether can, his head, the cone and his tail at the same time? I'm really not trained for this job," he said, troubled.

"Rest his head on the cushion near the cotton, it doesn't have to be in the cone. One hand will be free for the ether can, the other for his tail, and stop worrying. You're doing fine!"

Soon I was finished and held up the glands in triumph. I had operated on my first and last skunk. I dropped them, with the gloves into the garbage can and smelled my fingers. I might as well have worked bare-handed. It took me three days and a gallon of tomato juice, to scrub away the aroma. One week later, Mom gave the little bugger a bath and with the help of cologne he actually smelled civilized.

I returned to Foster General and Mom's letters kept me informed. Inky thrived on dog food and fresh vegetables. At six months of age he weighed five pounds, was bright and lively and had a beautiful glistening coat. Inky was one foot from stem to stern, with a beautiful white stripe down the middle of his back, gently tapering to the end of his fine fluffy tail. Mom described his stripe as Inky's pride and joy. She said if I could have seen it, I would have to agree that it was unusually bright and shiny for a skunk's stripe. He would alternately show it off by prancing about the pet shop with it high in the air. He'd regally polish it, by spending hours scouring the hairs with his rough tongue. At night Mom put Inky with the puppies for play and companionship. He took to pet shop life like a bird to the heavens and was one of the happiest of all its denizens.

One day Inky proudly dropped a limp white mouse at Mom's feet. It had escaped from its wire-covered aquarium, allowing Inky to prove himself an able predator, not realizing white mice were friends and fellow boarders. He kept jumping on Mom, begging for approbation, but instead his freedom was terminated. He was caged like all the rest, patiently awaiting a new master.

For years the store had been pillaged by mice. They would chew holes in the cardboard containers of dry dog food and boxes of bird seed. Their droppings were everywhere and Mother was desperate for a solution. She had to place all the cardboard and paper containers in metal barrels each night. She tried traps, rat poison, even cats. The traps only caught the idiot mice. Poison was too dangerous around pets and the cats would play with their victims until bored, allowing most to escape. Then came the brainstorm! Inky! He was small enough to get through the floorboards into the cellar where the mice and rats lived, and he wouldn't play like cats did. Dad had heard that skunks were great mousers and ratters. He gave his okay.

Mom changed Inky's routine, He was no longer confined at night. He now had free range after 6 PM and all day Sunday. He was an immediate success. Within a few months, his hunting acumen had the store free of vermin. With each success he demanded a pat, a hug or a place in mom's lap.

Inky had developed some cute habits and had his own unique sense of humor. Every morning he would drop the night's catch at Mom's feet. When there was nothing to show off, he substituted one of the puppy or kitten toys Mother left for him to play with. Whenever he was annoyed or hungry on in need of affection he would jump up on her with his forelegs, spin around, landing on all fours and jump up again, repeating the dance until he was noticed. He accepted other humans but adored Mother and would perform his dance for her exclusively.

Sundays the store was closed to the public. Mom would come in about 10 o'clock to feed and clean the livestock. One Sunday morning in September, she was doing her usual chores. Dad had designed a stack of glass cages. They were built and supported by metal frames and used to display toy breeds and kittens. They stood between the counter and the front door. The cages were about five feet high, a little taller than Mom. The glass doors were opened and closed by sliding them along a metal track.

On this particular Sunday, after feeding the pups in the upper section, Mother slid the door closed. All of a sudden the glass came loose and shattered with a boom like a rifle shot. A shard pierced her wrist. The pain was sharp and she stared with surprise as blood spurted to the rhythm of her heart. She felt faint and tried to support herself on the sales counter, but could not. She slipped to the floor, her arm sweeping the counter of papers, pencils, bottles, toys and other loose articles.

Bleeding profusely, her first impulse was to apply a tourniquet but there was nothing close that would work. A bottle of chlorazene, a mild antiseptic, had fallen from the counter close to her. It had a perforated cap that allowed a small amount to be sprinkled when turned upside down. Chlorazene had cured ringworm, eczema, conjunctivitis, purulent ears, infected wounds and sore gums. Mother soaked the wound hoping the miracle in the bottle would work again. Nothing stopped the pulsing fountain of red and her consciousness began to ebb again. She saw her life slipping away but fought the faint using a method that she had taught us. "Put you head down as close to your feet as possible." She rolled on her knees, lifted her backside up and put her head in her cupped hands. The blood soaked the side of her face and blouse. There was no feeling in her cut hand. The nerve was severed she thought, compounding her terror.

Mom kept forcing the faintness away. She mustn't give in to that beckoning haven of sleep. The bleeding! She must stop the bleeding! I once showed her a trick I played on my friends that stopped the pulse in my wrist. I would surreptitiously slip a bulky object under my arm pit, usually a roll of socks or a rubber ball. When pressed against the humeral artery by hugging my arm tightly to my chest, it would stop my pulse. Thank God she remembered. She reached for a rubber ball that had fallen from the counter and placed it under her arm, leaning her shoulder heavily against the wall near the door and hugging her chest as hard as she could.

There was a wino in the area who routinely staggered along Sixth Avenue from Fourteenth to Thirtieth Streets, looking for hand outs. His name was Dugan and he'd check the garbage cans on the west side of the avenue going south, then cross the street to the east side, and proceed north. He knew his people. Those that ran him off he avoided, but the few who were understanding and sympathetic, he touched for a few coins, a cup of coffee or a sandwich. Mom was one of his favorites. To her he was just another lost puppy. She never refused him a bite to eat or a kind word.

Dugan knew her Sunday routine, and never bothered her on her half day. He passed by at about 11 AM. The subdued traffic noises allowed him to hear the puppy's excited yapping more than a block away. On Sundays, the shades were drawn. As he approached, this time, he noticed a different look to the front door. Something was rhythmically striking the drawn shade. He swayed toward the door supporting himself against the show window and peered in between the shade and the door frame. My mother was on the floor, slumped against the wall, blood covering the side of her face, her arm and her hand. He thought he was hallucinating as he watched a skunk frantically jumping at her, spinning away and hitting the shade with both forepaws, repeating the ritual persistently.

His first impulse was that he needed a drink real bad. He thought he'd better clear out and forget the whole thing, but the animal was so tenacious and Mrs. Zim was so nice, he had to help. Dugan pounded on the door and shouted for the animal to let her alone. Mom stirred and looked up. She saw Inky's frantic dance and Dugan's face peering from the door. The blood was still spurting but at a slower rate. Thank God I'm still alive she thought. She reached for a letterhead amidst the debris. Using her own blood and her finger, she wrote the word "HELP". With her good hand she slid it under the door and croaked, "Police, give it to the police!"

Inky had stopped his dance and sat quietly next to her. Mom reached out and petted him then replaced the rubber ball that had slipped away. 'Dugan will get help'. She got on her knees again, reached up and unlocked the door. She tried her fingers again. They were still lifeless. My hand! I can't use my hand! There was no pain, no movement. She picked up a loose rag and wrapped it around her wrist as tightly as possible. With her good hand she emptied the bottle of chlorazene on the bandage.

Dugan staggered away wondering what to do. Sixth Ave was deserted and he looked north towards busy Thirty-Fourth Street. He rarely walked that far from his beat but he had to unload that note somewhere. The sobering experience gave him added incentive and he managed to reach Thirty-Fourth where a policeman directed traffic.

"Get back on the side walk." The officer shouted as Dugan lurched towards him. Dugan stopped short. He hated policemen anyhow and didn't care to talk to him.

"I got a note." He sputtered holding out the paper. The cars had stopped for the red signal and cross traffic was light. The officer, curious, walked over and reached for the paper gently pushing Dugan toward the sidewalk.

He looked down and recognized the letterhead. He had window shopped the London Kennels pet shop many times. He saw the message scribbled in mother's blood and looked up at Dugan.

When the Ambulance crew arrived and told her they had to take her to the hospital, she panicked. She hated and distrusted doctors and hospitals. She rushed into the bathroom and locked herself in. When the police finally talked her out, she was weak and dizzy and mumbled something about Gimbels and her husband. Someone had to take care of the animals. The ambulance rushed her to French Hospital, a Catholic institution on the west side of Manhattan.

Dr. Grady, a renowned hand surgeon, happened to be on duty. He was making Sunday rounds when Mom was brought in. He took one look at her wound, heard the crew's description of the splintered glass, and instructed the staff to transfuse a pint of blood and prepare her for the operating room.

Dr. Grady specialized in traumatic sugery. He had many cases with glass induced wounds and used special lamps to illuminate the operative field. He spent two hours debriding the wound as hundreds of tiny glass splinters had infiltrated the area. Three more hours were needed to repair the damage. When he finished he shook his head sadly and sighed deeply, anticipating that certain infection would ruin a masterful piece of reconstructive surgery. He instructed the sisters in the post operative care. "The dressings must be changed hourly for the first few days. Infection is inevitable. I've left a drain in the wound that will have to stay until we have controlled suppuration."

Dr. Grady checked mother's wound on Tuesday. The nurses were happily perturbed that the healing did not follow the prescribed course.

"Doctor," chief nurse O'Hallahan reported, "There has been no swelling, no tenderness, no suppuration. I've handled hundreds of these cases of splintered glass contamination and this is the first one I remember that is healing by first intention."

As Dr. Grady removed the drain and surveyed the wound, he smiled. "Mrs. Zimmerman, what magic do you employ? This was supposed to hurt, swell, ooze and be generally a nuisance for the first few days. Aren't you ashamed to upset my staff so?"

Mother thought for a moment, then recalled. "Chlorazene," she said.

"Meaning what?"

"Dr. Blamey, the English vet that we use for the animals told us about the wonders of chlorazene tablets to make mild Dakin's solution. We've been using it for years to cure everything from ringworm to mange. I must have poured some of it over my wrist before the ambulance arrived."

"Fantastic!" He said. "Would you mind if I showed you off to my students?"

Mom stayed in a general ward with twelve beds for ten days. The sisters couln't keep her quiet after the third day. She got to know all the other patients and their problems. When the nurses were busy, even with her arm bandaged she would help them sit up, get in and out of bed, adjust their pillows or just read to them. She missed the animals and had to take care of anything or anyone within reach. She had Dad bring in oranges which she peeled with one hand and fed to her new friends. "You'll get better much faster," she told them. "Vitamin C." Mom had a thing about oranges and oatmeal. She entertained them with her stories, especially the one about Inky. "The experts say that animals can't reason. Well, they're wrong!"

When she was discharged a week later, Dr. Grady gave her a rubber ball. "This is a very unusual invention," he said with a twinkle in his eye. "It not only controls bleeding, but it helps hands heal. Wait a month or so for the tendons to mend, then squeeze this ball four or five times a day to start, increasing gradually till you can do it twenty or thirty times. If we're lucky, and you work diligently, you may have 75 percent function in a year."

Mom worked hard and almost wore out the rubber sphere. She visited the hospital once a month as Dr. Grady's guest patient. He boasted to his class about the infection free surgery and rapid recovery, then admitted dryly, that Mrs. Zimmerman's case was a one in a million chance. "And don't forget," he reminded them, "how important it is to have a pet skunk on hand to alert our medical services."

At the end of the year she surprised him again with an almost ninety percent return of function.

Basketball practice, Rodholm's tennis lessons, Washko's social calendar and the duties of Post Veterinarian kept me on my toes for the winter of '44.

At home, Norman, now twenty years old, was drafted into the army and left for Europe on an army transport. His last letter had told me how happy he was to finally be able to do his part for the war effort.

Len Rafael, when he went off to war, asked my ex-roommate, Marv Steinberg (classified 4F) to take care of his girl, Reneé Wolf. Marv was a good friend of Lenny's and did just that. I received a wedding invitation for their June 24th marriage (Reneé and Marv), which I couldn't attend. Destiny was molding its inexorable pathway; Reneé's skinny kid-sister, the one I had ushered at a football game, and the one that launched a ship as a result of the war bond drive, was cast for an important role in my karma. The switching of roommates was evolving.

I received a midnight call from Captain Peter Washko, that their Cocker Spaniel was having a difficult labor. She needed help with a breach delivery. The first of five turned out to be a little black female. I demanded her as my fee for services rendered. I had planned her destination. She was to be Reneé and Marv's wedding gift.

The war was winding down and many of the wounded were being transferred to other Army hospitals. I got orders to proceed to Camp Blanding, Daytona Beach, Florida, for six weeks of detached service. Little Blacky, finally housebroken, was hurriedly crated and shipped, via the American Railway Express, to Marv and Reneé in Mount Vernon, New York.

In a typical Army snafu, Camp Blanding had never been informed of my orders, and had nothing for me to do. I had an army paid, six weeks, detached service vacation at fabulous Daytona Beach and the days flew. I headed back to Foster General Hospital, to help with its demise.

The patients had left as did most of the medical staff. Captain and Mary Jane Washko, their daughter, "Buttons", and dog, "Blacky", said a teary farewell as they left for a General Hospital in New Jersey. Most of my other friends were gone.

The quartermaster was tightening its belt and selling everything the Army considered surplus. Instruments, beds, drugs, linen, uniforms etc. Colonel Campbell, Parker's replacement, told me to sell or give away everything in the Officer's Club that moved or could be eaten.

The medical labs were closed, but the rabbits and the hutch were still my responsibility. There were about fifty furry rodents that I had visited twice weekly for two years, treating minor ailments and a chronic infestation of ear mites. To my surprise, I had became allergic to them and, in those last few weeks, sneezed and coughed a farewell to rabbit medicine forever.

Strolling the silent corridors that I would never forget, I waxed poetic. Foster General had served its country well and I couldn't allow it to ever fade from memory.

Ode to Foster General Hospital

Born 7 September, 1943
Died 15 December, 1945

The endless corridors dwindle,
The crutch's song is dead.
The empty wards are searching
For some young, blond soldier's head.

The MP gates are fastened shut,
The flagpole's sleek and naked.
The motor pool's without a hum,
The green lawns long forsaked.

No more the mess hall's clatter,
No whistle, no pretty nurse
To turn those heads of fighting men
Who battered a tyrant's curse.

The surgeon's gloves are idle,
His mask and knife lay bare.
The ether cone is put away,
There's no more tension there.

The swimming pool is dry and sad,
The gym doors closed and sealed.
The shouts of play no longer swing
An echo from yon football field.

The theatre's screen is dim and cold,
No train of light cuts through.
The chapel's altar long lay hid
From prayer and care of Gentile, Jew.

There is no more noise in the Red Cross hall,
Those rooms of cheer and games bereft.
Headquarters sleeps with its work well done,
For the CO has long since left.

Fashioned by claws of need and war,
Slumbered by health and peace.
Nestled quietly in rural charm,
May your dreaming never cease.

Dream with your sons of a world to come.
Dream of God's wish for peace.
Born of freedom's bid for right,
Foster General, for your cares, surcease.

I sat in my room at the bachelor officer's quarters alone and perspiring. There was no place to go and no one to talk to. Jezebel had been packed and ready for weeks. I telephoned my goodbyes to Melna and Ann, promising to write and begging them to do the same. I called the Jones's and spoke to Babe. I told them that I would fill up at their station on my way out, just as I did coming, on my first day two years before. I visited with Dr. Chadwick and Martha, discussed a few cases and thanked him for the opportunity to practice small animal medicine.

At last. The orders! The Welch Convalescent Hospital in Florida, was to be my first destination. From there I was sent almost immediately to Camp Blanding, Florida. Then the news I had dreamed about for forty-one months. "Report to the separation center at Fort Dix, New Jersey."

My last day in the army was unforgetable. The drive from Camp Blanding was a happy, summertime experience. Jezebel and I arrived at Fort Dix, New Jersey, on July 10, 1945. *I was going home*, and everything was bright.

Before signing my separation papers, I was offered the rank of major if I would remain in uniform. Thanks, but no thanks. Almost four years working for Uncle Sam was enough and I was happy to be a civilian again.

Melna Nichols and Lieutenant Ted Zimmerman, in Jackson, Mississippi, in 1945

JACKSONIAN Aids WAC Recruiting: Miss Anne Buchanan, left, reporter for the Clarion-Ledger, observed the on the line training of airplane mechanics at Keesler Field's B-24 Liberator Bomber school during her visit to Keesler's Army Air Force Training Command Station. She is shown here with 2nd Lieut. Kathleen Burger, assistant WAC Recruiting officer at Keesler. (Official Photo U. S. Army Air Forces Command.).

Ann Buchanon, reporter for Jackson, Mississippi's Clarion Ledger, with friend.

VII

Home

The following Sunday I was home. Dad had put a down-payment on a broken down four-story brownstone building about to be condemned. It was at 47 East 30th Street, where it had been abandoned for several years and looked it. Dad was very excited about its potential and was planning to use his carpentry skills to prove it. It was located just off Fourth Avenue. This was where I was to begin practicing veterinary medicine.

"I'm going to make the main and basement floors as the animal hospital," he said, enthusiastically, "the second floor for Mom and me. Joe will have his own room on the third floor and the rest of the third and fourth floors, seven rooms in all, will be furnished and converted to rentable, income producing rooms." Dad figured the renovation would take about six months.

Norman was home from the army also and took one of the third floor rooms. He had been an enlisted man for a couple of years and brought back a bitter taste for officers. He even looked at me with suspicion.

"Relax Norm," I said. "I'm going to take you and Joe on a cross-country trip in Jezebel. We'll see America the right way, by car, and get reacquainted."

Joe had been accepted to Ohio State University and was free for the summer. He was thrilled at the thought of touring the United States with his big brothers.

"I can't afford to share the expense." Norman said.

"It's on me." I told them, "I have about $700 in terminal leave pay and I think this might be the last time we three will have the time to be together."

Before our projected pleasure trip, I had the planning of the hospital to consider. We needed capital! The brownstone would require a new heating plant, hot-water boiler, new pipes, a new roof, some new walls, paint, wallpaper, furniture and veterinary equipment for the office.

"The back yard is ideal." I told my Pop, "There is no way of animals escaping, even agile primates."

I looked up at the three surrounding buildings towered twenty or more stories high. The yard was sixty feet deep and twenty feet across. "The runs will require a concrete floor and metal fencing to separate the animals." I told my Dad. "It will be large enough to exercise fifteen animals at a time."

We figured it would take about $5,000 to pay for repairs and equipment. We tried local banks for a loan, but were refused. We didn't have sufficient collateral. Uncle Stein was a possibility but we would only go to him as a last resort. He had been so good to us through the years that we hated to ask him again.

I called Rosy. What are good friends for? "Do you think your Dad will consider a loan so I can start my practice?" I asked.

"I'll get back to you." He said.

Mr. Rosengarten had a string of successful supermarkets. We thought he might be willing to lend us the money at a fair rate of interest.

Rosy called me back in less than ten minutes. "Come on over." he said.

"Thanks, Rosy," I told him. "I've got an appointment with Dr. Corwin in Jamaica. I'll send by brother Norman for the necessary papers. And Rosy. . .we can't thank you and your dad enough."

We expected Norm to pick up a loan agreement from Mr. Rosengarten. Instead, $5,000 in bills were stuffed into a brown envelope and given to poor Norman. He was plenty nervous. That amount of money was a fortune in those days, and carrying it on the streets of New York was nerve-racking.

I called Marv and Reneé to see how they were getting along. They had an apartment in Mount Vernon where I sent their wedding gift, Blacky Jr., the Washko's Cocker Spaniel puppy. I couldn't understand why I hadn't received a "thank you."

Marv answered. "High Squinch, where are you?"

"Just got home. I can't wait to see you two. I don't have any female connections any more. Get me a date and we'll go out double."

There was a pause. Then. "I'm trying to think of a girl who's single."

"She doesn't have to be a beaut. Just anyone so we can be together."

"The only one I can think of is my kid sister-in-law. She's a little young but very nice."

"Okay," I said. "If she's Reneé's sister she has to be okay. I remember her all right. I met her with her folks at a Cornell football game years ago."

"By the way, how is 'Blacky'?" Another long pause.

"We. . .uh. . .gave him away." I could see him squirming.

"You WHAT?"

Defensively, "He made too much of a mess. He wasn't housebroken."

"Marv, I spent a month training him myself. He was perfectly housetrained."

"The first thing he did when he got here was mess under the piano. . .on our new rug!"

"Marv, how many days did it take for the crate to get here from Mississippi?"

"The man said three days."

"Was the crate clean?"

"Spotless."

"Did you take him out for a walk? Three days is a long time for a puppy."

(long pause. . .)

"We never thought of it.". . .

"Who'd you give him to?"

"He got a great home." Animatedly, "Uncle Leo and Aunt Ruth. They love him and he's very happy.

"I'm glad." I said resignedly. "It could have been a great idea."

"Reneé never had a pet and she was too busy fixing up the apartment. But we really appreciated the gift, it was just that the timing was off."

"Okay. When are we going to get together?"

A few days later Marv phoned. "We decided to get tickets to a show in two weeks, on a Saturday night. Reneé says you should call Elaine first and maybe just drop over to see her."

The following week I made the trip to fourteen Alameda Place in Mount Vernon, New York. I rang the bell and waited. I could hear laughing in the background. A maid answered and I asked for Elaine. The maid was Irish, looked me over carefully before calling out.

"Elaine! Your date."

A young lady in long pig-tails, nothing at all like the one I remembered, scampered down the stairs chasing a girl friend, both hilarious.

They came over impishly goading each other. The other one said, "I'm Selma Seltzer, glad to meet you."

"Glad to meet you." I answered.

"Let me introduce you to Elaine." She said mock seriously and then howled with glee.

Elaine apologized explaining that they were roommates in college and always giggled and carried on like that. The three of us small-talked for a while and I couldn't take my eyes off Elaine. I tried not to show it, but I was smitten. Before I left, Elaine and I confirmed the date.

I went to a fraternity party alone that night and was surprised to see Elaine. She had a date with Harvey Gladstone, a frater we called "Happy-Rock." I think I saw more of her that night than he did. That magic spark of love was simmering. I couldn't get her out of my mind.

Saturday, next, was the appointment with Marv and Reneé. We had tickets for "King Edward III", an off-Broadway show but I was obsessed with a drama of my own. I picked her up at 7:00 PM. Marv had called to tell me that Reneé wasn't well and they couldn't join us. Elaine and I went to see Shakespeare alone. We sat in the back of the theater. Neither of us heard one line of the play.

The following Monday my brothers and I loaded down Jezebel with our gear and $700 worth of traveler's checks (every cent of my terminal leave pay). The three of us were off for the West. Elaine's face was with me every mile; I wasn't happy about leaving-- however, a promise is a promise and the boys had my word.

I returned home three weeks later and went to work for Dr. Corwin. I crammed in all I could about running a successful small animal practice. Weekends were spent helping Dad fix up 47 East 30th Street. I also spent a lot of time on the phone with Elaine. She was still at college in Ithaca.

Thanksgiving brought her home. I couldn't believe that I could miss anyone so much. She was the answer to real fulfillment. I'd wondered for years how I would ever know love if and when it came. Mom always said that when the real thing arrives you will know it and there would be no doubt. How right she was and how happy I was!

We were married on Christmas eve, 1946, at the Essex House in New York.

The Beverlie Animal Hospital was finally completed and I was ready to go. The drugs, pills and medicines had been delivered. Thanks to Dr. Corwin I knew just what to order. Dog and cat foods were in the storage room downstairs and my name was outside the front door on a small copper plaque. "THEODORE ZIMMERMAN, D.V.M". It was a modest size to satisfy the ethics of the veterinary profession. A small blue awning stretched from the door to the roadway, serving the dual purpose of protecting my customers from the rain and telling them in new, white letters that "The Beverlie Animal Hospital" had arrived. Over the door, again in freshly painted, white letters and numbers, "47 East."

I was the luckiest man in America, married to the greatest, prettiest gal and a member of the most wonderful, caring, loving family in the entire universe!

"Beverly," was Elaine's middle name. At city hall I was told that some laundry already had that title and I couldn't use it for the name of my hospital. A quick spelling change to "BEVERLIE" was approved and I was official. We took the small, modest, half inch listing in the phone book, and were assigned, "Murray Hill 4-2784". We were ready for business. . .almost.

Dad said, "Before you open you doors for business we need a C.O. from the Building Department."

"What's that and how do we get it?" I asked.

"Certificate of Occupancy, and don't worry. The inspector was here last week and we had a few small violations. Some plumbing and electric problems that were corrected."

The inspector returned, a short, kindly sort of man, very sympathetic and encouraging to me, the new businessman and New York City entrepreneur.

"I know you'll do just fine." he said as he started his inspection trip through the building. When he finished, he hesitated a moment and said almost embarrassed. "There are just a few infractions, not serious, but the city can't be too careful." He handed Dad the list. "I'll be back next week to check them."

The little man returned several more times, each instance finding something wrong and postponing my opening. One day, I mentioned my dilemma to Rosy and he asked, "Didn't you give him something? Grease his palm?" From the astounded look on my face he surmised what was wrong. "Dummy! You don't get anything in this city without at least a twenty dollar bill."

"I don't believe it." I said. "He knows I'm a veteran with just enough money to get started."

"Try the twenty," Rosy said, "You'll have your C.O. the next day."

I did, and we did, but I was a little hurt and disillusioned, as I finally opened our doors and waited for business. I hoped that eventually clients would discover that I was alive. The first month I grossed $50. The second $153. Each month was a little better as people got to know me and told their friends.

The tale of my Dad's first business in America, came to mind. In a way, his choice, in its inexorable way, had designed the blueprint of my future.

My father, also about my age, walked along New York's Amsterdam Avenue near Eighty-Ninth Street looking for work. He had spent six years in the army, learning English, earning money to start his life in America. He had met and married my Mom and it was time to earn a living. He was an expert cabinet maker ready to put his skills to work.

A store sign caught his eye. "Bird Store" was posted above a glass door entrance. He paused, shaded both eyes against the street reflection, and peered through the window. Shelf upon shelf of tiny cages, with little yellow birds in a melody of motion, filled the opposite wall. They fluttered from side to side, from side to floor, from floor to perch, stopping for a quick drink or a nibble at a white seed dish. Some had their little yellow heads outstretched, tiny throats pulsating like an operatic soprano.

When Dad opened the door, a symphony of trills from a hundred tiny throats magically transformed the street from the usual city clamor to enchanting chords of fairy-tale sounds. He was mesmerized, had never experienced anything like it.

An aged gentleman, stooped and slow-moving, wiped his hands on his soiled apron and stepped out from behind the counter. My dad looked around and was filled with envy—imagine getting paid for caring and listening to these beautiful little creatures.

He didn't leave the shop until closing, and the next day he was back with a hundred questions. Cabinet-making was forgotten. He made an offer to buy the bird store and it was accepted. The shop, and the young Mr. and Mrs. Zimmerman were joined.

Mother's previous job (she worked with sisters Anna, and Ella for Rose, the master milliner), with its fussy women, long hours and inadequate pay, proved too trying for Mother's temperament. Happy to join Dad and the birds, she became the brains and heart of the operation. Sarah was bright, alert, completely fearless, and possessed an innate ablility to manage. In addition to raising a daughter and three sons, she managed a business, was an expert bridge player and ultimate confidante to her family and friends.

Our lives were closely bound to Mom's immediate family. Her oldest sister, Rose (Mrs. Stein), brought her to this country from Europe. It was in Uncle Stein's house that Dad met my Mother. Uncle Adam, the oldest in the family supervised my Bar Mitzva. He was the one my sister Evelyn named our Pet chimp after. It was Ella, another older sister, whose maid, Lena, introduced us to Elise. The youngest of the sisters, Florence, was pressed into service when we were desperate for another nurse to help care for five baby gorillas, hospitalized with pneumonia.

Aunt Rose hosted our family for the annual Passover dinner. This holiday tradition started when I was a child and continued until my uncle's death in the late forties. I loved the Stein home. It was so elegant and clean. The coffee table in the living room held a dish of delicious looking chocolates I never had the nerve to taste. National Geographic magazines, with their fantastic pictures, sat next to the candy. I made up my mind when I grew up, I would get those magazines every month, for the rest of my life.

Passover seders were a time of boredom and starvation. The pre-dinner, religious service seemed interminable. I felt as though I would die before the first course was served, to signal the start of a wonderful feast. Hard-boiled eggs, crushed in salt water were so delicious, why weren't they served during the year? Broiled chicken, always the main course, was usually preceded by fabulous, matzo balls and noodles in chicken soup.

Cheek-pinching always accompanied the Passover dinner. As we got older, it also became college funding time. My sister's cheeks were abused with no reward until then. The tweeking didn't stop, but at least there was an excuse for the pain. Uncle Stein loved to pinch little girls, his way of showing affection and caring.

Evelyn dreaded it. "Why does he have to pinch so hard?" she whispered to Mother, with her cheek red and tingling.

"It's his way of kissing," Mother answered. "He's telling you he loves you."

"I'm glad he doesn't love me," I said. "Thank goodness he just shakes my hand."

"He has to show you in a different way," Mom assured me. And she was right. As the years passed and circumstances changed, Uncle Stein made it possible for us to get college educations."

During those college years, as one hand pinched or shook, the other thrust two, one-hundred dollar bills in our palms. We were lucky, because we were in colleges where state residents had no tuition. Uncle Stein made it possible to buy the books and pay the fees that most lab courses required. He never questioned its use or said one word to anyone about his gifts. Uncle Stein gave us a lesson in anonymous giving we never forgot. He knew our needs, because both his sons, Mike and Sam, were Cornell graduates.

The first pet shop prospered and, in a year or so, they leased a second store on Broadway and Eighty-Third Street. Puppies and kittens were added to the inventory.

Soon my sister, Evelyn, arrived and, two years later, I was born and nicknamed the "war baby", because the First World War had just begun, and young fathers with two children were exempt from service. But I was born into the animal business and like my parents, remained for life.

Dad's first pet shop, "The Bird Store" in 1914

VIII

Trefflich's

As my practice got off the ground, I wondered how and when I could get started working in a zoo. In early 1948, the Beverlie Animal Hospital awaited recognition. My practice was confined to dogs and cats except for the few pet monkeys recommended by my Mom or by Gimbel's Pet Shop. I waited impatiently for a call from Dad's old friend, Henry Trefflich.

The Trefflich's Bird and Animal Company, the huge, department store pet shop, was located at 228 Fulton Street in lower Manhattan. It occupied an entire four-story, brownstone building, located where New York's Twin Towers now stand. Dad had worked at the retail store at Trefflich's five years earlier.

When I was in high school, Mr. Trefflich encouraged my goal of getting into veterinary college. He said, "Work hard, Ted, and some day you can work for me. I'll need someone to travel to Africa, Asia and South America, to care and treat all the wild animals America will need for its zoos."

That fired my imagination and I dreamed of faraway lands with their myriad species making their way to the United States, with me in charge.

"Maybe Mr. Trefflich forgot about me and his promise," I complained to Dad.

Dr. Goss, from the Bronx Park Zoo, examined and treated the animals arriving from overseas and consigned to Trefflich's. He would submit the necessary health certificates needed for re-shipment to Trefflich's customers, and his clients were the zoos of America. Goss had the job I was promised, but I kept dreaming about someday having my aspirations fulfilled.

During the Second World War, rhesus monkeys, desperately needed for basic research on Infantile Paralysis (Polio), were officially embargoed by India. President Roosevelt, our most famous polio victim, intervened to secure a high priority for Trefflich to import them, but the U. S. Health Department wanted proof (by standard intradermal T.B. testing) that tuberculosis was not being introduced into the United States. Once the embargo was lifted, Henry could import approximately 3,000 per week. There were sufficient animals to fill the needs for a polio vaccine, as well as the requirements of many other research laboratories and pharmaceutical houses.

Dr. Goss had neither the time nor inclination to do TB testing; a time-consuming and relatively dangerous undertaking so he suggested to Trefflich that he hire a hungry young vet for the job.

I found out that Henry hadn't forgotton me. I was young and hungry and delighted when his secretary called.

"Dr. Zimmerman," she began, "This is Francis Lenz calling. I'm calling for Henry Trefflich. He'd like you to drop over and discuss a T.B. testing program for imported monkeys."

My experience with T.B. testing had been limited to tailfolds in cattle. I had no idea what lay ahead but was sure that adapting to monkeys would be simple.

"In addition," she added, "he would like you to keep an eye on the health of all the other pets in the shop, and occasionally back up Dr. Goss when imported animals need examinations and certificates at Port of Entry."

Francis Lenz was bookkeeper, telephone receptionist, treasurer and general all-around helper. She was invaluable to Henry, a quiet, efficient and very likeable lady in her mid-forties. In addition to her regular duties, she handled hiring and firing at the pet shop, contacted institutions interested in purchasing research animals, and wrangled with them on prices.

"We have a lot of losses, and insurance is expensive!" she told me in confidence. "We're going to need your certificates to prove our claims." I never gave her remarks a second thought, but learned later that more than my medical expertise and professional ethics would be tested.

I was happy for the work, and God knows I wanted wild animal experience. During my four years in the army, I hadn't saved much and the extra income would be substantial. In addition to the T.B. testing, I would be exposed to a variety of jungle creatures, large and small, wild and tame. It would be like going to school all over again, but now I would be learning about the animals that I cared about most.

"Too bad the war tied you up, Ted," were Henry's first words. "I could have used you four years ago. Now you will be T.B. testing primarily, but there are always animals arriving ill or getting sick around here."

T.B. testing was routine, but very exciting. The only objection I remember was the noxious odor that permeated our hair, skin and clothing afterward. Elaine would greet me at the door, holding her nose, and immediately put my clothes into the laundry hamper and me into the shower.

The expensive primates were kept on the third floor. There were gorillas, chimps, orangutans and baboons representing the large monkeys. The marmosets were the tiniest. Between the extremes were the ringtails, woolys, howlers, macaques, gibbons, capuchins, green and squirrel monkeys.

My work with John and Harry (Henry Trefflich's helpers) was on the fourth floor where huge, room-size cages held hundreds of newly arrived, wild, stinking rhesus of all ages and varied stages of health. Once a healthy monkey, weighing fifteen pounds, dragged John, piggy-back, the length of the room by his powerful legs, as John clung desperately to his arms, pinned behind his back.

Entering one of the cages, each man had a home-made burlap net and a whispered prayer. They hoped they wouldn't be attacked from behind by a frightened or angry rhesus. To minimize the hazard, they worked back-to-back. The frenzy that ensued had to be seen to be believed. Wide-eyed animals hurled themselves across the cage, defecating as they flew, getting as far away from the men as possible. But John and Harry were so skilled with the nets, they could nab an agitated rhesus in midflight, with the ease of a butterfly catcher. Once a monkey was in the burlap, the catcher stepped outside the cage, swinging his catch back and forth before setting it down between his legs. Looking down through the open end at the helpless, snarling catch, he would pin it to the ground with a lightning grab around the waist from outside the net. Then kneeling, with the ape between his knees, would reach inside to pin the monkey's arms. As he dropped the net and lifted him out, his other hand would grab both legs, rendering the wild creature helpless and stretched taut. They were then offered to me head-first, for testing.

I had to grasp their heads in my left hand— quick reflexes saved many a nasty bite at that stage. A single bleb of tuberculin, injected with a tiny quarter inch, 26-gauge, intradermal needle went into the paper-thin skin of the right eyelid.

It took a couple of dozen tries before I mastered the technique. John laughed as they jerked their heads, letting the needle slip out or go right through the eyelid. "Keep trying, Doc," he would say. "It takes most doctors forty of fifty eyes before they get it right."

"Don't laugh," Harry would say, embarrassed for me. "You' doin' jes fine, Doc. It ain't easy hitten a movin' head with a tiny needle."

Forty-eight hours after the injection, a return visit was necessary to "read" the test. A swollen eye meant positive, and euthanasia for the infected monkey. The healthy ones were certified and could be shipped out.

The Trefflichs, father and son Henry, emigrated from Germany in the early 1900's. They had already collected animals and birds from all over the world, and stocked the zoos and zoological parks of Europe.

Father Trefflich had the notion that a fortune could be made by employing natives from the jungles of Africa, India or South America, have them capture indigenous species, and sell them for profit where there was a demand.

Henry's genius, carefully nurtured by his Dad, was in making deals with the hunters, the poachers, even the native governments, and arranging the creatures for transfer by ship or plane to the United States. As a child, Henry made many a pilgrimage, and learned about safaris from his father. He became expert at securing and managing shiploads of rare animals and birds, attempting to treat many of the sick and dying creatures himself. It was heartbreaking to toss rare, valuable animals overboard because no veterinarian or experienced handlers were available. He even contemplated hiring a traveling taxidermist to preserve the magnificent specimens lost en route to America.

The logistics of shipping wild animals and birds were complicated and expensive. Cages had to be constructed strong enough to hold some of the world's most powerful creatures. Food, water and medicine were assembled to feed and care for them. Keeping them alive, confined for many weeks, with little exercise and no fresh air or sunlight in holds of tramp steamers, was a monumental task, until jet aircraft arrived. Then, restraining full-grown elephants, hippos or baby giraffes on cargo planes was a risky and sometimes dangerous mission, as well. Insurance was expensive, and the losses tremendous.

Once in the Port of New York, strings had to be pulled to ease them through customs quickly. Once released, an immediate asylum was needed for the miserable, seasick, weakened, frightened animals and birds that survived. The three New York City zoos, and the privately operated New York Zoological Park (the Bronx Zoo) were the closest available havens. John Fitzgerald, the Central Park Zoo's chief keeper, worked part-time at Trefflich's (where I met him), giving Henry an "in" at the closest zoo to the port of entry.

Trefflich was one of the first importers to use air transport to hasten the journey from jungle to zoo. Every zoo and circus in the country had one or more of his animals. In addition to the New York parks, a nationwide network of municipal zoos existed. They included the cities of San Francisco, Pittsburgh, Chicago, Kansas City, Forth Worth, Colorado Springs, Rochester, Denver, Buffalo, Dallas, Cleveland, Detroit, St. Louis, Washington, D.C., Racine, Toledo, Milwaukee, Little Rock, San Antonio, Boston, Omaha, Baltimore and Indianapolis.

Working for him, I learned about and treated birds of such infinite variety and beauty that just recognizing them was a monumental task. It wasn't easy adapting what I studied in Poultry Husbandry and Avian Diseases, under Dr. P. P. Levine, in Vet School. There we learned about chickens, turkeys, geese and ducks, but nothing about the myriad of wild and exotic birds I would be exposed to.

Their diet alone proved to be a study in nutrition that had to be improvised and applied, to maintain them in prime condition. I overcame my initial fright about mastering the perplexities of avian medicine, and took on the responsibilities with exhilaration and excitement.

I told Elaine, after my first exposure to a shipment of rare, ailing birds: "Except for the differences in size, feather-coloring and origin, a bird is a bird. They all have crops and gizzards to aid digestion, and air-sacks in their bones to allow them easy flight. They're all susceptible to bacteria, viruses and genetic disorders, whether from the Amazon or Antartica and respond to sound medical treatment." I told her I thought I could treat them like any other patient and I wouldn't allow myself to be intimidated by their diversity, beauty or value.

The singing canary was the most common bird in my dad's pet shops, as well as at Henry's. As a child, I took canaries for granted, thinking they were born and bred in a cage, but in college, I researched their history, and found that canaries are very much native to the wild outdoors. They have always been friends of farmers because their short, strong bills were built for crushing seeds, particularly the types that choke and kill a garden by growing into prolific weeds.

Trefflich said, "The finest and hardiest canaries came from the Hartz Mountains of Germany. Nearly every peasant, farmer, woodcutter, and anyone else who had a house or barn, raised a few birds. Careful breeding gave us the hardy bird we have today."

England, Holland, France and Belgium took up the breeding and selling of these birds, specializing in large, colorful pets.

"Look at these colors, Ted," Henry said, proudly, "developed by the English through years of experimentation. Aren't they breathtaking? Orange or pink or deep yellow. The English called these birds, 'Pepper-fed', because the colors are produced by feeding them large quantities of sweet pepper, pimento or saffron, or combinations of them. Compared to the Hartz Mountain birds, they are overfed, fat and lazy and don't sing well. Keeping these birds healthy will tax your ingenuity."

From my point of view, they were always becoming ill, needing treatment and therapeutic changes in diet. Recently the Japanese began raising canaries, and captured a large part of the American market. However their birds have never attained the song quality of the Hartz Mountain strain.

I thought many of the seed-eaters needed some meat in their diet, because insects supply the needed protein in their natural habitat. I told Henry my idea and he said, "Go ahead!" I added egg white and milk protein for the thirteen essential aminoacids, and the creatures thrived.

Exotic birds like the Quetzal, one of the most beautiful birds in the world, originate in the forests of Central America, from Mexico to Costa Rica. I was enthralled with its crested head, bronze-green back, and crimson and white underparts. I appreciated why it became the national bird of Guatemala. Their diet consists of grated carrots, sweet potatoes, Pablum, corn flour and honey, in the morning, and fresh plums, grapes or cherries in the afternoon. The first two Quetzals I examined had a chronic respiratory infection. I hid the medication in their food balls and, in a week or so, they were cured.

Sanitation and fresh food are essential in raising, selling and shipping the birds. Along with feeding and watering daily, they must be cleaned—an enormous chore when thousands of birds are shipped from a foreign country on a slow boat, on rough seas. A trained expert must accompany each shipment. Originally, when I was in highschool, Henry envisioned me making the trips, but time changed that. Now my responsibility was for the new birds to leave Trefflichs for their final destinations in good health, good song and looking beautiful, besides.

I was at Trefflichs on a routine visit and I saw a woman holding a baby ape that I hadn't seen before.

"Henry," I asked, "who is that? She seems very much at home here."

"Haven't you met Sadie Taylor?" he asked. "She's our infant primate expert. She keeps the babies healthy and away from you doctors. Come meet her."

"Nice to meet you, Sadie," I said. "I'd like to learn more about the baby apes and I understand that you are the one to see."

"And I've heard about you, doctor. Mrs. Lenz tells me that you are pretty good yourself."

"Thanks, but I'm still learning."

Henry interjected with, "Sadie developed a formula for the baby apes that has been used all over the country. I'm sure you two will be working together."

"I hope not," she said. "I want these babies to stay healthy so you will never have to be consulted."

I didn't know too much about their treatment but I found out all that was known about their origin, natural diet, habits, life span, temperament, etc. Sadie, the infant primate expert, mothered them as if they were her own. She was holding a young gorilla at the time but Henry mentioned she took care of orangutans and chimpanzees as well.

I read that gorillas are found in two places: the steaming, rain-soaked forests of East Africa, and the mountains of the Belgian Congo. The lowland ones have shorter hair and thinner coats than their mountain cousins.

I thought the apes were close enough to humans for me to talk to a good pediatrician. Dr. Janice Nightingale, a specialist in pediatric medicine from Scarsdale was the wife of Eddie, my close friend and former college roommate. She advocated a careful physical examination and described how she examined her patients.

As the months passed and I became more comfortable with my duties, I went to Idlewild Airport (now JFK) to examine a consignment of eighteen-foot-plus pythons, that were arriving in a heatless cargo plane from South America. Henry was worried about their condition and wanted Dr. Goss to examine them. Goss was busy at the zoo and snakes were easy to examine, so he sent me instead. Some of them weighed over 150 pounds, and arrived in crates that were about four feet square and two to three feet high. I was told to see the pilot, check the number of snakes and their condition, then pay the bill. Fifteen crates were stacked on a loading rack. I had Harry with me to help open and close the boxes. Snakes don't make any noise so it was hard to tell how they were without looking at each individually.

Standing on the ramp was a worried looking young man who seemed to be in charge. As we approached, he looked at my medical bag. "You're from Trefflich's." He said.

"Right, I'm to examine a shipment of pythons."

As he spoke, I realized he was the pilot of the cargo plane. He began apologizing for his route from the Amazon.

"We had terrible storms and I had to fly above them. We have no heat in the hold and I'm sure it was freezing back there. I dropped back down as soon as I could but we were pretty high for a couple of hours."

Harry pried open the first crate. A huge, coiled, net-like python lay quietly; its polychromatic skin glowed in the subdued light. It didn't move. Carefully, I reached in and grasped him just behind the head. Dr. Goss and his assistants always handled big snakes that way. The skin was cold and there was no reaction. The huge reptile had frozen to death. My first reaction was shock.

Slowly I turned, "Open them all up, Harry."

Crate after crate revealed the same. One medium-size specimen I decided to examine more thoroughly. I tried to open the jaw, in a manner I use for a dog or cat, slipping the lip over the teeth and forcing the mouth apart. I should have known better—a snake doesn't have a lip. I tried to force the frozen jaws to move, and one of the more than nine dozen teeth pierced my thumb. It was as sharp as a razor and caused immediate, profuse bleeding. I couldn't believe I had been bitten by a dead snake. I sucked my thumb as Harry opened the remainder of the boxes. We found three snakes clinging to life. They had been stacked on the bottom of the pile. The ones piled on top had partially protected them from the freeze.

The pilot watched in silence, saddened by what he was witnessing. "God, I'm sorry," he said. "It's the first living cargo I've ever lost."

"We'll have to get heated planes," I answered, wondering what Henry would say. I phoned him to get instructions.

"Bring them in," he said. "We're insured. Tell the pilot I'll send him a check as soon as the claim is paid."

We saved two of the three frozen pythons with warm baths and special food (heated warm chopped beef, fortified with vitamin and mineral suppliments), forced down their throats. Mrs. Lenz had certificates for me to sign for the insurance claims. Fifteen snakes were listed on the itemized request.

"Frances," I said, "we saved two of those phythons. We only have to collect on thirteen." From the look on her face, I could see she knew also. She was only following orders but I made my point. I was never asked to fake insurance reports again.

The following week, I was back at the airport (different pilot and plane) to examine and pick up a load of very large birds from Europe. Henry warned me to be particularly careful because they were swans. "They're mean as hell, so don't try to touch them unless you have to."

He proceeded to tell me about those graceful, beautiful avians. I'd always admired them but at vet school we saw them only in books.

"There are many different strains," he said, "but one thing they have in common is their disposition. They breed from Southern Alaska to Idaho and Indiana, while some winter in South Texas and California. Whooper and Bewick swans nest across the Eurasion tundra, migrating in winter to Great Britain and northern Europe, and some go as far as Japan and China. Whistling, Trumpeter, Bewick and Mute swans are all pure white, while black and black-necked swans come from Australia."

I thought about recent golf games at our country club in Westchester. I remembered that imitation swans were anchored in the lakes. They were very well made white birds with arching, graceful necks. "They're supposed to keep the Canadian Geese from messing up the fairways," our golf club supervisor told me when I questioned their use. "They really helped for a few weeks--but that was all." Live swans would have worked much better because all too soon the floating scarecrows were ignored by the waddling, messy invaders from the north.

The plane handlers unloaded two crates with a black and a white bird in each. I looked them over through the well-spaced slats before prying open the lids, and it was obvious one white female was in trouble. She was down and one wing sagged awkwardly. It looked broken and I knew a metal pin would be needed to set the fracture. When we brought the crates to Trefflich's, Henry showed me how to restrain them without getting bruised by powerful wings or nipped by sharp bills. It took three men to restrain the fowl in spite of her injured wing. They put her in a burlap sack, leaving only her head exposed. I took her to the hospital and set her wing with a steel pin.

The recovering swan had the run of one of our fenced outdoor exercise areas for two or three weeks, intimidating every dog and person she saw. The staff became accustomed to her and an affection grew between her and my attendant, Ken Haffner. No one else could get close without getting chased by the ill-tempered bird. When she was fully recovered, Trefflich shipped her out West where she had a tranquil lake to swim in and other waterfowl to boss.

*Henry Trefflich's department store pet shop at 288 Fulton Street,
New York City in 1960*

Henry Trefflich's African Connection

*Six men supporting a twenty foot boa constrictor on Fulton Street.
Henry Trefflich holds its head*

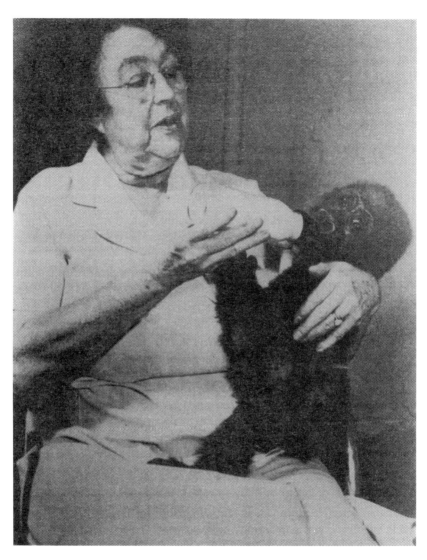

Sadie Taylor, a genius at handling baby anthropoids, feeds an infant gorilla a bottle of Simlac, a special formula used successfully in rearing these animals, which are very delicate in their early months. (Trefflich)

The Beverlie Animal Hospital

"There are killer rays in New York City," I told my mother with a wink and a smile. "They're never mentioned by the media because Mrs. Prettyman, is the only one that sees them."

"Bless her heart," mother said. "She's a dear and I don't want you making fun of her. It's only the one of her many cats that she's worried about. She's sure that her Trixie is safe here, and any excuse she has for feeling that way is okay with me. Don't try to discourage her and don't let her think you don't believe her."

"Don't worry, she's been peculiar for years, but these fantasies are wierd. She swears they streak secretly across the skies," I gesticulated with an out stretched arm, "like the myriad of high powered night-lights at a premier theater opening. She sees them radiating from the 78th floor of the Empire State Building and one of them, a sinister one, is trying to kill her Trixie. How did she put it to you, Mom?"

"Well, there was the usual office full of concerned animal lovers, sitting patiently awaiting their turns." She stopped, trying to recall exactly. "Mrs. Prettyman arrived, wearing her 'turn of the century' wide brimmed hat with a fresh flower tucked into the ribbon. She wore a full flowered blouse that covered her arms down to her wrists. Under one arm was Trixie, the other supported a huge black pocketbook. Two dogs were jumping and barking at each other from opposite sides of the waiting room, and poor Mrs. Prettyman flinched with each exchange. Another lady held her cat on her lap, also annoyed by the commotion."

Mom continued, "Mrs. Prettyman was having obvious difficulty with her load and she told me her problem in a deep masculine voice, forcing it to be heard over the din. I strained to listen to the poor, nervous lady who was both frightened and annoyed. She kept glancing at the noisemakers as the owners attempted to quiet them."

"Trixie isn't ill, but it's very important that I see the doctor immediately," she said.

"Is it an emergency?" Mom asked, looking at the cat in her arms. "These people have appointments and have been waiting."

"Well. . .er. . .no. I'll wait," she said, and turned to sit as far away from the jumpy dogs as she could. Mrs. Prettyman sat with her back to the window facing 30th Street and every few moments turned to look outside apprehensively. Finally, her face showed relief when Mom ushered her into the ward on the first floor of the hospital.

As she walked in and looked around, she nodded to Ken Haffner, always busy with some hospital chore. Then she turned to me and said lightly, "Doctor, you have been blessed. You have the one place in this entire city that can be a haven for Trixie. This kennel right here." And she walked over to an end cage in the battery of twelve that faced the floor-to-ceiling swinging doors leading to our back yard. "Trixie and I are lucky also because, though I know she'll miss home, and we'll miss her, she must stay here until the noxious beam is stilled. I've alerted the police department, but I don't think they will act." Her face hardened as she mentioned the police.

"What beam do you mean, Mrs. Prettyman?" I asked, attempting to get her to verbalize her fears.

"Why do you think I am here, Doctor?" she asked nervously, apparently worried about my reaction. Lowering her voice, she looked anxiously from side to side, and waited for Kenny to move out of earshot, before she spoke, "A death ray has been chasing Trixie for weeks. She is only safe in my arms. I'm exhausted from running and hiding. A friend told me about your kennels. I've been your client for years but never had the need to board my cats. That's why I'm here. Won't you please let her stay?"

"The police are pretty good at tracking such things," I assured her, wondering how much of their time was wasted, chasing fantasies. I probably should have suggested the psychiatric ward of Bellevue, rather than the police. "Tell me more, Mrs. Prettyman. If you know where it's coming from, I'm sure the police will find and stop it."

Her answer was a look of frustration and a shake of her head.

I opened the door of her chosen cage so she could set Trixie down, finally resting her arms. "This kennel is available for as long as you need it," I told her reassuringly, "but what makes you think she is safe here? The diabolic ray you are talking about might follow her anywhere."

She massaged her aching arm, as she explained, "You and I, and Lieutenant Flanagan, of course, will be the only ones who know. On July 28th," she paused and thought for a moment, counting to herself, "it was two years ago, July of 1945. Do you remember when a twin-engine army bomber, lost in a blinding fog, crashed into the Empire State Building?"

I was in the army at the time, but everyone heard about that tragedy, so I nodded.

"By chance, at that exact moment, I was looking out my window, over Trixie's head. She loved to sit on the window sill. I could just make out the Empire State Building. The upper stories were blocked by fog." She closed her eyes and sighed, picturing again one of the most remarkable accidents ever to hit New York City. "A brilliant, orange flame burst from under the fog-covered heights, and I could see debris showering down the side of the building." Tears showed in her eyes, "That's why the rays are chasing us. They were bottled up on that side until the plane crash broke open the brick and mortar of the Empire State Building."

She dabbed at her eyes with her handkerchief and continued, "Look at my arms." She rolled up her sleeves. Her arms had raised red and bluish blemishes. "I must wear long sleeves all the time, thanks to the burns I've received protecting Trixie. She loved to sit by the window, looking at the world for hours at a time." Again she stopped and gathered her thoughts. "The next morning the sky was clear. I could see the 78th floor where the plane struck. It was on the northwest side, facing us and, as we looked, the ray shot out for the first time, looking for Trixie. It found her. That was two years ago and I've been hiding her since." She rested her hand on the wire meshed door. "Thank God that satanic ray can't follow us here."

Mrs. Prettyman never explained why the rays could not penetrate our walls.

Trixie boarded with us for the better part of six months, checked daily by her mistress who also monitored the deadly beam and reported it, personally, to the police lieutenant at the local precinct.

"They are the most inefficient police department in the whole world," she complained, her face twisted in anger. "I've gone to the trouble of pin-pointing the exact window. You'd think they would at least go up there and stop them." She paused with a new thought, "Doctor, would you please talk to Lieutenant Flanagan and insist that his department do something to protect Trixie? I think, as her doctor, he might listen to you."

Dutifully, I phoned Officer Flanagan, a patient and understanding policeman.

"She's been driving us crazy for several weeks," he said. "She hasn't missed a day, coming up here and wasting my time. The first day, she showed me some lesions she said were from the rays. She has psoriasis. My wife has the same condition. The skin gets red and inflamed. But she insists it's from the rays. I know she's harmless," he said kindly. "We've had other people with unfound notions. Isn't there something you can do?"

"It's very real to her, Lieutenant," I said sympathetically. "I suppose eventually the rays will go away as quickly as they appeared."

It took about six months for that to happen and Trixie finally went home. The deadly beam was stilled, and Mrs. Prettyman was left with a six-month boarding bill. She paid it happily, with a lovely and valuable antique gold and garnet necklace; a family heirloom. Her face glowed as she handed me the jewels. "I want Mrs. Zimmerman to have it," she insisted. To this day, Elaine values it as one of her treasures.

It was a ritual for Trixie to see me once yearly for her examination and shots. Mother knew something was wrong when she showed up only three months after their last office visit.

"It's her constipation," Mrs. Prettyman told Mother confidentially. "Nothing helped, and believe me I've tried everything."

Mother scrawled "constipation," across her card for my information. She knew from experience that many clients impart bits of information to her, rather than the doctor.

"Has she been straining?" I asked a moment or so later, motioning Ken to place her on the examination table. I noticed Alicia Prettyman was wearing a short-sleeved blouse and her arms were white and normal. No sign of psoriasis today, I thought. The damaging rays were gone.

"Well, yes," she said, "and besides the straining, Doctor, she is always licking herself."

"How long has it been going on?"

"About three weeks, more or less. She has lost a lot of weight and I'm so worried. After all she's been through, I do hope she'll be allright."

Trixie was painfully thin to the point of emaciation. I weighed her and marked less than four pounds on her chart. Her long, silky hair had all but disappeared, leaving a dull, patchy, mange-like skin. The examination revealed a tumor about the size of a golf ball encroaching on her rectum and effectively blocking her bowel.

Mrs. Prettyman looked away, a little embarrassed. "Is it serious? Can you help her?"

"I'd advise a biopsy. A malignancy would require surgical removal, then follow-up radiation therapy. If it's benign, the surgery will remove the growth and eliminate the problem.

The tumor proved to be a squamous cell carcinoma, highly malignant, very vascular and difficult to remove because of its location.

"Do you think those rays got to her, after all?" she asked. "I was sure Trixie was safe here."

"It's hard to tell, Mrs. Prettyman. These things frequently happen without cause."

"Try to help her, Doctor," she said finally. "I don't want to lose her."

I discouraged surgery because in my opinion the chance of recovery was nil and I told her so.

"I want you to try," she said, "I don't want to look back and wonder what might have happened."

I operated on a very friable, bleeding mass that broke apart so easily that a sterile sponge was more effective than a scalpel to remove it. Trixie went home after surgery and one radiation treatment, returning weekly for three more x-ray exposures.

As Mother made out her bill, she knew the visits were hopeless, but necessary therapy for Mrs. Prettyman's psyche. I was sure I'd never see Trixie again.

A year later, Mother checked in Mrs. Prettyman's cats for their annual, prophylactic inoculations and examinations. Ken Haffner was helping and lifted one of her cats to the table. It was, I assumed, a new member of her family, as Mother made out an unmarked clinical card. My mind turned to Trixie, probably because this cat resembled her. Mrs. Prettyman hadn't told me when Trixie died and I never had the chance to express my sympathy. Because of her usual, solemn nature, I didn't know whether or not she was still upset about Trixie.

As I checked the cat, it was easy to see Trixie's replacement looked as much like her as was possible and I wondered if I should mention it. The new cat was normal, weighed close to ten pounds and had a shiny, healthy coat. Her mouth indicated a rather mature animal and, except for a mild periodontal condition, was in good health.

Before asking questions about medical history, I brought up the subject of Trixie's demise. "You never did tell me how Trixie made out." I finally said, hoping I wasn't digging up painful memories.

She looked at me oddly then turned to Ken, "Don't you recognize her?. . .How could anyone ever forget Trixie?"

In October, 1949, a tall, blonde, blue eyed, well dressed gentleman walked into the waiting room and confronted mother.

"Is the doctor here?" He asked in an unfamiliar accent.

"I'm the receptionist. Can I help you?"

"I'm looking for a job. I'm a graduate veterinarian from the University of Bologna Verterinary College in Italy. I need to work while I prepare for the New York State Board Examinations."

Mother was surprised and asked, "You went to school in Italy?"

"I'm Polish and I always wanted to be a veterinarian. The closest school was in Italy so that's where I went. I learned to speak Italian and married an Italian girl."

There was something about him that Mother liked and she wondered what I would say. His frankness is refreshing, she thought, putting his cards on the table at the outset. She walked him back to the treatment ward and introduced us.

"This is. . ." she looked at him for help.

"Jerzy Kseizniak." he repeated, smiling. "Call me George."

"He's a vet from Poland and. . ."

"From Italy," he interrupted. "I'm Polish but I studied at Bologna University." As he talked his eyes took in the entire room and they widened as he spied one of Trefflich's baby chimps in a treatment cage.

I shook his hand, "Glad to meet you, George. Have you any experience with small animals? You seem surprised to see a baby chimpanzee."

"I am. I've seen them in zoos, but never this close. I just arrived and this would be my first job." He couldn't take his eyes off the chimp and slowly shook his head. "We never learned a thing about chimpanzees."

I hadn't considered hiring an assistant, but realized I could certainly use one. Commuting from Westchester took its toll on my time and patience as I sat mired in New York City's all too frequent traffic gridlock. With Henry Trefflich's exotic animal demands in addition to my practice, George could ease the tedious, time consuming hospital procedures. From his reaction to the chimp, I was sure he would be willing to treat wild animals.

The next few weeks proved that hiring George was the best administrative move I could have made. Mother smiled, taking credit for George's presence. She felt responsible for his family and asked him the usual motherly questions.

"Are you happy in your new home? Does your wife speak English? Is she happy with the neighborhood?"

His answer was, "Thank you, yes. We love the neighborhood and she speaks pretty good English. It was a required course in High School. She had much more trouble with Polish. She was the reason I learned to speak Italian so quickly. I needed that for college and we learned English together."

Mother asked, "Do you have any children?"

It gave him the opening to mention the pride of his life, his son, Angelo. "Here is a picture," he showed us proudly. "My son and my wife."

"She's lovely," mother said. "and Angelo is a beautiful baby."

Angelo was all of eleven months old at the time, and George admitted he could only utter a few unintelligible words, but he was convinced that his brilliance was so apparent, that it had to be shared. Grandma was quick to produce a snapshot of Ricky, her first grandson, and she received appropriate raves in return.

Bologna probably couldn't meet New York State's standards for veterinary procedures, but it did a fine job on George, nevertheless. He must have been an outstanding pupil, a stickler for detail with a gift for digging out obscure diagnosis. If he got a negative slide on a stool analysis from one of our patients, he followed up with daily testing for a least a week. On more than one occasion, George picked up elusive ova that I would have long given up on. A difficult diagnosis, solved by his medical footwork, would have made his professors smile with pride.

Henry Trefflich was soon to benefit from his rare expertise. One day I took George with me to Fulton Street to see the huge pet shop. George had a thousand suggestions for Henry to improve the health of his menagerie. One might have thought he had extensive expeience in pet shop medicine. He showed confidence, knowledge and plain old horse sense as he paraded through four floors of exotic and domestic animals.

"I like your new assistant," Henry told me on my next visit. "He spotted an ailing lizard and I didn't even know we had. He thought one of the chimps was coming down with something and he was right."

For some reason chimpanzees were plentiful, and consequently, their demand was weak. American zoos hounded Trefflich for baby gorillas and orangutans. Henry had been nagging his African and Asian connections for them. He knew if he could get his hands on some he could name his own price.

It was a routine day at the Beverlie. Rain beat down from an angry New York sky as my staff and I busied ourselves with dogs and cats. Mother picked up the phone for the third time in five minutes. She buzzed me from her desk in the waiting room.

"Son, Trefflich is on the phone. Please pick up. He said baby gorillas are on the way."

"Ted," he crowed, "I just got a wire that two male and four female baby gorillas, are finally arriving. They're costing me $5,000 each but if they are in good health and saleable, I can turn a tidy profit!"

My first thought was how they were captured. It would be my job to examine them initially and then take care of them if they were sick.

George was listening and was becoming excited as I asked Henry for more details. "How old are they? When will they arrive?"

"Tomorrow. At Idlewild. As soon as you pass them through we have a place ready for them. They are from seven months to a year or so in age, and the bill of lading has them at ten to twenty pounds in weight."

The next day I waited impatiently at Idlewild. They finally arrived by plane and I certified that they were in acceptable health and would be confined until T.B. tested or Xrayed. In spite of my certification I saw that two were very thin, one had diarrhea and another, dermatitis. Even so, I checked them through. I planned to follow up with a more detailed examination.

The following day, I couldn't wait for office hours to end so I could drive downtown and complete their checkups. In spite of rain, the usual New York crowds were congregated in front of Trefflich's show windows on Fulton Street as I approached number 228. I joined them, trying to see, between drawn umbrellas, what new animals were featured that day. A couple of primates, a Woolly and an unusual Howler monkey. Also a Coatamundi (a rare South American anteater), a five-foot python and the huge lizard from New Guinea—the one George had spotted a few weeks earlier, now looking fine after taking antibiotics for a week. In addition, a litter each of puppies and kittens; always a crowd pleaser.

I entered, shaking my umbrella, and waved to Mrs. Lenz, standing lookout from behind her office window. She waved a greeting then motioned me to the second floor.

Henry was all smiles as he pointed to the six confused, unhappy little gorillas in a make-shift, baby-pen nursery.

"They're all ready for you, Ted. How do you like them?"

I put down my bag, twisted out of the raincoat and stared at the immigrants from Africa. They sat listlessly on shredded newspaper-- six blobs of jet-black, staring at us, each other and their strange surroundings. They returned my look fearfully and my heart went out to them.

I told Elaine that evening, and her expression mirrored my feelings. "They are like the babies we treated a few years ago, before Sadie Taylor retired. They looked so human, so sad and lonesome." I recalled Uncle, my pet chimp who taught me the hard way, about feelings and yearnings by the great apes for loved ones.

"What about the stories I heard, Henry? You told me that the African governments were very strict about protecting the gorillas. There has been poaching and unbelievable cruelty to adult gorillas." He had to admit that too much money was made by poachers; natives selling gorilla hands as ashtrays, and mounted heads as wall-hanging souvenirs.

"But the African authorities are trying to stop all that," he said defensively.

"Well as long as they're here," I said, "let's do our best for them." I looked around the makeshift nursery. "Do you think you could keep coughing New Yorkers away from them? Remember how Sadie Taylor protected them from casual exposure?"

Pigheaded Henry had a short memory, "Six rare primates sitting together make a rare and exciting exhibit." He said. "We can't keep them away from the public. I'm moving them downstairs as soon as you're finished. I have customers for all of them but I want to show them off for a couple of weeks."

My bag was crammed with all sorts of medical paraphernalia and I pulled out the stethoscope, thermometer and otoscope.

Mrs. Lenz had followed me upstairs with her pencil and pad ready to keep the medical records. "Henry," I asked, "would you do the honors and hold the babies while I look, poke, listen and smell?"

We used a small product scale to register their weights and placed it on the counter which I used as my examining table.

"Let's start with the smallest one," I said, lifting the little female and setting her gently on the bobbing, squeaky scale. She had a cute, gentle face and was so frightened, she piddled as she clung desperately to my arms.

"I'll need a towel," I said, lifting her again, the urine dripping to the counter, "Get me a few C.C.'s for the lab, as long as she cooperated," I said to Henry, nodding toward a small syringe and vial I had taken from my bag.

Mrs. Lenz left to get toweling, and soon the baby was on the scale, scared but dry, and I had my first gorilla urine sample.

"She's almost eleven pounds. Let's call her Matilda."

As it turned out, Matilda was the "lady" of the lot; refined, demure, never lost her temper, and maintained a composed expression on her little, black, wrinkled face.

She objected to the cold stethoscope. "I'm sorry." I said each time she brushed it away. After the weigh-in I lay her on the counter and covered her bottom with a diaper. "We'll need specimens for stool analysis, so keep them all diapered." I requested. "We have to know who's sample is whose. They can't be allowed to soil themselves or each other."

The next baby was a skinny male, much taller than Matilda, had bigger bones but looked fragile. He was frowning and averted his eyes as Henry set him on the wiggling scale.

"Number Two," said Francis, writing, "a boy, twelve and a-half pounds."

"He's the one with the itch." Henry pointed to an area on his forearm where white scales were vivid against the black skin. He was nervously digging at it.

"Dermatitis on right forearm," I repeated for Mrs. Lenz. "He's too thin, Henry." I added, "and his heart rate is rapid. Let's try some penicillin ointment for his arm. If that doesn't work, I'll make a scraping for mange. Have someone file his nails before he digs a hole in his arm."

Mrs. Lenz made the notes and I wondered who would follow up on my instructions. I diapered Two, applied the ointment and returned him to the play pen.

"Ready for the third," said Mrs. Lenz. "How about we call her Bantu?"

Bantu clung to the big male for dear life, and he, in turn, wouldn't let her go. Again Francis' face mirrored concern. "They love each other." she said, as she held the boy's arms, so Henry could lift her out.

I reported, "about fourteen pounds, a nice, solid Swiss girl." I lifted her off the scale, and set her on the counter. She twisted and turned her head, never taking her eyes off the young male.

"How about calling him Samson?" suggested Francis as she jotted his name down. "He's a real lover boy and someday will live up to that name."

"Good idea," Henry said as he returned Bantu to Samson's open arms.

"Let's do number four," I said, and Francis took that for her name. I casually mentioned that Four was the ugliest of the group.

Francis looked hurt. "I'm sure she was considered a beauty in the African jungle."

"You are probably right." I said as I called out her weight, "fifteen pounds. She has a mild infection in her right ear." She allowed me to clean the ear with Q-tips, and apply penicillin ointment.

Number five, Samson. At twenty pounds he was a proud young fellow, sitting upright, holding Bantu with one arm, his other hand pounded an empty tin water cup rhythmically against the floor. "I think you'll need help with him, Henry." I said, "he's not about to release Bantu again." I helped force them apart, but he clung to the cup. Mrs. Lenz smiled as she took notes. Samson was a handsome, healthy specimen, but his dark, wrinkled, masculine face contorted with worry until he was returned to the pen and his Bantu.

"How about Lisa for number six?" Henry suggested.

Lisa, was a petite, normal looking baby girl with a pretty face who kept peering about, as if looking for something. She weighed ten and a-half pounds.

As I returned the instruments to my bag I gave final instructions. "We have to give each baby a separate cage," I said. "except during supervised playtime. Also, each must be given his or her own doll."

Henry listened, but I don't think he heard one word. He was thinking of the publicity and the profit.

"Also," I looked at him and paused to be sure his eyes were focused on me and not a dream, "remember Sadie's baby formula?"

He nodded and smiled. "We'll put them all on the formula. I'll see that they all have dolls. Anything else?"

Mrs. Lenz said. "These are lonely, grieving youngsters and they are so troubled. Someone has to hug them and make a big fuss over them, just the way Sadie did."

I added, "Right! In the wild, baby gorillas are carried, hugged and nursed for at least a year."

There was no doubt that Samson and Bantu would have to be kept together. "They are the exception that proves the rule, Henry." I said. "They really need each other. Tell the handlers to keep them diapered, and label the stool specimens for me. Don't forget to catch urine for the other five."

When I returned to the Beverlie Animal Hospital with my samples, George was happy. It was his first chance to test the great apes and he took special care in doing it. He couldn't wait to tell me his success.

"I've found a heavy infestation of roundworms in Two's stool." He reported. "That explains his emaciation and lethargy."

George took care of the stool analysis and the urine went to the diagnostic lab. The other five babies were normal.

Henry cornered me, "I thought only dogs and cats got round worms and how come only one gorilla has it?"

I explained to Henry about ascarids (round worms), and detailed their life cycle. (my years of research was now bearing fruit).

"They get them from their mothers when she is pregnant. Luckily, only one mother was infested."

"Thank goodness we know the problem." Henry said. "Now let's do something about it."

Even with the two sick babies on hold, Trefflich had a monopoly. Zoos all over the country heard about them through word of mouth. Henry was deluged with requests for their purchase. Before they left his shop he wanted as much exposure as possible, so he kept his word and moved the makeshift nursery to the first floor. He knew it was against my advice, but he was the boss.

"I get a shipment like this once in a lifetime," he boasted. "and I'm going to make the most of it. I'll separate them as you suggested, except for Bantu and Samson, but I want maximum publicity."

Ten days later, the frantic call arrived, "Matilda is coughing and can't breathe. Her temperature is over 105, and her mucous membranes are blue."

"Get her here as soon as possible," I said, with the intoned, 'I told you so.' Here we go again, I thought, remembering Uncle. But now we had penicillin, the sulfonamides. . .and experience.

Baby Matilda was in a police emergency car, racing to the hospital. It seemed I had just put the phone down, when I heard the siren. It rose to a wail as it neared. Henry Trefflich's nerve to use the police for help didn't surprise Mother or myself. We looked at each other knowingly. He could get the United States Army mobilized if he needed them. The emergency lights flashed their intermittent warning as the car screeched to a jarring halt where George had already posted himself. Henry had Francis Lenz accompany the patient. George lifted her out of Mrs. Lenz' arms and rushed in.

He lay "Matilda" on the table and hurried inside to prepare the oxygen tent. It didn't take long to see there wasn't a second to spare. She lay on her back, her terror-stricken eyes pleading for help. Her mouth was open, gasping, her tongue blue, swollen and hot, lolling with each frantic breath. Her body was desperate for oxygen, her forehead burning, her heart pounding.

Mother gazed horrified at her terror-stricken eyes, then up at me, waiting for me to do something. "You've got to help her, she's gasping for air. Her tongue is blue!" My stethoscope picked up an orchestra of discordant string instruments. Matilda had acute bronchial pneumonia.

"George," I called ahead, "is the tent ready?"

Mother's face relaxed as I lifted the baby and backed quickly through the swinging door of the examining room. I hurried toward the Kirshner small animal oxygen tent, my stethoscope wildly swinging with each step. George had the door open and was emptying an ice tray into the acrylic container. I saw the precious element bubbling through the cooling water. George had placed a clean towel on its floor and I set down the terrified infant and shut the door in one motion.

Four pairs of worried eyes watched through the window at the pumping little chest fighting for life. Slowly, worried to death, Mrs. Lenz turned and left. She took a cab back to Fulton Street. Mother went back to the waiting room and I returned to the routine treatment of dogs and cats. George stayed and observed for another minute before he stepped away. He made sure his work allowed him to look inside the cage every few minutes.

Within the hour George saw Matilda perk up and reach for her bottle. "Her membranes look normal, Doctor, and the frightened look is gone." He called over his shoulder obviously relieved. Mother heard and came in to look, a satisfied expression on her face.

Sharing their mood I called Janice Nightingale once more to find out how a pediatric specialist would handle pneumonia and dehydration.

"It doesn't sound good, Ted." Janice started, "You're probably right about pneumonia. With human babies, as long as they keep eating, there is a chance. We'll just hope that baby gorillas are close enough to humans to share similar symptoms and physiology. I don't like the cyanosis (blue membranes showing oxygen need), but it sounds like she's responding. Remember, don't keep her in the tent too long, only a few hours at a time until her mucous membranes are pink. Pure oxygen will dry out her tissues and then she'll need fluids."

"How do I treat that?" I asked, "I don't think I should try to hit a vein on such a baby. It would take such a tiny needle and her skin is like leather. If she struggles the slightest, it will exhaust her. What would you suggest?"

"Saline and dextroxe subcutaneously," she advised, "depending on the degree of dehydration. It's not too painful, and you can give it several times daily. Over the ribs works well and in the abdominal area the skin is usually loose enough to take a hundred or so CC's. I'd advise an antibiotic also. Her pneumonia is probably viral, but secondary infection is what can kill her."

I thanked her and crossed my fingers.

Mother took over the job of holding, hugging, bottle and spoon feeding, plus diaper changes. When the phone rang or a client came through the front door mother would hand Matilda to whomever had a free hand. When finished she rushed back to resume her mothering with the rest of us looking over her shoulder. Matilda was so cute that we all fell in love with her.

As she responded to treatment, we didn't think about the magnitude of the crisis that lay ahead. We assumed the rest of the babies were doing fine but Trefflich had run into an epidemic. Two days later, he called again, cursing his luck. He rushed two more babies to the hospital.

We didn't have any more oxygen tents so we'd have to improvise to accommodate the new patients. The ward had metal dog kennels in a battery of fourteen stacked in three tiers. The middle and lower rows were four across, while the upper—out of reach without a stool--were six small cat cages.

"We'll have to use the metal kennels for additional tents," I told them, and I could see from Mom's expression, she didn't think it possible. "They're not air-tight." she said.

"How about it, George? Do you think we can do something about that?"

He thought for a moment, his face in a frown of concentration, one arm across his chest, the other supporting his chin. "If we can get some rubber sheeting. . ."

"We can use five-inch adhesive tape to seal the edges." I interrupted, walking to the kennels and showing him what I meant.

"I think hardware stores carry rubber sheets," Mother added.

We all agreed it was possible. We had to get started immediately. George was enthusiastic and rushed out to find the sheets. Mother called our veterinary supply house and talked them into delivering a couple of cartons of five inch adhesive tape immediately. As she got off the phone I gave our oxygen supply house an emergency call for five cylinders of oxygen. I hung up smiling and turned to Mom. "The man said they always have extra cylinders on had for just such a happening. They'll get them right over with extra gauges."

Mom called Ken Haffner from the yard, explained what was happening and told him to take all the hospital patients downstairs to the boarding areas. George found rubber sheeting in a local hardware store and to be sure, bought enough for a dozen tents.

The three of us stood before the now empty battery of cages, contemplating the task ahead. For a few moments nobody spoke.

Mom broke the ice. "We have to use the middle row for the tents because I want to see what's going on without using a stool."

When Dad walked in for lunch he was drafted for his expertise. He supplied plastic tubing from his fish tanks, to bubble the gas through ice water, using our stainless steel feed dishes to hold the ice.

George hummed a foreign lullaby as we measured and taped the rubber around each kennel. Holes were made for the hoses. Dad taped them air-tight to each tent. The doors presented a problem. As George and I frowned and pondered, Dad solved the puzzle by using the five-inch adhesive tape to seal the doors every time they were opened or closed. "They will have to be changed as soon as they lose their sticky." he said.

George cut little windows in the sheeting that covered the doors, his hum breaking into song, and he taped plastic over them so we could look inside. We were all set except for the oxygen tanks and the gauges.

No one was surprised when Two, the weakest of the lot, arrived with Bantu, Samson's soul mate. Two caught our attention immediately.

"I'm afraid he is gravely ill," I told them. "He can't even sit up. Look at his chest." He needed oxygen so desperately that Matilda had to leave the Kirshner cage, and Two took her place. Bantu, would have to wait her turn. The oxygen tanks hadn't arrived.

Now, I thought, we need to get some help to take care of the new patients. I talked it over with Mom. "Florence is still here. I'll talk to her," she said, and scrambled up the stairs.

Aunt Florence was mother's youngest sister and had just suffered the traumatic loss of her beloved dog, Jockala, a ten year-old Scotch terrier. We had operated on her dog the previous day, and lost it to a neglected pyometra, an infected uterus. It was a hopeless, messy procedure.

"Why did she wait so long." George had asked during the operation. "This should have come out weeks ago."

"She's a Christian Scientist," I answered, "and was having her practitioner read to Jockala." George raised his eyes in disbelief, "Finally, Mom convinced her that no dog could understand English, and the incantation might not work."

It was difficult for her to decide. Tearfully she had talked to her husband on the phone. "Jackala isn't getting any better and Teddy and Sarah advise surgery."

"Dogs are different, dear," Guy said consolingly. "Your family knows what they are doing. I really don't think we should have waited so long."

"I'm so scared. . .She won't die. . .?"

"God's will, Honey. She had a good life and you know she's suffering. If she can be helped, they'll do it."

"Okay. I'll tell them to go ahead. I'm going to spend the night here with Sarah. Will you be all right?"

"I'll be fine dear. Good luck!"

It was Mom's chore to tell her what happened and her heart broke as she looked at the shocked, disbelieving face. Florence choked back her grief but her eyes cried out.

Florence grieved silently 'till she was alone and then the tears flowed. She was so sad, rings showed under her eyes from lack of sleep and her shoulders drooped from remorse and depression. She had been such an "up" person, like my mother, but the loss of Jockala was too much.

My aunt was an extraordinarily gifted and sensitive lady. Years ago she married Guy Martin, a Dane with a thick accent and a great outlook on life. They opened their own millinery shop on Broadway and Eighty-Third Street and it flourished. He watched adoringly as she designed and hand-made all of the merchandise.

Florence was childless and yearned for motherhood. She had adopted all Mom's family as her own and she in turn, was our favorite aunt. I was sure she would help out once she saw the little wild babies.

"What do you say?" Mother asked, "Will you help?" Tears streamed down Florence's cheeks and it broke Mother's heart to see her sister cry. She took her in her arms.

"At least come down and look at them," she whispered, "they are so rare and human, you'll get a kick out of them."

Florence didn't speak, but Mom took her hand and led her downstairs and continued talking. "There are enough hats in your stockroom for Guy to sell for a few weeks. And I know that it would be like a vacation for you, a break in your routine."

I picked up Matilda, wheezing and coughing, and put her in Florence's arms. Matilda clutched her as if she were her mother. My aunt looked down at the worried, little black face, and I could see her heart melt. George's eyes were moist as he watched.

"Exactly what they need," I told her, "a woman's touch."

Suddenly Florence looked up at me and I knew what she was thinking.

"This baby will be fine," I assured her. "She just needs a couple of days on medication, and oxygen every now and then. You have Matilda, but I'd like you to take care of Bantu." I took her over to the kennel under the oxygen tents where Bantu sat, eyes tearing and nose running. She was clutching her doll and rocking as she looked up at the new stranger. I opened the cage door and lifted Bantu out. Mom made the exchange.

Florence didn't speak, but looked down at the infant in her arms with such compassion, I knew she'd been won over. She reached for a tissue to clean Bantu's nose, and wipe her eyes, as she murmured loving words of assurance.

Mother demonstrated diapering, preparing formula, and bottle feeding. "We give them a bottle every two to three hours, depending on their need." she explained. "If they are in the tent, we wait a few more minutes."

I showed her how to detect oxygen need from the blue color of the eyes, lips and tongue, and instructed her to call us for a tent immediately, if necessary. "There's a love affair going on between your Bantu and Samson, a little male you haven't met." I told her. "She is going to miss him so give her lots of holding and cuddling. When you leave she has her own little doll that she holds all night."

For the next week or so, I rarely saw them apart. Florence never let Bantu out of her sight except for a few hours at night. We set up a cot in the treatment ward for George. He, Mom and I alternated the night shift. Mom watched with a satisfied grin as Florence brushed Bantu's hair, cleaned her face and wiped her nose. George monitored Florence out of the corner of his eye as she made the formula and tested it on her forearm before allowing Bantu to suck.

"You're doing great, aunty," I said as diapers were changed and baby oil applied to little black bottoms. The new "Nurse Florence" ate her lunch with one hand as the other cradled the sleeping ape. Sometimes, when the rest of us were busy, she kept an eye on Two as well. After the second day, with the new routine established, Mother told Florence to go home at night. Florence left after 7:00 o'clock every evening, and I could see the guilt in her eyes when Bantu cried for her.

Most of the time, "Two" was looked after by George and mother. He was critical and took precedence over Matilda. Mother did the hugging, diaper changing and worrying. George tried to give him fluids orally, immediately after his arrival and, after two hours in the oxygen cage, as Dr. Janice suggested. We injected saline and dextroxe subcutaneously. Florence, with a concerned frown, rocked Bantu and watched the heroic medication needed for Two. She winced every time the needle was used. Two worried us all because he wouldn't take his bottle, was weak from the worms, and toxic from pneumonia. The little fellow coughed and wheezed and hung on desperately to his two-legged nurses. Every time George had a free moment he held him and tried to get him to drink. When called away, he set him down with his doll or Florence took double duty.

During one afternoon, everyone stopped what they were doing because Two began retching, aggravating the dehydration and weakness. Florence bounced Bantu on her knee, cooing sweet nothings, but her worried eyes were on the little male. She turned to George, her eyes asking what he could do to help. When I walked into the room, they both asked at the same time, what could be done for the vomiting. "George," I asked, "Would you stay with him tonight? I'll be upstairs if you need me."

George nodded and I gave Two an antemetic that controlled the nausea. "If he throws up during the night we'll give him saline again," I said. "We have to control dehydration."

Between five and six A.M., George, thoroughly exhausted, cat-napped. When he awoke and peered through the window at six o'clock, he saw a lifeless Two, with vomitus covering his chin and chest. Huge, ugly, white round worms were crawling and wiggling from his nostrils and out between his teeth and tongue that had turned a deep blue. They were four to five inches long. The leeches were deserting their fallen host, succumbing themselves, to the hostile, cold, arid environment of air and light.

George, with tears in his eyes, reported what happened. "It's not your fault, George. I think everything was done that could be." He blamed himself for falling asleep, but of course. . .

Trefflich took the news in stride. His premonition about Two had proved true. He asked for an autopsy. "I think it would be good for you and George to learn more, and of course, it would be a back-up for our insurance claim."

Henry, now subdued, was unwilling to take a chance with Four and Samson. He sent them to the hospital to be checked. Everyone had heard about Samson, and when he was carried into our treatment room, Mom, George and Florence stopped what they were doing and waited to be introduced. He had a deep, productive cough, a running nose but was eating well. Bantu, for the first time tried to wiggle out of Florence's arms to get to him. Samson and Bantu had a noisy, wheezing, happy reunion, only to be separated when Bantu needed oxygen. Florence had her hands full holding them both on her lap. They were only content and willing to bottle feed if they were touching. Florence went to work on Samson's neglected coat--combing, brushing and oiling, till he was as neat and clean as his girl friend. Fastidious Matilda, when she felt better, tried to keep everyone's face clean. Four was still normal, but had to be watched because he might be incubating; the interval between exposure and the start of symptoms.

Lisa was the only one who stayed well. Blessed with natural resistance, she never left Trefflichs and was shipped to one of the zoos in the mid-west.

The Beverlie Animal Hospital, during a normal week, was a veritable mad-house. The addition of five sick gorillas turned it into a frenzied, time-consuming circus.

I tried to examine each baby at least once every four hours. If they were out of the tents, they had to be watched constantly for tell-tale cyanosis. George was a God-send and my other pair of eyes. I stopped commuting to Westchester. Florence didn't want to neglect Uncle Guy, and managed to get in some sewing for the millinery shop before bedtime. At 8 A.M. sharp, she was back to accept the happy greetings of the lovers. She changed diapers, then fed Bantu and Samson breakfast.

The day after we lost Two, Trefflich called to tell me that a news crew would be down to take pictures. Would I mind?

"We don't have the time or space for any more people, Henry," I answered truthfully. "Maybe in a week or more, when they've recovered enough not to need oxygen, it might be better."

"They won't take much room or time, Ted. It would be great publicity."

I couldn't argue, because Mother stuck her head through the door to announce that reporters and cameras were in the waiting room.

I looked over the ward. Sitting on a blanket in the center of the room was Aunt Florence. Bantu sat between her legs, sucking a bottle with her other arm around Florence's neck. She alternated playing with her hair and teasing Samson. He sat next to Florence, with his bottle in one hand and the other trying to catch Bantu's free hand. He suddenly had a severe coughing spell, and I decided to leave him in a tent until the strangers were gone.

"How would you like to have your picture taken?" I asked Florence casually.

"I'm too busy to put on makeup. Some other time." She answered.

George was diapering Matilda. "She still has diarrhea," he said, "but it's better formed. I'm going to check for parasites again." He was still traumatized by Two's demise, and wasn't about to let another succumb to worms.

"Don't put her back yet, George, photographers are here to take gorilla pictures. How about holding Matilda and Four on the operating table? We'll put a blanket under them. That will make a nice picture, and we can get rid of the press quickly." Four had been in an oxygen tent about an hour, and would be strong enough for the distraction. Samson was coughing badly, but after a couple of minutes in the tent he was quiet. He was sitting up and playing with ice cubes. The door from the examining room swung open, and two men and a woman, with photographic gear, pushed through.

"Hi," the first one said.

"Hi," I answered. "Can we do this quickly? These little guys are pretty sick."

"Sure. Why don't you just continue your routine, and we'll take some candids. I'm Jim, this is Mary, and he's Pete. We're from The Daily News. Henry Trefflich told us about the baby gorillas."

"Glad to meet you. I'm Dr. Zimmerman. This is Dr. Ksiezniak, and on the floor there is Mrs. Martin. Let me introduce the patients: on the floor with Mrs. Martin is Bantu; sitting on the table with Dr. Ksiezniak are Matilda and Four. They all have pneumonia in various stages of recovery."

"I understand one already died. What are their chances?" Jim asked motioning toward the babies.

"Hopeful. There isn't much medical experience with baby gorillas, and," I injected a little sarcasm, "I don't think many psychiatrists have observed them in sufficient numbers to grasp the effect of being abducted and traumatized by loneliness and grief. They endured an arduous trip to this strange, hostile environment," I explained, "and we are doing everything in our power to insure their survival."

"They really are cute," Mary said, as she prepared to shoot. "We'll try to finish quickly." Flash bulbs exploded as the photographers worked. "I thought Mr. Trefflich said there were four."

Suddenly in the silence, before an important shot, her question was answered. A rhythmic banging interrupted the action. Samson was feeling better. He had dumped the ice cubes from the stainless steel dish, and was using it to summon Bantu.

"You haven't met Samson yet," I said, opening the door to his tent. "He's all wet, but feels a little better." As I lifted him out and wrapped him in a towel, he started coughing. I set him on the table near Bantu, and they rushed into each other's arms.

"There's a picture for you," I said, as the cameras aimed their lenses.

"They're just wonderful," said Mary, admiringly. "I could stay here all day."

"I think they've had enough. In a week or so, they'll be back at the shop, and you can take all the pictures you want."

Except for George's fancied guilt about Two's demise, there was a story-book ending: New York loved the news report and the pictures; Trefflich got more than he dreamed possible, in publicity. When the babies were back in the store, he was mobbed by the curious. The Daily News sold the pictures to syndicated papers around the world, Trefflich made his killing selling the babies to grateful zoos and we basked in the euphoria that followed the successful medical crisis.

Six years later, we smiled with satisfaction at a newspaper article and photograph of a 600 pound grayback gorilla, celebrataing his birthday at the Milwaukee zoo. He didn't look the least bit familiar, but we knew him. His name was Samson.

After our gorilla family left, Mother and Aunt Florence watched the oxygen tents dismantled, and the cots returned to the storage room. George and I, slept in our own beds.

Mother put the veterinary hospital back on course and I resumed taking care of the routine tasks of morning office hours, afternoon small animal surgery, caring for hospitalized patients and the boarding and grooming of dogs and cats.

None of us realized the impact those little apes had on us. Aunt Florence forgot, for the moment, her darling Jockala. George had used his talents as a most capable veterinarian. Mom was in her element taking the entire crisis in stride while her son acted out the dream fulfilled.

Our college course in jurisprudence never alerted us about the everyday hazards of running a small animal practice. Our learned professors never informed us about perverse clients or irascible patients. Boarding animals provided small animal hospitals with "bread and butter" income, but few dog and cat veterinarians knew the pitfalls that accompanied that simple service. Mom and Dad, thanks to twenty years of pet shop-boarding, prepared me for what was to come.

The first trap, besides the health and well being of the boarder, was identifying and returning the proper leash. I had been warned that returning a boarder to its owner, freshly bathed and groomed, and in perfect health, went unnoticed and unheralded, if the leather leash that accompanied his admittance was dirty, damaged or lost.

George's mouth fell open in amazement as I outlined the precautions necessary to prevent such a catastrophy. A special clip board, with appropriate hooks to hold the priceless strips of leather, carefully identified with owner's name, Fido's name, plus date of entry, assigned boarding ward and projected date of departure.

One day, Mother greeted Mr. and Mrs. Henry White, old clients, who brought their two Persian long haired cats, one brown, the other black, into the hospital to board for ten days. They had used our service many times before. Mr. White was hard to please and suspicious, despite the fact that he was a diplomat by profession. If he didn't complain that his pets came home covered with fleas, bothered by hairballs, or suffering with diahhrea, it was a minor miracle.

Henry White was a State Department employee. He confided to me proudly, "I've just been assigned a position in the ambassador's office in Panama. My Mrs. and I are traveling to Colon to set up our new household. It should take about ten days. As soon as we're settled, we'll send you a cable. Can you ship "Brownie" and "Blackie" to us?"

Mom was tickled. For once he wouldn't be there to fuss about imagined ailments, conjured up by his suspicious mind. "Don't worry, Mr. White," she assured him, "We've shipped animals all over the world and they do fine. The Railway Express Agency is wonderful with the animals under their care."

Mrs. White was never one to compliment our facilities and never contradicted her husband's criticism. Mother noticed that she rarely opened her mouth at all. This time, however, she said, "They always do so well boarding with you. I hope we can find as good a vet in Panama. Please have George brush them before the trip. They always look so wonderful when he sends them home." Mother listened, wide-eyed at her admission of fact. Mrs. White left, assured that the move to the South would be smooth and uncomplicated.

Several days later, the John Hurleys arrived with their brace of pure white short haired tabbys, for a ten day stay. Mother, always happy to sign up new clients, filled out their clinical card. "Are you new in the neighborhood?" she asked politely, seeing their address in the Murray Hill Section of Manhattan.

"Yes," Mrs. Hurley the spokesman, answered, "We're going to visit our children in Kansas. You have been highly recommended by the Horvaths."

"Thanks," Mother replied, noticing Mr. Hurley's reticence. His eyes took in every inch of the waiting room, including several clients waiting for the doctor.

Just then the front door slammed and two men struggled to carry a limp dog into the waiting room.

"We have an emergency!" rasped one of them, his face drawn and completely out of breath.

The reaction was dramatic. In one motion Mother pushed back her chair and pressed the "Emergency" button on the wall behind her. A loud, strident clang sounded as she sprang from her chair. She pushed back the swinging door to the examining room motioning the two men with their burden to follow. Ken Haffner, who was cleaning the examining room was right on their heels pointing to the operating table for the men to place the unconscious animal. When I heard the alarm, I was downstairs. I grabbed my stethoscope and raced up to the treatment ward. The comatose dog was on the table and the bell of my stethscope found his chest, just over the heart. I picked up a slow, shocky heartbeat.

"What happened?" I asked, as Kenny picked up the animals lip to show blue mucous membranes.

"He was hit by a car about five minutes ago."

"He's not breathing. Ken, oxygen!"

It took me two strides to reach the instrument cabinet for the intra-tracheal catheter as Ken rolled over the oxygen cylinder. He held the patient's jaws ajar for the introduction of the life sustaining plastic as Mother opened the flow of oxygen. I applied pressure on the rib cage to the rhythm of a normal heartbeat and soon the mucous membranes appeared normal.

In a few minutes, Mother returned to the waiting room all smiles. She reported to the waiting people who were spellbound by the crisis. "He'll be okay! You can go back in, Mrs. Farrady. The doctor is ready."

The two men were seen leaving through the side hall, talking normally and obviously relieved.

"Mrs. Hurley, you were saying?"

Enamored by the reaction to the emergency played out before him, Mr. Hurley found his tongue. "Would you be sure that "Tom" and "Melinda" get their annual examinations and boosters."

He was smiling now, no longer unhappy to leave his pets.

It was Thanksgiving weekend. Our kennels were holiday full. The hospital was a symphony of mews, barks and howls. The expected cable from Panama arrived on the tenth day.

"Ken," I called into treatment ward, "call the Express Company and crate the White cats. They are flying out today."

Ken Haffner, meticulous as usual, prepared the crates with shredded newspapers and filled the water cups. Six cans of cat tuna were attached with feeding instructions for the shipper. The Persians were readied for the trip. They were checked, brushed, and sprayed with insecticide.

The Express company arrived late that afternoon and Mother was busy helping me with a new case. "Ken," she called to our harried hospital attendant, up to his ears with over a hundred boarders, "put the White cats in their crates." He complied. But that afternoon, two white cats, instead of the two White cats, left for Panama.

Later in the day the happy Hurleys returned home and phoned us asking that their pets be delivered to Park Avenue.

"Ted," Mother called, "Hurley's cats are going home today."

I relayed the news to Kenny, "You'll have to deliver those white cats later today."

Ken pulled the two carriers with the "White" tags from storage. He hurriedly checked the different wards until he spied the "White" labels. He put the two Persians in the carriers and brought them to the Hurley's home on Park Ave. The doorman accepted the carriers and took them upstairs.

Anne called to her pets as she released the catches. "You poor babies. I'll bet you're glad to be home."

"My God!" she screamed as two longhairs jumped out. "John!"

"What's the matter," he asked, rushing in.

"John," she cried, "Look! They sent us the wrong cats. Call Dr. Zimmerman this instant!"

Cables flew between N.Y. and Panama.

The Whites weren't about to send the tabbies back until the Persians arrived safe and sound.

Mrs. Hurley wanted her pets back, like yesterday!

I did my best to placate the Hurleys. I assured them that their cats would be home in three days. A phone call to Panama assured the Whites that their cats were on the way and to please send the white cats back, at our expense, of course.

When the Persians finally arrived in Panama, the hostage tabbies were released. They arrived home, safe and sound, enriched by their world travels.

"We did everything right," I told the staff when the dust settled, as Mother gaffawed, "one must never overlook "Murphy's Law.""

*Approximately $40,000 worth of baby gorillas, the biggest shipment
of these rare animals ever to enter the United States, before they
came down with pneumonia. They were treated at the Beverlie Animal
Hospital at 47 East 30th Street, New York City.
Backrow (left to right): Samson, Two, Matilda, Four, and Lisa.
In front, Bantu*

*Aunt Florence, my sister-in-law Ruby and Uncle Guy before
Jockala's death and the baby gorillas*

*Samson, a young gorilla that weighed 20 pounds when
Henry Trefflich sold it to the Milwaukee Zoo in 1950. When this photo
was taken, in November, 1965, Samson weighed about 600 pounds.
(Milwaukee County Park Commission)*

X

New York Versus Mount Vernon

As Ben Levy, owner of Ben and Nat's grocery store on West Grand Street put it, "I look up from arranging my fruit, and I see a limp, full grown tiger, being carried down West Grand Street. I see a full-grown wooley monkey roaming around like a pet dog. It frequents the friendly pub down the street. Boy, has this neighborhood changed!"

I opened my Mount Vernon, New York office in 1951. This was the time when doing double duty between my two practices was enervating, to say the least. As usual, every time a crisis would arise in Mount Vernon, I was in New York or vice versa.

For two years, it was daily commuting and attempting to run two offices efficiently. Finally, with urging from Elaine, I chose Mount Vernon to be the site of my sole practice. There was room and facilities for the wild animals. I put the New York office up for sale and sold my practice to Dr. David Suss. My parents remained there, at his request, to help him get started.

Six months was as much as my parents could stomach under these circumstances. They decided to retire to Florida. They chose Tampa and settled down to what I thought would be a life of leisure and bridge playing. Mom and Dad were in their seventies but had the vigor of fifty year olds.

After about two months Dad told me excitedly, "I'm just not ready to retire. I got myself a job in the local Hillsborough Avenue pet shop." Before long it was a full time endeavor, and within the year he bought the shop and Mom and Dad were in business again.

It was impossible to find anyone in Mount Vernon who could match Mom's expertise as a vet hospital receptionist. "Mom." I asked, "how am I ever going to find another you?"

"No one is indispensable," she remarked sagely, "you must interview and give people a trial run. A year from now you'll look back and wonder what all the fuss was about." She was right as usual, but it took four tries.

Mercedes Hadley was the fourth and successful applicant. It had taken patience, hope and faith to finally score a ten! My need for an experienced, sober, honest and dedicated attendant and receptionist was met. Mercedes arrived for an interview with her baby pet macaque monkey, Etu. Also her brown, male standard poodle, Ledgie. She had a six-year old son, Jerry, from a previous marriage.

"Call me Mike," she insisted. "I know bookkeeping. I've had experience nursing all types of animals. I learned grooming and bathing all breeds of dogs when I worked in a fancy pet shop."

Ledgie, her poodle was groomed to perfection and looked as though he was ready for "Best in Show", at the Westminster Dog Show.

"Did you clip him yourself?" I asked, admiring his perky, professional appearance.

"Of course!" she said. "I wanted you to see my work."

The way she handled Etu, a clever, juvenile ape, was as skilled as a zoo keeper. The monkey was clean, diapered and well behaved. As the interview progressed, I mentioned that the hospital was getting busy and needed a kennel man also.

"I know just the man for you." she said excitedly. "His name is Peter Mueller. He lives with his mother and two sisters right here in Mount Vernon. They are German immigrants. Peter has been working at Sloan Kettering as an attendant in their animal research department. He's wonderful and just as gentle and caring."

Peter was an animal lover and disinchanted with Kettering's treatment of the animals. He would have been an ardent anti-vivisectionist if he had known what the word meant. He wanted a job with animals and Mike promised him she'd find one.

I agreed to interview him and hired Mike on the spot.

Peter was a dwarf. Self-conscious and shy, he had a problem with people that didn't exist with animals. He was in his early twenties, about 5 feet tall, with the typical build; bowed legs and arms, large head and waddling gait. He was gentle-looking with brown eyes and hair, a soft speaking voice with just a hint of a German accent.

Mike was exactly right. In the twenty-plus years he worked for me he handled lions, ocelots, margays, chimpanzees, gorillas, orangutans, pumas, skunks, and a variety of small monkeys and other wild life.

Peter had two great attributes. One was the love and respect he inspired in my clients. When they boarded their pets, Pete would be there. When they went home they were always clean and well groomed. Most boarders left Peter with reluctance, to the dismay of some owners, and many couldn't wait to see him when they returned.

The other plus was a magic gift. An innate, uncanny ability to develop the trust and affection of the meanest, wildest, and most untrustworthy of the dogs, cats or wild animals. Boarding full grown ocelots was a responsibility no other animal Hospital in our area, took on. Most of these wildcats couldn't be safely handled by anyone but their owners. I insisted that they be cleaned and exercised twice daily—a chore customary for a professional animal trainer, but rarely practiced by a small animal hospital attendant. Peter handled them all with skill, daring and proficiency. He was a polite, thoughtful, reliable and honest person, never talking back or raising his voice to animal or man. He never asked for a raise in salary or an extra day off in the many years of employment. I rewarded him appropriately and he became one of the highest paid veterinary hospital attendants in Westchester County. My nurses and receptionists, working with Peter all those years, liked and respected him. I owe him a debt I can never repay for the peace of mind he afforded me and my family when I was away for a day, a week or a month.

Pete and I became expert in handling and restraining wildcats, especially during the '50's and '60's, when the ocelot and margay craze swept the New York metropolitan area. We saw as many as twenty per week for routine visits, treatment, surgery and boarding.

An exciting event unfolded in late June, 1959. I purchased a six week old Peruvian ocelot from the Trefflich's pet shop. He was the most affectionate, intelligent, adorable creature we had ever encountered. We named him Buddha, and he took over the hospital, our home and our lives.

"We need to experience, first hand," I told my employees, "the problems and pleasures of raising an ocelot. How else can we council our clients intelligently."

Buddha had to be in someones arms constantly. He loved to suck on the fleshy parts of our hands, betweeen the thumb and forefinger. He talked constantly in a low persistant growl if he were set down. At night, he would curl up and substitute the end of his tail for our palms, and suck 'till he fell asleep. Ocelots are nocturnal and it wasn't until I took him home to meet our sons that I realized his preference to stay up and play all night. Everyone loved him and competed for his attention so that by the time he was four months old, he was as spoiled as a first child.

When he was five months old, I neutered him and extracted his permanent fang teeth; procedures routine for male exotics. He was going to be raised principally in the hospital, and had to be rendered harmless to the other patients and boarders.

Peter was his mentor, pan-training him, teaching him some degree of obedience and catering to his idiosyncrasies.

Buddha had a thing about telephones. He loved the sound, their odor and movement. It wasn't long before Peter had him answering the rings. He taught him to knock the receiver off its cradle, then patiently wait for Peter to pick it up. After the conversation ended and the phone put back, he'd spend many minutes beguiled, showing his fascination by sniffing and rubbing against the instrument.

One day we were engaged in minor surgery, cauterizing a corneal ulcer on a pup's eye. Local anesthesia was used over slight sedation. Buddha was napping on the floor beside the instrument cabinet and the telephone was nearby on the desk.

"This pup has to be quiet," I cautioned. "I don't want the head bobbing about when I am about to scrape his cornea. Speak softly, if you have to, because with this sedative, sounds are magnified and anything will make him jump. I'll need all four hands to hold him steady."

Peter and Mike were the assistants and they supported his head and body. My scalpel was poised to make the first move when the phone rang and the pup's head jerked. We were anchored to our tasks and powerless to move. With the second ring came another head-jerk. Without moving, Peter said, "Buddha! Answer the phone."

Already alerted by the peals, Buddha, in one quick leap, was on the desk. He pawed the receiver off the cradle and the operation proceeded.

John Cronin was killed in a plane crash. His remains were found in a heavily wooded area west of the Hudson River, three months after being reported missing.

I met John for the first time, two years earlier, when he walked into my office with his chic, slender, classic Whippet, "Toulouse." Wherever he went, eyes turned to admire the sleek canine. Cronin was a gifted artist and photographer who came to us on the recommendation of a close friend. Toulouse was getting old and needed medical attention. Cronin sat quietly, awaiting his turn, when suddenly his mouth opened wide. Buddha, in all his glory, pranced into the forbidden waiting room. He stopped, stretched, forelegs extended straight out against the floor, his hind end and tail raised high in typical feline fashion. Cronin sat mesmerized, unable to take his eyes off the stunning, gold and black, striped and spotted wildcat. He recalled the newspaper account of the artist, Salvatore Dali's pet. John Cronin had to have one of his own. Buddha, all stretched and relaxed started toward the waiting patients, curious and ready for play.

All Cronin talked about in the privacy of the examining room, was his new obsession. For the moment, Toulouse was forgotten.

A month later we met our new patient. His name was Spot, a big-boned cat, originating in the jungles of Central America. He had more spots than Buddha and no stripes. Like all ocelots and margays (miniature wildcats), he demanded constant affection. If Spot was awake, John wasn't permitted to pet or show any attention to Toulouse, but that didn't stop Spot from endlessly chasing and teasing the dog.

The Whippet's long slender tail was the best plaything he could find and when he collapsed, exhausted from play, he would curl up against Toulouse's warm body and suckle the end of his tail.

Spot's attitude towards the hospital, Peter and myself was typical and anticipated. He growled and complained from the minute the door closed behind him until he left for home. He hated needles, stainless steel tables, stethoscopes and veterinarians. When Cronin had to be away on business for more than a weekend, he was brought in to board with Toulouse. Thank God for Peter. Spot grew to love and trust Peter as much as his master and Peter catered to him by letting Toulouse stay in the adjoining kennel, for company.

In the first year, Spot only had to stay at the hospital two or three times, once for surgery and other times to board. He was already bigger than Buddha, weighing thirty pounds and still growing. I neutered him when he was five months old but John refused to put him through the declawing. "You are leaving some pretty potent weapons, you know," I warned when he came to pick him up the following day. "And he'll do a pretty good job of tearing up your favorite sofa."

"He never once scratched Toulouse or me and I don't think it's necessary." He said, stroking the spotted fur adoringly. "And I can always get a new couch."

Toulouse passed away from natural causes about a year later and all of John's affection and attention focused on Spot. One day, Steve Cromwell, John Cronin's nephew, whom I had met when he accompanied John to our office several months before, called us hysterically. His uncle had left for a weekend trip and hadn't returned. A three day supply of food had been left for Spot, and it was now almost a week. Neighbors were complaining because of the roaring sounds coming from the Cronin apartment. The superintendent of the building opened the door a crack to see Spot pacing the floor in a nervous rage. He phoned both Steve and the A.S.P.C.A. They arrived at the same time.

Steve brought food, peeked in the door and when Spot was far enough away threw it on the floor and slammed it shut. "I'll go in after he's eaten," he told the authorities, "then try to get him home."

"No way," the officer said, "you're not going in there with that leopard. I'm not going to have a mangled person on my conscience. I'd sooner shoot him first."

"No! He's my uncle's pet. Let me call his vet." Steve said, "He can handle him."

"They want to shoot Spot," He explained, excitedly. "You know he wouldn't hurt anyone, he's just hungry and lonely. I never was too friendly with him." He babbled on, "To tell the truth I was afraid and never trusted him too much. He really didn't like anyone but John. I tried to feed him but he's too agitated to eat anything. He needs to see someone he knows and trusts. I hoped you could help."

"Let me talk to the officer in charge. If he'd just wait an hour we can get him out of there and into the hospital."

Steve put the A.S.P.C.A. officer on the phone. "This is Chief O'Reilly."

"Dr. Zimmerman, here. I've been taking care of Spot for a couple of years and I can assure you that he's no threat to anyone. I'll send my man to pick him up. He's Peter Mueller, and he can handle him easily. We'll keep him until Mr. Cronin returns. It might take an hour for Peter to get there."

"Okay," he said, "you have three hours."

Peter traveled to Brooklyn lugging our largest carrier with some tasty tidbits he knew Spot loved. He grinned as he told us what happened.

"The A.S.P.C.A. cops were scared to go in even though they were armed. When I arrived they opened the door. All the guns were raised and ready. I yelled, 'Here, Spot, come and get it.' He ran over to me almost purring, and when I opened the carrier and he smelled the food, he jumped in and began munching. I stroked his back, closed the box and here I am."

Four months went by with nary a word from the family until a phone call from Steve Cromwell shocked the entire staff. In the wooded areas, west of the Hudson, a police helicopter spotted the downed airplane. A relief party found his remains.

As a memorial to his uncle, Steve took reluctant Spot into his own home. Before long a bond was consumated. We saw Spot at least once yearly for the next ten years. We were sure he was content with the relationship that lasted the remainder of his natural life.

After dinner and before bedtime, my sons, without fail, demanded a story. "Okay," I agreed, "what's the plot tonight?" The boys made me proficient at the art of spinning yarns, a gift I hadn't used since the days of camp and Max Ray. They picked the topic and I improvised the tale. Ron jumped on my lap and snuggled up while Rick, very mature at nine, sat beside me on the couch, more poised, but just as excited.

"How about tigers?" Rick said, trying to please me.

"No! Racing cars!" Demanded Ronny.

"Dad," Rick asked, "can I have Buddha for "Show and Tell?" I told Mrs. Peters about him and she said I could bring him to school."

"He'll have to stay overnight, and you know how Mom hates wild animal smells. If it's okay with her, I'll bring him home."

"Maybe he won't make doodoo this time." Ronny giggled.

"I'd better check with Mrs. Peters myself to be sure it's all right," I said, "some schools don't like wild animals for Show and Tell."

"Buddha's not wild, Dad. Please! Please?"

"Can I ask Mrs. Anderson if I can bring him too?" Ron begged.

"Say! How about that story." I said as I tickled Ronny sending him into a paroxysm of laughter.

So the story was told and as I tucked them in and sang, "Good Night Ricky, Good Night Ronny, Good Night Tigers, I'm happy to see you sleep. Merrily we roll along, roll along, roll along," with more tickles and bed bouncing, lots of giggling and hugs and kisses and finally, quiet!

A few days later, Buddha, smells and all, arrived riding in the back seat in his special dog carrier. He was scheduled for Show and Tell the next day.

Rick, upon wakening, asked, "Dad, can I put some aftershave on Buddha? I want him to smell good."

"Good idea. After all, he's civilized now." I put my arm around his shoulder. "Now, Rick, we have to plan this day carefully. Buddha is our special friend, but he is a wild animal and it will be the first time most of your classmates have ever been this close to one. You can't ever be sure how a wild feline will act, or how he will behave around certain people. Some times, what seems like a quiet, peaceful place, will spook an animal, provoke some wild instinct and sent it into a rage. I'm going to school with you to be sure he behaves himself."

Rick sighed, "Whew. I was hoping you'd come but I was afraid to ask."

Elaine chimed in, "Honey, will you ask Mrs. Peters and Miss Anderson to dinner next Tuesday. I was going to call but an invitation in person is better than a phone call."

The boys were thrilled that their teachers were coming to their house.

Buddha was both curious and aggressive. When walked on a leash, he pulled against the restraint like a Pit Bull, anxious for the next smell or the next animal to bully.

We decided to carry Buddha the quarter mile or so to the school grounds, then put him down to walk. Rick took command and proud as Frank Buck, walked him into the schoolhouse. This "Show and Tell," would be one they'd never forget.

The home-room door opened and the little tiger burst through with his usual impatience, dragging Rick with him. The girls screamed with delight and some fearless boys rushed to be the first to stroke the vivid yellow and black fur. Rick sat down proudly with Buddha on his lap. After a moment, the affectionate cat settled down, took Rick's palm into his mouth and sucked contentedly.

Ricky stroked his head, then scratched his neck, as Buddha closed his eyes in ecstasy. I sat in the back of the room as the role was taken, announcements made and the plan for the day's activities explained by Mrs. Peters. When it was time for Rick to "Show and Tell," he carried Buddha to the head of the class and placed him on Mrs. Peters desk, held the leash with one hand and his prepared notes in the other. The children buzzed with excitement with this unusual happening. Rick informed the group that ocelots come from the South and Central American countries.

"They hunt at night and feed on small rodents, birds and insects." He explained that Buddha was from Peru and was declawed and defanged for our safety. "He was pan trained," he explained, "so he could take his place as a pet in a normal household. However in the wild," he informed them, "he had the capability of grabbing his prey with forelegs and talons, and tearing their bodies apart with his hind, razor-sharp claws. Finally," he said as he finished, "because he is a feline, and domesticated, he was inoculated for all the diseases of the domestic cat."

After his talk, the children who hadn't approached before, took turns in getting a close look, some even touched the tame ocelot. Mrs. Peters was so impressed with Buddha and the interest he generated that she asked if I could bring some other exotic animal for the children to see and study.

"How about a baby chimp?" I asked, knowing that we always seem to have one or two a week from Trefflichs.

Her eyes opened in desbelief, "Could you really? We'll be the envy of the entire county."

"I'll set up a date with Rick, the next time one comes in. By the way, Mrs. Peters," I remembered, "my wife would like to have you and Miss Anderson to dinner next Tuesday. We promise a quiet dinner with no wild animals."

"Thank you, Doctor, I'd love to. I'll ask Helen and give Mrs. Zimmerman a call tomorrow."

The following Tuesday, we entertained the teachers. The boys eye's reflected their surprise as the teachers, looking so different, arrived in "dress-up" clothes, makeup and evening hairdo's. Ronny, giggling and embarrassed, hid his face in his mother's skirts. It wasn't long before Elaine paraded the ladies up and down stairs, showing off our home.

The teachers were intrigued by a portrait of my wife, wearing a magnificent red, low cut evening gown, that hung in our living room. Mrs. Peters read aloud the name of the painter, Raymond S. Pease.

"He's wonderful," she said, "he really captured your look and expression. I'd love to have him do my husband. Is he very expensive? Does it take him long?"

"I don't think so," Elaine said, "I only sat for three, one hour sessions, but he also did an uncanny likeness of our pet poodle, Cherie, from just photographs. We swapped my husband's fee for the paintings because he ran up quite a bill. There's a story the Doctor might tell you, about paintings exchanged for medical service. His wife, Ann, happened to be my teacher in elementary school when I was about Rick's age. She taught art and I adored her."

As we sat down to dinner, prodded by Elaine, I proceeded to tell the yarn about Jerry, the Pease's Brittany Spaniel.

"Ray and Ann Pease lived in an apartment building just around the corner from my office. They had chosen a first floor apartment in a six story building, right over the common garage, because Jerry was just a puppy and was being house-trained."

"Ray was one of my favorite people, and as you can see, a very talented artist. He was a quiet, soft-spoken, sensitive man with a special love for Brittanys.

"'I'd never own any other breed,'" he told me, and as it turned out, his brown and white long-eared pets were the only Brittany Spaniels I ever saw in my practice.

"Jerry was about ten when I first saw him. Ray told me he was gradually declining in health and wondered if I could help him. His breath was fetid, his teeth and gums were diseased and arthritis had attacked his joints. Cataracts robbed him of his sight but his tail never lost its wag and his heart was full of love for his owners and the joy of just being alive."

"One day, a young man that lived in their apartment building, returned home from a party. He had a little too much to drink. He automatically closed the garage door, staggered out of his car and weaved his way into the elevator and then to his apartment. He forgot to turn off the ignition. It was a mid-summer evening. After an investigation it was learned that one of the intake hoses on the common building air-conditioner had broken, carbon monoxide, odorless and deadly, began seeping into the Peases first floor apartment."

Everyone, including the boys, were quiet, intrigued by the story as they munched on their food.

"Their neighbors, Jim and Estelle Ryan, loved old Jerry and took care of him occasionally when the Peases were away. Jim was a tall, taciturn man and Estelle the direct opposite. She was short and round, talked easily, made all social arrangements and lived on the telephone.

"That night, Jim Ryan was awakened by an odd sound. A low groaning noise slowly rose to a howl then subsided. This continued incessantly for over fifteen minutes.

'Are you awake Estelle?' he whispered.

'Yeah. What in God's name is that racket?' She said, as she switched on the light.

'I think it's Jerry,' Jim said, 'Jesus, I never heard such a scary howl.'

"Estelle Ryan, already slipping into her robe said, 'He's never made a sound this late, ever. I'm going to call them. They're probably awake anyhow. Maybe they'll need some medicine for him.'

'Don't disturb them,' Jim said, 'Go back to sleep.'

"Estelle was already dialing the phone," She waited. There was no answer. 'That's strange. Something must be wrong. I'm calling Regatti,' She said.' He's got a pass key.'

'You're making a fuss at 3:00 AM. They'll all think you're crazy.'

"After three rings, a tired, 'Hello.'"

'Mr. Regatti,' she said, taking charge and ignoring Jim.' Estelle Ryan here. Sorry to wake you. Something is wrong at the Peases.' Please hurry with your pass key.' She hung up before he could answer or object."

'Awake or not, there is no harm finding out.' She told Jim."

'In a few minutes Regatti arrived, disheveled and annoyed. He had pulled his trousers over garish pajamas, the tops hanging over his belt. The Ryans were waiting outside the Peases' door.

'You're waking up the whole house. What's wrong?'

'Jerry was howling. He never does that.'

'That's all?' he asked incredulously. He turned and started away. 'Go back to sleep.' he tossed over his shoulder."

"Estelle walked over and rang the Pease's bell. Regatti turned and they all waited. 'You know as well as I, that Jerry always answers that bell with a bark.' Mrs. Ryan challenged."

"Regatti paused and thought. He knew she had a point. He reached into his robe and pulled out the pass-key."

"The key opened the lock but he had to force the door as the limp dog had fallen against it. Open about a foot he poked his head through, to see what was blocking it. 'Move Jerry,' he said when he saw it was the dog. When he couldn't arouse him he reached behind the door and pulled him away. The three entered the hall and hesitated. Estelle didn't waste a second. She charged into the bedroom and found the Peases, unconscious."

"Regatti threw open the windows while Estelle Ryan grabbed the telephone. Police and Fire Departments arrived quickly, accompanied by an ambulance."

"The superintendent then checked the garage and found the automobile, its engine still running, and noticed the broken air conditioner hose. His next move was to call me here. Regatti was a client, his cat had been my patient for years. With the Peases on their way to the hospital and Estelle Ryan sitting and giving the attendants orders, he picked up the limp dog, carried him to his car and met me in my office.

"Jerry was critical, as were his master and mistress, now in the emergency room of the Mount Vernon hospital. By some miracle, I thought, Peter, my attendant had slept in the hospital that night. He came through the door from downstairs, checking on the unusual activity at 3:00 o'clock in the morning. We had to give oxygen and stimulants immediately if he were to be saved. Peter prepared the oxygen tent while I attached an I.V.

"Did they die?" Rick asked, worried about the tale's ending. Ron was too nervous to talk.

"No they didn't. Oxygen and stimulants saved them all." The faces of both boys broke into wide grins. "The amazing thing is how the dog sensed trouble. Monoxide is odorless and tasteless. The only possible explanation was Jerry's perception that something different and unusual was happening in his little world. It might have been that the Pease's breathing sounds were just a little different. The average dog reacts to anything out of the ordinary. That's why they usually make such a fuss when their master and mistress occasionally dance together in the home. It's a miracle that he remained conscious long enough to attract attention."

"That's a great story, Dad." Rick said, "You never told us that one."

"It was much too long. Now finish your food. Show your teachers how good boys eat."

We retired to the living room where the portrait of Elaine hung. The boys were excused. Miss Anderson couldn't wait for the rest of the tale.

"In the Mount Vernon Hospital, the following day, both patients were awake and feeling better. The first words out of Pease was, 'How is my wife?' When reassured; 'what about Jerry?' He was told that his dog was in my care but insisted that the nurse call me immediately.

'Doctor,' she said, 'he feels so guilty that he is not with him. We told him that the dog alerted everyone to the accident and saved their lives. Is he all right?'

"I think you should say everything is okay until Mr. Pease is out of danger." I told her. "Jerry is an old dog and his accident just exacerbated existing pathology. I'll talk to him about it later."

"Jerry, being the old dog that he was, had some serious after-effects. A routine blood check showed his BUN, (blood urea nitrogen) was far above normal. He had become uremic.

"A week later Ray and Ann Pease visited Jerry.

'God! I love this dog, Doctor.' Tears began to flow as he threw his arms around his neck, getting his face washed by his excited pet. Ann was next as the poor pooch tried to kiss everyone at the same time. 'You saved our lives.' He said, then to me, 'Will he be all right?'

"I explained to him about, "chronic interstitial nephritis," the most common, complaint we have for our old dogs. "Jerry is a carnivore, as you know, and the heavy protein intake during his lifetime, slowly wears out his kidneys. Heart disease and cancer are the principle cause of death in man. Kidney failure and uremic poisoning account for almost eighty percent of the old age mortality in canines."

'He did love his meat,' he told me thoughtfully. 'I thought dogs had to eat it.' Then he asked, 'What can we do for his kidneys now? Can you help him?'

"We can try. As a dog ages it becomes more and more difficult for the kidneys to function at a 100% level. The urea backs up into the blood stream and uremic poisoning is the result. The Hill's K/D diet that I am prescribing for Jerry, is low in crude protein and contains high-quality amino acids, like milk and egg white, to satisfy his nutritional needs. The older he gets the less his kidneys can handle stress, and believe me, carbon monoxide can cause severe stress."

"'But he's only ten, that's not so old.' He said. I've heard of many living fourteen or fifteen years,' he wailed, 'ten is just a baby.'

"He's as old as a seventy year-old man." I told him. "My oldest patient was twenty-four, but she was one in a million. Dogs average twelve to fourteen years."

"Pease wasn't happy about the prospect of ever losing Jerry and I couldn't blame him. He went home with medication and his special diet. A month later Ray was back with a very depressed Spaniel. "I thought he was doing fine, Doc, but he stopped eating yesterday." he said dejectedly. "He's been throwing up also."

A BUN Check showed highly elevated levels. "I guess it's time to consider alternatives." I told him, quietly. "He's been such a good friend. Don't allow him a miserable end." He looked at me grimly as my meaning hit home.

"I can't put him down," he said, finally. 'He was eating until yesterday, and is still glad to see us when we come home. We just love him too much. Isn't there anything you can do?' His eyes were pleading, desperate.'

"His blood urea nitrogen is doing the talking." I told him as gently as possible, "If it gets much higher he will be in real distress. Constant nausea, depression, diarrhea, and dehydration." My heart went out to Ray. He was about to break down completely.

I thought for a moment, "We might try peritoneal dialysis. It's a temporary measure and it might not even work, but, theoretically, it could give him a few more months."

I stopped and looked from Mrs. Peters to Miss Anderson. "This might be getting too technical and boring. Should we change the subject?"

"No way!" they said together. "So what happened?"

"I've taught dialysis in biology," Miss Anderson said, "and I know Mrs. Peters has also. We've discussed it."

"Right." Mrs. Peters said. "We used a salt solution, and a potato as the semipermeable membrane."

"Right. And the salt in solution went right through the potato to the hypotonic water until an equilibrium was reached."

I laughed. "You know as much about dialysis as I do. Anyhow, I explained it to him as simply as possible, as a separation of substances from solution by means of their unequal diffusion through a semi-permeable membrane. I was really trying to convince myself, also, because I had read about dialysis, but never used it. "The shiny peritoneum that lines the intestines and internal organs is the semipermeable membrane, and the urea is the substance to be separated. It sounds a lot more complicated than it is," I assured him. "We inject a couple of quarts of sterile distilled water, a hypotonic solution, into his belly. It sits for a half to one hour, diffusing the poison from his blood to the water. Then we aspirate the urea-filled solution. The procedure does the work of the kidney, and must be repeated frequently."

"'Is it painful?' he asked.

"It shouldn't be." I told him. "We'll warm the solution to body temperature and they hardly feel the needle. You can stay with him if you like."

"'I want to try it,' he said, 'it sounds sensible and I'll do anything to prolong his life.'

"Bring him in tomorrow after office hours." I said "We'll infuse him, leave the catheter in, plugged and bandaged. Once we drain the fluid you can take him home."

"The next day, Jerry dragged himself in behind Pease, exhausted, out of breath, his tongue hanging out of the corner of his mouth. Looking up at his master, he seemed to be apologizing for his illness. As I prepared him for the infusion, he spit-up.

"He had a terrible night." Pease said, almost in tears. 'Nausea, diarrhea, moaning, I really can't stand to see him like that.'

"Don't give up on him yet, Raymond," I said. "Let's give it a chance. I don't want you to suffer through it. We'll know in thirty or so minutes."

"Jerry lay on his back. His belly was shaved over the umbilicus and the clear hypotonic solution dripped into his abdomen. It was painless, but the dog was so depressed he couldn't react, even if it hurt. I waited forty minutes. Jerry hadn't tried to move. Using a 100cc syringe, the size used for horses and cattle, I began to aspirate the fluid. It had a yellowish, unhealthy cast. Slowly, all the solution was removed. The abdomen was wiped clean and a band-aide applied to the puncture site.

"It took an hour for the magic moment. Jerry's eyes cleared and his panting ceased. His tail beat a new tempo as he greeted his master.

"I think it worked," I said, amazed. "Our artificial kidney is a success!"

"It became a routine that did well for both Jerry and the Peases'. His BUN was checked frequently. Sometimes he could go a couple of weeks without dialysis. As the months passed, however, it became necessary at least twice weekly.

"One night, two years later, Jerry passed away, quietly, in his sleep, and tearful Ray and Ann Pease carried him in for his last visit. He was wrapped in his favorite blanket and his feed dish and cherished toy were to accompany him. Ray wanted him cremated but couldn't part with him easily. He lay his head on the blanket and both sobbed uncontrollably as they said their last goodbyes.

The teachers smiled ruefully. "What a wonderful, touching story," Miss Anderson said wiping away a tear.

The Westchester-Rockland County Veterinary Medical Society was a service and educational organization formed to keep local veterinarians up to date on the latest developments in our field. In addition, an emergency service program was initiated with two objectives. One was to serve the public with guaranteed emergency coverage at any time, day and night, for both large and small animals. The other was to give the individual practitioner a degree of uninterrupted freedom with his family after normal hospital hours. For that bit of delight each of us pledged two weeks a year of dedication to the service.

When it was my turn I alerted Peter that he might be needed after regular hospital hours. "I'm on call again next week. Seems like it was only yesterday."

"I'll sleep in the hospital to be sure I'm available."

"Thanks Pete." I recalled that he had slept in, the night of the Peases' Brittany emergency.

It was Wednesday, about 11:30 P.M., when I received the call. It had been quiet both Monday and Tuesday nights. I wondered if I was going to have a lucky, crisis free week.

A mishap had occurred on the Bronx River Parkway. Elaine and I had just turned out the lights after mentioning our good luck. While picking up the phone I said to her, "We should never count our chickens!"

She turned on the lamp and looked to me to find out if the emergency could be handled by telephone.

The operator described the case and I repeated the words to Elaine. "A horse is down and in trouble, could I please hurry." I smiled reassuringly to my wife and said to the operator, "You have the wrong list. I'm on call for small animals." I almost hung up when the harried voice made me pause.

"Dr. Gandel can't be reached. The police are desperate. A young woman was walking her standard bred home from a horse show in The Bronx and was hit by a car. The horse and the girl were hurt. They asked me to try you."

I covered the phone and turned to Elaine.

"They can't get the large animal vet. I guess I'll have to go. I just hope you don't get a call for a sick dog or cat while I'm out treating a horse."

I uncovered the phone, "Okay, operator, I'm on my way. Where exactly is the accident?"

"Where the Bronx River Parkway crosses under the Cross County Parkway."

I dressed hurriedly, opened my medical bag and glanced inside. I must have looked bewildered because Elaine sat up in bed and asked. "What's the trouble?"

"I don't have a single item I can use on a horse. Suppose it's something I can't help?"

"You told me you treated horses in the army."

"That was a million years ago and I had horse medicine and equipment besides. And a colonel behind me that was a real horse doctor."

"You'll do just fine, Honey. Stop worrying. Drive carefully and hurry back. I won't sleep a wink 'till you're home."

"Neither of us will have many winks from now on. Everything happens in cycles and I'm sure one is starting. I'll be glad when my tour is over."

I drove as fast as I could on the Cross County toward the Bronx River Parkway. It was less than a mile away from my office and I knew the roads well. Approaching it, I could see the flashing lights in the night sky. I neared the bridge that bisected the two highways. The traffic slowed to a crawl on the Cross County and finally stopped due to rubbernecking. I pulled on to the shoulder, got out of the car and looked down from the bridge. The Bronx River Parkway was completely blocked. A high retaining wall lined the roadway and hundreds of onlookers were hanging over it. I couldn't see much of what was going on because of the ambulances and police cars.

How was I going to get my car through? I would have to approach from South to North against the traffic flow in order to get down to the lower road. The only way would be to use the exit ramp from the Bronx River Parkway to the Cross County. The trouble was that the ramp, just ahead, was one way in the wrong direction. There wasn't enough room for me to make a right turn down the ramp so I drove slowly past it. I proceeded to back down the one lane road. It was dark and I didn't know if it would be better to stick my head out of the window or just turn in my seat to guide the car down the narrow, curving, hardly visible road, or look over my shoulder and out the rear window. I inched my way, hoping there wouldn't be any exiting cars.

I hadn't gone a hundred feet, bumping the curb, stopping, straightening the wheels and starting again when a police car with flashing lights came straight at me from behind, frantically waving me to stop. I opened the door, clutched my black bag and waited.

The officer got out. He wasn't wearing his jacket. Out of uniform, I thought. He saw my bag and put his summons book away.

He said, "Leave your car and come with me." I turned out my lights, turned off the ignition and obeyed his command. He backed down the rest of the way leaving my car in the middle of the ramp. He turned toward the accident with his siren screaming and lights blinking, against the now stopped normal traffic flow.

"We never thought you'd get here," he said. "We've been waiting over an hour."

"I'm Dr. Zimmerman. I don't take care of horses," I said, "I do small animals. They couldn't contact the horse specialist."

"I'm Reilly. My patrol car was the first to reach the accident. Two guys had already freed a young woman who was pinned against the retaining wall. She was unconscious. They probably saved her life.

"Does anyone know what happened?" I asked.

"One of the passing motorists, the guy that helped pull her out, saw the whole thing. She was walking the horse in the right lane when this drunk hit them from behind. He was going fast and probably didn't see them. The horse fell forward knocking the girl against the wall. The driver then swerved, missing the downed horse, and crashed into the wall, pinning the poor woman against the concrete."

"Was he hurt?"

"Just stunned I guess. Nobody looked at him. The passing motorists used crowbars and plain muscle to back the car off the girl's leg. It looked like it would fall off--just held by skin and sinew."

"Is she still here?" I asked.

"The ambulance just took her away."

"What about the horse?" I asked.

"I'm sure his leg is broken. The poor animal is suffering. He was bashing his head against the road trying to get up. I put my jacket under his head. I couldn't put it out of his misery without a vet's okay and we couldn't find one," he said sadly. "I couldn't watch it any more."

As we pulled up to the scene I saw the ambulances and police cars up close. The horse, a deep brown gelding was on his side, Reilly's coat wedged under his bloodied head. As I neared the animal I could hear his rasping breath. He was covered from head to foot with foamy perspiration, and his body shivered uncontrollably every few seconds. His head was quiet from exhaustion. His searching eyes were desperate, pleading. As I walked around to his rear, I saw the grotesque shape of his thigh and the jagged end of the broken femur. I didn't have to be a horse specialist to know that it was hopeless. Nothing in anybody's bag could help.

"This has gone on long enough." I told Reilly. "Hand me your revolver." I'd never shot a horse, but there is always a first time and this was it!

"You have to sign a release before he can be destroyed." He said. The papers, lying on the hood of a police car, were ready. I scratched my name on the official form and turned to see Reilly standing over the animal.

The noisy, restless crowd peered down from the towering retaining wall. Suddenly there was only a hum echoing from the height. I reached out for his gun.

"Excuse me, Doc, but we are not permitted to release our weapons to anyone and I don't know how to handle this. I guess I'll have to shoot, but you gotta show me where." he said. His voice cracked as he spoke.

He drew his revolver and cocked the hammer. The hands of that tough New York cop were shaking. I pointed to the spot where the lines from ear to opposite eye crossed. Reilly tried to follow my instructions. He was embarrassed by his trembling hands and tears trickled down his cheeks. He tried to control himself.

"I'll help you," I said gently. I put one hand under his, steadying the gun, then pin-pointed to the proper angle with the other. The report reverberated eerily against the stone wall, ending the torture. The people looked down at the pageant with front row seats to carnage. . .but after the curtain. . .total, chilling silence.

XI

Mount Vernon Zoo Clinic

Mike Hadley, my receptionist, my groomer, my all around right hand man, became Mrs. Heidenreich and had to leave.

I was happy for her but miserable for myself. I knew I could never replace her. As it happened, my fears were unwarranted. Mike suggested Joan Anderson as her replacement. Barbara Scheid, an expert groomer, also passed Mike's rigid requirement to work at the Beverlie. Both girls were accepted by Peter and though Mike would be missed, the transition was smooth and effective.

Mrs. Anita Kraus was in tears when she phoned my office. At that time she learned I was going away for two weeks. She was more than beside herself. Her dog, "Cricket," was an old friend and patient of twelve years. He was a mutt-collie, lean and rangy, with the collie's long silky hair, gentle disposition and great intelligence. He had the mongrel's genetic strength.

They told and retold the story of "love at first sight," every time we were together. Mr. Kraus met Cricket at the Yonkers Animal Shelter where he had gone to get Anita a kitten. It was to be her Valentine's gift.

The attendant said, "Take your pick," and he pointed to where five or six kittens were playing in a common pen. Kraus had to walk past some puppies. A dozen young mongrels were playing and tumbling around, except for one serious, brown-eyed baby with a white spot on his forehead. The cavorting stopped for a moment as all eyes turned to follow Kraus' steps. Little brown eyes caught his attention. He stopped and fingered the friendly snout through the bars. A warm affectionate tongue caressed his hand. They looked at each other for a moment. Kraus strolled away and glanced back. Those tender eyes never left his. He slowly returned, caught in the spell of mutual intrigue. The kitten was forgotten.

Kraus brought the pup home to his wife—she adored her gift.

Cricket was black and brown with that lone white dot on his forehead. The Krauses were childless, and the years of pent-up love and affection was released on that puppy. It was more than a love affair. Cricket filled the void when Kraus was away on business, supplying the kind of companionship and security only a dog affords. When Mr. Kraus passed away, Anita and Cricket grieved together. He was the bridge and last emotional tie between the departed lovers.

He had been in good health until that desperate phone call. His annual exam six months before, showed him in fine shape except for some loose incisor teeth.

One day, Mrs. Kraus noticed a cough accompanied by frequent swallowing. It persisted, and a slight bloody exudate appeared on the corners of his mouth.

She called my office. "Joan, I have to see the doctor. I'm worried about Cricket."

We squeezed him in late that day. Cricket was too old a friend to put off. With the electric spotlight behind my shoulder I looked down his throat. My fingers replaced the tongue depressor to visualize his pharynx. An angry reddish growth at the base of the tongue just in front of the epiglottis near the windpipe was oozing a sanguine exudate. I palpated the mass. It was hard to the touch but elicited no pain.

"Mrs. Kraus," I said, "Cricket has a tumor at the base of his tongue. It's small, painless, about the size of a marble. The seepage, so close to the windpipe is causing the cough. I don't like the look of it. I'm going to make a smear for the lab."

"It's serious isn't it doctor? He was fine when you checked him out only a few months ago."

"I'll know in just a few days, Mrs. Kraus. It's in an awkward area. I'll call you as soon as I hear."

The lab's report was dismal; lymphosarcoma. I informed Mrs. Kraus of the cancer, and explained about the location.

"I want to be with him at the end, doctor." she wept, "and you're going to California. I couldn't let a stranger put him down!"

"We have a few weeks, maybe a month." I said gently, "I'll be back in plenty of time. Don't worry, we won't let him suffer."

"How will I know when it's time?"

"It's like falling in love, you think you'll never know until it happens."

In the canine, and especially at an advanced age, the tongue is too vascular and too vital an organ to mutilate. In addition, cutting into a hot carcinoma would be inducing diseased cells into explosive, deadly metastasis. Before discharging him, I ran my hands across his throat, palpating the pharyngeal lymph glands. They were normal. It hadn't spread.

I dreaded the necessity of destroying any animal and as evening approached on my drive home I thought of nothing else. Elaine could always tell when there was something on my mind.

"What's the trouble, dear?"

"An old patient that I can't help." I paused. "I'm sorry, Honey, I shouldn't bring my frustrations home, but I've always felt that I should be able to cure anything that walks in the front door."

"Not everything is treatable. You've told me that a hundred times."

"I know, but it's still frustrating. Remember that mongrel "Cricket," I told you about years ago? It was one of the good stories."

"I don't recall off-hand. Remind me."

"Well, he was the pup Mr. Kraus picked up from the pound. He went there for a kitten to give as a gift for his wife, but he fell in love with a dog. Remember, I told you about the gentleman who made an appointment for a kitten and walked in with a puppy?"

"Yes. I do recall. What about him?"

"It may be time for me to put the dog to sleep."

"Is he that old already? How bad is it?"

"He's fourteen. It's an inoperable tumor in his throat. I figure he has about a month."

"Well, there's time for our vacation. Weren't you telling me about a veterinary meeting or seminar in New Orleans?"

"I thought you made plans for California." I felt guilty about constantly changing vacation plans to fit my needs.

"Nothing is uncancellable. I think you will be happier mixing a little work with play. You mentioned a seminar. What's it about?"

"I've been reading about cryosurgery during the past four or five years. I saw an ad in one of the medical journals. They are having a symposium of veterinarians with experienced practitioners acting as professors. It's a new, intriguing procedure. The course takes three days. I would like to take it. There may be long hours of lectures and demonstrations during the day. You could go antiquing and join me and at night we could investigate Louisiana's gourmet dining and Basin Street's music." I thought for a moment and added, "Afterward, we could take in a little of the South; Charleston, Savannah, maybe even Florida.

Elaine agreed and reservations were changed to New Orleans, Louisiana.

It was a fascinating, enlightening seminar. I had a notebook crammed full of notes describing pathological conditions in small animals that were treatable with freezing. The teachers imparted their enthusiasm to us about cryosurgery on birds as well. That subject was right up my alley because I've seen birds bleed to death from what seemed like minor hemorrhage during a simple procedure. With cryo, they assured me, only light sedation was needed with little chance of bleeding.

They demonstrated its use on dogs and cats as well. The instructors encouraged us to practice with the new instruments. They had huge pieces of raw beef for us to work on.

After the lectures we were bombarded by a flock of veterinary supply house salesmen all trying to convince us to buy their products. In addition to the standard equipment used for the dispensing of the liquid nitrogen, I decided I needed a few specialized instruments so I could put some of my notes to use. It was important to have a dewar (a container used to transport liquid nitrogen). It looked like a large thermos bottle and it would hold a week's supply. The instructors warned me to strap the dewar in the front seat of my car so a sudden stop wouldn't cause a spill. Then I bought a set of metal probes to use for freezing different sized tumors. Finally, I needed a special and very expensive thermometer to insert at the base of each lesion so the temperature of the ice-ball could be calibrated. A successful treatment should measure the ice-ball at 20 degrees below zero. Three successive freezes were recommended to kill the cancer cells. As I studied the thermometer, I realized that it was too large to be used on small birds. I would have to use judgement and good old horse sense for them.

During the three days of study and enlightenment, I couldn't get Cricket out of my mind. I asked a lot of questions wondering if somehow the new procedure could help him. They told me that freezing hadn't been effective for basal cell carcinomas and they didn't have much experience with cases of lymphosarcoma.

Elaine was making plans for the final ten vacation days. I phoned my office to make certain all was well.

"I'm glad you phoned," Joan said, "I was about to call you about Cricket Kraus. Mrs. Kraus called and she was frantic. I sent him to Dr. Matthews, as you suggested. He gave the same prognosis you did but Mrs. Kraus wouldn't let him put Cricket to sleep. I told her I'd have you call her."

"Good, Joan. I'll call Matthews too. Give me Mrs. Kraus's number."

I called her immediately. "It's Dr. Zimmerman, Mrs. Kraus. I just spoke to Joan and she brought me up to date. I'm sorry Cricket isn't doing well."

"He feels a little better now, Doctor. Dr. Matthews gave him a shot." She started to sob. "I thought he was dying. He started to choke. Could you please come back just to take care of him. I don't want him to suffer anymore."

"Mrs. Kraus," I explained, "I'm not just on a vacation. There is a continuing education course here and I want to talk to you about some new procedures. It may be helpful for Cricket. I'm coming home immediately. We'll just put off our vacation."

"Thank you, Doctor." She said and I could hear the tears starting again. "I remember what you said about knowing when it's time, and I'm afraid it's close."

I apologized to Elaine, "Thank goodness we didn't travel too far. I have to go back and see Cricket immediately."

"Can your new treatment cure him?"

"If it does I'll take you to Paris for a month."

"You're on." She said. "Let's go home."

I was enthused with my new weapon to challenge formerly untamed pathology. Conditions previously written off as untreatable were now reclassified, at least in my mind, to the realm of curable disease. The use of freezing as a therapeutic and surgical tool was so simple and sensible that I couldn't believe I had not investigated its use before. What I liked most was that only sedation was necessary because it was practically painless during its application and there was very little discomfort afterward. It was actually medically applied frostbite. The diseased tissue, after treatment, painlessly dropped away.

When I arrived at the office with my notes and new equipment, I knew I would have to explain what I learned to my staff. I started with Peter who would be assisting on most of the procedures.

"Liquid nitrogen, at 164 degrees below zero, is the medium producing the freeze. Be careful, Peter," I warned. "Liquid nitrogen is cold and it can burn if you're not careful."

"I will be," Pete said, "I'll wear gloves."

Joan stuck her head in the door. "What's all the talk about burns? I thought you said we were now in the freezing business."

"You'll be assisting also, so come in and listen. 164 degrees below zero is pretty cold and if you happen to touch one of the instruments, while in use, it will stick to your hands and give you a severe burn. It splashes also and the splashes burn. I've felt them, so be on your toes every minute."

I showed them the dewar I would be using for the transportation and storage of the liquid nitrogen. "It is so volatile, it boils away at room temperature in less than a week."

I read from my notes how the nitrogen is used. "The simplest way is spraying on the lesion itself. A disadvantage of the spray is the intense mist that is generated by the boiling of liquid nitrogen at room temperature. Using the spray, surrounding tissue must be protected by vasoline. Liquid nitrogen can be dabbed on with a cotton swab or poured directly if surrounding tissue is protected with petroleum jelly, and finally," I explained showing them several metal probes, "as you can see, these probes are different in size and shape depending on the size of the tumor." The use of the probes was explained by the salesmen. The nitrogen was confined to the channels on the inside of the instrument, giving better control to the freeze.

I called The County Welding Company of White Plains, New York. They had been supplying me with oxygen in heavy metal cylinders, for many years. Betty O'Conner usually took my calls, and, as an animal lover, inquired politely about what strange creature I was treating that day.

"I need liquid nitrogen," I started, "can you get some for me?"

"I wondered when you would be asking about nitrogen," she said, "we've been delivering it to the hospitals and dermatologists for over a year."

"Really!" I answered, "Why didn't you tell me about it? You could have saved me a trip to Louisiana and an entire year of ignorance."

Then seriously, "I bought a dewar in New Orleans. They said it would hold about a week's supply."

"We always have it on hand but we don't deliver small amounts. You'll have to pick it up. The dermatologists come in once a week."

It became routine for me to carry the volatile liquid once or twice a month, depending on my need. I planned to carry it in my car strapped to the front seat.

I arranged for Joan to have Mrs. Kraus bring Cricket in the first thing in the morning. I was supposed to be on vacation and except for boarding and grooming, the office was quiet. If I could win her over to allow me to try, we could do the procedure the following day.

"Mrs. Kraus," I began slowly, "Cricket is in pretty good health except for that tumor. I think we can give him at least two or three more years by using a new technique called crysosurgery."

Her face lit up, then clouded and she said. "Dr. Matthews said there was no chance. He explained that almost any other organ could be removed, but the dog's tongue. It's too important in keeping him cool, cleaning himself and expressing affection." She sobbed. "I won't let him suffer."

"Neither would I, Mrs. Kraus. And cryo doesn't remove the tongue at all. It freezes the tumor. It's a procedure that is practically painless. It doesn't bleed and doesn't require hospitalization."

She wiped her eyes. "Why didn't he mention it? If it's so good I'm sure he would have."

"It's a new procedure, Mrs. Kraus. I told him about it and he is very interested in hearing more. I'm sure if he had taken the course he would have suggested it.

"Tell me about it, doctor."

"It's so simple it's scary. The tumor is frozen with liquid nitrogen, a harmless gas taken right from the air we breath. Freezing doesn't hurt. It's a little uncomfortable, and when it's applied, mild sedation is all that's necessary. When the tumor thaws, the frozen cancer cells burst and die. It takes from ten days to two weeks and then it just sloughs off. In Cricket's case he'll just swallow without even knowing what it is."

"And I can take him right home?"

"The same day. He'll walk out the way he came in. He'll cough occasionally during the first week from the oozing and there will be a horrible odor. Don't forget that dead tissue putrefies, but it's temporary. When it falls off nothing will be left but a tiny scar at the base of his tongue."

"Can you do it now?"

"I just need a day to get a supply of liquid nitrogen. Bring him in tomorrow morning and he will be ready to go home by three. I'll call Dr. Matthews. I'd like him to be here, if he can make it."

I spent a sleepless night going over the surgery in my mind. Most of my experience had been on raw meat at the seminar in New Orleans.

The following day I left home early to pick up the nitrogen, visualizing all the way about how the surgery might go. I'd be using the tissue thermometer, similar to the housewive's gadget when roasting a turkey. I'd place it in the root of the tongue just under the tumor. The entire lesion will be frozen to 20 degrees below zero.

I had the choice of applying the nitrogen as a spray or use it through one of the metal probes that would be embedded into the growth. The tumor at the base of the tongue requires an intratracheal catheter to protect the lungs from the freezing gas and any exudate that might result during the procedure.

The instructors had explained that the spray method would only be practical on skin lesions or small tumors because it freezes the tissue slowly. They showed us how to remove a portion of a tumor with an electric cautery loop, which seals tiny blood vessels as it cuts. Then they demonstrated the use of a proper size probe placed right in the scooped out tumor for a more rapid freeze. I planned to remove about a third of the tumor, enough room for a medium sized probe. I remembered from the seminar that the liquid nitrogen, as it flows through the probe evaporates and creates a thick fog, obscuring the operative field. I practiced it repeatedly in New Orleans. Every few seconds I would have to blow into his throat, clearing the view. Once the probe was in place and the tissue commenced to freeze, my eyes would be on the thermometer.

That morning Cricket arrived, his tail wagging vigorously. Mrs. Kraus was smiling and optimistic. I hoped she wouldn't notice my nervousness. Dr. Matthews couldn't be there. He was busy and promised to observe the procedure some other time.

Cricket was tranquilized, an oral speculum kept his jaws open for the insertion of the intratracheal catheter. Sterilization was unnecessary, except for the placement of the thermometer under the tumor. He jumped slightly as I forced it under the growth.

I turned on the nitrogen and watched the ice-ball enlarge slowly between my blowing to clear the view. The freeze started at the edges of the probe, gradually growing until it completely enveloped the cancer. When the tissue thermometer read twenty below zero, I turned off the nitrogen to await the thaw. The procedure was repeated three times. The freeze for that size growth took about five minutes. The thaw lasted almost twenty. In a little over an hour we were finished.

The operation went without a hitch. Cricket hardly moved.

At three o'clock Mrs. Kraus arrived. Cricket was wide awake and apparently normal.

"He looks fine, doctor. What do I have to do for him?"

"Nothing at all. Treat him normally. You'll never know when the tumor falls off. Bring him in about Wednesday or Thursday, next week, for his post-surgical exam. That's ten days from today."

That night I confided to Elaine that I wasn't at all sure what would happen. At the seminar the instructors assured me that at least no harm would be done by the procedure. It was so new that there wasn't enough scientific evidence for every possible condition to be encountered.

On Wednesday Cricket was back. Mrs. Kraus said the odor was like a rotting animal corpse.

"He did plenty of coughing all right. I'm glad you warned me about that. Now that has stopped and I don't see any more blood on his lips. I think he is cured."

"We'll know soon, Mrs. Kraus. I'm as curious as you about the result. Open up, Cricket." I said as Peter lifted him to the table, "Let's have a look."

I saw a tiny white scar, nothing more. I pressed the area with an index finger. It was soft and normal to the touch.

After the successful operation on Cricket, Nat Matthews called to tell me that he heard from Mrs. Kraus.

"She thanked me," he said, "and I didn't do a thing but tell her that her dog had to be put to sleep."

"I know," I answered. "She was so happy that she had to thank everyone. She knew you were honest because I told her the same thing."

Cricket lived another three and a half years, finally succumbing to natural causes. Mrs. Kraus buried him at the Hartsdale Animal Cemetery.

She called me the next day. "A house without a wagging tail is not a home," she told me. "I went back to the Yonkers Animal Shelter for a new puppy, Cricket Jr., and this time, a kitten also, just to keep him company.

A week after the Kraus success, Dr. Matthews phoned. "I have a case I want you to take that looks as hopeless as Cricket's did."

"Another throat job?"

"No. Not as simple but it's your specialty. A talking lovebird with a rapidly growing cancer on its cheek. I've operated on a lot of them and they either bled to death or died from the anesthesia. The owner is tougher than the tumor and I'm not going to touch this one. First I told her it was hopeless and then said that you had a new treatment. I hinted that it was something about freezing and maybe worth a chance."

"Thanks a lot. I love the simple ones."

"Anyhow, she's going to call you. Her name is Wolfson. Good luck, and if she agrees, I'll come and watch your magic."

Mrs. Wolfson, encouraged by the hint of a new therapy, brought in her blue, male, talking parakeet. Her "Budgy," an amazing little bird, had learned almost fifty words with the clarity of a linguist. Mrs. Wolfson talked as much as her bird. She loved the little thing and went on about its intelligence and sense of humor. It sat on her finger talking its head off, walked around the table while she and her husband were dining, sampling everything on their plates. He was more fun than any pet they'd ever had, and the healthiest.

The bird was three years old, when a small lesion, like a pimple, appeared on the left side of his head just behind the corner of his bill. It didn't seem to bother him but kept growing. Mrs. Wolfson finally called Dr. Matthews.

Since then, it had grown in size to almost a quarter the size of Budgy's head. That type of rapidly growing tumor, as Matthews mentioned, was usually malignant. Treatment had formerly been surgical excision with an electrocautery knife under deep anesthesia. The double danger resulted in a poor prognosis. I explained the pitfalls of the routine treatment to Mrs. Wolfson, and told her about the new hope of cryosurgery.

"It's a new, exciting avenue that's opened up. Freezing can destroy unwanted cells without much damage to the normal ones surrounding the lesion. It's superior to conventional surgery because cancer cells would not be spread, accidentally, by the scalpel.

"How is this any less risky?" she asked tearfully, realizing the gravity of the condition.

"The anesthesia is light," I explained, "and there is no cutting, so it is relatively painless to the bird. The biggest plus is that there is no bleeding. You know how we use ice for a nose bleed. The liquid nitrogen is fifty times colder than ice. In about a week or ten days the tumor simply falls off."

"How do you know it will work, Doctor?"

"I don't, Mrs. Wolfson. I've just returned from a seminar where the experts themselves had limited experience and still don't have all the answers. With Budgy, we don't have much choice. If we go the old way the odds are too great that he won't make it. Dr. Matthews agrees. With cryo, at least the procedure won't hurt him. If it fails we can always go back to electro-cautery as a last resort."

Mrs. Wolfson thought about it. She didn't want to lose her pet by doing nothing, and had to decide what, in her mind, was least risky. She thought my explanation made sense and finally agreed.

"How long will he have to stay, Doctor?"

"If you bring him in at 9:00 A.M., you can pick him up at 3:00. If all goes well, the tumor should drop off in a week or ten days. I can't be exact because at the conference there was limited experience with birds."

The appointment was made and I called Matthews to reserve the time so he could observe and assist.

In a week Budgy arrived, ready for surgery. Dr. Matthews took Peter's place and held the tiny patient for his sedative. We estimated his weight at about eighteen grams and I sedated him with Ketamine. The injection was made intramuscularly in his thigh. Within minutes he was down.

Matthews gently wrapped him in Kleenex tissue with his head exposed. I used the smallest cryo probe available and within minutes the tumor was frozen. The bird was too small for the monitoring thermometer. The thaw took about eight minutes. We repeated the procedure three times as we had done for Cricket. Soon afterwards Budgy began to object to the restraint, which was Matthew's hand, so we put him back in his cage, still wrapped in tissue, to keep him warm until fully awake.

Ten days later Mrs. Wolfson was back for the post-operative exam. I looked at him through the cage bars and couldn't see much change in the growth except that it was a trifle smaller and darker in color.

"It's not much smaller, but at least it hasn't grown, Mrs. Wolfson. I think we should repeat the procedure."

"He certainly didn't mind the first one. He came home talking as much and as fast as before. If you think so, Doctor, go ahead. Where is Dr. Matthews today?"

"I didn't call him because I thought I'd just be taking a look. I'll call Matthews later and bring him up to date. If you leave him with us now, I'll work him into our surgical schedule and you can have him back by 6:00 P.M. Peter, my attendant, will assist."

The freeze was repeated without a hitch. Budgy went home talking his head off at the indignity of the entire experience. A week later the expectant call came from an excited Jeanne Wolfson.

"Doctor, I can't believe it! It's gone. The tumor fell off and I can't even see a scar, just a tiny white dot. I can't thank you enough, it's like a miracle. I know you said it would happen but I never dreamed it really could."

"Hold on, hold on. I know you're as excited as we are. It's our first bird patient. Was there any bleeding? Is he scratching at the area? Would you bring him in so we can examine him?"

"There is no sign of anything. I can't even find the tumor. "Doctor!. . .Do you think he might have eaten it?"

"Probably not. It just dried up and fell off and it was so small you couldn't tell it from normal droppings. Don't worry about it."

"Thank you again Doctor. I'm going to drop him by the first chance I get. First, I'm going to teach him to say 'Doc Zimmerman is great! I love Dr. Zimmerman.' And by the way, I'll never be able to thank Dr. Matthews enough either. He referred me to you when he thought there was a chance to save him."

"Be sure to show Dr. Matthews how he looks." I said, "I've been trying to get him to take the next cryo course. Budgy will certainly convince him."

Joe Lipsio was a barber on South Broadway in Yonkers, New York. He had a hobby. He was a big game hunter who never used a gun. He was an expert with bow and arrow.

It was the winter of '54. The snow was falling heavily, the wind was whipping into his face with the sting of a sand storm. He was ready, positioned behind some trees. "Hold at full draw at least five seconds," he repeated to himself. "Establish an anchor. When the draw fingers touch some part of your face at full extension, you have it. Pull the bow arm to its full length until the fingers are anchored at the same spot." He rehearsed the sequence for the hundredth time, remembering that the arrow head has four cutting edges and kills by hemorrhage. It must be sharp to cut large blood vessels.

Just ahead something dark moved. It was low in the snow. He heard the far-off roar of a thousand running feet. The migrating Caribou! There it was again. A full grown Timber wolf came into view moving slowly in the midst of the heavily blowing snow. Joe steadied his quivering arm as best he could and finally let the arrow fly. One yelp and quiet. By Gad he did it! He hit the target!

Joe approached slowly, looking for signs of life. He heard several scurrying movements. As he got closer he could see that the female wolf was down and quiet, the single arrow protruding from her heart. It had been a lucky, uncannily accurate hit. The blood was scarlet against the snow. Then he saw a little cub trying to get close to her. For one brief moment he was flooded with guilt. Killing a brood bitch meant the death of an entire family. The scent and sight of man forced the others to flee. This baby must have been six or eight weeks old. He was whimpering as he sniffed his mother's bloodied wound and watched the warm red flow melt the snow.

Joe approached the youngster slowly. The cub looked up and his tail flickered in submission. Joe picked him up without resistance. Funny, the hunter thought, he didn't follow his brothers and sisters. He took him back to camp and fed him some warm milk and bits of meat. The least I can do, he thought. The pup accepted gratefully.

Marie never minded her husband's trophies or his stories of hair-raising adventure. She admired his sport that showed a real hunter's courage and daring. The mounted animals and heads hanging at home and in his barber shop were okay. However, she wanted no part of a real, live wolf cub.

"Get rid of it, Joe. I won't have a wild animal in my house."

Reluctantly he walked down the street to the local pet shop. As he cuddled the furry bundle of love he felt a pang of remorse. I should have left him near his litter-mates, he thought, but he realized they could never survive without their mother. God knows what will happen now. As he looked down, the puppy looked up at him and affectionately licked his nose. Joe felt responsible for the little fellow. He thought of the legend: save a life and he is your responsibility forever. He's my obligation now, he thought.

He entered the store, "Jim, can you sell a full blooded timber wolf?" He asked as he held out the white ball of fur. "Marie wants no part of him." He narrated the story of its capture. "Would you please take it off my hands? Maybe you could pass it off as a Shepherd. Maybe you could even keep him, Jim. It could live in the shop and be a great advertisement."

Linda Bismark was a young attractive newly-wed working the switchboard at a hotel. She helped supplement her husband's income, a law student attending night school. He was a part time waiter and cook at a New York City hotel. Tall and handsome, full of ambition and hope for their future, he relished hard work. Some day he would be successful and rich.

Every day after Linda finished work she took a bus to within one block of her home on Bronx River Road in Yonkers. One day, a moment after she got off the bus, she sensed someone following her. She turned and saw an unshaven, angry vagrant. He grabbed at her purse. She resisted, aiming a kick at his groin. The man was quick also. He dodged her leg and grabbed it throwing her to the ground and knocking her dizzy. When she sat up her bag was gone with its few dollars and some make-up. The man was no where in sight. She felt miserable, spent and vulnerable.

The mugging had left Linda with the rage and helplessness of a rape. She had to do something and her husband agreed. "I'll go to school and learn karate." she said, "or join a gun club and get a license for a revolver."

"No!" Fred said, "I have a better idea. I know you hate dogs, but if you get a Shepherd pup and raise it, it will give you all the protection you'll ever need."

Fred had been raised with pets as far back as he could remember and missed them terribly. He was really looking for an excuse to induce Linda to try a puppy. Women don't get attacked with a dog at her side, he reasoned, but Linda's mother was always afraid of animals and instilled that fear into her only daughter.

"I don't want a dog." She said. "I'm afraid of them. I'll never feel comfortable with one around."

Fred decided he'd take the chance. He'd get a puppy that was so cute and adorable she would grow to love and trust it. It was just chance that a baby Timber Wolf looked like a cute, Shepherd puppy.

"Please don't mention to my wife that it's a wolf," he begged the proprietor, "It will be hard enough for her to accept a dog, much less a wild animal."

"It might grow to be a little larger than a Shepherd." Jim Courier warned. "This puppy was brought back from the wild. We don't have a pedigree to judge him by, or any idea about how a wolf matures."

Fred looked down at the puppy in his arms. The little fellow looked up at him and licked his hand in assurance. "I think he'll be okay," he said to Jim. "I have a feeling he's exactly what we want!"

After the mugging incident, the Bismarks bought a Volkswagen Beetle so Linda wouldn't have to take a bus any more. She was wary of the new pet, but he was so young and defenseless, needed love and affection so desperately, that within a week she agreed to give him a chance. Fred would have to supply the petting and affection because she couldn't bring herself to accept him completely. She named him Silver and took him wherever she went but in her heart, just tolerated him. He would sit and look at her so lovingly, so enraptured, that it made Linda uncomfortable. The back seat of the car belonged to Silver, because Linda couldn't have him sitting next to her and staring at her. It was a common sight in Mount Vernon and Yonkers, to see the "Bug" with its three occupants, Silver's head sandwiched between the two Bismarks. Silver depended on Fred for overt caring. Fred romped with him, played with him and hugged him with genuine love.

I knew during Silver's first visit to my office that Linda was far from enamored with her pet. Fred warned me that Linda didn't know his background. He would tell her himself, when he thought the time was right.

My sub-conscious was troubled by a sense of foreboding the first time I saw the wolf puppy. I recalled our first telephone conversation. "Dr. Zimmerman," Fred Bismark began. "Dr. Sternfels told me to call. He said that you were the expert on wild animals."

"Thank you," I answered, "How can I help you?"

"I bought a Shepherd puppy. Actually, it's a wolf cub. I want it for my wife but she is frightened of animals and I don't want to tell her yet. I brought him to Dr. Sternfels on Broad Street and after a couple of visits he suspected the truth. The puppy grew too fast. He told me he thought it might be a wolf and I admitted that it was. I want to know if I can raise it and train him to protect her." He proceeded to tell me about the mugging.

"Why don't you consider a well trained Shepherd or a Doberman?" I asked, "I'm sure they could give you all the protection you need."

"I really was looking for a Shepherd," he answered, "but now that we've had him a couple of months, I think my wife really likes him. I can't part with him. Will you take him as your patient?"

"Mr. Bismark, I'll tell you the same thing I tell everyone who asks about adopting wild animals. Most people see tham as cute, adorable babies, never stopping to consider what may happen to them later."

"Animals lose their cuteness," I told him, "the same way children do. The trouble is they have no place to go when you want to discard them. They get too large," I continued. "Too strong and sometimes too mean for a private home. At that point in their lives, they aren't equipped to return to the wild, even if you could get them there. Sometimes, if you're lucky, a zoo will take them. Most of the time there is no room for them or they just don't want them. These animals, raised with affection by humans, will be distraught when separated from the family. They wind up in an animal shelter where there is neither the love nor the care they have become used to and need. Most of them are put to sleep, or die of a broken heart."

I spoke not only as his veterinarian but as a casualty that had learned the hard way when I was only fourteen years old.

Four years after the Wall Street crash of 1929, the United States was in a deep depression. People had problems feeding themselves, let alone having money to spend on pets. My dad not only lost his manufacturing business, but the pet shop, his great love, was failing. Miss Price, our bird lady and cashier had to be let go. Our attendant John Velez, was put on notice, and most of the exotic livestock, including monkeys and large parrots, were sold. Some animals, like half-grown chimpanzees, couldn't even be given away. The small birds, puppies and kittens were transferred to a new little shop on Sixth Avenue.

A place had to be found for Uncle, now a four year-old, sixty-pound, female chimp. I was fourteen years old, and still had a close relationship with her. Bill was gone and, except for Prejie, our Siamese cat, Uncle was my only Pet. We couldn't play together the way we had in the past and she was too old and powerful for us to walk the streets of New York. I spent as much time as possible just keeping her company. Her patience and gentleness were sometimes frustrated by her imprisonment, and she became restless. We always parted in the same way--I gave her an affectionate hug and told her I loved her; she looked me in the eye and, with her right, index finger, gently touched my "love spot," the little birthmark under my lip. Dad had kept her in a large cage, in the basement of the store, where she was isolated from people and other animals. He had to put a heavy leather collar on her, attached to a strong metal chain for restraint. When she acted up, he was the only one strong enough to control her. Besides, he had Uncle's love and respect, being the only parent figure she had ever known.

I'd had many a heart to heart with my dad about Uncle's confinement. "Shouldn't we ship her back to Africa where she can be free?" I asked, repeatedly. "I love her but would give her up if I knew she could be happy."

The answer was always the same. "Uncle is like a child. She loves us and is happy in the place she's grown up in and is used to."

I was convinced that keeping her was the only answer. But in spite of us both, circumstances changed and she was about to lose the family and the security she enjoyed. She had to be placed somewhere else.

The Steel Pier in Atlantic City made Dad an offer. They wanted a fifth chimpanzee for their "Great Ape" display. That lovely summer day turned into a solemn and unforgettable one. With tears in my eyes, I implored my father, "Can't we please keep her? She doesn't know anyone else. You said so yourself. She'll be miserable away from us." I never considered the everyday, worldly problems facing my folks. The falling income, the national recession sliding insidiously into depression, and the need to change our lifestyle. Uncle, though one of the famly, wasn't really a natural child. I never thought I'd see the day when circumstances would jeopardize our relationship.

"She'll be with four other chimps," Dad explained. "She needs more freedom and companionship. Besides," he continued, "we can't afford to keep her any longer. We must sell the store and move the business to smaller quarters."

That was my first inkling of a profound change in our lives. My parents never complained. They tightened their belts, did what had to be done, without burdening any of us about the perils of the future. Our brownstone house on Eighty-Seventh Street had been sold in 1929, four years earlier, and we had to move into our first apartment, on Ninety-Seventh Street near Riverside Drive.

Mom and Dad also decided to tell Elise we had to let her go. We loved her, but couldn't afford the luxury of a cook. I was losing Uncle, the London Pet Shop and now Elise. It was more than I could understand. My whole life was coming apart.

"I'll get a job, Dad," I said. "I'll make enough to keep Elise." I didn't like school too well anyhow, and we had to keep the family together.

"Forget it, son," he said, putting his arm around me and holding me close. "Nothing interferes with school. Things aren't that bad. You leave the problems to me. We have a home, a smaller business perhaps, but we'll get along just fine."

"In a few years," he addressed Elise, "we'll be able to afford you, and we hope you'll come back."

"I don't need a salary," she said, tears streaming down her cheeks. "I'll stay like the rest of the family. I'll work for room and board. I'll be with my children, and the Lord will provide."

I hugged her and we all cried. We'd be together a little longer.

On Sunday, following the arrangements for Uncle's sale, we were to drive her to her new home. The shop was closed to the public, although as long as I could remember, pet shops were never really closed, because the pets had to be cared for the same as every other day. On Uncle's last day with us, my cousin Bill gave her extra treats as a going-away present. As he cleaned her cage for the last time, he knew it was the end of an era. Uncle knew also. She wouldn't take her eyes off Bill and "ooh ooh'd" at him as if asking what was happening to her world.

No one looked forward to the long, car ride to Atlantic City. My brother Norman and I were to accompany Dad. We used the family car, a large, luxurious, red Nash. An old blanket was spread across the front seat, on the passenger side, for Uncle and me. Under the blanket was a rubber sheet, as she had grown too big and strong to diaper and was not toilet-trained. She never traveled by car, but she loved and trusted Dad, and would follow him anywhere.

Norman, curious and lively, hated riding in the back. Sitting in front was always special. Dad sometimes put us on his lap, let us hold the steering wheel and pretend we were driving. Norman was appeased by holding Uncle's bag of fruit and nuts and giving her some if she got hungry. Uncle sat between Dad and me. Sensing an impending crisis, she sat quietly, and I affectionately kept my arm around her shoulder.

Dad spoke, "She can't be in a cage all her life. The people from the Steel Pier promised a large area with trees, a brook, and natural-looking surroundings. And. . ."

"But," I interrupted, "you're taking her away from her family. They may not like her and, besides, just think how much she needs us. And I'm really going to miss her, Dad."

"I know, son," he answered consolingly, "but don't forget she's an animal. Instinctively she'll know she is one of them. She'll get to know them, and they will accept her in their family. Believe me, they will all live "happily ever after."

"I hope so." I said dejectedly, "Can we please come back and visit her?"

"Of course! Atlantic City isn't far away. You'll see, we can get there in a couple hours."

It was closer to three hours, by the time we arrived. We followed signs to the Steel Pier, a giant, commercial area, packed with a variety of stores. A security policeman directed us to the zoo area.

Dad left Norman, Uncle and me, sitting in the car, as he completed his business transaction. I spent those last few minutes worrying about what would happen to her. From the time she was a baby, I considered her my special pet. When she was sick, I prayed for her like she was a baby sister. As she matured, it never occurred to me that someday she would be too big to keep.

I looked at her face, so sensitive and expressive. She looked back with a hint of understanding. Then, her patience wearing thin, she stood up, restlessly rocking back and forth. I wished Dad would hurry.

Quieting her the only way I could with the instinctive ritual that she loved. For three years we practiced the scratching, picking and searching each others skin for bugs or salt or whatever. She would be suddenly successful and put it in her mouth, chewing contentedly. I then reciprocated by scratching her and pretending I was looking for that elusive something. I played the game and pretended to eat it also. I coaxed her to sit, realizing this might be the last time we would share this intimacy.

We waited. Now Norman became restless. He opened the bag of fruit and nuts, and offered them to Uncle. She wouldn't touch a thing, so Norman ate them.

Finally Dad returned and said,"Come on out. Let's take her to her new home. No more cages for her. She'll be free, and the other chimps look great and friendly, too. Uncle will love it here!"

We started along the sidewalk. Bystanders stopped to watch the strange procession. I held Uncle's right hand while her left knuckles touched the ground with every step, in the typical chimp gait. My father held the chain in one hand, Norman with the other. We strolled nonchalantly as though it was the usual and only way to have a pleasant walk along the famous Steel Pier.

Arriving at the huge window fronting the chimpanzee's quarters, I saw four, fairly large apes sitting on the floor nibbling bread, fruit, nuts and vegetables. I shaded my eyes, face pressed against the glass, to get a better look. "Dad," I asked doubtfully, "where are the grass and trees? There's no sunshine!" The floor was packed earth, covered with wood shavings and straw. It looked dirty, dull and artificial.

Dad replied defensively, "It's certainly better than her cage in the cellar. I guess they did exaggerate a bit."

I bit my lip, but the tears started. I turned my face to hide my hurt. Did my father really care?

The chimps listlessly picked and poked at the food. Occasionally, one would finger some fecal droppings, investigating whatever from the aroma. They ought to be cleaning up that stuff, I thought.

Three females, dominated by the larger, mean-looking male, acted out their ceremonial feeding. He would grab any interesting tidbit out of their hands, carefully smelling it before sampling its taste. Uncle won't care too much for him, I thought. These were Uncle's new companions. To the average person, all chimpanzees look alike. I easily made out the difference in their features and expressions, and I didn't care for the looks of any of them.

I counted four artificial trees scattered about the compound, with swings fashioned from old automobile tires, hanging from the branches. The stagnant-looking, wading pool with scum and algae floating on the surface, was visible way back on the right side. A heavy mesh, wire door was at the far end, near the pool. I suppose it really is better than her cramped quarters back at the shop, I admitted to myself.

We walked to the back where a short, narrow hall led to a locked metal door. One of the attendants was there waiting to open it. As it swung open, a second door of heavy wire mesh, the one I had seen from the outside, allowed an easy view of the animal quarters.

As we neared, Dad introduced us to the keeper, "Mr. Lieber, these are my sons, Ted and Norman. And this is Uncle," he said, as he laid a gentle hand on her head. "She's been our pet since she was a baby, and I'm sure she won't give you any trouble."

"Don't worry," he said gruffly, ignoring us. "We can handle her!"

He unlocked the second door and motioned Dad to lead her in. They had decided to leave the collar and chain on her until she became acclimated. There was a four-inch threshhold separating the hall from the compound. Dad, gripping Uncle's chain, backed over it, gently pulling as he tried to coax her along. Uncertain, confused and a little frightened, she objected, wedging both feet against the threshhold. I pushed against her back.

"Please go in, Uncle," I begged. "Go meet your new friends."

She wouldn't budge. Uncle wasn't about to be dragged into that strange, unfamiliar place. A sixth sense told her she might be abondoned.

Dad, knowing her strength and stubborness, had anticipated this reaction, and made an alternate plan. He knew Uncle loved him and would do most anything to protect him. Would love prove stronger than muscle?

"I'll go in alone," he explained to Lieber. "When I stir them up, they should threaten me. If I know Uncle, she'll come to my aid."

I saw the chimps behind Dad, anxiously backing away from the unusual commotion. As he stepped further into the compound, Dad confronted the already alarmed and pacing foursome. He began making threatening gestures, throwing his arms into the air and shouting. They, in turn, reacted by hooting and slapping their hands against the floor. They showed their teeth, screamed and waved their hands above their heads. Led by the male, they charged a few steps, then backed up for collective security. Dad, trying to entice Uncle through the door, kept a wary eye on the frightened apes. Suddenly, they charged!

With an angry, answering scream, Uncle moved. She jumped over the threshhold and ran right at the four, the chain swinging wildly from her collar. Dad stepped back through the doorway as the attendant pulled the wire door shut.

I watched horrified. Uncle rushed to help Dad, only to have the door slammed in her face. I began to cry. I had resigned myself to leaving her there, but I thought it would be a different kind of goodbye with sad hugs and kisses and some understanding. After all, she was family. Dad tried to console me, "She just needs a little time to adjust to her new home. She'll be fine. Let's say goodbye to her from here."

Uncle had returned to the door. She squatted, her hands holding the wire mesh, and looked right at me, her anguished eyes begging. She pursed her lips and uttered a long, plaintiff, "Oooh." Uncle was trying, in a final desperate way, to say she loved us, wanted us, needed us.

Finally, resignedly, she poked her finger through the mesh and touched my "love" spot.

She was saying goodbye.

Dad waved and said, "Bye bye, Uncle, be a good girl."

Then I realized that Uncle would no longer be my pet and my friend. She was, from that moment on, just another zoo attraction. In spite of her inability to understand why, she sensed it, too. She had been duped and her heart was broken. Dad tried to say goodbye again. Uncle glared for a moment, then turned her back on us.

We walked around to the front and peered through the window. She was still sitting near the door. The other apes had backed away from the charging stranger, but, with the human menace gone and no longer threatened, their natural curiosity returned. They made overtures to Uncle, in typical chimpanzee fashion, holding one arm outstretched, wrist bent, fingers pointing straight down, "ooh-oohing" in a friendly way. Uncle ignored them.

I tapped on the window to get her attention. I couldn't walk away leaving her so unhappy. She turned away again. Would she ever forgive us?

"She won't watch us go, Dad. She just knows we're deserting her!" I looked up at my father imploring.

A tear streamed down his troubled face.

"Oh please don't feel bad, Daddy" I sobbed, as I threw my arms around him. "It'll be all right. It's the only thing we could do."

My dad couldn't talk. He put one arm around my shoulder. With the other, he took Norman's hand. Slowly we turned, never looking back.

I learned later that she never lived out the year. Broken-hearted and lonely, she refused to eat, she mourned, withered away and died.

To this day, her memory brings pangs of remorse and guilt. I didn't realize, nor did my Dad, that the great apes are enough like us to love completely, to suffer mental anguish, and to grieve deeply the agony of a lost love.

I pledged my mother's words, "Cross your heart and hope to die," to never subject a wild animal to such misery again.

I tried my best to convey that feeling to Bismark.

"Doctor," Fred said, "I might never have taken him had I known the implications, but it's too late now. We really intend to keep this animal! The bigger he gets the better. Will you take care of his medical needs and help us raise him?"

"I won't refuse to treat him" I answered, "I'm only advising you about the future. I'll do my best to keep you and your pet healthy and happy."

I met Silver for the first time when he came for his initial examination and inoculations. He was a beautiful, healthy specimen of full blooded timber or gray wolf, indigenous to parts of North America. In spite of my zoo experience I didn't know how he would behave in a civilized environment. When he walked into my waiting room, everyone fussed over him. Linda Bismark was the only one that seemed reserved. But what a cute, adorable, gentle animal he was. At four months of age, he came for his second series of shots, which, for most of my young patients is somewhat traumatic. Silver behaved better than most.

"How are you coming along with house-training?" I asked, anticipating the primary problem with new puppies.

"He never had to be taught." Linda said proudly. "He just wouldn't go inside from the first day."

"I'm sure he eats well, but does he like what's good for him. Puppy chow and vitamin and mineral supplements?"

"He likes everything I put in front of him and then wants more. I think he is a normal adolescent. And doctor," she added reassuringly, "he is gentle and I'm not afraid of him any more."

He weighed thirty five pounds. A month later his final shots were due and he weighed fifty. Still happy, playful, completely tractable and the apple of everyone's eye. He had reached sixty pounds when he arrived for his rabies vaccination. It was obvious he would not need much training as a guard dog. All he had to do was show himself! He would demand the respect of the world's meanest muggers!

Silver filled the back seat of the Volkswagen "Bug" completely and was very agile, leaping in and out. He loved to ride anywhere and everywhere. He would sit on the sidewalk on the passenger side, patiently waiting for the door to be opened. In one leap he would be in his seat, his huge head nestled between theirs. Silver adored them both. It was mutual, and returned with the same warmth any parent would bestow on a child.

During the day when Fred went to work, Linda and Silver would be together. He would ride with her to work, wait patiently in the car till noon. Then drive home for lunch and his mid-day run. There was a wide expanse of lawn adjacent to their apartment running about one hundred feet along the Bronx River Parkway. This area was perfect for dog owners to run their dogs. Silver would frolic with them, and though he was big and strong he was gentle and never overly aggressive.

After lunch it was back to the Bug and on to work. Linda was off at three o'clock. Back home, the ritual of running and playing was repeated for a half hour or so. In the evenings Fred and Linda would walk him again.

The call came one early Saturday morning while I was treating hospital cases. Joan answered the phone.

"It's Mrs. Bismark." She said, "She sounds terrible."

"Can I call her back?"

"Better talk to her now. She sounds emergency-like."

"How does somebody sound emergency-like?" I asked in an attempt at levity.

"When you're crying, begging to talk to the doctor and saying 'It's Silver, it's Silver,' you can sound like a screaming siren, clanging bells or a racing motor."

Peter heard the word "Silver" and popped into the examining room. "What's wrong with Silver?" He queried.

Peter loved him, our only wolf patient. He held him for his shots and gave him baths, necessary after a roll in the mud. Peter, in his usual way, had made a fast friend in Silver.

"We don't know yet, Peter," I said, "hold this pup." I let him take the little speckled Cocker Spaniel puppy I had been treating.

"Hello Linda, Dr. Zimmerman here."

"Doctor," she began, her voice quivering with emotion. "I'm afraid we may be in for some trouble with Silver. We need your advice."

"What's happened?" I asked, wondering what could be wrong with an eight month old, ninety five pound, full blooded Timber Wolf.

"Something very peculiar. He grabbed Fred by the arm rather viciously when he opened the door to get into the car. It's the first time we've heard him growl in anger. It was as if he was trying to protect me from my own husband."

"Were you in the car?"

"Yes. I was picking Fred up at the station. We've done the same thing a thousand times before."

She continued her story, "I had been shopping. Everything was normal and Silver and I were in the car waiting for Fred to arrive from New York. As my husband opened the door to get in, Silver bared his teeth, growled and grabbed his arm. Lucky thing Fred had his jacket on. He didn't break the skin but bit pretty hard."

"Then what did you do?"

"I shouted, "Silver!" And he let go. I jumped out and he followed. When he was out of the car he seemed normal and responded to Fred's talking and petting with the usual tail wagging. What do you think could be the trouble?"

I remembered the last hospital visit. His huge head with gigantic teeth surrounded by exquisite grey-white fur. Gentle disposition, but with the potential for mayhem. He had normal protective instincts.

"It sounds like we'd better be careful," I told her.

"I don't want to lose Silver," she sobbed. Her husband took the phone. "Doctor, I've told Linda all about Silver. We've decided to put him to sleep before we let a zoo have him. I don't know if we should take the chance and keep him if he's getting vicious."

"Hold on," I said, "don't be so hasty. Lets talk about it."

"Can you figure any reason for this behavior?" Fred asked.

"It might have been an unusual scent that provoked him, something that you inadvertently brushed against, or touched. The canine smell is much keener than sight and Silver might have been reacting to that. "Or," and I said what I really thought, "it's possible that 'the call of the wild,' is rearing its relentless, uncompromising head."

"You mean a wild male animal is growing up to be wild, just as the pet shop proprietor warned?"

"Silver is a normal, healthy male approaching sexual maturity. He has no other way to show his adulthood. Your wife may be the substitute object for that male instinct. Did she by any chance start her period recently? Male dogs have been known to become very attentive to their mistresses during the menstrual cycle."

After a moment of reflection, Fred Bismark answered my query. "My God, doctor, you may be right. I think she did start." He covered the phone and I could just make out the muffled query and the affirmative reply.

"There is a chance that we can solve the problem." I told him. "First of all, you can't ever try to enter the car or any room or even home when Silver and Linda are inside. Try to plan your life so he rides with one or the other. When you and Linda go out, Silver stays home! When you get home, you enter first. I have a feeling that as he gets older it may get worse. Remember that it's a confusing instinct. I'm sure that he still loves you very much." I paused, "Do you want to take the chance?"

"I think so. What else should we do?"

"The next step is to neuter Silver. Castration is not complicated surgery. Compared to a spay it's not at all risky, especially with epidural anesthesia. The only worrisome thing for you is that it takes about six months or so to become effective. If you love him and want to keep him as a pet and guard dog, that's the way to go."

"Why does it take so long?" He asked incredulously. "A spayed female is sexless immediately."

"Two reasons. The male sex hormone lingers in the blood a long time. Secondly, the pituitary gland stimulates the production of male hormone in other parts of the body." I remembered Dr. Danks imparting that bit of information on the green lawn behind the large animal clinic before demonstrating the neutering procedure. 'A gelded stallion can mount a mare for six months after this operation.' I'm sure you have heard and read about eunuchs serving the queens of yore. Anyway," I continued, "think about it and let me know. But remember; there is a possibility it may not work."

"Why not?"

"If it's a character defect, not related to his sexual maturity, he'll only get worse. He may just be too mean for us to take the chance.

I put down the phone and turned to my staff. "How would you like to help castrate Silver? The Bismark's are thinking about it. He's getting to be a big boy and doesn't want the lady of the house touched."

The potential for disaster was real. It was very possible that someone or something was going to get hurt and my job was to protect both owner and animal.

The young couple discussed their problem that night. Was keeping Silver worth the risk? What would happen to him if they didn't keep him? They just couldn't visualize that wonderful free spirit apart from them. They decided to go ahead with the surgery and prayed that it would work. His operation was scheduled for that week. Because of his size and strength, restraint was a real consideration.

"Stay with him till I give the sedative." I suggested to Linda. "He likes Peter and just puts up with me. He's very perceptive and he may suspect something. Act as though he's coming for an office visit."

We prepared him for surgery. Epidural anesthesia was administered after the initial sedative. Silver weighed ninety-five pounds and even asleep was a magnificent, frightening specimen. His head was twice the size of the largest shepherd. His teeth were out of proportion to the size of his jaw, nearly three times as large as any dog's I had ever seen. The damage this animal could inflict, if provoked, was terrifying to comprehend.

He slept like the proverbial angel during surgery. The only problem was lifting his huge, relaxed body from the table when we were finished. He was too big for the hospital's largest kennel so we put him on the floor of the operating room and watched him carefully until he came out of the anesthesia. Joan sat with his head in her lap until he was awake. She looked up and said, "Why don't we keep him here until he's ready to accept Mr. Bismark?"

Peter smiled and nodded his agreement.

"Forget it! They aren't about to leave him one minute longer than necessary."

He was discharged from the hospital a few days later completely recovered. As he was leaving I cautioned Linda and Fred again. "Don't put him in a situation where he might have to confront you,

Fred. Be patient and in a few months we hope he'll be normal and dependable."

Six months passed with no news; then the happy call from Linda.

"We tried Fred and Silver in the car today," she said joyfully, "His tail almost came off, I never saw such wagging and licking and," she emphasized, "I'm having my period. He got hugs he hadn't felt since puppyhood."

The trio was seen driving around Mount Vernon once more. Silver's glorious head sandwiched between his masters.

Fred graduated Law School and took his little family to Peoria, Illinois, where a top position in a prestigious law firm, awaited.

Their new vet sent a request for Silver's medical records and any hints, clues or suggestions for the safest way to treat a 160 pound full blooded Timber Wolf. In his post script he offered to pay my fare once yearly if I would please come to Peoria and give Silver his annual examination and shots.

Xmas cards were exchanged between the Bismark's and The Beverlie Animal Hospital for years. A son and two daughters were added to the family, all accepted, loved and protected by Silver. The sad news of his inevitable demise, from old age, at the age of twelve arrived with a portrait of all six Bismarks. It was added to our growing gallery of unusual exotic patients.

Henry Trefflich called, out of the blue, to tell me about a surprise he had, just for me. "If it's just for me, Henry," I answered, "I know it's nothing I can take home to my wife and family."

"I guess not," he laughed, "but you'll enjoy it just the same. I have it on the second floor (which meant monkey). Come on down and take a look."

"Should I bring my medical bag or a thank-you note?" I teased.

"Make it an official house call." He said. "There's no rush but you have to see this."

I arrived the next afternoon and Mrs. Lenz waved me upstairs.

There he sat. A little redhead. A cute baby orangutan huddled on the floor of a fairly large, straw bedded cage. Looking down at him, he looked normal. Henry wasn't around but I saw Harry cleaning monkey cages at the far end of the room.

"Hi, Harry. Where's the boss?"

"He's around heah somewhere. Can I help you?"

"What's the story on this baby? Henry called and said he had a surprise."

"A surprise for you is something he wants you to do for him. You should know my boss by now."

"I was sure of it, Harry. I just couldn't figure out how much my surprise would cost me."

Harry laughed. "Heah he is now. You ask him."

"Hi, Henry. Is this my surprise?" I asked looking down at the orangutan.

"I got him for nothing." He said gleefully. "He's got a big hernia on his belly and they couldn't sell him. I made them throw him in with a large order. They couldn't refuse because there was nothing else to do with him. If he were normal he'd be worth more than all the others combined."

I stooped over for a better look because his belly had been hidden from above.

"It looks like a congenital umbilical hernia." I said. "I never have seen one that extensive. How is he otherwise?"

"He's just fine. Eats and plays like a normal baby. You can repair it, can't you Ted? I'm sure you can. I can get $5,000 for him when he's right. I knew you'd love the experience. That was my surprise."

"You know Henry, I've never operated on an orangutan before, and I've never seen a hernia that size. What makes you think I can do it?"

"I'll take the chance, Ted, I have nothing to lose. Dr. Goss is gone and you might as well do the surgery. Chances are it will turn out fine."

Henry wouldn't take no for an answer and had Harry put him in a dog carrier for the trip to Mount Vernon. I knew I'd have to research the surgical technique and discuss the case with Janice Nightingale.

There was nothing in the literature about hernial repair in orangutans and Dr. Nightingale wasn't a surgeon. After thinking and worrying about it, I decided to just adapt the method I'd learned at Cornell for the umbilical repair of dogs and cats. The same muscles are involved and besides, I would get another look at the internal organs of an orangutan.

My staff was thrilled with the new baby. He made himself very much at home and had free run of the kitchen. He learned quickly, and within a few days had mastered how to open the refrigerator door. One day, Joan had a dish of spaghetti prepared for her lunch. She had to help in the examining room for a minute and when she returned we heard her scream. We all rushed back.

"I need help!" she shouted, "He's eating my lunch."

An orang doesn't just have two arms and two legs. When he wants to, he has four very effective hands. The little ape had opened the refrigerator door and was helping himself. As Joan gripped his hands, each holding a fistful of spaghetti, his hind legs reached into the bowl, grabbing two more fistfuls. As she held his arms, both feet were stuffing pasta inside his mouth. Joan gave up in disgust as Peter and I roared.

We planned the surgery for the following Monday. The staff listened attentively as I allocated their duties. They had assisted in surgery many times and were excited about their first orangutan patient.

Ed and Janice Nightingale's tenth anniversary party happened to fall on the Saturday before the operation. What a great gag it would be if I hid the little orang in a gift package and surprised Ed and Janice at the party. I couldn't resist the chance to test Ed's squeamishness again. Janice couldn't have cared less and I knew she would go along with the gag.

I gave Elaine the plan. She agreed it would be all right as long as it was a gentle baby. "Little Red," was about four months old and weighed about ten pounds. Just small enough for a discreetly sized gift box. Elaine fussed with the plans for wrapping paper and ribbon. It had to be inconspicuous, as it would sit on the living room floor with the other gifts.

I took him home the day before the party and Rick and Ron had a ball playing with him. He required Sadie Taylor's formula in a baby bottle every three to four hours during the day, in addition to bits of fruit and other foods from our table. The boys wanted to take him to school immediately, but I had to explain that he was sick and had to be operated on that week.

"Can we catch his disease?" Rick asked.

"Not that kind of sick," I explained. "He was born with a muscle on his tummy that wasn't normal. See right here." I explained, as I showed them the hernia.

"He doesn't even know he has it." I told them. "He feels fine, and eats well. He played with you both today and you didn't even notice."

"Then why do you have to operate on him?" Rick asked pragmatically.

"Because when he is a baby the hernia doesn't matter. When he grows up and weighs a hundred pounds, it can be very serious. You must have strong muscles under your skin, protecting vital organs like your stomach and liver and everything else in your belly."

The boys were satisfied and chuckled when I explained how we were going to put him in a gift box and surprise the Drs. Nightingale.

"Can we stay up and watch?" Rick asked.

"Yes." Ron echoed. "Can we? Can we?"

"I think it might be too late." I said. "But I'll check you two before we surprise Dr. Nightingale. If you're still awake, you can watch from the stairs."

"Oh, thanks, Pop. We'll be awake."

The party was at our house on Fayette Road, Scarsdale. I didn't mention the ape to the other guests. Most of them were our fraternity brothers and their wives from Cornell. I figured they might as well enjoy the surprise with Ed. All the presents were piled in a heap around one easy chair. We toasted the happy couple at dinner, and retired to the living room to open the gifts.

Trying to anticipate every eventuality, I had my boys put a handful of grapes in the orang's gift box. Except for screaming when hungry or frustrated, the little ape was always quiet.

I had my sixteen mm. camera with all the lights needed for indoor movies. I wanted to have a picture record for them and posterity. Ed and Janice "oohed" and "aahed" over the many gifts with, "You shouldn't have," and, "what a surprise," till they came to the fairly large, square box decorated with vivid paper and a beautiful bow.

The others knew there was something special when I wound the camera, turned on the brights and got ready for an important "take". Off came the ribbon and Ed impatiently tore at the paper. The omnipresent grin was on his face as he peered in, too excited to notice the air holes perforating the carton's sides.

As he bent over the box his necktie fell in. A furry red hand reached up and grabbed it. Before Ed could react the other hand appeared and encircled his neck. As he straightened in dismay, up came the little ape, all diapered and dressed for the party, both feet wrapping themselves around Ed's waist, holding fast.

"Jerome!" He cried, christening the baby. "What I always wanted!" The entire audience convulsed as he begged, "Take him away! PLEASE!"

I had forgotten Rick and Ron, but they had never closed their eyes. From behind the banister two little heads were bobbing with mirth.

"I'm sorry guys." I said when I heard them. "I didn't mean to forget. Say hello to everyone."

They waved, turned and ran back to their room still giggling.

My fraternity brothers crowded around the little red celebrity, but their wives were just a little reluctant.

I handed Jerome to Stan Kates. He passed it on to Chuck who couldn't get rid of it fast enough to his wife, Estelle.

"He's adorable." she said. "What a wonderful gift. As usual, Ted, you outdid us all."

I told Ed and Janice that despite the importance of their anniversary, we hadn't brought Jerome just for them. I lifted his skirt, and showed everyone his problem. I explained that it had to be corrected before he was saleable. All were interested, especially our pediatrician, Janice. She examined him carefully and discussed the technique for the repair. Though she had referred many a child for similiar surgery, she had never witnessed the procedure.

Monday morning, goodbyes were said, before the boys went off to school. They were worried about the operation.

"Will he be all right?" Rick asked, giving Jerome a hug.

"When he's all better can I take him for, "Show and Tell?" Ron echoed, holding the little ape's hand.

"He'll be just fine boys. And no Show and Tell. He has to go back to Mr. Trefflich as soon as the bandages come off."

I brought Jerome back to the hospital for his surgery. My staff was ready. Joan gave the ether and Peter assisted at the table. It was a rather difficult procedure compared to a dog or cat because of the orang's huge belly. Peter had to hold two large retractors for over an hour as I dissected the atrophied muscle away from the skin. I was afraid the shrunken abdominal muscles wouldn't bridge the gap across his belly, and contemplated doing the surgery in two stages. Finally, with gentle stretching, the suture line was completed and holding. The skin took more than thirty stitches to close. A tight bandage strengthened the area and would remain at least a week.

Jerome was up and drinking his formula within hours. We had to prevent overeating for fear of putting too much pressure on the sutures, a real challenge for a hungry baby. He resented the restriction and fussed for the entire week. Joan and Peter took turns feeding him a swallow or two, every hour.

A week later the bandage was removed. The skin had healed perfectly but I was appalled and disappointed to see the entire hernia as large as before. What could have happened? All the muscle stiches had failed. I couldn't imagine what went wrong.

I phoned Janice and asked if she could refer me to a good pediatric surgeon. She told me that their friend, Ed Miller, whom I had met socially at dinner one night, was an excellent surgeon and they were sure he could help. It wasn't the first time I called an MD to consult on a puzzling primate case.

I explained what happened and Dr. Ed Miller went into detail about what I used as far as technique and sutures were concerned. He knew immediately what happened.

"You used ten-day catgut the way we did on dogs in Medical school, didn't you?" He asked laughing.

"Of course," I said, "the best quality! Just as I have for all my patients."

"The trouble is," he answered, explaining the complication, "The greatest stress on muscle tissue after surgery in primates is the tenth day. Your catgut dissolved when you needed it most. You have to use stainless steel and a muscle overlap technique. I'll be glad to show it to you anytime."

"Ed," I answered, "how would you like to demonstrate the procedure in person? I'll administer the anesthetic. You say when and I'll set it up. How about it?"

He surprised me, "I'd love to do it, Ted. I'll have something unusual I can report on at my next medical seminar."

We scheduled a date and I invited Ed and Janice to watch. Trefflich was thrilled that I had obtained the use of a skilled surgeon, and as usual made the most of the incident, for publicity.

The muscle overlap method he showed me, was so simple it was ingenious. The stainless steel sutures would never break and would remain forever. Ed assured me that they would in no way inhibit the growth of the muscle as Jerome matured. I practiced exotic animal medicine another forty years and never had a chance to use Miller's method on apes again. It wasn't wasted, however, because I improvised the technique and used it on dogs and cats. Stainless steel sutures became standard procedure for muscle closing on all abdominal surgery.

Jerome went home to Trefflich's with his new figure. He was sold to the Chicago Zoo and ultimately weighed nearly one hundred-fifty pounds.

A month after Jerome's departure, a day at the Beverlie began with old office hours and a new receptionist. Joan had separated from her husband and decided to stop working. Barbara left to have a baby. One of their mutual acquaintances, Sophie Shupin, came to work. With no one left to do the clipping and bathing, and the load of a ponderous clinical practice, I decided to give up grooming, entirely.

Nick Corrado's business and hobby were chimpanzees. He bought two babies from Trefflich, about a year apart, and raised them like his own children. They were washed and dressed daily, taught discipline, good manners and even toilet training was attempted.

Nick was a soft-spoken Italian. A husky, dark haired, powerful man with experience in the martial arts, yet, a gentle sensitive person.

Nick was in show business. His wards were rented out for children's parties, and occasionally did bits for advertising companies. Before long his babies were on T.V. shows and movie shorts. At the New York World Fair of 1964-65, on a huge billboard, Nick's Kokomo and Kokomo Jr, dressed to kill, towered over the Fair's entrance.

He brought Kokomo to me, that first day, straight from Trefflichs. Peter placed a blanket on the examining table to protect the little fellow from the cold, hard, metal surface.

Nick Corrado asked questions about diet, preventative measures on health and any hints I could give him on training.

"Are you married?" I asked.

"Why?"

"Raising a baby usually takes a woman's touch."

He looked inquiringly. "how come?"

"Have you ever changed a diaper?"

"Why would an ape need a diaper?"

"Then you've never put a diaper on a baby, much less changed one." I said.

"That's right." He said defensively.

"Are you going to keep him in a cage or allow him to run free."

"I don't believe an animal should be caged. Especially one of the great apes. They are so human-like, I am going to bring this baby up exactly like a child."

"Exactly. We've discussed the diet and health of primates. Now let me show you how to diaper one. Pete," I said as I took the chimp from him, "bring me one of the cloth diapers we used on the baby gorillas. And don't forget the safety pins."

"You had gorillas here?" Corrado asked incredulously.

"And we kept them diapered."

"Them? You had more than one."

"We had five. We were treating them for pneumonia. But you really have to keep this baby covered. Can you imagine what your apartment would look and smell like if a naked baby had free run?"

He was silent for a moment as he reflected. "I never thought about it." he admitted. "I intend to raise him, teach him tricks and use him as a business. You know, children's parties and such. I'm going to dress him in children's clothes, even shoes. I got the idea from some teacher friends. They said there was quite a demand for trained chimps to be shown in schools. I've always loved chimpanzees," he said simply.

Peter came in with a diaper and we demonstrated putting and pinning it on.

I held him up when we were finished and handed him to Corrado. "Now he won't get you wet, or mess up your car. You were lucky he didn't have to go on the way here. Didn't Henry tell you anything about caring for him?"

"No. He said I'd learn myself and encouraged me to call him if anything came up I couldn't handle." He looked down at the little fellow in his arms and coo'd.

"I'm sure you'll do fine but it's going to take patience and a lot of time."

"I'm prepared for that, Doc." He said. "And eventually I'm going to get another one. I think they'll need company growing up."

"Don't rush yourself. This baby will take up most of your time, especially if you plan to train it to perform."

A funny look came over Nick's face and he suddenly held the chimp away from him. "I think he's gone. My arm feels very warm. . .and wet." He looked at us sheepishly. "Can I borrow another diaper?"

Corrado spent a year nursing, worrying, learning and teaching little Kokomo. He bought the second ape, and like an experienced parent, relaxed and enjoyed his new family. His efforts proved his original idea as sound business sense. His first ward was producing an income and by the time Kokomo Jr. was two years old, Nick Corrado was a familiar name in New York's world of advertising.

Kokomo went through the usual travail of teething, and was soon sporting his new set of large, sharp, incisors. There was nothing wrong with Kokomo's teeth, but there was a problem. He used them for more than chewing bananas and eating nuts. Several years earlier, as he was just entering the modeling profession, I removed his upper front incisors. He was using them to nip his fellow models. The advertising agency was getting nervous about insurance claims. With the incisors gone he learned to use his fang teeth. Biting or pinching was his way of showing independence and superiority. He was never hostile, but like a naughty little boy, he loved the way his victims reacted. Nick decided it was time to see me again.

We were running about a half hour behind schedule, not unusual during office hours. At 12 noon, there were still three ladies with two small dogs and a cat, patiently waiting their turn.

The front door opened with its irritating buzz. All heads turned as Kokomo appeared in the doorway, one hand on the door knob. His eyes surveyed the office. He was dressed in a plaid shirt, grey trousers, suspenders, and a jaunty Tam-o-shanter with a long sweeping feather. High black shoes, laced and shined, completed his attire. He stood erect, shuffled to the nearest chair and sat down. He very nonchalantly crossed his legs and put an unlit corn-cob pipe in his mouth.

A few moments later Nick entered the waiting room and, ignoring the ape, sat in a chair directly opposite where long practiced signals could be given.

Nick was full of hell as usual. Astonished eyes were on the chimp, especially Sophie's, our new receptionist. Nick had Kokomo do his routine. Uncrossing his legs, then recrossing them. He took the pipe out of his mouth, turned the bowl upside down, and pounded the back of it, as if emptying the ashes on the floor. He then casually placed it into his breast pocket.

I walked in just about them, to view the open mouths and disbelieveing faces.

"Morning Kokomo," I said, going along with the gag. "Did you come alone this morning?"

One raised finger from Nick and Kokomo answered with a vigorous "Ooooh" and a nod of his head.

"That's nice," I answered, "I hope you had a nice drive. You're a little early and you'll have to wait your turn. These people are ahead of you."

Nick, still unnoticed, clenched his fist and rubbed his lapel, like a third base coach signaling the batter.

Kokomo responded. He stood up, stamped his foot in anger, spun completely around and plumped himself back in his chair. Out came the pipe, jammed into his mouth, legs crossed again, and both arms akimbo.

"Ladies," I chuckled, "I'd like you to meet Kokomo, the famous television star, and his handler, Nick Corrado."

The waiting room erupted in hilarious laughter and spontaneous applause. Right on cue, Kokomo stood up and bowed low from the waist.

"What's he here for?" Mrs. Reese, the tabby's owner asked, "He looks fine and healthy."

"Just his yearly checkup." Nick said grinning as he threw a wink at me.

It wasn't long before we could turn all our attention to Kokomo.

"I think we had better do the extractions before we have lunch." I said after the waiting room had emptied, "He'll be tougher to handle if he waits too long. He's got a good memory and I'm sure he knows why he's here."

We decided to tranquilize him in the waiting room which was well lit, roomy, and free of the smells and sights of the hospital. Kokomo was justifiably uneasy. His only recollection was probably the operating room so I wanted him sedated first. We locked the front door and turned to the patient.

"Okay, Doc." Nick said, laughing, "Look at his face. He knows what's coming." Kokomo kept staring at Nick, his eyes pleading. His face asking, why are you doing this to me again?

"Can you restrain him for the shot?" I asked nervously. "He put up quite a battle last year."

"I'm a Black Belt Doc. He doesn't even weigh a hundred pounds. Get the shot ready and let's go!"

The tranquilizer was to be given in the back of the thigh and we figured a hammerlock would be the easiest restraint. Nick was very muscular, weighing about two hundred-twenty pounds. Kokomo was quiet and almost too restrained as he allowed Nick to remove his trousers. Talking to him softly, Nick applied the hammerlock.

Nick had cared for Kokomo since he was three months old. He loved his master and would do most anything for him. Nick schooled his charges with love and patience, even the difficult task of toilet training had finally been accomplished.

I prepared the needle and approached the nervous ape. Nick was sitting, his arms under Kokomo's armpits and up behind his head. Wrestlers break the hammer-lock by relaxing, throwing their arms straight up, and dropping to the floor in one motion.

As I knelt along side of Kokomo and dabbed his thigh with alcohol he did just that. The hold was broken in one second, the needle went flying, and Nick, mouth open in amazement, was left with up-raised arms and no ape. In the same flash, Kokomo grabbed my hand, pulled to his mouth and slashed it with the canine tooth destined for removal.

Nick and I stared unbelieving at my bloody hand. It happened so quickly I hadn't the time to react.

"I'm sorry, Doc." Nick said finally, "he's never done that before. I was sure I could hold him. Is it bad?"

"I'll get some ice to stop the bleeding. It's not my first bite, Nick." I said philosophically. I examined my hand closely. "Thank goodness his incisor teeth are gone. It looks like I'll need a couple of stitches but I'll wait until we're through. I think you'll have to tie his hands together behind him to keep him from breaking the hold."

"I just happen to have handcuffs which will do the trick. We use it in one of the acts. I'm really sorry, Doc."

I washed the wound. It was just below my left knuckle on the index finger. The bleeding was minimal so I slipped on a rubber glove and prepared another syringe.

With his hands locked, resistance was fruitless. In five minutes he was down. Nick carried him to the operating table like a baby. I gave each of the four canine teeth local anesthesia and within a half hour we were finished. Before packing each of the dental cavities with antibiotic soaked gauze, the teeth were replaced firmly in their sockets to control bleeding. We were amazed at the depth of the fang teeth's roots. Two thirds of the entire tooth was below the gum line.

By the time we were finished, my left hand, still inside the glove, was covered with blood. I called Dick Neudorfer, my golfing buddy and the club's orthopedic surgeon. He was at the Saint Agnes Hospital in White Plains. He met me in the emergency room and administered four stitches and a tetanus shot.

"How did that happen?" He asked.

"I'm just getting old and slow." I answered. "I should have moved quicker." Then I explained the incident, the waiting-room humor and wrestling match.

Luckily, that weekend Elaine and I had tickets to fly to Rome for a two week vacation. I wouldn't have to scrub for surgery for at least fourteen days, and by that time the wound would be healed.

Elaine didn't relish the idea of removing sutures, especially on a vacation. She agreed to hold the surgical silk ends, with forceps, eyes closed, as I snipped each of the ties with my left hand. We were now free and clear to tour Italy. The vacation was a success but trouble was brewing at home. I spoke to Sophie long distance. Steady, reliable Peter was neglecting his duties and drinking beer during his work time. His mother forbad him to drink at home so he slept at the hospital and was hung over every morning. He never got along with Sophie and picked on her incessantly.

Back in the office on my first day home, Sophie told me she had decided to quit. She wanted her pay.

"Peter wouldn't do his work. I had to feed the animals, clean the kennels and act as receptionist while he goofed off. I would have walked away except for the animals. I've had it. I waited for you to get back and now I'm going."

Reluctantly I paid her. She picked up her few belongings and stomped out the door. I hated to see her leave with such ill feeling. I was grateful that she had held on 'till I returned.

I confronted Peter. "What happened to you? You never allowed an occasional beer to interfere with your work. Does this mean that every time I turn my back you're going to get soused?"

"No Doc, I'm sorry. It won't happen again."

"You know Sophie left because of you. You told me that you could get along with her."

"I'm sorry. I'd like another chance. My mom hasn't been well and I was worried."

His remark brought me up short. I knew he adored his mother and she was always over-protective toward him.

"Why didn't you say so?" I asked. "I could have postponed my vacation or even come back early. What's her trouble? Anything I can do?"

"No thanks, Doc." he said, "she's getting old I guess."

His mother was an agreeable, quiet little woman. He told me that she nagged him to the point where he wouldn't go home. Night after night he had curled up in a kennel, disregarding the cot, and drank himself to sleep.

"What about Sophie?" I asked. She told me she had to do your work in addition to hers because you refused to lift a finger."

"She's exaggerating. She doesn't like me and I don't like her."

What was done couldn't be undone and the hospital couldn't function without a receptionist. Elaine had helped in the office when we were first married and I asked if she would cover until a new girl could be hired.

"I've always wanted to see how the Mount Vernon office works," she said. "Your stories about the lion cub and gorilla, intrigued me."

"They're not there now," I said, "but something interesting is always happening."

She came to work with me early the next morning and I explained her duties. Elaine was never comfortable with strange animals, especially large ones and though she loved kittens, and well behaved dogs, full grown cats were an anathema.

"All you have to do is sit at the desk and answer the phone," I instructed, "if the call is for me, press the first button once. Twice is for Peter, but he rarely gets a call. When people come in you can find their clinical cards in the metal file right here next to the desk."

"What if it's a new patient?" she asked.

"Blank cards are here in front of the files. Just fill out the cards." I showed her the forms and explained the information I'd need.

It had been a busy, noisy morning starting at 9:00 AM sharp. Elaine had been working for about an hour and a half. It was 10:30. Peter had taken the Cocker Spaniel puppy she had just admitted for surgery to the hospital ward in the rear of the first floor. There were still three noisy canines and a couple of felines, huddled in the safety of their carriers, awaiting their turn when Elaine pushed through the door from the waiting room. She closed it and leaned back on it, a troubled look on her face. I looked up at her and smiled.

"Everything okay?" I asked.

Elaine breathed a long plaintive sigh, "I just had to get away for a minute," she apologized. "I'm exhausted!" She looked down at me accusingly. "It's heaven in here. Quiet, no bells, no one jumping on you. Practicing medicine is easy compared to that tumult, that uproar. There's pandemonium every minute," she complained, "I no sooner finish answering the phone to take care of a client, when the door buzzer starts and someone else comes in with a noisy animal. The floor is a mess, the smell is awful, the phone won't stop and I want to go home!"

I grinned, never realizing how unnerving that job was.

"Relax," I told her, "Pete will be right out with the mop. You stay here and help me for a few minutes. Pete can pull cards and answer the phone."

It was tranquil in the examining room and soon Elaine relaxed. Peter returned from the surgical ward, through the kitchen door. "Pete," I said, "Take the office for now. Mrs. Z will help me do the examinations."

I gave her the heavy leather gloves to use on the skittish patients and between her and the owners, we handled the examinations and shots adequately. The next day Elaine was back at her desk, knowing that she could always take refuge with me. Her fourteen days were fun for me and an unnatural torment for her. I loved having her nearby, and appreciated her ordeal.

Darryl Mauro was Elaine's replacement. What a Godsend! She loved animals better than anything in this world and became a marvelous receptionist. She had two adorable seven-year old twins, Chris and Tom, that always visited on her days off. She had a fantastic memory that saved me from many an embarrassing moment. I remembered my patients but could never recall the client. She whispered, very artfully, and I came off as the dedicated, perceptive and very bright doctor who never forgot a name. She even got along well with Peter. She was so down to earth and logical, that he accepted her occasional suggestions, without rancor.

The call came on a busy Monday. Darryl was on duty that day and I could tell from her expression that it wasn't routine. She cupped her hand over the phone and said quietly. "A referral from the Long Island Ocelot Club. She sounds weird." Weird was one of Darryl's most descriptive adjectives. As she listened, her face took on that look of annoyance reserved for a special few.

"Wait till you hear her. She says her ocelot, "Baby," that she loves sooo much, needs a good doctor. She demands that you get on the phone."

I took it from her. "Dr. Zimmerman speaking."

"Catherine Cisin of the LIOC (Long Island Ocelot Club) told me to call. My name is Irene Fratello and I have a very sick ocelot. I love him doctor," she said passionately. "I just love him so much, I don't want him to die."

"Can you bring him in to be examined?"

"I live in Flatbush, Brooklyn, but I'll bring him anywhere to save him. Oh Doctor, I love him so much, I'll die if he does. He's been to another vet and he almost killed him. He has a growth on his chest and the vet couldn't treat him. He sent him home to die! Doctor I love him so much, he's such an angel. I've had him since he was a baby. You have to save him doctor. Mrs. Cisin said you could save him."

"My receptionist will give you an appointment and directions to get here, Mrs. Fratello. Just hold on."

Now it was I who cupped the phone. "Get her vet's name and number and as much of a history as you can. I'd better check with him first. Be sure you make the visit after lunch; early afternoon."

The ocelot and margay craze was still in its initial stage and Mrs. Cisin, president of the newly formed LIOC had asked me to talk to as many veterinarians as possible to appraise them abut handling, restraint, diet and treatment. Her office had been bombarded with complaints about vets that wouldn't treat them. Ocelots and margays are small spetacular looking wildcats, with dark black spots or sripes or both. They were as ornery as they were beautiful.

The appointment was made for Wednesday and we wondered what was in store for us. I called her veterinarian but he didn't help too much. "She's a nut," he said disgustedly, "and her ocelot is wild and mean. He had an abscess and I tried to drain it. I got bitten, my attendant was mauled and we never got paid. Good luck!"

"Did you take Xrays?"

"No way! I got him out as quickly as I could. I didn't think they were indicated anyway. It looked like an abscess pure and simple."

After lunch on Wednesday we put off surgery waiting for the Fratello office visit. Finally, at about 1:30, a very weary, overweight lady, carrying a heavy dog carrier, in addition to a tremendous pocketbook, plopped herself down in our waiting room. She was out of breath and exhausted. The poor woman had taken the subway to Grand Central then the NY Central Railroad to Mount Vernon. There was a quarter of a mile steep hill from the station to our office and Baby weighed about twenty pounds. She evidently struggled up the hill rather than pay for a cab.

A noxious odor accompanied her entrance. Pet ocelots always stank from the combination of their natural wild odor, combined with the fright induced diarrhea; one of the reasons we schedule their visits after office hours.

In this case, adding to the unpleasant aroma, there was the obvious stench of an unclean woman. She was dressed in an old house dress, stockings rolled halfway down her legs, worn black flat heeled shoes adorned her feet. Her hair was short and unkempt, her face was pale and puffy. The smell of stale urine added to the unpleasant aura of Irene Fratello. Her eyes had a vacant stare, though her face was contorted with emotion.

It took several minutes for her to catch her breath. Finally she reached down and unsnapped the cover of the carrier, swinging it open. Cowed in the box was Baby, now growling in a low continuous hum, communicating his displeasure. Ocelots are nocturnal and prefer the security of the closed, dark interior of the black boxes.

"Is he leashed?" I asked. Most clients know that handling a frightened ocelot is impossible without a snug collar and leash.

"No." She said, reaching down into the box to caress her pet. "Oh I love you, Baby." She bubbled, kissing the top of his head as he continued to growl with displeasure and fear.

"Be careful! He's frightened and he'll bite you as quickly as he will us."

"I don't care I love him so much. You have to help him, Doctor. I can hold him for you. He doesn't need a leash."

I turned to Peter, who heard the talking and had entered the waiting room with the thick leather gloves we used for wild or intractable animals.

"Get the towels and the loop, Peter. This is going to be messy."
I could see that the box was dirty and Baby was lying in his own filth.

The "loop" was a six foot hollow pipe with a ring of strong rope
at one end and a handle at the other end to pull it tight. The loop
around an animal's neck is perfect for restraint, keeping one's
hands safely out of reach. We use the gadget for half grown lion
cubs, baby pumas, even the great apes before they are tamed.
When attached properly it acts like a rigid leash.

"We'll have to loop him to get him out and examine him." I told
her. "If it makes you nervous we'll do it in the examining room and
you can wait here."

"No! I'll get him out. He'll do anything for me." She reached in
to grasp him and got a nasty bite for her trouble. "Ooh Baby!" she
screamed, "you bit your mommy." And she put the injured hand
into her mouth, sucking her own blood.

"I told you that when he's frightened he'll bite anyone." I slammed
the cover shut and motioned Darryl to get the first aid kit. Some
owners are stubborn and think their pets will behave the way they
do in the quiet and tranquility of home.

"Peter and I can handle him without any trouble. We treat five
or six wildcats a week so leave Baby to us."

Darryl took Mrs. Fratello into the washroom to treat her hand.
I knew she didn't like her but I saw the look of concern on her face
when she looked at the wound. We all had our share of bites and
she was used to giving first aid.

Pete arrived with the loop and towels. We opened the lid again
and Baby was crouched low. "Why can't they put them on a towel,
or at least strip newspaper for them. He's a mess." Pete said disgustedly.

"Loop him, Pete. See if we can snare him."

It took a minute or so to work the rope around his head as Baby
kept his chin as low as possible. Finally Peter succeeded, and using
the pipe as a leash, tried to get him out. Baby would have no part
of it so we used an old trick. I took the loop with both hands,
keeping upward pressure on his throat. Pete gave the side of the
carrier a sharp kick. It sounded and reverberated like a drum. Baby,
sprang out to get away from the noise and was restrained by the loop

The next step was grasping his hind legs and stretching him taut.
One had to be quick and experienced and Pete was both. We used
the towels to wipe him clean. Pete held both hind legs with one

hand just out of reach of his flailing forepaws and with the other hand, toweled him. The waiting room smelled like a zoo. Now to get him on the stainless steel table. Working in tandem, me with the loop and Pete lifting his hind legs, we carried him to the examining room and set him on the table. We called Darryl to lend a hand when she was finished dressing Mrs. Fratello's hand.

Within a minute she arrived and took the loop, holding his head at a safe distance and I proceeded with the examination. Baby was very unhappy about being held rigidly and his loud growls expressed his displeasure. Mrs. Fratello could hear him from the next room and she called to him to be good. His forelegs were free and trying very hard to find something to grasp so I put the empty fingers of the thick leather glove on my left hand for him to hold or chew while my other hand probed the growth. I palpated the superficial lymph nodes draining the area. There were no enlargements. Good! If it is a tumor it's still localized. The growth itself was very soft and I agreed with my colleague that it felt as if fluid might be just below the surface. He thought it was an abscess but was unable to drain it. He was correct not to lance it without being sure. The only way to be certain was to try to aspirate fluid through a large gauge needle. If it was dry, a biopsy would be necessary, if pus showed in the syringe it could be safely lanced and drained.

"Hang on folks," I said as I left them holding the fuming feline. "I'm going to get a large gauge needle and a syringe."

As I walked to the instrument cabinet, Darryl whispered. "Her hand's okay, Doc, but she's a freeloader! She's on welfare, she's separated from her husband and has two kids. You'll never get a nickel from her!"

"So what else is new?" I whispered back, "it sounds like she is as low as a human can get. Imagine her compelling need for love, gleaned from a reeking wildcat! No wonder she looks harried. And Darryl. . ."

"I know," she interrupted, "don't dun her for money." She said disgustedly. Darryl was like my mother. She thought I was always selling myself cheap and needed prodding to collect what was due. Probably they were both right but when there was a need like this. . .why make it worse!

I turned back to "Baby." A small area was shaved and disinfected which took a couple of minutes. I grasped a handful of tissue with my left hand and applied pressure. The syringe penetrated the mass and I tried to aspirate. It was dry. I thought about what to do next. He would have to come back for a biopsy because there was no time to do it now. There was a full afternoon of surgery scheduled. I felt guilty about having her make another trip all the way from Brooklyn.

"Ease him to the floor. Let his legs go but hang on to the loop. Pete, clean out the carrier and strip in enough paper to keep him clean. I'll talk to her."

We arranged an appointment for the following week. I cautioned Mrs. Fratello that on her next visit to put a leash and collar on Baby. "Use an old towel, blanket or newspaper to keep the carrier clean and don't feed him anything." I planned to get a tissue sample from the base of the tumor. I wasn't sure what the mass was and would have to wait for the lab report.

"Oh Doctor, do you think he'll be all right? I'll do whatever you say."

I told Darryl to give her a bill for the visit but not to insist on payment. I wasn't about to deprive her kids, and the fanatical look on her face told me Baby was first on her list of neediest.

"And be sure to have her call from the station next time so Peter can give her a hand up the hill."

A week later Irene Fratello and Baby arrived in a much less distraught fashion. Pete lugged the carrier for her and all she had to worry about was the huge handbag. She had followed our instructions to the letter. The frantic look was gone, her hair was neat and there was a meager hue of red on her lips. She didn't smell much better and I was sure her private life was still far from idyllic.

Darryl, unhappily, was left alone with her in the otherwise empty waiting room as Peter carried the box inside. This time Baby wore the leash and collar but needed Pete's boot once more to drum him out, claws flailing and throat growling. In a few minutes he was on the operating table, sedated and quietly accepting local anesthesia.

After the initial incision it was obvious there was no abscess. The tissue was dry, soft and pale. There was a fistula at the center that allowed a gloved finger deep entry into the mass. I felt something hard and reached for forceps. With my left forefinger on the object, my right hand manipulated the foreign body and brought out a broken bevel of a large guage needle.

I thought of what may have happened. Possibly, another vet tried to aspirate without proper restraint or anesthesia and the needle broke in the ensuing fight. The doctor might still be wondering what happened to it. That would be negligence, pure and simple. If it was already there when he tried to drain the abscess, he wouldn't have known about it either, unless he used Xray. There was the chance that the growth was a reaction to a foreign body; the broken needle. It was also possible that it was a tumor.

How the needle became involved was the mystery. Perhaps Mrs. Fratello wasn't telling the entire story. Maybe there was a third party, who could have been giving a routine injection. Without proper restraint the outburst of any normal wildcat could have broken the needle leaving the beveled end under the skin. It could have happened months before.

I decided to go ahead with the biopsy and question Mrs. Fratello a little more closely. The sample was taken, Baby's skin sutured, and he was returned to his carrier, quiet as a mouse. As I entered the waiting room, Darryl gave me a big shrug and raised eyebrows indicating nothing more was learned. I decided to try.

"Mrs. Fratello," I asked kindly, "how many veterinarians have taken care of Baby?"

"Only three. Including you."

"I spoke to the vet whose name you gave me last week. He told me he tried to treat Baby, but couldn't handle him. Tell me about the other doctor you used."

She had an outraged look on her face. "He only took care of him when he was very young. He gave him all the baby shots and when he got big he wouldn't even give me an appointment."

"Mrs. Fratello, we found a needle tip at the base of Baby's growth. Can you tell me how it got there?"

"I don't know." she said defensively. "I wasn't in the room when the doctor treated him."

"Did the first vet ever have trouble handling Baby?"

"No." and she began to cry. "I couldn't pay him and he wouldn't take care of him any more. I didn't have any money. My husband hated Baby and said if I didn't get rid of him he would leave. I begged him for money to treat Baby and we had a big fight. He yelled at me, and said he would treat the damned cat himself. He had a syringe he used for drugs. He put a big needle on it and stabbed poor Baby in a fit of temper. Baby screamed and attacked my husband. The syringe got smashed and he scratched and bit him pretty bad, but he was only defending himself." She tried to make me understand that Baby had ample provocation. "Maybe it was then that the needle broke off." She sobbed and continued. "I tried the other vet but he was afraid of Baby. I didn't know what to do and I called Mrs. Cisin from the Ocelot club."

"What about your children? Do they get along with Baby?"

The crying became more hysterical. "Nobody loves Baby but me! And nobody loves me, only Baby." and she began to blubbler. "From the time he was a little kitten in the pet shop he needed me and loved me. I need Baby to stay alive. You have to save him, doctor. I love him so much. Mrs. Cisin said you would save him. Please, doctor, save him for me!"

I looked at Darryl. There were tears in her eyes. If I knew her, she was thinking of a pair of neglected children not getting what kids need of a mother. Pete was uncomfortable with the emotional outburst and slipped out of the room. . .

"I've taken a biopsy, Mrs. Fratello. I'll know the answer in about a week. I'll call you if it's a tumor that has to come out. If it's inflammatory, now that the needle is out, it will disappear in time. Now pull yourself together. You have a long trip home."

"I'll call you, Doctor. They turned off our phone."

The report from the lab was good. Baby had a slow growing benign connective tissue tumor, the result of a long standing foreign body, the broken needle. I waited for Fratello's call.

Darryl spoke to her a few days later and set up the surgery schedule.

When she arrived carrying her handbag, Peter right behind with Baby, she was glowing.

"Baby saved my live!" She plopped herself down and couldn't wait to tell us the story. There was fresh blood on her dress and hands. Peter set the carrier at her feet, the leash handle protruding from the edge of the closed lid.

"I did what you said, Doctor. I put the leash and collar on him, good and tight. When I carried him on the subway the loop of the leash handle was around my wrist just like you said so when you open the lid you wouldn't have to dig for it. I was so happy about the report, I knew you would save him. Even he knew. He hardly growled when I put him in the box.

"Anyhow, he doesn't smell too good I guess, and people in the subway always move away. I don't care. I like to be alone with my Baby. I always talk to him and pet him because the subway noise is so loud I know it frightens him. I left the lid unlatched because I open it and pet him several times. The trip is so long that he needs to know I'm near and that I love him."

"I was kinda day-dreaming when I looked up to see two colored kids lookin' at me funny. I know them looks. They were out for no good, believe me. Then the train stopped for some reason between stations, hardly anyone else was around, they came over and told me to give them my bag. I was scared because I had almost ten dollars from my welfare and I have children to feed. I just hugged my bag, terrified, with both hands so they couldn't get it.

"One wore a black leather jacket, the kind most gang members wear. They had black and white sneakers with crazy striped socks. The laces were long and loose, almost touching the ground. I remember those socks because that was what I stared at. I was afraid to look at their faces after the first glance. They were mean and hard looking. The bigger one had a long, ugly, sneering face, and short, nigger-hair. The other's face was fat and pock-marked.

"They began cussing and the biggest one pulled a knife and stuck it right against my neck. I was shaking so hard all I could do was shrink back and hug my bag even tighter. The carrier was between my legs and I remembered what Pete did to get Baby out. I gave the sides of the box a kick with both feet, one on each side. The lid sprang open and Baby charged.

"He ran right through the legs of the kid in front of me, jerked to a stop by the leash. It almost pulled my arm off. He flipped over on his back and grabbed the nigger's leg with his sharp claws then pulled hard and growled as he sunk his teeth into his leg, just behind the knee."

"The big one screamed," Mrs. Fratello related, "A fuckin leopard,' and the other kid ran. You should have seen him trying to shake Baby off his leg. The striped socks saved that nigger's leg. As it was, when Baby's hind claws raked the leg, it slit his skin, sock and sneaker like four razor blades. Baby released his hold on the kid 'cause he probably couldn't stand the taste. The big nigger ran off screaming, his blood all over Baby and the floor. I picked him up and hugged and kissed him, 'You saved my life and I love you,' I told him and I put him back in his box. It's against the law to have

ocelots loose in the subway, you know. He saved my life, Doctor.
Now you know why I love him so much.

Baby, in his own way, proved again, all the intrigue of wild life
and nature. In a hundred millennium of natural selection, the feline,
from house cat to lion, tiger and leopard learned the most efficient
way to fight. When standing on all fours they had but one weapon,
a vicious set of long, sharp fangs. When attacking with hind legs
planted, there were three; the jaws and two sinewy paws with
needle-like, powerful talons. But on their backs they had an even
more deadly arsenal. With the ground protecting their backs, all four
mighty, muscled limbs were ready for action. The ocelot perfected a
method of attack that was singular in its deadly effectiveness. As
mouth held its prey steady, the fore-legs hugged the unfortunate
with unrelenting claws while the hind legs, striking with uncanny
accuracy and power, could eviscerate its victim in seconds. No
planning was needed; instinct directed the attack. Irene Fratello
could thank that intuition for her deliverance.

After her story, the surgery and recovery were anti-climactic.
She came back once more to have Baby's sutures removed and a
final check-up. Mrs. Fratello left with Baby's carrier in one hand,
the huge pocketbook under the other arm. She turned and looked
back. She didn't have to say a word. Her eyes, moist with gratitude,
had their own eloquence.

*The New Beverlie Animal Hospital, opened in 1951,
17 West Grand Street, Mount Vernon, New York*

Westchester County Parkway Police
SAW MILL RIVER PARKWAY
HAWTHORNE, N. Y. 10532
914 Telephone ROgers 9-3100

EDWIN G. MICHAELIAN
COUNTY EXECUTIVE

PARKWAY POLICE BOARD
JOSEPH J. BRADY, CHAIRMAN

WILLIAM S. NELSON
CHIEF OF POLICE

August 5
1971

Dr. Theodore Zimmerman
17 West Grand Street
Mt. Vernon, New York   .

Dear Dr. Zimmerman:

        On August 2, 1971 at 10:00 P.M., the
services of a veterinarian was sorely needed by
this department as a result of an accident on
the Bronx River Parkway at Oak Street.

        Without regard to any personal incon-
venience, you responded to our call. This department wishes to express our appreciation for
the cooperation and assistance rendered to us.

                Very truly yours,

WSN:dd

                WILLIAM S. NELSON
                Chief of Police

NICK CARRADO
MANAGING DIRECTOR

SIDNEY O. HERSHMAN
PUBLIC RELATIONS COUNSEL

JERRY KRUTMAN
STAFF PHOTOGRAPHER

ADVISORY COUNCIL
MARTIN CARRADO
LEO DAVIS
RUTH DOOREMAN
ROBERTO DUQUE
NAT GOLD
RICHARD HARDENBROOK
HELENE HERSHMAN
MARY KEENE
DORA McLANE
ART POMERANTZ
KEN STOUT

KOKOMO, JR.
America's Favorite TV Chimp

TV—Network & Local   Modeling
TV Commercials   Public Appearances
Films   Private Parties

CARRADO ENTERPRISES
640 WEST END AVENUE
NEW YORK 24, N. Y.
TRafalgar 7-8655

March 5, 1969

Dr. Theodore Zimmerman
17 West Grand Street
Mount Vernon, New York

Dear Dr. Zimmerman:

I have recently formed the Carrado Research, Experiment and Training Center for Chimpanzees. The purpose of this center is to make a concentrated effort to better understand man's closest relative, physically and mentally, the chimpanzee. Special emphasis will be given to exploring the depth of intellect the chimpanzee possesses.

We are compiling a book-length manuscript on the chimpanzee, Kokomo, Jr., for John Hopkins University Press. Both the Chief Editor and Scientific Editor showed definite interest in our project and have asked us to send them our manuscript when completed. I am also arranging for a lecture tour to colleges and universities covering the subject matter in our manuscript.

I will be the Executive Director; Lawrence LaShan, Ph.D., Scientific Director; Gary Null, Program Director, and Jerry Krutman, Research Photographer. Thusfar, the following individuals have accepted our invitation to serve on our Advisory Council: Ada Fridman, M.D., Henry Trefflich, wild animal importer, and Robert Dietch, curator of the Dietch Zoo. We are now ready to print our stationery, and would like very much to add your name to our Advisory Council. This would not entail any responsibility (either financial or timewise) on your part, but we would thus feel free to ask your advice about prospective developments. You would be informed of all events that occur with the center in advance and would receive a copy of the lecture program and book manuscript, when completed.

If you would be agreeable to our adding your name to our Advisory Council, please send me a short letter or note to this effect. I would appreciate it if you could do this at your earliest convenience as our stationery is ready to go to the printers.

Sincerely yours,

Nick Carrado
Managing Director

NC:srw

Buddha, our pet ocelot at four months of age

XII

Central Park Zoo Veterinarian

"Ted, say hello to John Fitzgerald." Henry Trefflich introduced me to his long time friend and Central Park Zoo connection. Henry's company had branches in Africa and Asia. He placed newly arrived exotics temporarily in the local zoos. Both parties benefited as the zoos had extra attractions and Henry's wards were parked rent free.

I was working at Henry's in the early sixties, TB testing and checking out some of the new arrivals. I was happy to meet anyone connected with the zoo. I held out my hand to the tall, pleasant looking gentleman with crow feet cornering his eyes and a soft, half-smile. I said, "Glad to meet you, John."

"Likewise," he said, with a firm, friendly grip. John took two sniffs in the air like an alerted bird dog and grinned, "Been on the third floor, eh? Henry mentioned that you enjoy working with his animals."

Enthusiastic Henry loved people almost as much as he did animals and he couldn't wait to see my reaction, "John is in charge of the Central Park Zoo. They're looking for a good vet."

Fitzgerald saw the light in my eyes and said, "That's right. We need an attending veterinarian to make rounds once or twice a month, check the Children's Zoo, and be on call for emergencies."

I was happy that Henry thought enough of my work to recommend me.

"I'm your man," I said, trying to sound casual, but my heart was pounding. I knew that Henry and John Fitzgerald had discussed this offer beforehand.

"When do I start?" was all I could get out.

"How about Friday?" Fitzgerald asked. "Say about eleven o'clock. I'll meet you at the Children's Petting Zoo, and we'll walk the grounds and meet the keepers." I was speechless so Fitzgerald continued telling me how to park my car at the end of the service road, just off the city's busy intersection of Sixtieth Street and Fifth Avenue, next to the zoo garage. I had been working for Henry Trefflich at the Ports of Entry for almost a year. If animals arrived by air at Idlewild Airport, they were even more intractable following the trauma of a noisy plane ride. If they came by boat, arriving at the piers in New York harbor, the long, sickening ocean voyage left many of the animals and birds depressed, dehydrated and ill.

I explained to Elaine when she asked how one could possibly examine an animal or bird without handling it.

"I look them over as best I can without taking them out of their cages." I explained, "If the animals or birds looked healthy, they were passed and sent on to the zoos that had ordered them."

"And if they are sick?"

"I dispensed medicine for the midly ill and send it with instructions to both the shipper and the zoo attendants for giving it as needed. The unfortunate ones, too ill to eat or drink have to be sedated for treatment before Uncle Sam allowed them in. Many are too sick to respond and die. Others we just put to sleep."

"What a terrible waste." She said when I told her the numbers involved.

I remembered envying the zoo vets. They had the time to study and get to know their charges intimately. Their patients were hospitalized, observed as long as was necessary and treated until they recovered. Now I was finally going to join their ranks.

Friday came after an eternity and, as my black Pontiac bumped down the service road, I could make out zoo sounds between the taxi-honking and brake-screeching of New York's traffic just behind me on Fifth Avenue. I looked to the left where the Plaza Hotel with its beautiful architecture and multi-colored pennants fluttered in the breeze while seals from the zoo were honking, birds chirping and I thought I heard an elephant trumpeting. I couldn't wait to treat my first elephant.

From my earliest days, when I resolved to some day treat exotics, I read everything published about wild animals and birds. I knew the habitats, diets, and was familiar with their evolution and their precise scientific classification. What I was never taught, even in vet school, was how to treat them.

Elaine sagely noted, "Experience is the key to success."

I thought out loud, "That key is still too new at my stage of proficiency."

What qualifications I did have, started early. As a child I went to the Central Park Zoo on school field trips and with my family when we had a free Sunday. Working in our pet shop just whet my appetite for close looks at wild animals. I went to the zoo alone as soon as I was old enough, and always ran to my favorite house-- the "Great Apes." Those human-like gorillas, orangs and chimps intrigued me from the start, and even then, something rubbed me the wrong way about their housing. It hurt me to see twenty-five year old Caroline, the vintage gorilla of New York, having to sit on a cold, concrete floor, picking through the fruit, nuts and vegetables of her daily repast.

I reported to my Dad, "They even taught her to smoke. That's no way to treat a lady!"

Her outside quarters weren't any better than her parlor with metal fences, a swing fashioned from an old automobile tire and a slimy, artificial pond for drinking and bathing. It reminded me too much of the heartbreak I lived through with Uncle and her abandonment at Atlantic City's Steel Pier.

My dad tried to console me. "It's the best way to keep confined animals clean. They can hose the floor a couple of times a day, because even the highly intelligent great apes are not toilet-trained Remember "Uncle?" (As if I cound ever forget). "We always kept her diapered until she was too old."

My Dad's explanation, in spite of Uncle, justifying concrete and water hoses didn't completely satisfy me. It didn't make sense. Animal droppings on the great savannahs of the Masa Mari in Africa, were absorbed by natural processes (sun, rain, specialized bacteria and carrion eating animals, insects and birds). In the zoos, because of the water-tight concrete floors, hosing was a must for the predators and great apes who were closely confined. The few grazers, such as zebras, antelope, gazelles and wildebeest were allowed on turf where natural processes did exist with help from man's broom and shovel. The environments were better for the seals and polar bears. They had a more nautral set-up.

I envisioned an ideal man-made paradise for all zoo residents. Maybe someday, they would be constructed so that nature would take over again. The predators would never be hungry and wouldn't have to chase and kill for food. The range animals could graze without the constant fear of the cheetah's charge or the hyena's powerful jaws. I pictured the ideal: fences and moats only when necessary to prevent escape or keep natural enemies apart. No concrete and lots of room to run and play, unless the inhabitants were ill and needed help.

Parking under a tree near the garage, I shut the windows, locked the doors, and carried my black bag filled with equipment and medicines I hoped would be adequate for large and small animals alike.

I did little but meet people and observe procedures, but my first day at the zoo was a milestone. Many exciting events took place in the succeeding years, but this day is etched vividly and indelibly in my memory bank.

Walking toward the zoo, a dozen or so pigeons, busily pecking at seeds and grass, were startled by my approach and noisily flapped off as one. I followed them with a keen eye. I vowed to train myself to notice anything out of line, even studying their droppings and feathers on the stained sidewalk for a diagnostic clue. The common pigeon, forever taken for granted, would become like the barnyard fowl, carefully dissected by freshmen in Anatomy 1 class. The acquired skill from close observation would help me diagnose and treat birds from all over the world. My biggest problem would be the perpetual enigma of the veterinary profession: patients unable to communicate verbally. I recalled Professor Milk's sage observation about diagnosis; "They can't answer questions but they talk to us nevertheless." Eyes, ears, nose and fingers would have to discover their malaise, and eventually the perception of healing will become apparent and hopefully, intuitive.

Benches lining the path to the zoo's entrance were occupied by tired old ladies, petting over-weight dogs, and one bench served as a bed for one of the homeless. I never noticed before that the trees along the way were identified by arborists, on small metal plaques, in Latin, followed by their common, more familiar names.

My black bag was the badge of authority, as I strode in eager anticipation. It made me different, and people's eyes looked impressed and respectful.

At the main gate, directional signs pointed to the various areas of the park. I had visited the zoo a hundred times before and never paid any attention to them. Today, I needed to pinpoint exactly where the Children's Petting Zoo was, a section dedicated after I left for college, and unknown to me.

I obeyed the directions and soon the location was obvious—children were everywhere. A "Noah's Ark," ramp was busy with screaming youngsters going aboard. Inside, they made faces and teased the caged animals--a tame ringtail monkey, a dozen hamsters, six rabbits and three pygmy goats. Hanging out of reach were the birds. A red macaw and black mynah talked and screeched at each other above the din. Twenty or more kids jammed the three-foot aisle of the fifteen foot-long boathouse.

Further on was the "Whale," another fun house shaped like its name, with the entrance the huge mouth and a double-finned whale's tail for the exit. It harbored goldfish and tropical fish, an ant colony, small reptiles, tame African Green talking parrots and more rabbits.

In the barnyard outside, the children leaned over wood partitions to pet baby ducks and chicks. Other kids chased baby lambs and playful, bleating, pygmy goats. One little boy sneaked away from his parents and had a baby chick by the legs, holding him above his head and waving him back and forth in triumph. I rescued the frightened bird and asked the child where his mommy was.

Looking in a picture window of the main house of the children's zoo I saw Fitzgerald talking to one of the lady keepers, a tall attractive brunette. He looked up, saw me, and beckoned me in.

When I went inside Fitzgerald said, "Ted, this is Mrs. Infante. She's in charge here and was telling me she needs some medical advice. There's trouble with a rabbit, one of the snakes is sick, and the llama has a bad eye."

There was a problem with one animal she mentioned that I hoped to hide—my allergy to rabbits! And here it was to be one of my first patients. Who would have dreamed a zoo would have common rabbits on display. My nose picked up that funny, burning feeling and I knew I would sneeze or cough in a very few minutes. No matter! I wasn't going to mention it or let it interfere. "Glad to meed you, Mrs. Infante," I said. "Let's look at the snake and llama," hoping to put off the sneezing. "We can check the rabbit later."

She spoke with a slight southern inflection, "Call me Tatey, please."

"Why don't we walk the rest of the zoo before you see her sick charges?" Fitzgerald interrupted. "I have to get back to the office and you can come and talk to Infante after our tour."

I waved a friendly goodbye, my eyes telling her I'd be back.

John pointed out a pair of Fallow Deer, and said, "President and Mrs. Kennedy presented the pair to us this year."

"Did the Kennedys come in person?" I asked, impressed.

"No, but we got a nice, personal letter at the presentation," he said. "They wrote: 'A miniature deer for the little people of New York, from the White House to Central Park.' And they signed it, 'President and Mrs. John F. Kennedy.' They went to considerable trouble importing them for us. The deer are a small European strain, with broad antlers and as you can see, a pale yellow coat, spotted with white in the summer."

We continued walking, and Fitzgerald turned his thoughts to Mrs. Infante. "Believe it or not, Tatey was a debutante from North Carolina. She lives on Park Avenue. In the late 40's she walked over here almost every day to watch the Children's Zoo evolve. The zoo was donated to the city by Governor and Mrs. Herbert Lehman. You can tell, she doesn't enjoy the role of socialite.

"One afternoon in 1960, she was sipping tea at the park restaurant, over there," John said, pointing to the outside tables and chairs on the edge of the grounds. "A young llama got loose from the petting area and walked over to where she was sitting. Since the restaurant serves breakfast and lunch, but is closed for dinner, no one else was around, and Tatey and the llama stared at each other for a moment. Infante didn't know what kind of creature was giving her the friendly eye, but she liked him and remembered seeing him inside the Children's Zoo. Running her hands along his large, graceful neck, she touched the silkiest, whitest fur she had ever felt. His ears stood straight up, and his big, black eyes never left hers. She told me later it was a peculiar looking beast—short legs holding up a disproportionately large, compact body, with a tiny, flicking tail and a very tall, tapering neck. The only thing she could think of was to offer him something to eat. She found some scraps at a nearby table and he gobbled them up gratefully, then nuzzled up to her. Tatey was so taken by the friendly animal that she wanted to adopt him. After several minutes of mutual adoration, she knew he had to be returned."

"The furry creature wasn't wearing a collar, so she found an apron near the kitchen and put the straps over his head. She led him back toward the children's area. He followed obediently and she found the door to a pen slightly ajar. She gave that big neck an affectionate hug, pulled him into the enclosure, took off the apron and fastened the hasp on the door as she left. Tatey then circled the fence till she found the small, informational sign. It listed the names of the animals inside: mininiature horse, deer; lambs; calves, and Peruvian Llama. So that's what he is! What a wonderful creature for the children, she thought.

The next day, at about the same time, that clever llama managed to flip the hasp and sneak over to where Tatey sipped her tea. She was thrilled, and prayed he would continue his visits forever, but she was disappointed. The next day he didn't come. She decided to go to his pen to visit. They were delighted in their reunion. She studied the lock on the door. That's the trouble, they changed the mechanism, she thought. Well, I'll just come by occasionally and open it. Surreptitiously she would walk by, unlock the door, then hurry back to the restaurant. Their rendezvous continued."

"One day I caught her walking him back," Fitzgerald continued, "one arm around his shoulders, the other leading him with apron strings. Quite an unusual sight! After questioning her at length, trying to hide my amusement, she admitted their love affair and explained the clandestine meetings. I told her that only Park Department employees could walk animals outside of their designated pens. She looked so miserable, tears welled up in her eyes and I thought she would cry."

"Why don't you consider working with animals?" I suggested. "We can always use another keeper." The next day, Tatey showed up at the personnel office and applied for a job. Little did she realize the effort it would take to get one. She had a Bachelor's Degree in Arts and Sciences, but needed courses in Animal Husbandry, Feeds and Feeding, Poultry Husbandry, Psychology, Accounting and Mathematics. She studied, working part time when she could at the zoo, took the civil service tests and, last year, after five years of study, she's in charge of the Children's Zoo." He smiled and shook his head. "She watches that llama with a worried mother's eye. She wants you to check it, probably because it sneezed once."

The elephant stockade was close by, and I met Ed Rodrigues, the keeper-in-charge, a small, serious-looking man, with a gold tooth that glistened on every word he spoke. Ed shook my hand and said, "Glad to meet you, Doc, we really do need our own vet." With his Spanish accent, I assumed he was Puerto Rican, and I looked at him with respect and admiration. That little man in charge of elephants! Behind him were his charges. A huge, adult, Indian cow elephant, shifting slowly from side to side, laying her trunk over the shoulder of a young male, like a caress, with each sway of her body. The little one, I guessed, weighed about nine hundred pounds and kept a loving eye on his keeper. I knew they were Indian elephants because of their high foreheads and two prominent "bumps." My research, years before, differentiated them from the Africans who had much larger ears. Adult Indian females had no tusks and the tips of their trunks had but one "finger" rather than the African's two.

Rodrigues, like Tatey Infante, mentioned the health of his charges.

"Tina, the big girl, had been here a couple of years and she's fine, a little temperamental with strangers, perhaps, but in good health. I was told that as a calf in India, she had a frightening childhood; Tina's mother had been killed by poachers before her eyes. They maltreated her for months. Half starved and desperate she was rescued by Trefflich's safari employees.

She was fattened up and two years later was shipped to America. Chang, the baby, just arrived. He has a large swelling on his left hip, there," he said, and pointed to an obvious growth easily visible from where I stood. "I'd like you to examine it." Those last words were music to my ears.

"I'll come back, Ed, as soon as I finish the rounds with Mr. Fitzgerald." I started away, and looked back because I couldn't take my eyes off the friendly mastodons. Chang broke away from Tina and ambled toward Rodrigues. I stopped a few yards away, wondering what was going on, as Chang's prodigious, mobile trunk searched the keeper's pockets.

"He loves roasted peanuts," Rodrigues called when he saw me pause. "They both do, so I keep my pockets full, and they help themselves anytime they have a fancy." He reached back and affectionately patted that busy, hairy and very dexterous organ.

"I'll get some nuts later so he'll let me examine him," I said as I turned away.

"He'll be your friend for life," Rodrigues called after me.

Our next stop was the polar bears. They were penned in a large area, much like their natural habitat, at the side of a hill, with waterfalls, a large pool, and rocks around it, with a cave big enough for them to nest. There was an extra fence separating the main enclosure from the public.

"Now this display was well-conceived," I said to FitzGerald. "I can picture this scene in the Arctic. The concrete could well be the floor of a glacier." I'd spent many hours, in the past, watching them cavort. I remembered, at feeding time, large fish were tossed to them over the fences.

Joe Scimmo, was their keeper and he explained, "They'd fight in a flash to protect their catch, so we avoid trouble by tossing fish as fast as possible, to keep them busy and satisfied."

"They're treacherous bastards," FitzGerald said. "Good thing they're a healthy pair. We'd have to use an anesthetic to treat them for anything. It's one of the few exhibits our guards won't enter. See that coil of hose near the outside fence? That's a high pressure water hose and Joe cleans the pen from there. It's as close as he can safely get for daily sanitation. Normally, even with the big cats, we hand feed through the cage bars, then chase them into adjoining rooms and clean their pens with brooms from the inside."

We moved on to the sea lion, or seal pond. Scimmo and Herb Clemant took care of them as well as the bears. It was in the center of the zoo, and the public's most popular display. FitzGerald introduced them to me, "That's Sara, sitting on her favorite rock. You should see the commotion if one of the other seals tries to get on it. The others play, "king of the hill," just to tease her and the hooting and honking is unbelievable."

A deep moat gave the five sea mammals a perfect place for swimming, diving and feeding. The rocks in the center gradually rose about ten feet, creating an authentic environment. Twice-daily feedings were the most crowded events at the zoo. People were gathering now, as Scimmo's helper approached the pool carrying a big bucket of fresh fish.

The proud zoo director said, "That's Herb Clemant, about to feed. Herb spent many years in the Antarctic and loves water mammals. He makes a request to the brass every year, asking for a pair of walruses so he can feel more at home."

Sara left her perch and swam with the others toward the food bucket, hooting for dinner. Clemant chose a youngster from the crowd to assist. It was a girl about eight years-old with a blonde pony-tail swinging to and fro. He fed a silvery fish to each of the seals, then offered the pail to the little girl. "Go on, take one," he encouraged, "they're hungry."

She wasn't about to put her hand into the bucket, and backed off, embarrassed and shy. A lad, probably her little brother, couldn't wait to take over. He threw fish as far as he could, like playing fetch with his pet dog. The seals loved it and retrieved every one. It was so easy that finally the young lady timidly reached into the bucket and dropped one fish into the pool.

The audience applauded, and FitzGerald, a big smile on his satisfied, handsome face turned, and led me to another large, red brick house, with "Big Cats" etched over the entrance. The cages and confinement had been one of my pet peeves for years. Maybe, I thought, now that I'm an important part of the zoo, I might influence some higher-ups who signed checks to pay for improved environments. I didn't understand about city budgets but there were lions, tigers, pumas, a black leopard, a jaguar, a civet cat, a pair of ocelots, a margay and an African lynx who could use some natural sod, a few trees and a larger area to roam.

Each specie was kept separate. The pair of lions occupied one end of the house, while the tigers called the other end home, like a duplex, with large concrete stalls for each couple, and a door between to separate them if family arguments erupted. There was a trapdoor to the fenced, outdoor runs.

I learned from John FitzGerald that Elvira, the female Bengal tiger, was in her first pregnancy. Her mate, Stripe, was to be a happy first time father in two or three weeks. I'd never seen a big cat whelp and I wondered if they ever needed help. After saying hello to keepers, John Spabola and Dick Clurman, we discussed the mating and I questioned the two on the tiger's care and feeding. I asked about her temperament, in case I was called to assist the delivery. The men were experienced and assured me she would cooperate when the time came. "Stripe might not appreciate a stranger, but Elvira is a pussycat."

We moved on to meet my favorite animals, the apes. John was proud of the primate exhibit and, except for the living conditions, I agreed with him. Caroline was showing her age—graying gradually, like any older lady. Close by was Maggie, a mature, breeding, female orangutan from Borneo. Her companion and very disinterested soul-mate, "Big Mike," the potential sire, sat quietly in his house, looking for a handout. He displayed the cheek pads and throat pouch of an adult, breeding male, weighed over one hundred fifty pounds, stood four and a-half feet tall, with an arm reach of seven feet.

Maggie was sitting quietly on the floor of her house, picking through the array of fruit that had just been delivered in a metal dish. She wore another pan on her head like a hat.

"Does she always do that?" I asked, thinking about Suzie, the macaque, and her inclination to wear a hat and hold a pocketbook full of pennies, so many years before.

"She mimics human behavior all the time," John said, grinning. "I think sometimes she's just making fun of us. See that wood box in the corner?" He pointed to a trunk-size crate, sitting in the corner of Maggie's house. "It's full of old clothes, shoes, socks, scarves and gloves. John Gamn has a fashion show with her. She pulls on socks, tries to put shoes on, drapes a scarf over her head just the way John shows her. At the end of the day, clothes are all over the floor, just like my kids' room."

I couldn't resist telling him about Suzie, and as I spoke the years drifted away, taking me back at least thirty-five years.

In addition to Uncle, my pet chimp, the other primate in my life was Suzie. She arrived in a shipment of wild rhesus monkeys from my father's old friend, Henry Trefflich. He received a shipment from India, and he knew Dad was looking for some young monkeys to train and sell. I happened to be in the shop when they arrived and was fascinated by our new boarders. They were young and wild and like most primates it took months of patience, kindness and skill before one could be tamed. (Mom was the expert and somehow got their trust quicker than the others could.)

All six were crowded into a shipping crate, bedded with straw to absorb the droppings. They smelled awful because half of them had diarrhea, and fear made the condition worse. When anyone approached, the straw flew as they tried to hide or escape. The exception was one young female who sat in the front of the crate, quietly observing the outside world. She weighed about five pounds and had beautiful hazel eyes. Her serene demeanor contrasted with the hysterical thrashing going on behind her.

The other five were netted and placed in individual cages bedded with stripped newspaper. The little female allowed Mom to handle her immediately. Mother named her Suzie and, because she was so unusual, it was decided to make her a house pet. My father sent me to the library to research rhesus monkeys.

Suzie was an old-world monkey, an Asian macaque, a ground dweller with food pouches in her cheeks. I marveled that she kept stuffing monkey-chow in her mouth until her jowls and neck were distended to the breaking point. It was a trait of old-world monkeys. The macaques weren't gluttonous; it was a feature that evolved when the specie developed a way to store food.

A lady came into the store one day, wearing a wide-brimmed hat, and stopped at Suzie's cage to talk. Suzie reached through the bars and tried to touch the hat. The lady stepped back, laughing and saying, "Not today, little one, it's much too expensive for your little hands."

But Suzie couldn't take her eyes off that hat. When the lady left, she lifted a handful of stripped newspaper and placed it on her head. Mom noticed the exchange and handed Suzie a small colored hanky. She immediately placed it on her head. The next day mother bought her a doll's hat. She loved it, put it on and there it stayed. Mom had to buy her another one, because she became so upset when it was taken away for washing.

Suzie was remarkable and mimicked every move and motion of Mothers'. One day she reached for Mom's pocketbook, the same way she did for a hat. Mom gave her a little change purse and showed her how to work the catch. Suzie took to it right away. When she wasn't opening it and closing it, she tucked it under her arm just like my mother did with her pocketbook.

I put two pennies in her purse, and tried to teach her the value of money. She opened the catch, lifted out the change, promptly put them both in her mouth and down they went. I was appalled. Suppose she swallowed them and got sick. I called to Mom and told her.

"I don't think she'll swallow them," Mom assured me, "they're just in her favorite hiding place."

"They're so dirty," I said, "she'll get sick for sure."

"Let's train her to use pennies properly." Mom said, "She loves juicy plums. Be sure she is watching. You hand me a penny and I'll give you a plum."

We played out the lesson slowly, hoping she would get the idea. I took her on my lap, fearful that she had already swallowed the coins. I was relieved when I felt them through the skin of her throat.

"She hasn't swallowed them yet." I told my mom, "Let's try the plum again."

I held it out to her. "First give me a penny," I requested.

She reached for the plum and I held out my hand for a penny. She was confused but wanted the fruit. Mom, took a penny, showed it to her and handed it to me. I said thanks and handed Mom the plum. Suzie watched and we could see the wheels turning. Mother then offered the plum and Suzie slowly reached for it, looking at me for approbation. "Give Mom a penny." I coaxed. She put her hand down and watched me give Mother a penny. Mom exchanged it for the fruit.

"Maybe she forgot where she has her money," I said. I gave her another penny and held out her hand with the coin to Mother. Mom took it and handed Suzie the plum. She ate it with relish and somehow it didn't dislodge the other coins.

When John Velez, the shop attendant, cleaned her cage that evening, he found the two pennies on the floor. He knew what had happened earlier, so he took the purse, snapped it open and put the coins back. He offered her a banana, and with a big grin held out his hand for payment. As yet, she wasn't quite sure what to do. John opened the purse, took out a penny, placed it in his pocket and handed her the banana.

The next day I approached with another ripe plum. Suzie looked me in the eye, opened her purse and handed me the coin. I gave her the plum, and when she was finished, she got a big hug as well. We kept her supplied with money and from then on she stored them in her purse, using her fortune to ask for anything she wanted.

The next week a pretty young five year old was walking through the store looking at the pets and wares while her mother shopped. She was wearing a cute white bonnet with flowers attached to its band. She approached Suzie's cage and stopped. Suzie was wearing her hat and she stared at the little girl who returned the look. Neither moved or made a sound for a long moment. Mother was watching the confrontation as she waited on the child's parent and motioned the woman to look at the two young ladies apprising each other.

Suzie looked straight at the little girl, then raised her eyes to the hat. She opened her purse, pulled out a penny and offered it to her. The little girl smiled, shook her head and walked away. Suzie was furious. For the first time, Mother saw a display of temper and heard her chatter angrily after the child. Both women laughed. Mother had another blue hat she was holding in reserve. She walked to Suzie, took the penny, opened the cage and exchanged chapeaux. Suzie placed the hat on her head in rather a rakish angle and glared triumphantly at the world.

Maggie's zoo house was neat and clean and FitzGerald explained, "She's been slowing down the last month or so. For some reason, she doesn't play as much as before. Mostly interested in food."

"Do you keep them together?" I asked, looking at Big Mike, next door.

"Six months ago they were inseparabale. Then we had to separate them. They made each other so nervous, they never rested. He picked on her constantly, "FitzGerald commented. "Now they ignore each other completely."

"She may be pregnant," I thought aloud. "I read somewhere that after mating, the male goes off by himself, until the youngster is weaned."

"If they have a baby, we'll be one of the first zoos to accomplish that feat in the States," said FitzGerald, hopefully. I was disappointed in her maternity house and showed it. "It's a shame we don't have better conditions for an expectant mother. She'll need a more natural setting to raise her young," I admonished. "Orangutans are arboreal, compared to the gorillas and chimps. In the wild, they spend most of their time foraging and sleeping high in the trees. They build huge, saucer-like nests that protect the young from falling. I've read that infants hang on to Mom day and night for at least a year. Here," I pointed to her cage, "Maggie sees rock, glass and an artificial tree without leaves or loose branches to build a nursery. She certainly won't spend nights on the ground with her new baby." I looked up at the over twenty-foot height of the artificial tree, set in unforgiving concrete, and shuddered.

"She'll do all right," FitzGerald said. "If she's pregnant, the powers that be may fund a more natural habitat for them."

"Who takes care of the apes?" I asked.

"John Gamn is in charge, but everyone chips in. You met most of the keepers. There is still Ralph Suza, Joe Kolinka and Bill Sherada. Ralph and Bill are in the aviary, but they're bird people and spend all their time there." John looked behind me and said, "Here's Gamn now."

A tall, serious, dark-haired keeper, wearing glasses, looked into the cage as he approached, said affectionately, "Hi Maggie." She raised her head, fastening her eyes on him for a moment, before going back to her tidbits.

"John, this is Dr. Zimmerman. He'll be making rounds at least once a month."

"I know" he said, reaching out to shake my hand. "I just left Rodrigues, and I was looking for you," he said, "Maggie has a urinary problem. She's drinking a lot and wetting more often than usual."

The concrete drain conduit, at the front of her cage, had some urine in it, and I reached for my bag to get a lab vial and syringe. "I might be able to get enough urine for a test," I assured him. "It won't be sterile but may show leucocytes if there is an infection." As I stooped over to aspirate as much as possible, I said, "We may have enough to do a rabbit test. Might as well find out if she's pregnant.

"That would be great," John FitzGerlad glowed. "I never thought of using the pregnancy test on her.

Gamn stayed behind and, as we walked outside, another, uniformed park employee approached, saying, "Fitz, they need you in the office. The commissioner is on the phone, needs some answers."

"Fred this is Dr. Zimmerman, the vet I was telling you about. Doc, Fred Sandman is the Menagerie Supervisor, he'll show you the hippos, the African range animals and the birds."

I shook hands and, as FitzGerald hurried away. Fred, who looked familiar, said, "I think I saw you at Trefflich's. You were busy and I was in Mrs. Lenz' office on zoo buisness.

Fred Sandman was much like FitzGerald. He carried an air of authority and confidence. "John probably mentioned," he said, "that we are proud of our breeding program. We're expecting a litter of tigers; we have a breeding pair of orangs and the small monkeys are always surprising us with new arrivals. Our hippo just had her first baby, and we didn't even know she was pregnant." He laughed, "She's so big, she always looks pregnant. Let's go check her."

The Hippo House had a tremendous swimming pool with a graded ramp so the huge animals could lumber out of it for feeding and nesting. Happily swimming in the pool was the new mother and her baby. I frowned when I thought about the hard floor awaiting them out of the water. It was a far cry from the soft, swampy terrain they were used to in Africa. When I met keeper Jim Holmes, he agreed there was room for environmental improvement even though his charges were obviously enjoying their swim. In spite of the civilized accomodations that allowed hosing and scrubbing, the animals looked as well-adjusted as possible to the contrived tile and concrete imitation jungle home, in the heart of New York City, not far from Fifth Avenue's fine shops

On the way to the aviary, we passed the African mammals grazing contentedly. One of the zebras was limping, and I mentioned it to Fred. I felt sure I could handle zebra problems okay—just a striped horse, and they don't have to be shod which eliminates a myriad of hoof problems.

Sandman said, "John Kinsig is my assistant and is a good handler. I'll have him help you make your examination. There's John now." He beckoned a uniformed keeper coming into view.

"Kinsig, this is Dr. Zimmerman, our new vet. He'd like you to help him take a look at the zebra's hind leg. He's noticed a limp."

"Hi, Doctor," he said, "glad to meet you. I can hold him now if you like."

Kinsig entered the compound and the animals moved toward him, en masse, obviously expecting a handout. He slipped a lariat around the zebra's neck. "Shoo, you guys," he said waving the others away, "no treats now."

Sandman and I walked toward the striped equine, and Sandman took the rope. Kinsig turned his back away from the animal's head, ran his hands down the right leg from the hips, gently picked up the hoof and pulled the zebra's leg over his own bent knee, exposing the underside of the hoof.

"The frog looks healthy," I murmured, then ran my hands around the periphery of the leg just above the hoof. The surface was cool, normal I thought. I felt a sticky area where exudate had dried somewhat, just above the hoof line. I probed it with my fingers and the leg flinched. "It looks like a penetrating wound of some kind caused some bleeding. Let me clean it up and apply some antibiotic ointment. I'll give him a tetanus shot tomorrow. You fellows can follow up daily 'till it heals. And be sure to keep this guy's hooves filed down. There are no predators to chase him and they can get overgrown in a hurry." I stepped away, opened my bag and reached for the alcohol, cotton and tube of ointment. After the treatment, Kinsig released the leg and the zebra ambled away, not the least perturbed by the incident.

The aviary was a large brick building, lined on the inside with four, wire-mesh areas to separate different species of birds. As we entered, the sound of a thousand fluttering wings mingled with bird-song and chirping. There was motion everywhere as the happy flyers dove and streaked back and forth, finally perching for an instant before winging away again. Little skirmishes, punctuated by flapping wings and serious chirps, took place everywhere. Then, just as quickly, the players took flight again.

Two keepers were busy sweeping droppings, "Ralph Suza is the big fella and Bill Sherada is wearing the glasses," Fred informed me. "Boys!" he called. "Dr. Zimmerman, the new vet is here. Come say hello."

"Hi, Doc," said Ralph.

"Glad to meet you, sir," echoed Bill.

"Any problems, men?" Fred asked, for my benefit.

"We have an epidemic of the runs, sir," Ralph answered. Then to me, "They seem to be okay otherwise. Anything we can use to treat it, doctor?"

"Let me check their droppings." I said. Birds eliminate bowel and kidney wastes simultaneously through the cloaca. Kidney infection, as in animals, is more serious than an upset bowel, and takes much longer to respond.

They had more than ample samples to present and luckily, I had medicine that would correct the upset.

"As long as they are normal otherwise, eating well and not fluffing their feathers (a sign of fever), I can leave you some soluble sulfa to add to their water. It's tasteless and works pretty fast. If they don't respond, be sure to let me know."

"Thanks, Doc," Sandman added, "What should we do to prevent another outbreak?"

"Diet is the key," I told them, "fresh seeds with plenty of healthy, fresh greens and egg white for protein. Some of your exotic species should have meal worms for their protein needs. The parrots love variety. Anything you eat, share with them. It's also a good idea, when a batch of new birds arrive, isolate them for a week or two to eliminate trouble."

"Come to think of it," Sherada said thoughtfully. "One of the macaws escaped last week. We thought we lost her, but she showed up a couple of days later and roosted in that big oak, near the front door. She was hungry and might have picked up something and introduced it to the rest of the gang."

"Entirely possible." I said. "Lucky you got her back at all."

I thought of Miss Price when I was a teenager and the red macaw that was a fixture in my Dad's new pet shop on Fifth Avenue. It had bullied me for years and I was happy when it found a new home.

The London Pet Shop was huge. Mom planned a section for the birds, one for dogs and cats, and the third for exotic animals.

"The cash register will be in the middle section, opposite the door to Thirty-First Street." Mom said. "From there, Miss Price can be both cashier and bird maven."

Following her directions the store was fully stocked. The doors separating the sections were topped by open transoms—a nuisance to me, years later, when I was old enough to work part-time, feeding and cleaning the birds. Two or three always managed to escape through my fingers, and their flight was over the doors into hostile sections.

Miss Tillie Price, our former summer-camp counselor in Rivervale, New Jersey, was perched with her cash register in the avian section. She was as attracted to the birds as they were to her. Tillie was the only one who could coax the escapees back to their proper nests.

One day, a Fire Department engine roared down Broadway, swerved into Eighty-Third Street on the upper west side, and came to rest between West End Avenue and Riverside Drive. Their destination was a tree harboring an escaped red macaw parrot. The London Pet Shop and the Fire Department had simultaneously received an urgent plea from the owners (our customer), to capture and save their pet. A tropical macaw could never survive the frigid, snowy winters of New York.

The engine arrived with sirens blaring and bells clanging and, for the first time, the rescue was not intended for a terrified, treed kitten. The young enthusiastic firemen pulled out two ladders, and placed them on the tree under the macaw. A crowd gathered, all eyes on the beautifully feathered bird, perched on a distant limb. Firemen rushed up the ladders, their nets prepared and ready. The parrot adroitly fluttered into an adjoining tree. Down came the ladders and were replaced twenty feet away. As they climbed, this time more slowly, they were frustrated again—the graceful bird changed perches. The play was repeated time and again, to the glee of the crowd. The firemen ran, the ladders dragged and the nets remained empty. The crowd roared with laughter.

Amid all the confusion, a lady, our Miss Tillie Price, arrived and quickly took command. "Take the nets away and lend me one ladder," she ordered. Miss Price began to climb as the frightened bird, crouched with half-open wings, set for another getaway. Tillie cooed, "Remember me, pretty bird? Come get a cracker."

Magically, the bird relaxed. Instead of taking flight, it cocked its head sideways, took a better look, remembered, then dropped gratefully on Tillie's extended arm. Miss Price was just greeting an old friend.

The crowd cheered as she, blushing, stepped to the ground, returned the itinerant avian to its grateful owners with the admonishment, "Have Polly's flight-feathers trimmed and she'll stay home."

The firemen replaced their ladders, folded their nets, and rumbled back to the station house, subdued, and much the wiser.

I ambled back to the Children's Zoo and Mrs. Infante's problems. Tatey led me to the rabbits first. I couldn't object, without going into a long story about my allergies. There were a half-dozen bunnies, all white and pink and cute. One of them had deep, self-inflicted gashes on the sides of her cheeks from scratching--probably her ears. Some of the wounds were infected and needed treatment. "Tatey," I said, "this little gal has ear mites. It's easy to treat, but very contagious. Put a few drops of insecticide in her ears daily and I'll leave you penicillin ointment for the scratches. Keep an eye on the other rabbits." I gave her the medicine, sneezed twice, wiped my eyes and suggested we look at the other patients.

Infante sighed, "The young python has a skin, or rather scale, condition."

"It's skin, Tatey," I corrected. "They look like scales, and used to be. Evolution gradually changed scales to derma. When a snake sheds its skin, it comes away in one piece."

"I see," she said, and continued, "He's gentle and the children adore playing with him and taking pictures with him hanging around their necks. Those that aren't scared to death, that is." she smiled, "I was like that at first. Boa constrictors take a little getting used to."

My love affair with snakes, as a child, had me looking forward to one as a patient. None of mine were ever sick and, once again, I wondered how I would treat whatever he had. He was a far cry from the frozen giants I examined for Trefflichs after the disastrous freeze on the air-transport.

Mrs. Infante walked over to the huge aquarium where the reptile was kept. His head was facing the glass, and his body coiled beneath it. She lifted him out so I could see the troublesome lesion. There was an area on his never-ending abdomen that was inflamed.

"Looks like dermatitis, Tatey. Use some of the penicillin I gave you for the rabbits. Massage it into his skin a couple times daily. If it's going to work, we'll know it in a week or so."

"Now, I want you to meet my pride and joy," she sighed, "Lulu the llama. She's the reason I work here. The white beauty you passed in the outside pen. Lulu must have been playing too hard. I'd like you to check her eye."

We walked outside and I saw Lulu. She stood at least a foot taller than the fence. Infante introduced us, and, for a moment, we stood nose to nose, inspecting and smelling each other. There was a dark, almost black streak of hair, caused by moisture under one eye where the tears had stained the white hair. She wasn't blinking or showing any signs of discomfort.

After using the magnification of the otoscope to examine the cornea, I said, "Her eye looks fine, Tatey. Tearing is a natural defense when something blows in your eye. Here's some ophthalmic ointment. Just a little medication, twice daily for maybe a week. Can you do it?" I asked.

"Sure." She screwed off the top, held Lulu's eye open with thumb and index finger of one hand, and squeezed in about an inch of ointment. Lulu never budged.

"She's a great patient, Tatey, but that's more salve than is necessary. You'll never have enough for two days at that rate. About one drop at a time will be fine."

"Okay," she said "I'll be careful." She sighed as she looked over her little kingdom. "We have too many rabbits, hamsters and goats. I've been hounding the powers that be, to start a "trading" arrangement with other zoos. We need baby elephants, zebras and chimps to round out our program."

The mention of elephants reminded me that Rodrigues and Chang were waiting. I excused myself, told Mrs. Infante that I'd see her on my next visit and started for the elephant compound.

I bought a bag of roasted peanuts from a sidewalk vendor, and emptied them into my side pocket. Now for baby Chang. Ed Rodrigues was waiting. I said to him, "I've got a pocketful of nuts. Let's go."

Both elephants ignored me as I approached. The behemoths were munching on hay, oblivious to the sounds and movement of children and parents alike. I thought a distinctive sound would differentiate me from the casual spectators, of which there must be thousands. I used the shrill whistle Les MacMitchell taught me. Without using any fingers. I made one undulating, three note call, as if I were hailing a cab, and they turned their heads. I never approached their compound again without using that very distinctive greeting.

Leslie MacMitchell lived directly across the street from our brownstone on West Eighty-Seventh Street and had become one of my closest friends. Marty Rosengarten (Rosy) lived on the same street in an apartment over the food market on Broadway. We three were inseparable, went to high school together and to this day (1994) we are as close as ever.

A major accomplishment in my life was when Les taught me how to give a shrill whistle by manipulating my lips and tongue. He tried to teach Rosy the same art but it was useless. Rosy could whistle but he had to use at least two fingers. It's a skill I've used and cherished for a lifetime. I can hail a cab with my arms loaded with packages, call my wife if we get separated in a crowd, tweet every time I come home from work to let everyone know I've arrived. My most recent pleasure was teaching David, my eight-year old grandson the very same skill. What a wonderful legacy for the new generation.

Thanks to that whistle, I had their attention as Ed and I approached the young elephant. Ed reached into my pocket, took out a peanut and showed Chang that I also carried them. I gave him one, stroked his trunk and said a few words of greeting. It was the first time I'd touched an elephant's hide and especially for a youngster it was hairier and rougher than I anticipated.

"Pet his side and work back to the swelling," Rodrigues advised.

I did, and as I walked slowly toward his hip, he turned his head, his trunk searching my pocket. He helped himself and didn't seem to mind my probing fingers. "It feels like fluid, Ed. Do you think he would object to a needle? I'd like to aspirate some for the lab."

"They don't mind shots as a rule, if they like you. I think he'll be fine. Most doctors I've worked with give the injection area a smart slap, and then just jab the needle through the skin."

I opened my medical bag and took a five-c.c. syringe out of its sterile metal container. An eighteen-gauge needle seemed about right for an elephant. Cleaning the epidermis with alcohol, I pinched the leathery hide over the swelling to bring any fluid to the surface, and jabbed the needle through the skin. Serum flowed easily into the barrel of the syringe.

"Good!" I said. "It looks normal. Clear and most likely sterile."

Curious, Tina ambled over to see what I was doing to the youngster. When satisfied that he was okay, she reached into my pocket and helped herself.

"I think she likes you," Rodrigues said. "She's never done that to anyone but me."

That pleased me as much as anything that happened that first day.

"I can see she loves you very much." I said.

"We do get along well," he said and explained, "She's got a sense of humor, too. One day I gave her a peach. When I was emptying my pockets before going home, I found the pit. She had dropped it back into my pocket."

"Just returning the favor, I guess," I said, envying his closeness to the huge, loveable, ponderous beast.

"More than that, I think," Ed said thoughtfully. He looked at the cow rummaging again, now competing with Chang. There was really room for only one snout at a time.

"She shows her love by the size of her presents. The peach pit was just for fun. When I return after a day off, she's overjoyed and I find a small, smooth stone."

He thought a moment and continued, "Once I was out for a week and we really missed each other. She rewarded me with a suitable gift, a large, rough, many sided paving-stone she had worked loose with her huge flat foot and powerful dexterous trunk." He smiled, "She was thanking me for coming back."

"How many times a week do you have your uniform cleaned?" I asked grinning, as I felt my jacket pocket, "they really leave them wet."

"It goes with the job. Now that she likes you, your Mrs. will start complaining."

"It's worth it." I said. Maybe Tina understood how much I wanted to succeed. Perhaps she could feel my love enough to ignore ineptitude. Mother always said, "You can't fool children or animals."

When I returned to Mount Vernon, I was all smiles. Joan greeted me and I handed her a small package, "These are your doctor's latest accomplishments--an elephant's serum sample and an orangutan's urine."

She grinned and put the vials into the refrigerator for the next morning's delivery to the diagnostic laboratory.

"I know how you feel," she said simply, "and I never doubted for a minute that one of the zoos around here would eventually call you."

When I got home that night, Elaine could tell it had been a turning point-day in my life. She exulted with me, remembering that it was my first official trip to the zoo. My eyes told her before I said a word. Fourteen year-old Rick and eleven year-old Ron were all ears as I reported on the lions, tigers, orangutans, gorillas, seals, hippos and zebras. "And now I'm taking care of them all." I said.

After dinner, I was off to the den with my umpteen references on "exotics," unused for months. "Did you know hippopotamuses are related to pigs?" I called out. "And llamas are first cousin to camels?"

The lab report for Maggie, the orangutan, showed leucocytes and a trace of albumen. I called John FitzGerald and recommended Maggie get a penicillin injection. "Do you think she can be restrained for a shot?" I asked dubiously.

"Sure, we'll get you our three biggest keepers and John Gamn. She's fairly gentle and, if you're quick, I don't see a problem. How was the rabbit test?"

"It takes about a week," I said. "And if she's in an early pregnancy, a urinary infection could be debilitating."

"How about tomorrow for Maggie's shot?" FitzGerald asked.

"Would one o'clock be okay? I'll be finished with office hours and I'll grab a bite at the zoo restaurant after we're through."

Visualizing a wrestling match between the keepers and a full-grown, lady orangutan, I arrived at the primate area to find Maggie in the small holding pen, between her's and Mike's living quarters. It was about six feet-high, with wire mesh on all sides, including the ceiling. She had been lured in with bananas the expectation of visiting Mike. Squatting on short-bow legs, the fruit untouched, Maggie's harried eyes looked from keeper to keeper, then to me, wondering what was going to happen. I swallowed hard. She was so far from the swampy, coastal forests of her home in Borneo and Sumatra. These beautiful, trusting animals are revered by the natives who call them "forest people," and here we keep them imprisoned. I felt ashamed to be a party to their incarceration, and I swore to myself--somehow, some way, their lot would be improved.

Three tremendous men were waiting with Gamn. He was instructing them on how best to hold her, "You, Pete, and Marty. You're the strongest. Grab her arms. They're powerful. Be careful not to hurt her, and stay away from her face. She can bite hard. Lee and I will hold her legs. The Doc will come in after she's restrained."

"Don't do anything till I'm ready," I told them. "I'll fill the syringe and get the alcohol swabs set. It's an intramuscular shot, and the thigh is usually the best spot to hit, so try to have her hind end toward me." The men looked a little nervous, and I could see it was the first time Maggie had to be held for anything. Somewhere I'd read that "one orangutan is as strong as any four men." I wondered what lay ahead.

I nodded my head and Gamn opened the door. The keepers slid through the narrow entrance, one at a time. Maggie sensed trouble. She reached up with her long arms, grabbed the wires on the ceiling, and swung her legs up, holding on with all fours. She hung there, her head turning back and forth, watching us. We, in turn, looked at her in amazement. I hadn't planned on a ventral approach, but there was no choice. If she stayed in that position, the injection could be given from beneath and without any restraint.

"Don't move," speaking softly, "just stand looking at her so she'll stay put. I think I can do it alone."

The men froze, and I walked slowly under her. The ceiling was low enough for me to reach her backside. "If she doesn't let go and land on me," I thought, "this might be easy."

I wiped the target area with alcohol and jabbed the needle straight up into her exposed thigh. She didn't move. I emptied the syringe and pulled it out in one motion, giving the hide one more alcoholic wipe. We moved away quickly and filed out. Only when the door was closed, and we walked away, did she let go with her legs and swing down to the ground. She touched her wet thigh with one finger, then put it to her nose, snorting with displeasure.

Obviously relieved, Gamn said, "That was easy. For a minute I wondered what you would look like with a full-grown orang sitting on your chest." He grinned, "Nice going, Doc."

He turned to one of the men, "Let her back in her house and give her this present." He pulled out a brightly colored bandana he knew she'd love.

By the end of the week, the pregnancy test came back <u>positive</u>. I called FitzGerald, "Pass out cigars, John. Maggie is with child. The only thing I can't tell is when she's due."

"We'll be ready, from now on," he answered gleefully. "Here's hoping for a normal healthy baby."

"I'll talk to Gamn about Maggies' diet when she starts to nurse," I assured him. I thought for a moment and said, "John, who could I talk to upstairs about improving Maggie's pen? It wouldn't cost too much to cover the floor with sod and give her a large natural tree to nest in. Have you seen the "Great Ape" display at the Bronx Zoo? Maggie could raise a youngster there the way nature intended."

FitzGerald answered, "How about you breaking the news of Maggie's pregnancy to Sam White? He's our Director of Maintenance and Operation, and he has the ear of Park Commissioner Newbold Morris."

I called Mr. White, introduced myself, congratulated him on Maggie's pregnancy, and poured out my heart about the primate, hippo and big cat displays.

"Thank you for calling, Doctor," he responded. "I'm thrilled about the expected blessed event. I'm going to tell the commissioner about both the good news and your concerns. Maybe we can get something started."

Maggie gave birth to a two-pound, baby boy, all head, arms and legs. It happened quietly at night, atop the artificial tree. Clothes from her box were scattered all over the floor. Instinctively, she had grabbed anything movable to fashion a nest on the hard branches of the leafless tree. The birth must have been quick and easy. The new mother cleaned the baby, devoured the afterbirth and, by the time I arrived, only a wet spot, some of the amniotic fluid that had dripped to the concrete floor, attested to the event. Everyone celebrated, the media coverage was similar to a celebrity having a baby. Champagne, cigars and congratulations were directed to both Maggie and Big Mike, the disinterested father.

The zoo's maternity programs were flourishing. Three beautiful tiger cubs were born just one week after Maggie's "Little Mike." And a healthy macaque delivered a tiny baby girl weighing less than a half-pound at the Children's Zoo.

On my next visit, I entered the Big Cat's Building to get my first look at the new babies. The cubs were three weeks-old, as large as full-grown tabby cats. There were two males and one female named "Winky," "Blinky" and "Nod." John Spabola, was seated on a stool in Elvira's cage, holding Nod, the female cub. He was bottle feeding and, as I neared the cage bars, I could see the other two babies suckling their mother's breasts. Stretched out on her side, displaying the vivid black and yellow Bengal stripes against the cement floor's gray background, she looked as contented as a nursing mother could be. Every few moments, she lifted her huge head, highlighting long blonde whiskers, and turned to the nursing kittens to smell them and wash them with her large, reassuring tongue.

Spabola looked up, as I peered through the bars, and proudly explained, "Elvira has only two milk stations that work, so I'm helping her out."

"They look husky and healthy from here," I said. "How did you ever get her to trust you?"

"She loves carrots. I had my pockets stuffed with them for the zebra, a year or so back. Elvira smelled them and wouldn't leave me alone till I figured out what she wanted."

"Would she mind if I came in?"

"Not as long as I'm here," he said. "She trusted me from the time of the delivery. I helped her clean them. Three babies seemed to confuse her. It's her first litter, you know. Come on around to the side, and I'll let you in."

He said it so casually that I was encouraged to enter the cage. I knew that an animal can sense fear, so I put trepidation out of my mind.

He handed me the little one with the nipple still in her mouth. She was warm and soft and seemed to like me. At least the kitten didn't act any differently to me than she did for the keeper. She was fuzzy and brown, the stripes not yet present. The bottle slipped out, as I cuddled the ball of fur in my arms, but she was saited, and yawned. I lay her on the stool, my improvised examining table and checked her mouth and throat, palpated her abdomen, and listened to her chest and heart with the stethoscope. She didn't even mind my taking her temperature.

I kept one eye on Elvira as I looked and probed. I made up my mind that the baby was just another cat. She appeared perfectly normal. John took her from me, and pulled one of the boys off his mother's nipple, allowing Nod to take his place. Elvira turned her head, and peacefully watched the exchange. She accepted me on John Spabola's faith, and I examined all three babies uneventfully. I breathed a sigh of relief and satisfaction as the cage door closed behind me.

I watched their growth and maturation at least once or twice a month. Stripes appeared, baby teeth erupted and were used playfully on each other as well as their mother, mine and the keepers hands. Elvira accepted me and allowed me to play and examine them at will.

Four months later, the cubs were weaned. I asked John what he planned to feed them. He showed me by throwing three, large chunks of meat into their cage. They had been playing, mock fighting and growling at each other. The snarling increased in intensity and depth as they mauled their portions protectively. We saw their innate, hunting traits emerge.

"They're meat lovers all right," I said. "But don't neglect the roughage. Predators rarely eat each other and depend on their kill for that." Then I turned professor and lectured. "I'm sure you've heard that in the wild, carnivores feed on the grazers--zebras, gazelles, wildebeests, etc. They first devour the semi-digested hay and grass in the entrails and internal organs. Then they feed on the muscle meat." I added thoughtfully, "A good ration that I've used on ocelots and margays are equal parts of horse meat with canned dog food, like good old Ken-L-Ration. It makes an excellent diet, well balanced and palatable. It costs half as much as beef, and you'll have to consider cost when they start consuming twenty or thirty pounds daily."

"How about milk or cream?" He asked.

"No way," I told him emphatically. "Only man drinks milk after weaning, and I'm not sure it's good for him, either."

"Don't worry," Spabola said, "they'll be well fed. I'll personally see to that."

"I'm sure you will," I answered, "we all want the best for them."

Four weeks later, an anxious John Spabola met me at the Big Cat's entrance. "Winky is lame. He's been favoring one leg for several days. I thought at first he just played too hard or was bitten by those sharp baby teeth."

"Let's look at him," I said.

John picked him up and carried him to me, and Winky complained all the way. I palpated the leg and the arm bones. They were tender to the touch and slightly bowed.

I felt a knot in my stomach. I had seen this before in the exotic cats. Something was happening here that was not right. A poorly balanced diet in young, developing animals can raise havoc with their calcium metabolism. I recalled my talk with Spabola about the cub's diet.

"What are you feeding the babies, John?" I asked casually.

"They're on the best, most expensive meat we could buy," he cooed proudly. "Gamn's father is a butcher. All the guards chipped in and we bought the best quality beef at wholesale. These babies eat like kings!"

"What about the diet we discussed last month?" I said, my anger rising and my fears becoming a reality. I had come to love those cubs. The first babies I'd taken care of at the zoo.

"Well, you recommended a cheap canned dog food and horse meat." He said defensively. "We weren't going to settle for that, and they didn't seem to care for vegetables. These cubs are a first for us, and real special."

"Can you recall the calcium-phosphorus ratio?" I challenged. "I'm sure it was discussed by John FitzGerald in your nutrition seminars."

He stopped and thought. "Calcium two parts to one of phosphorus. The normal calcium phosphorus ratio," he repeated by rote.

"Your expensive quality steak, fed without proper supplements and natural roughage, is so rich in phosphorus, it's depleted the bones of calcium. We're in trouble here. Don't you remember the discussion about 'Cage Paralysis,' in monkeys? Droopy wings and lame legs in caged birds? All caused by an excess of phosphorus in the diet!" I was furious. "I have to talk to FitzGerald," I growled. "I'd like to take Winky to the office for X-rays. If what I think is happening, this is not simple rickets. I wish it were. This may be irreversible." I paused to let it sink in. "We may lose our cubs."

FitzGerald was aghast. He had heard about secondary, nutritional, hyperparathyroidism, and knew its implications. "How could Spabola and Furman feed them meat only?" he asked incredulously. "I assumed they were following your instructions. They love those cubs. The entire staff drools over them."

"It's partly my fault," I admitted sadly. "I suggested he feed a cheap canned dog food when we discussed diet a month ago. I didn't emphasize that an inexpensive balanced ration could be more nourishing than a filet mignon. John, I'm afraid we'll lose the litter, even if we change now."

I took Winky to the office and poured out my heart to my staff. We had seen and treated that condition, many times. I X-rayed his body. His bones were almost completely devoid of calcium. It was a ghostly plate, barely showing a skeletal outline.

I told Joan I'd look up the condition and make copies for the zoo personnel. I read aloud, "Hyperparathyroidism: abnormally increased activity of the parathyroid, causing loss of calcium from the bones and resulting in a condition marked by pain and tenderness in the bones, spontaneous fractures, muscular weakness, abdominal cramps, and osteitis fibrosa."

One by one, the cubs became lame, their legs deformed, and they lost their desire to play or move. With tears in our eyes, we watched them crawl on their stomachs to reach their feeding bowls, now filled with canned Ken-L-Ration! Too little, too late. My most difficult chore to date, euthanizing those three, lovable Bengal cats. Spabola cried as he held each one. "It's my fault, and I thought I was doing good!"

The lesson was painful, but well taught. The following year, two healthy cubs were delivered by Elvira, and raised on dog food and horse meat without incident.

John Gamn called me, complaining about Little Mike, the orangutan youngster. He wasn't happy about the way he looked or acted. "He's not thriving, Doc. He's just not the same playful ape he was a month ago."

I had seen him the previous week and thought he was all right. Maggie was nursing him at the time but Gamn said she seemed to be impatient and frequently pushed him away before the little one was satisfied.

I peered at the mother and baby through the bars. She was sitting on the cold floor nibbling on fruit and nuts, some green vegetables, tomatoes and cooked potatoes. I had instructed Gamn to feed her the widest variety possible. It was mid-winter, and all the tropical animals were confined indoors. I felt chilly with my overcoat on.

Little Mike clung to Maggie's back, coughing, occasionally sneezing and was generally depressed and disinterested. Gamn was right. He wasn't what I would expect from a healthy primate. In just a few weeks he had become dehydrated and thin. Small deposits of yellow exudate covered the corners of his eyes. I remembered Uncle as a baby, when she had pneumonia, but hoped maybe orangs are just different.

"Can we get close enough to examine him?" I asked Gamn.

"Fred Sandman asked me to try to snatch him. I used to get close, when I brought Maggie her food, but when I made a move at Little Mike, she grabbed him and climbed as high as possible to get away. Now, every time I enter the cage, she climbs to the top of the tree."

"We may have to sedate her." I said. "Every day is important. We can bottle feed and try to get his strength back."

"Sandman thought about asking you to do it, but we thought you might consider it too risky. If she got dizzy, twenty feet above the ground, she might fall and hurt herself and the baby."

"We'll have to figure a way to catch the little fellow if we knock out Mama. If Maggie climbs up the tree, gets sleepy and drops him, we'll need a blanket or a net to break the fall."

I thought for a moment. "We could try to get her into the wire run between the two pens that we used for her penicillin shot.

There's no place to climb and we might get the baby away from her. Maggie's milk may be drying up. It seems as though the little one is suckling with nothing to show. If we could supplement Maggie's milk it might turn the entire problem around. Let's try for the chute."

"We tried that already, Doc. Since the time you treated her, she refuses to go near it."

"Let's not put off the sedation too long. I'll tell FitzGerald that we should go ahead immediately."

I caught John in his office before I left. He said, "let's give her a couple of more days, Doc. Then, if she's not nursing normally, we'll risk the shot."

I left the zoo worried and frustrated. I was the vet-in-charge, and I couldn't even figure a way to treat an obviously ailing baby. I decided to insist that FitzGerald allow me to sedate Maggie the next day. The risk would be worth the try. We could post a few men under her and if Little Mike fell, one of them would catch him.

That night, I had a nightmare about Sumatra, caring for wild orangutans in the forest, listening to the wind rustle through the trees. I sat on the soft, swampy, leaf-strewn ground, peering up, looking for my ailing apes. As I shaded my eyes against the sunlight filtering through the trees, I held my medical bag with the other hand, and wondered how to get to my patients.

Tasting the forest fruit--the round red mongosteens, the durian and wild plum, I found they were delicious! Next I cut down some of the climbing bamboo, but before I could taste them, some lightning-fast baboons stole them. I decided to try enticing the orangs with some brightly colored ranbutans, covered by the wonderfully fragrant, strangling figs.

I looked around and saw John Gamn holding a huge, elephant-ear leaf, full of the jackfruit, langsat and breadfruit. The food was suddenly covered by a swarm of hungry, buzzing wasps. He dropped everything and was frantically brushing the wasps from his arms and face. As he moved away, his arms flailing, he backed up and fell into a deep, dark pit. I rushed toward him to help, but fell into the hole with him. It was large and roomy. There was a tree trunk, shaped like a table, in the center. We heard grunting and looked up. Several mature orangutans were looking down at us. The heads of young apes would pop over the rim, stare down for a moment and disappear. Other heads appeared. A zebra, an eland, the head of a lion and then a tiger. "How did tigers get to Africa," I thought. They were all quiet and curious. The orangs dropped some of the jungle fruit to us.

Suddenly I spied Maggie and Little Mike. Her breasts were full of milk, and the baby suckled contentedly, as he played with his mother's long red hair. When I looked up again, Maggie was there but Little Mike had disappeared. Gamn began to scream, "We have to get out! Let us out!"

The more noise we made, the more they dropped things to us--nuts, some strands of hay, the tender underside of tree bark and more fruit. I looked up and shouted to Maggie, "Help! Help us out!"

I woke with a start, wringing wet from nervous perspiration, Elaine was shaking me, "You're having a bad dream. You were screaming."

"I was traveling in Sumatra," I said dazed. "Gamn and I were trapped in a pit. We were on display!"

That dream ended my sleep for the night. A veiled notion stirred beneath the surface of my consciousness.

The call came that morning. I was in surgery, and Joan took the message. My heart skipped a beat as I looked at her face. Little Mike had fallen. They thought he was dead. Could I please come? Gamn told Joan how Maggie held her bleeding baby and how she was trying to evoke some response.

By the time I arrived, Maggie had climbed the tree, holding the limp baby in her arms.

"I think he's gone, Doc." FitzGerald said, choking back his tears.

Half a dozen keepers were there, all staring sadly, not knowing what to say or do.

Maggie made the decision for us. She descended slowly, coming to rest at the base of the tree. She set her baby down next to her and poked an index finger once in a last desperate attempt to arouse him, then sauntered away to a dish of food that had been brought in earlier.

FitzGerald opened the cage door and I followed him in. Maggie was disinterested as I bent over her son.

His eyelids were swollen. I opened the little mouth, cold and clammy to the touch and worked his upper gum back and forth. His face moved with my finger pressure. Some type of maxillary fracture, I thought. Bones still soft and malleable. There were lacerations about the cheeks and eyes, blood oozing from them as well as the nostrils.

I glanced up at the plastic branches. He had survived for a few minutes, I reasoned. There wouldn't be any bleeding if his heart had stopped before the fall. Maggie watched expressionless, nibbling at the food in the pan. I looked at her impassive face. I felt sick. It was a needless, preventable death. I should have insisted on safeguards for her maternity ward.

"I'll finish the autopsy in my office." I told FitzGerald as I picked up Little Mike and wrapped him in a towel. A dozen pairs of misty eyes watched me leave.

My heart was filled with frustration as I searched out probable cause with scalpel and forceps.

After the autopsy, for the record, I dated my notes. . .Traumatic hernia of the abdominal muscles at the mediastinal junction. Lungs congested with several areas of hepatization.

Little Mike had acute, viral, double pneumonia, explaining the cough, anorexia, weakness and probably the fall. No protective cradle of branches and leaves to catch him as would have been the case in the wild nor the blessing of a warm tropical sun.

I strolled the zoo many times between 1965 and 1972. I still loved the apes, and adored the rest of my exotic family but for me, the elephants made the deepest impact. Chang matured in those exciting years and cherished his peanuts. Tina put up with me, accepted my gifts but I felt we were just casual friends. Ed taught me things I had never read about or experienced. After examining their mouths and huge grinding teeth with a flashlight, I learned that they have six sets during a normal lifetime and Tina was working on her second set.

"The coarse food in the wild demand it." he said, "When their last set gets worn down, usually at the age of sixty or more, they can no longer chew and so they die," he remarked sadly. "but that won't happen here," he brightened, "we'll make mush so they can live to be a hundred."

"Are they really afraid of mice?" I asked one day after some white mice had escaped from the petting zoo.

"No way," Ed assured me. "I've seen field mice in their enclosure and they didn't even notice them."

For seven years, I used my whistle, patted elephant trunks, filled my pockets with roasted peanuts a thousand times and became proficient in the practice of wild animal medicine.

When my private practice became too time consuming, it became my reason for leaving the zoo. I discussed it with John FitzGerald.

"There are young vets from the Animal Medical Center who could take over my duties."

He agreed and, when it was time for me to leave, I didn't know how to say, "goodbye." Finally the day came when I took my last official walk. The elephants were the hardest to part with. They were the most intelligent, affectionate and demonstrative. They soiled my jacket for the last time as I hugged each trunk with tears in my eyes. Each received an apple as a going away present. I knew I'd miss them as I turned and looked back at Ed and his family. I promised myself to come and visit when I could.

On January 4th, 1985, almost twenty years later, a startling headline made me gasp. It appeared in the second section of a New York Newspaper. "CENTRAL PARK ZOO ELEPHANT DOOMED." Tina, the mature cow elephant and long time zoo resident, attacks her keepers."

The story took me back to that magical expericence I had as attending veterinarian at the zoo so many years before.

I continued reading with a lump in my throat.

"Tina became distraught and incorrigible after the death of her keeper, Ed Rodrigues. He passed away from natural causes and the zoo directors have been trying to replace him with little success."

"Ed gone," I thought, disbelieveing. "He was too young."

The article went on to explain how the Central Park Zoo originally bought Tina, and how Ed Rodrigues took her under his wing. His kindness and gentle manner transformed a potential "Bad Girl," into a very acceptable attraction.

"Ed was one of the few humans she trusted and loved," it continued.

"A year after Rodrigues died, Chang, her young companion, was sold, leaving Tina sad and lonely. In April of '83, in a moment of bad temper, she attacked her new keeper. He was sent to the hospital. She had also charged at two additional replacements, crushing the arm of one and stomping the foot of the other."

I called to Elaine and said, "Read this. . . How could I permit anyone to put her down? I wonder if I could change their minds.". . . A notion materialized.

I called John Kinsig, now the head keeper and told him my thoughts.

"It might be worth a try," he said.

I made a hurried trip to New York. With pockets loaded with roasted peanuts, I returned to my favorite haunt. John walked me to the elephant house. "She's different, Doc. No one can get near her, not even me, and nobody wants her. Please," he warned, "be careful."

As I approached the compound I stopped, wondering if Tina could possibly remember. I let out a sharp whistle as I had so many times before and there was an immediate reply. She answered with a shrill trumpeting as I stepped between the bars to greet her. She was overjoyed. Her trunk didn't know what to do first. She layed it on my shoulder then dug into my pocket to see if the nuts were there. Her tiny eyes were blinking and deep grunting sounds of satisfaction and happiness came from her throat. Kinsig couldn't believe his eyes.

"Don't let them destroy her, John." I begged. "She lost Ed and then Chang. Why wouldn't she be upset?"

She began pacing, grunting, shaking her huge head, flapping her ears and pawing at the ground. She was telling me what happened. Suddenly she was at my side, again feeling for more peanuts. We touched and played for a long time. Finally, I turned to go, feeling a little like a traitor to be leaving her again. If only I could change their minds. .

As I walked away there was one last plaintive trumpet call. When Kinsig and I turned for a final look I brushed against him and felt something hard in my pocket. It was a large, rough, moist paving-stone Tina had worked loose when she was telling her story. She hadn't forgotten.

I was back in Florida when I got the call. It was a very excited John Kinsig. "It worked, Doc! Your idea worked! They realized that their decision to put her to sleep had been very wrong. Your visit changed their minds."

Less than a month after I saw her at the zoo, the Marine World/ Africa, USA, in Redwood City, California said it would take Tina.

Her new home would be near San Francisco and the owners were convinced by John Kinsig that she was a good animal.

Sedated and coaxed, she left by truck on February 2, 1985. Within a month her keeper, David Blasco, said she was adjusting so well they were about to try her for children's rides.

THE CITY OF NEW YORK
DEPARTMENT OF PARKS

ARSENAL
64TH STREET AND FIFTH AVENUE
CENTRAL PARK
NEW YORK 21. N. Y.

NEWBOLD MORRIS
COMMISSIONER

JOHN A. MULCAHY
EXECUTIVE OFFICER

ALEXANDER WIRIN
ASSISTANT EXECUTIVE OFFICER

SAMUEL M. WHITE
DIRECTOR MAINTENANCE & OPERATION

CHARLES H. STARKE
DIRECTOR OF RECREATION

January 8, 1965

Dr. Theodore Zimmerman
Beverlie Animal Hospital
17 W. Grand St.
Fleetwood
Mt. Vernon, N.Y.

Dear Dr. Zimmerman:

   Supervisor of Menageries Sandman has sent me your letter of
December 19, 1964 concerning your suggestions about some of the animals you observed during December 1964.

   Arrangements have been made to have a blacksmith trim the hooves
of the zebra during the week of January 3rd.

   The keeper in the elephant house has been instructed to closely
observe the small elephant and to report any change or enlargement in the growth on
the hip.

   Mr. Sandman plans to separate the Orang and her son sometime
during the week of January 11, 1965. Fred prefers not to use the tranquilizer because of the possibility of a fatal dose. He will open an adjacent cage and attempt
to lure the mother away from the baby with food.

   The civet cat will be isolated during and after her next pregnancy
in hopes of making it possible to rear her litter. Of course the antibiotics have
been discontinued as you suggested.

   The shy young lion would appear to be a good title for a children's
story. We are rotating the keepers who are handling this animal in hopes of overcoming his bashfulness.

   I regret to inform you that the male bison died on December 22nd.
Please forward the reports from the diagnostic lab at Cornell as soon as they are
available. We will have to arrange for the purchase of another male bison but do
not wish to do so until we have a test made on the female particularly if our fears
concerning the deceased male are borne out by laboratory tests.

         Very truly yours,

         Director of Maintenance
         and Operation

Henry Trefflich escorting "Chang", down the gangplank and heading for his new home at the Central Park Zoo, New York City, NY, in 1964

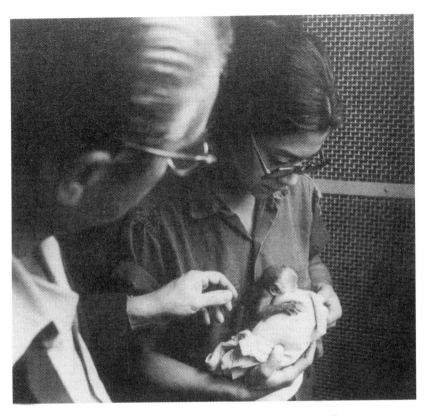

1965, examining a baby ape at the Children Zoo

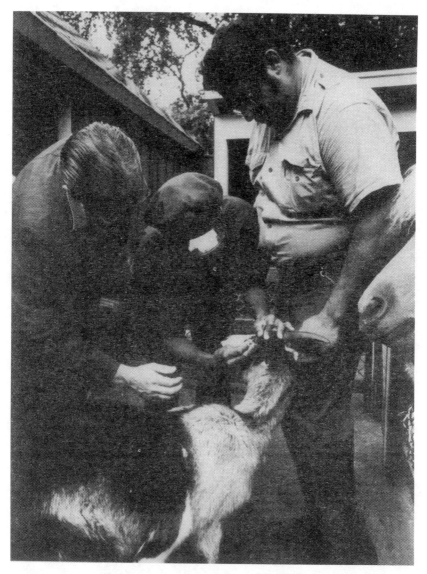

Treating a pygmy goat's eye at the Children's Central Park Zoo in New York City in 1969. Dr. Zimmerman and keepers

Dr. Zimmerman giving some advice to the Children's Zoo cockatoo

XIII

Winding Down

For the first time in forty years I thought about selling my practice. It was 1984 and Elaine and I talked about retiring to Florida. I had practiced so many years, loved every minute of it, but realized it was time to change trains. I had been incredibly fortunate with my staff. Little Peter, my right hand man for nearly thirty-five of those years would take the brunt of my decision. I realized later, that he was concerned about his own future. His mother repeated a remark that he made to her after working for me just a couple of months. "Who besides Dr. Zimmerman would ever give such an ugly dwarf a decent job?"

One day, during the last year of my practice, Darryl and her six year-old twins, Chris and Tommy, purely by chance, discovered something that troubled all of us. They had come over to help her clean up several basement storage closets.

"Pull all the junk out," she told them, "and make your own pile in the middle of the floor. I'll check what we need. The rest we'll put in the garbage. A coke to the guy who makes the biggest pile."

"Okay Mom," they squealed happily as they piled into one of the narrow, junk filled areas.

When they were finished, their mounds consisted of used newspapers, old collars and leashes, rags, discarded cans of dog and cat food, an old bird-cage, several pieces of tile, rolled up wallpaper left over from our last redecorating, a few mouse traps and the surprise—several large paper bags filled to the brim with something metallic. Darryl opened them to find hundreds of flattened beer cans. As she gazed at them open-mouthed, the twin's exuberance brought her back to reality.

"Who won, Mom?" Chris asked. "I think it's me."

"No. Mom. Look at mine. It's higher," Tommy shouted. He picked up the bird-cage. "Can we get a bird, Mom? Please."

"You're both winners." Darryl decided, ignoring the request. "Cokes and ice-cream for both."

Darryl told me about the find. "Mrs. Mueller has been complaining to me that Pete doesn't always come home at night."

She said, "I can see why."

Peter's mother, doing what mothers do, nagged him unmercifully about his drinking, so he opted for the quiet of one of the larger dog kennels, curling up on cold, hard steel after emptying an untold number of beer cans, rather than sleeping on the soft army cot that was folded and always available in the downstairs closet.

Despite the encouragement, compliments, praise and appreciation showered on him by our clients, myself and our entire staff, Peter suffered from chronic, low self-esteem.

After I discussed the situation with him, he showed his courage and tried very hard. He behaved normally for nearly an entire year. Then, the sale of my practice. That, unfortunately came at the same time as his mother's death. His world fell apart. Desperate and miserable, his only out was alcohol. I had no choice but to fire him, hoping the shock would turn him around so he could come back to work before the new doctor took over. I knew he loved being with the animals and needed the activity to occupy his hours. Peter had been such a loyal, honest, diligent friend and helper. I had a real affection and a deep concern for him.

Several weeks went by without a word, so I visited his home. No one answered the ring but the door was unlocked. Masses of newspapers were stacked so high near the entrance that I could hardly enter. Brownie and Blinky, his two dogs, greeted me as I pushed inside. The house was in shambles and smelled like a pigsty. Both animals were disheveled and grotesquely thin. Blinky, always one of my favorites, tried to wag his tail in greeting. He had Shelty breeding and immediately rushed to Peter, lying on the couch, then back to me, telling me to follow him to his troubled master. Brownie, just able to stand, looked at me with blood-red eyes, his tail tucked between trembling hind legs. He almost staggered into the kitchen for a moment then slowly returned carrying his bare food dish in his mouth, placing it at my feet. Blackie, the cat that Peter loved dearly, was lying at the foot of the couch, head between her paws, dreary eyes looked up at me but she didn't move. The animals were starved. Peter was on the couch, knees drawn up to his stomach in the fetal position wearing a filthy "T" shirt and dungaree trousers. His feet were bare. Beer cans were everywhere. I touched his shoulder and spoke to him. He didn't respond so I shook him and shouted his name.

He moved slightly and moaned something unintelligible in German. I walked into the kitchen where the dog and cat dishes were. The sink was overflowing with soiled and stinking dishes. The counter top littered with empty food cans, soiled silverware, a can opener and filthy glasses, some empty and some half filled with sour-smelling milk and coffee. I found a couple of cans of dog and cat food in one of the cabinets and fed the animals. The dogs were voracious but Blackie sniffed disinterested at her bowl. She was depressed and dehydrated and would need fluids and perhaps an IV feeding.

The bathroom door was open. Dirty towels and spread newspapers littered the floor amid the accumulated droppings of the neglected animals. The toilet cover was open where I was sure the animals drank. I looked for leashes so I could take the animals back with me. They were on the floor in the kitchen.

Pete was in a semi-conscious stupor. The police and an ambulance were my first call. Then his sister, Mrs. Elfrieda Green, who lived in New York City had to be notified. I found the phone almost hidden from view behind the living room couch.

"I'm sorry about your mother, Mrs. Green." I said, "I think Peter took it pretty hard because he hasn't stopped drinking since the funeral." I told her that I sent for an ambulance and wondered if she could come up and maybe supervise the cleanup. I mentioned the condition of the animals.

"I'm going to take them to my hospital. They need some care and building up. Then I'll meet you back here if that's Okay."

Mrs. Green agreed.

The next few minutes were spent moving the stacks of newspapers so the authorities could get in the front door. I leashed the dogs, picked up Blacky and waited.

The police finished their paper work and Peter was placed on a mobile stretcher. Both animals tugged at their leashes to follow Peter as he was rolled out the door. The strange loyalty that dogs have for their master, their need to be near them, especially when there is trouble, is incomprehensible. They only desire a kind word or a friendly pat on the head.

"He'll be okay, fellows," I said softly as I coaxed them back. They sat, watching the procession move out. Their heads turned in a final look, as if they knew, instinctively, that it would be the last time they'd see their master.

After they left, I walked the dogs and carried Blackie to my car and drove them to the hospital. Darryl took them from me and I hurried back to meet Peter's sister.

Elfrieda Green rushed to Mount Vernon, frustrated and in tears. She tried to clean up the house while hot coffee was brewing for me in the kitchen.

"Let the professionals clean up," I told her, "It's too much for one person."

"I'm so ashamed," she said. "Peter was doing so well for so many years I hoped it would go on forever."

"You can't blame yourself," I said. "Peter had problems we never knew. I was as close to him as anyone for over thirty years but he was a very silent person."

I accompanied her to the Mount Vernon Hospital where the ambulance had taken Peter and talked to the head psychiatrist.

"I'm afraid he's a very troubled young man. I'd advise the state hospital for a while. If he has any chance to get back to normal, he'll get it there."

Mrs. Green committed him to the psychiatric ward at Grasslands Hospital in Valhalla. I took the animals to the office hoping he would some day pick them up and resume his life. His sister made sure the house was immaculate, hoping for the day that Peter might return.

Blinky, Blackie and Brownie, fully recovered, went to New York with Peter's sister where they lived out their natural lives.

Peter was allowed to leave the hospital about six months later for a very short respite. He had to be returned and is there to this day.

The Animal Medical Center took over the zoo work as I had suggested in 1972. In 1983, out of the blue, I received a call from John FitzGerald. "I had to call and tell you that plans have started for the renovation of the zoo." he said, "I think your efforts may have been the spark that ignited the conscience of the Park Department."

"Where do the animals go during the renovation?" I asked.

"Some will be sold, like Chang the young elephant. He's left already. Most of the large animals will go to the Bronx Zoo." he said. "The birds and small animals will be easy to shift around as work proceeds. It's a perfect time for me to retire. It's about time I take it easy. John Kinsig will be promoted and take over."

In December of 1984, the zoo was closed for renovations, and Elaine and I retired to Florida.

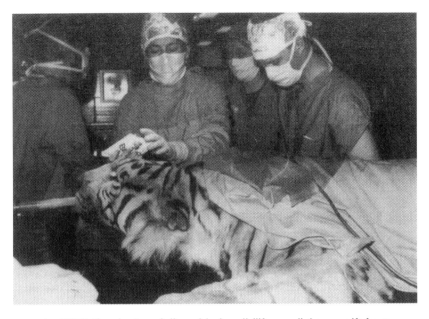

In 1992, thanks to a fellowship in wildlife medicine, a gift from Jay D. Hyman (DVM, '57) a bengal tiger is being treated at the Cornell Veterinary College.

Epilogue

Three years late and with a 25% over-run, the Central Park Zoo was reopened. It was August of 1988. The bars and concrete were gone and the displays accurately simulated the natural habitats of Africa and Asia. Walking through the new zoo, this time as a spectator, the heaviness in my heart was forgotten. The bells in the animated, Delacorte Clock, chimed with a new resonance. Those wonderful, sensitive, captive creatures would still roam in Central Park but would now feel free.

Almost fifty-five years after my request to the Admission Committee at Cornell University for a course in wildlife medicine, it finally happened. Wildlife, exotic pets and zoo animals were becoming frequent patients at the clinics of the Veterinary Medical Teaching Hospital. In 1992, the first professorship in wildlife medicine in an American veterinary college was established at Cornell. It was a gift from Jay D. Hyman (D.V.M. class of '57), at Cornell.

Elaine saw a Cheshire cat-like smile on my face and looked over my shoulder to discover why. A copy of the documented history of the first hundred years at Cornell University was open to a picture of a magnificent Bengal Tiger, anesthetized and surrounded by a group of veterinary students about to perform landmark surgery that was sure to become routine.